# The Ultimate Guide to Success

DR. MOHAMMED NAYEEM SIDDIQUI

Copyright © 2013 Dr. Mohammed Nayeem Siddiqui
All rights reserved.
ISBN: 0615496180
ISBN 13: 9780615496184

**In the Name of God, the Most Beneficent,
the Most Merciful**

# Dedication

*In Loving Memory of:*

*My father,* **Mohammed Viqaruddin Siddiqui**, *and my mother,* **Syeda Akhter Siddiqui**, *for their incessant efforts in all they did to try to make the world a better place, and their many efforts to make sure I attained the foundations of success, by study and by example. Built on this foundation, and with the Grace of God, the Most Gracious and the Best Guide, is the work I am honored to share with you, and from which I hope you attain as much benefit as I have, including* **Success**!

# Foreword

History provides us with evidence that the messengers of God have been sent to every nation. It was never the intention of the Almighty to differentiate people on the basis of the messages and the messengers. The spirit of all messages and the "Mission Statement" of every messenger has always been the same: showing the Right Path leading to "Success" both in this world and the Hereafter. It is only through the blessed prophetic mission of God's last prophet, Muhammad (peace be upon him), that the world restructured and rationalized the relationship between heaven and earth.

Today, the world's problem is essentially that of perfecting the life of man individually and collectively in every phase of life so that man may live a pure, peaceful and powerful life in this world and achieve success, salvation and eternal happiness in the hereafter. Therefore, it has become a world-cry, cherished by all right-thinking people of modern age, to adopt a superb ideology: a simple, practical and rational creed; a complete way of life which might offer solutions to all human problems of our own time and of the time to come. If ever there was a time in the annals of human history and culture which needed a message of guidance, peace, love, solutions and success, it is surely the time in which we are living.

The Holy Quran presents a magnificent message which is universal in its outlook, Divine in its origin, human in its subject-matter, simple and practical in its application, ideal in its pattern, comprehensive in its scope, and dynamic in its nature. This message is full of life and hope, love and tolerance, peace and progress, harmony and happiness, success and salvation, quality and justice, liberty and fraternity, and glorifies the future of humanity. This is the same message which has been superbly and diligently selected from the Holy Quran by Dr. M. Nayeem Siddiqui, for which he has also humbly tried to give the meaning of the Quranic text, especially as it relates to success. His approach seems to be most appealing to human reason and understanding. During the process of selection, he has shared with us the virtues like fortitude, gratitude, trust in God, hope, sincerity, modesty, contentment, humanity, the art of pleasing God, uprightness and the like. He has also listed vices to be abandoned, such as falsehood, back-biting, envy, pride, anger, impurity of speech, malice, casual passion, oppression, greediness, misery, bad disposition and the like. Thus, in a very comprehensive way, he is inviting everyone to self-purification, strictly, in terms of the Quranic injunction:

*"He indeed is Successful who purifies himself"* (87:14).

It is very difficult for anyone to explain the depth and glory of the original Arabic text. Nevertheless, Dr. Siddiqui's commendable and zealous spirit attracts our applause for this outstanding and amazing contribution to the field of self-development: The meaning of the Holy

Quran pertaining to success has been presented in an innovative and unique format to inculcate the ultimate guidance for mankind in a highly effective manner. In related context, it has rightly been said about the Quran:

It is a practicable code;
For high or low, and weak or bold;
Simple to read and understand,
To know, remember, and comprehend.
It endows man with what he requires on earth,
From womb to tomb, and for every breath he takes.

**Dr. Syed Muhammad Mohiuddin Habibi**

*Author of "Beautiful Names of Allah Mentioned in the Bible"*
*and "One God, One Religion".*

# Acknowledgments

As commonly accepted, Arabic is extremely difficult to translate without losing the beauty inherent in the original language - especially that of what is considered the undisputed masterpiece in the Arabic language, the Holy Quran . Throughout this collection of verses from the Holy Quran and their implications in regard to success, I have relied primarily on the excellent works Abdullah Yusuf Ali and Mohammed Marmaduke Pickthall. The beloved prophet Muhammad's traditions, or Hadeeth, as recorded in Sahih Muslim were also utilized to shed light on some verses of the Holy Quran, when necessary. Further details on the selected verses, when needed, were obtained from the voluminous masterpiece on the Commentary to the Holy Quran by the classical Islamic scholar, Ibn Kathir. I thank Allah (blessed be His Name) for guiding me to attempt to fulfill the void in current literature on self development in light of the Holy Quran, first in the English-speaking world, and if God wills, translated in other languages for benefit of non-English readers. I hope God, the Best Guide, Most Righteous Teacher, and the Most Forgiving One, accepts my humble effort and forgives any unintended errors or misunderstandings.

# Preface

Success: We all want to achieve it. There is no uniform description of success among two different people. Success to one person may mean being able to give a speech that elegantly relays the intended message of the speaker, leaving the audience captivated - while to another person, success may mean being able to run a mile in less than four minutes.

Because we all want to achieve success in whatever way we understand it, there have been thousands of books written on success. I still remember my younger days, more than twenty-five years ago, when I first became interested in deciphering the formula for success, as I was nearing the completion of my undergraduate college studies. I had already spent a sizable fortune purchasing the required textbooks in college, and I felt that spending another fifteen dollars voluntarily on a book instructing me in how to be successful might not be a bad investment. Needless to say, I became fascinated with the subject, and over the past twenty-five years, during which I have read more than one hundred books on success, I have been amazed to find in each new book an interesting perspective offering the recommended formula for that which we are all seeking consciously or unconsciously, i.e. Success.

During my utilization of the Quran for both spiritual as well as worldly guidance, I have come across numerous recommendations on achieving success. As a self-proclaimed seeker of books on formulas for success who found them to be interesting and useful, I have come to realize that the Quran is a treasury for such a seeker. From the literally thousands of recommendations in the Quran for achieving success, I have had an extremely difficult time selecting the three hundred sixty five recommendations to expound upon for my own as well as the reader's benefit. I will be the first to admit that there are scholars presently, who are more qualified than I, to expound on the Quranic verses. However, my aim is to analyze the Quranic verses as it relates to success, which we all are, or should be, seeking. In my opinion, the Holy Quran is foremost a guide on how we can achieve success - and that is how it should be utilized. I have merely sought to shed a light on those components of the Holy Quran that are most relevant to success and can be put to practice, for our optimal benefit, in the simplest terms, whenever possible. I believe there is a clear need for this kind of resource - which I hope the honorable reader will find useful both in today's milieu as well as the future, since the Holy Quran is intended for guidance through the end of times.

For those readers who already share my belief in the Islamic faith, this book may be considered a refresher, reminder, or a lazy man's approach to obtain the most benefit in the least amount of time. For those readers who are not of the Islamic faith, you are invited to set aside any preconceived notions about what is considered the most misunderstood religion in our time, and use its treasures for your growth. In my humble opinion, the Quran surpasses the combined wisdom of the more than one hundred books on how to succeed that I have read over the past twenty five years, particularly as the Source of the Quran is also the One Who will judge whether we succeed or not in terms of lasting success.

**Dr. M. Nayeem Siddiqui**

# Introduction

Quran in Arabic literally means "the Recitation". The first message from God, the Most Beneficent and Most Merciful, to the beloved prophet Muhammad and the first word chronologically in the Holy Quran is related to the word Quran, which is "iqraa", meaning "read". This revelation was first received by the beloved prophet Muhammad in 619 A.D., when he was at the age of 40 and on a spiritual retreat in a cave near Mecca. The noble prophet Muhammad continued to receive revelations through the Archangel Jibreel (Gabriel) from God, the Creator of all in the heavens and on earth, to relay to mankind, so that men might succeed both in their life on earth and for eternity.

The holy prophet Muhammad continued to receive revelations through the Archangel Jibreel from God, the Most Wise and the Best Guide, over the next twenty three years, and these revelations were immediately written down by scribes. The beloved prophet Muhammad himself was not able to read or write. The collection of revelations was rendered into book format in the current order during the reign of the first distinguished caliph and the most trusted companion of the holy prophet, Abu Bakr, at the behest of the another distinguished companion, Umar, who became the second caliph, and standardized in current form during the reign of the third distinguished caliph and companion, Uthman, may Allah be pleased with them all. The glorious Quran consists of 114 chapters and, with the exception of the first chapter, titled "the opening", the most important chapter in the Holy Quran and recited during all Muslim prayers, the chapters are generally arranged in descending order based on length, with no particular significance chronologically.

Central to the Islamic faith is belief in the Unity of God (from here onwards the word God in English and Allah, the Arabic word for God are used interchangeably), Who Himself was not created but created everything else that exists and Who, therefore, is the only object of worship: This is God. If man wishes to praise the grandeur, beauty or the order that exists in the universe, he must direct his praise to the One Who is ultimately responsible for the creation of all that exists, i.e. God. The second component of the central Islamic doctrine is that Muhammad (peace be upon him) was the messenger and the final prophet sent to mankind by God, the Creator and Sustainer of all, who received the revelations from God though the angel Jibreel and provided these revelations to mankind as instructed by God, the Most Generous and the Most Righteous, in what is now the Holy Quran.

Therefore, for Muslims, the Holy Quran is the Word of God, the Most Wise and the Source of all that exists. A Muslim reads the Quran for both spiritual rewards as well as to seek guidance on both spiritual and worldly matters. All Muslims recognize the Holy Quran as the final authority, and all Muslims will refer to particular portions of the Holy Quran to justify the range of differences seen in practice throughout the Islamic world.

All of us desire success, and would like to avoid failure. As noted above, part of the Islamic faith involves referring to the Holy Quran as the ultimate guide for all matters of interest to mankind, an important component of which is attaining success. As for those who are not of the Islamic faith, it is my belief that the Holy Quran also offers to them the most comprehensive and practical advice available for one who wants to achieve success – and if one is not convinced of this assertion, then at least what follows in this collection of meditations on success from the Holy Quran might help one better understand the psyche of those who follow the Islamic faith, which is also badly needed in today's world.

Regardless of whether anyone uses this book as intended, i.e. as a guide to attaining success, or to gain a better understanding of the one in five people inhabiting this planet who are Muslim, all praise is due to God, the Creator and Sustainer of all! Any shortcomings in this humble collection of meditations are my own. I take full responsibility for those shortcomings and seek the forgiveness of God, the Most Gracious and the Most Forgiving.

**Dr. M. Nayeem Siddiqui**

# Day 1

In the Name of God, the Most
Beneficent, the Most Merciful

Praise be to God,
the Cherisher and Sustainer of the worlds.

The Most Beneficent,
the Most Merciful.

Master of the Day of Judgment.

You Alone do we worship,
and Your aid Alone we seek.

Show us the Straight Path,

The Path of those on whom,
You have bestowed Your Grace,
those whose (portion) is not wrath,
and who go not astray.

(1:1-7)

# Day 1

The first chapter of the Holy Quran, aptly termed "The Opening", is one of its shortest, and is unequivocally considered its most important one. Indeed, the remainder of the Quran may be considered a commentary on the first chapter. No formal Muslim prayer is complete without the recitation of the first chapter.

From a spiritual perspective, the seven verses comprising the first chapter of the Holy Quran cover the most important components of any spiritual activity:

1. Praise directed towards one's Creator and the Creator of all that exists.

2. Affirmation of the primary tenets of one's belief.

3. Personal request to the Creator/Supreme Being/Supreme Authority for the improvement of one's condition.

The message relayed from these seven magnificent verses to the seeker of success is simple, easy to understand, yet quite comprehensive. First, the seeker of success is instructed to have belief in a Supreme Authority Who is in control of all that exists. Second, the seeker of success recognizes that he is responsible for all his actions, with the final result to be known on the Day of Judgment. Third, the seeker of success affirms that all help must ultimately come from God, the Creator and Sustainer of all that exists. Finally, the seeker of success recognizes that he has a choice - whether to follow the Straight Path, on which the Grace of God, the Most Glorious and the Best Guide, is bestowed - or conversely, to follow the alternate path, which results in God's displeasure. Those who are not on the Straight Path are aptly considered as lost or astray – certainly this situation is to be avoided by the seeker of success.

The seeker of success who wishes to reach his goal has unwavering faith in God, the Cherisher and Sustainer of the worlds, and in His beloved messenger, Muhammad, who received revelations from Him to relay to mankind as a Mercy to the worlds so that everyone may be guided toward success. He realizes that the beautiful selected passage of today is the most important of the revelations or instructions to mankind for success. He realizes the importance of strategic planning and knows that success is not a matter of coincidence but occurs as a result of patient and sustained striving against formidable resistance. He utilizes the beautiful selected passage of today that incorporates his core beliefs and the mission statement to help him reach his goal. As such, he refers to it more often than to any other source for guidance - and each time he does so, it increases his enthusiasm to reach his goal.

# Day 2

In the Name of God, the Most Beneficent, the Most Merciful

Alif Lam Mim.

This is the Book;
In it is Guidance sure,
without doubt,
for those who fear God.

Who believe in the unseen,
are steadfast in prayer,
and spend out of what we have provided for them.

And who believe in the revelation sent to you (Muhammad),
and sent before your time,
and (in their heart) have the assurance of the hereafter.

They are on (true Guidance) from their Lord,
<u>and it is these who will succeed.</u>

(2:1-5)

# Day 2

These are the first five verses of the second chapter in the Holy Quran, out of 114 chapters (or surahs, as they are called in Arabic). The second chapter contains more verses than any other chapter in the Holy Quran and covers a wide range of topics. The order of the 114 chapters in the Holy Quran is not based on the time of revelation, but generally on decreasing length of the chapter. The first verse of this surah consists of three Arabic alphabets and has no clear meaning, although much has been written about the mystical significance of these and similar alphabets at the beginning of this and some other chapters of the Holy Quran. The author prefers to draw the conclusion that it probably has spiritual significance, but remains an unsolved mystery. Our attention is directed instead to the remaining four verses, which are clear and succinct in terms what is required to succeed, as mentioned in the fifth verse; this is the reason for our selection of these special verses guiding one to success in life (and the hereafter). However, as indicated in these 5 verses, all of the Quran should be regarded as guidance for success. The seeker of success acquires from the beautiful selected passage of today, the following characteristics that will help him in his quest for attainment of lasting success:

1. He fears God, the Creator and Sustainer of all. Man's instinct is to be selfish - but in order to succeed, he must rise beyond his animalistic instincts and understand that he is accountable to his Creator.

2. He believes in the unseen. Otherwise, one would not believe or have faith in the Creator at all – which leads one to fulfill the duties for which he was created, which we will review in further detail in the meditation for tomorrow.

3. He is steadfast in prayer. Here, the injunction is made not only to pray but to also be vigilant about performing the required daily prayers. The five obligatory daily Islamic Prayers consist of praise to God, the Creator and Sustainer of all, in words and action. Additional supplications may be added based on personal needs.

4. He spends out of what has been provided to him by God, the Best Provider and Sustainer of all. One may feel that he may not be given additional provisions in the future and therefore, develop a fear of spending from one's own wealth for himself as well as others in need. But it is God who created all that exists, provided one with all his abilities and wealth and continues to care and provide for him as well as for all creation for eternity; an individual who develops miserliness tends to forget this aspect of God, the Most Great and the Most Wise. Besides the discouragement from miserliness, one is guided towards charitable spending, which is mentioned in numerous verses, as highly pleasing to God, the Most Compassionate and the Most Generous, which the author

places next to praise and worship of God – blessed be His name, in importance of the righteous actions.

5. He believes in the Holy Quran and also the previous revelations (now known as the Old and the New Testaments). The Holy Quran recognizes the scriptures sent before it and instructs the faithful that the Quran is a continuation of the instructions from God, the Most High and the Most Loving One, as were the previous scriptures.

6. He has assurance of the hereafter, or life after death. Otherwise one would have no incentive at all to behave other than in accordance with one's animalistic instincts of selfishness, being content with the instant gratification of this life and neglecting the future – which is more important, or the afterlife.

The seeker of success who wishes to reach his goal has complete faith in God, the Most Great, Who is the Manifest and the Hidden One, and in His noble messenger, Muhammad. His faith includes belief in his Lord even though he cannot see Him with his limited senses, although signs of His existence are everywhere; fearing his Lord because on the Day of Judgment he will be accountable to Him for all his actions and fears punishment in the hereafter; and having firm faith in the Holy Quran as the word of God given for the guidance of mankind and as a continuation of His earlier revelations, which have been modified by man and are now known to us as the Old and the New Testaments. As a manifestation of his faith, he is steadfast in prayer for praise and worship to his Lord, and spends from his resources for the needy and in the path of God, the Highest and the Best Rewarder.

# Day 3

O Mankind!
Worship your Guardian Lord,
Who created you,
And those who came before you,
That you may become righteous.

(2:21)

# Day 3

The seeker of success is instructed in the beautiful selected passage of today to worship God, the Source of all power and the Creator of all that exists. We will review the later verses of the Holy Quran later in this collection, which specifically clarify that man was created for the purpose of worshipping and serving God, Who created him and sustains him. In today's sublime verse, man is reminded that God, the Most High and Most Great, is to be worshipped because man owes his existence to Him and in order to succeed. Additionally, prayer and worship of God, the Creator and Sustainer of all, is recommended so that one might become righteous. One who is righteous has his reward both in this life and in the hereafter. As we will learn in later verses of the Quran, **success in the hereafter is considered the highest form of achievement in the sight of God, the Most Wise and the Best Guide, leading to eternal happiness and success of the highest kind.**

The seeker of success is instructed in the beautiful selected passage of today that engaging in the worship of God, the Creator and Sustainer of all that exists, leads to the individual becoming righteous. The wise person who regularly worships God, the Most Wise and the All-knowing, is engaging in the task for which he was created and thereby earning the pleasure of God, the Greatest and the Most Magnificent. And the one who earns the pleasure of God, the Bestower of all honors and also the Humiliator, will be rewarded with eternal happiness and the **highest success** – both in this life and for eternity.

Worship is a term which we must understand well, because that is the reason why mankind was created in the first place (as we will elaborate further in the later meditations), and therefore, would be the basis by which man can be termed a success or failure. Too often, the term worship is wrongly equated with the physical or verbal actions showing worthiness to the object of worship (and in terms of the monotheistic faiths, God). However, physical or verbal actions alone that are meant to convey worship, are unlikely to be considered as worship by God, the All-aware, All-seeing and All-hearing, as explained by his beloved prophet Muhammad, who explained that "actions are but by intentions and every man shall have only that which he intended". The focus of intention for all actions for the seeker of success, therefore, should be Allah, the Creator and Sustainer of all that exists. Subsequently, every action of the believer, then, can be considered a form of worship, resulting from the individual's consciousness of his Lord, from unison between his heart, mind, body and soul - of which the ritual worship is but one component. This explains how an individual can be occupied with the worship of his Creator throughout the day, and which differs from the common perception of worship.

The seeker of success who wishes to reach his goal has absolute faith in God, the Most Great, the Creator of all and the Best Guide, and in his beloved messenger, Muhammad. He makes worship of his Lord, with sincerity and awe, the reason for his existence, knowing that it leads him towards righteousness. And he realizes that his faith, worship, and acts of righteousness are the most important ingredients necessary to achieve lasting success.

# Day 4

And seek God's help with
patient perseverance and prayer.
It is indeed hard, except to those who bring a lowly spirit;

Who bear in mind the certainty
that they are to meet their Lord,
and that they are to return to Him.

(2: 45-46)

# Day 4

The seeker of success will no doubt encounter challenges, hardships and perhaps even setbacks during his quest of life. However, he is instructed in the beautiful selected passage of today to keep in mind the certainty that he will return to and meet his Creator in the end. If one is not cognizant of this factor, then one is likely to be lost as a result of the multitude of distractions he is likely to encounter during the quest of life.

It is recognized that the seeker of success might need help during his quest of life - for this, he is instructed to seek help from his Creator and Sustainer. The methods of seeking God's help have been listed as prayers and patient perseverance. Prayer includes praising the Creator, as well as supplications to fulfill one's personal needs. We must recognize that although other people can be of help to us in the short term, the best help is from the One who controls all aspects of existence. Another method of seeking God's help is with patient perseverance. Here, one is reminded that by being patient during one's trials and tribulations, he is being provided with help from God, who is indeed the Best of helpers.

It is acknowledged that being patient, and continuing to perform the scheduled prayers or worship, is difficult - especially during the trials and tribulations of life; but those who are humble and realize that the Creator and Controller of all that exists has His reasons for what He does and that they will ultimately return to Him, then will they be able to help themselves and realize their goal.

The seeker of success who wishes to reach his goal has unwavering faith in God, the Most Glorious and the Most Patient, and in His noble messenger, Muhammad. He is not proud and seeks the help of God, the Most Praiseworthy and the Most Kind, with patient perseverance and prayer – and he bears in mind with certainty at all times, including during the most difficult trials in his life, that he is ultimately to return to Him .

# Day 5

**And those who have faith
and work righteousness -
they are dwellers of Paradise;
they will dwell therein forever.**

(2:82)

# Day 5

The seeker of success is directed to the two factors that have been repeatedly mentioned together in the Holy Quran as prerequisites for **entry into paradise, which is the highest success one may attain**: 1) faith in God, the Most Beneficent and Most Merciful and in His noble messenger, Muhammad, and 2) performance of righteous acts as a result of this faith.

In chemistry, we may have two substances that have different properties separately, but when mixed together, the combination yields a desired product of use. Similarly, faith in the Creator of all that exists, God, and belief that His noble prophet, Muhammad, transmitted God's message to mankind, in combination with performing good (or righteous) acts, would lead one to the highest form of success: eternal paradise.

In life, man should work diligently so that he might obtain eternal rest and pleasure in paradise as a reward for his faith and good acts. The seeker of success is again reminded in the beautiful selected passage of today that the two essential ingredients for success, faith and good acts, when added together, yield success. And if one exists without the other, it alone is insufficient to yield success. The identified combination of faith (in God, the Most High and Most great, and in His beloved messenger, Muhammad) followed by good acts, has been most often mentioned in the Holy Quran as the prerequisite for entry into eternal paradise, the ultimate achievement for all seekers of success.

The seeker of success who wishes to reach his goal has complete faith in God, the Most Beneficent and the Most Merciful, and in His beloved messenger, Muhammad. He performs righteous deeds as a manifestation of his faith. **He knows that faith and performance of deeds of righteousness as a manifestation of faith together form the most important components of success.**

# Day 6

> Do you not know,
> that to God belongs
> the command of the heavens
> and the earth?
> And besides Him,
> you have neither protector nor helper.
>
> (2:107)

# Day 6

As mentioned in the earlier meditation in this collection (Day#4), encountering challenges, hardships, or setbacks is an inevitable part of life. The natural tendency when one encounters such resistance is to enlist others' help when one is not able to overcome such a situation himself. In the beautiful selected passage of today, the seeker of success is reminded that the entire earth as well as all existence is under the command of God, the Creator and Sustainer of all that exists.

Once the above point is understood, then one need not waste his energies on seeking assistance from others who have no control over events on earth or in the universe. Indeed, turning for help to anyone other than God, the One Who has complete control all that exists, could be considered a form of polytheism, i.e. the worshipping of others besides the One Source Who created all that exists. Does this mean that if one encounters a situation where one has to lift a 200 pound object to accomplish a task, that one should wait for God to help him? No. If a passerby is willing to help one lift the object, then one can enlist another's help, with the understanding and appreciation of God, Who created the other being and caused the situation to arise wherein one could be of help to the other.

Seeking help from others in itself is not an undesirable act, and which is closely related to being helpful to others, i.e. being mutually beneficial. If we could not help others, it would be difficult to fulfill part of what is expected from our stay on earth, i.e. performance of righteous deeds as a manifestation of faith. However, we must understand the fact that the Best Protector and Helper is God. The problem lies in expecting from others a solution to our problems and protection from harm. The individual who has faith in God the Source of all power and the Best Friend and Protector understands that relying on others instead of God for help and protection is as foolish as an individual who believes that a bank will help him with his financial needs in all situations, without realizing that the bank will only help if the individual has cash deposit in his account or a loan based on real or expected assets.

The seeker of success who wishes to reach his goal has absolute faith in God, the Cherisher and Sustainer of the worlds, and in His noble messenger, Muhammad. He knows that the command of the heavens and the earth is entirely under the command of God, the Most Great and the Source of all that exists. And he knows that besides his Lord, there is no one else that can help him.

# Day 7

To each is a goal
to which God turns him.
So strive together (as in a race)
towards all that is good.
Wheresoever you are,
God will bring you together -
for God has power over all things.

(2:148)

# Day 7

As we understand from the earlier meditation detailed in Day 2 of this collection, one of the prerequisites for success is having certainty that in the end, we will return to God, Who is the Creator of man and the Creator of all that exists.

All individuals have the option of either turning towards good or towards evil. The injunction made in the beautiful selected passage of today is not only to turn towards good, but that to turn towards good, one has to strive and expect to overcome obstacles. Additionally, the striving towards good is recommended to be done with others so as to encourage one another. Furthermore, the example of striving (as in a race) towards good implies competing with one another towards the reward of gaining of the pleasure of God, the Most High and the Most Generous, as children may compete with one another to receive the love of their parents.

An example of God, the Most Wise and the Most Loving, bringing people together as they strive towards good, would be the practice of the five daily communal obligatory prayers in Islam, encouraging all the faithful and the seekers of success to perform the highest form of good action, i.e. praising and worshiping one's Creator and the Creator and Sustainer of all that exists.

The beautiful selected passage of today closes with the reminder that God has power over all things, including the ability to turn one towards the good individually, and the ability to bring people together to perform good actions (as in a group during the communal obligatory prayers, or when people form a nation) towards Himself, which is the highest goal of all those who seek lasting success.

The seeker of success who wishes to reach his goal has unwavering faith in God, the Most Great and the Most Wise, and in His beloved messenger, Muhammad. He realizes that engaging in good actions for the sake of God, the Creator and Sustainer of all and the Most Generous One, is of utmost importance to him. He strives with the other seekers of success to do good, as in a race with others to seek the pleasure of his Lord.

# Day 8

Then do remember Me.
I will remember you;
and be grateful to Me,
and reject not faith.

O you who believe!
Seek help with patient perseverance
and prayers; for God is with
those who patiently persevere.

(2:152-153)

# Day 8

    The beautiful selected passage of today opens with a reminder not to forget the One Who created all that exists. If one is not focused, then there are plenty of distractions to keep one from remembering the Source Who brought into existence the individual as well as all that exists. It happens not infrequently that one may neglect the remembrance of God, Who is the Source of all that exists, until one is afflicted with a calamity. At that time, one then instinctively turns to God, the Most Beneficent and the Most Merciful, for help. The seeker of success would do well to remember his Lord at all times, including the times of ease, so that his Lord does not neglect him during his times of hardship.

    The seeker of success is instructed in today's beautiful selected passage to be grateful to God, the Most Kind and the Most Generous. There are countless things for which one should be grateful to God, including one's faculties of sight, hearing, intellect, etc. One is instructed not to reject faith in God, the Creator and Sustainer of all, as faith is the primary ingredient of success.

    The seeker of success and one who has faith in God, the Most Great and the Best Friend and Protector, is likely to encounter hardships in the path of life and his quest to successfully reach his goal. At such times, he is likely to turn to God, the Most Glorious and the Most Trustworthy, for help. The method of seeking God's help is relayed in the beautiful selected passage of today: prayer (including both the obligatory Islamic prayers as well as personal supplications) and patient perseverance.

    The seeker of success who wishes to reach his goal has unwavering faith in God, the Owner of all that exists, the Most Righteous Teacher and the Most Patient One, and in His noble messenger, Muhammad. When faced with hardship, he seeks his Lord's help with patient perseverance and prayer. When blessed with comfort, he remembers his Lord with sincere appreciation and gratefulness.

# Day 9

And say not of those who are slain
in the way of God: "they are dead".
By no means! They are living, though
you perceive it not.

Be sure We shall test you with something of fear and hunger, some loss in goods or lives, or the fruits (of your toil). But give glad tidings to those who patiently persevere;

Who say, when afflicted with calamity:
"Truly! To God we belong, and truly to Him is our return!"

They are those on whom (descend) blessings from their Lord, and Mercy, and they are the ones that receive guidance.

(2:154-157)

# Day 9

One is expected to encounter challenges of various degrees in life. The beautiful selected passage of today proclaims with certainty that one will be tested with hardships such as fear, hunger, loss of goods or property, or even loss of life. Is there any way other than judging one's performance on testing, to determine to what degree one has mastered a subject? Therefore, the tests of life as listed above will be given by God, the Creator and Sustainer of all that exists, to all of mankind.

The best approach to handling the tests in life, especially calamitous afflictions, is given in the beautiful selected passage of today: First, realize that one's goal is towards God, the Most Beneficent and the Most Merciful, regardless of the outcome. One can simply affirm this concept by mentioning the following saying, which is well-known to the faithful and is uttered at the news of another's death or of a catastrophe: "Truly! to God we belong, and truly to Him is our return!". Good news is given by God, the Most Great and the Best Guide, to those whose approach to the tests and challenges of life include perseverance; these are the people on whom will descend the Mercy, Blessings and Guidance of God, the Creator of all that exists. **These are the people who will be successful!**

With the limited knowledge that we have as human beings, we have designed a system wherein an individual is reimbursed for his knowledge, skills and services with monetary and material benefits. In the case of those individuals who perform beyond what is normally expected of them, we are not at all hesitant to reward them with impressive bonuses in recognition of their outstanding services. Indeed, the largest employers of our times, the hundreds of countries in existence at present, bestow their highest honors to those who have served them to the best of their ability and given their lives in the service of their country, as martyrs. Therefore, it is not surprising at all that God, the Most Powerful and the Most Rich, informs us in the beautiful selected passage of today that those who serve their Lord most selflessly and are slain in the process will be rewarded with **the highest form of success**; indeed, they will never die at all, but instead live at all times**, in the highest honor, for eternity**, although we are not able to perceive it at this time with our limited senses.

The seeker of success who wishes to reach his goal has complete faith in God, the Most Great, Most Generous and Most Wise, and in His beloved messenger, Muhammad. He realizes the importance of tests to distinguish between the mediocre and the gifted individuals. When afflicted with adversity in life, he patiently perseveres and reminds himself that everything in existence belongs to God, the Most Great and the Most Glorious, and to Him is the return of all. He knows that the highest form of service is that spent in the path of God, the Lord of all majesty and reward.

# Day 10

**And your god is one God:
There is no god but He,
Most Gracious, Most Merciful.**

(2:163)

# Day 10

This is a short passage, but includes the key elements that need to be understood by the seeker of success. If one can contemplate the wonders of life, including its beauty, such as the sun and the moon, the water and the trees, or a baby's laugh, as well the destructive forces in life, such as a hurricane or an earthquake, uncontrollable fire, an airplane crash, or a malignant tumor, it is possible to come to the erroneous conclusion that each of the individual factors described above are under the command of a separate being; it would be impossible for these separate beings to communicate with each other and coordinate their activities to the minutest detail that is required for the universe to function effectively. However, having all the forces described above, and those not described, when guided by a single commander-in-chief, would avoid chaos and result in an orderly structure, such as we can see in an individual cell or a galaxy.

Moreover, where did this matter come from that we have been discussing above, i.e. the matter that makes up an individual cell or a galaxy, and how was it structured and how is it being maintained? The answer: By the One Most Powerful and Most Merciful, Who gets no benefit in return. Should we not turn to this Source with praise, seeking guidance and help? It is crucial for the seeker of success to know where to turn for guidance, i.e. to the Source Who created all that exists, and to Whom is the return and goal of all: God.

A proper understanding of today's beautiful selected passage is essential for acquisition of the primary ingredient of success: faith, which can then lead us towards the other vital ingredient of success: performance of righteous deeds as a manifestation of faith. Additionally, we attain a better understanding of God's Graciousness, as manifested by the countless blessings He has provided us, including the vital components necessary for life, i.e. water, air, nutrition, and our bodies working in harmony with these factors to carry out our will, as well as His Mercy in giving us time and Guidance to learn to exhibit gratefulnesss and appropriate attention to carry out the duties for which we were created, until the Day of Judgment.

The seeker of success who wishes to reach his goal has absolute faith in God, the Most Glorious, the Most Powerful, and the Only One, and in His noble messenger, Muhammad. He knows that all that is in existence has been created by God, is sustained by Him and is to return to Him. He knows that there is no God but He – the Most Gracious and Most Merciful. It is to Him that he turns for Guidance, and He is the central focus of every single moment of his life.

# Day 11

When my servants ask you concerning Me, then (answer them), I am indeed close (to them). I listen to the prayer of every supplicant when he calls on Me. Let them also, with a will, listen to My call, and believe in Me, that they may walk in the Right Way.

(2:186)

# Day 11

Access to authorities such as the governor of a state or the president of a country is difficult, if not impossible, for most people. One must make appointments far in advance and go through various intermediaries to have an audience with such authorities. The beautiful selected passage of today is a notification to all that access to God, the Creator and Sustainer of all that exists, is available to all persons at all times, and without any intermediaries.

All are assured in the beautiful selected passage of today that when one addresses the Creator of all that exists in a supplication or prayer, that it is heard by the One for Whom it was intended. However, it is not guaranteed that one will receive everything he requested, just as a parent may not grant everything a child requests even though the parent is perfectly capable of granting such a request. One of the author's favorite parables of the Power of God as relayed by his beloved messenger, Muhammad, is one where it is explained that if all humans were to ask for whatever they desired and all were granted their requests from God, the Most Rich and the Most Generous, it would be like taking from the possession of God an amount comparable to a drop from an ocean.

We are reminded in the beautiful selected passage of today that the privilege of such direct access given to man by the Creator of all that exists as we discussed above, carries with it the responsibility to listen to the call and instructions from Him Who created everything, and follow the Guidance given in the Holy Quran, so that he may be guided to the Most Righteous Way and succeed.

The seeker of success who wishes to reach his goal has unwavering faith in God, the Most Great, the All-aware and the One Who listens to every being's supplication, and in His beloved messenger, Muhammad. He knows that his Lord listens to him every time he calls on Him. And the seeker of success knows that this honor and privilege carries with it the responsibility to listen to the call of God, the Most Wise and the Most Loving One, as addressed to all mankind through His noble messenger, Muhammad, so that he may walk in the Most Righteous Way and attain the highest level of success.

# Day 12

**And spend of your substance
in the cause of God, and make
not your hands contribute to (your)
destruction; but do good –
for God loves those who do good.**

(2:195)

# Day 12

People are so occupied by the dynamic nature of life, first acquiring the abilities to earn their resources, then optimizing their earning ability, and later in life maintaining or further increasing their resources, that they may not realize at all how they are actually spending their available resources.

In the beautiful selected passage of today, God, the Most High and the Most Great, instructs mankind to consciously spend from the (lawful) resources available to them in His cause. The consequences of not spending from one's resources in the cause of God, the Most Wise and the Most Forgiving, are described, including one's own demise. If one is not spending his available resources in the cause of God, the Most Beneficent and the Most Merciful, then one may alternately (and unknowingly) spend his resources in a cause against Him – in which case he is making his own hands and his own resources a cause of his own destruction.

Today's beautiful selected passage ends with the injunction to do good, for God, the Most Loving and Most Kind, is the Best Example of One Who does good, from which He expects nothing else in return. In some professional specialty examinations, we hear about the vague nature of the examinations, sometimes to maintain the exclusivity of a privileged group. However, we are fortunate that the Creator of all that exists, gives us clear guidance on how to successfully pass the test of life, which is indeed the biggest and the most important test for all of us.

The seeker of success who wishes to reach his goal has complete faith in God, the Most Beneficent and the Most Merciful, and in His noble messenger, Muhammad. He spends consciously from his resources in the cause of his Lord and performs good deeds as a manifestation of his faith.

# Day 13

**And there are men who say:
"Our Lord! Give us good in this
world and good in the hereafter,
and defend us from the torment of the Fire!"
To them will be allotted what they
have earned. And God is swift in (taking) account.**

**(2:201-202)**

# Day 13

There is no doubt that every individual wants to succeed, whether he is aware of it or not. Some seekers of success (including yours truly) start on a journey of actively seeking a formula to succeed – however, the success sought is usually still sought even up to death. Today's precious message goes beyond the transient success of this life and guides one towards the highest success: both in this life and the life after death, which is eternal.

The beautiful selected passage of today is a key supplication that used to be mentioned in most of the beloved prophet Muhammad's supplications, which includes the repeated personal supplications of a Muslim after the completion of the obligatory prayers five times daily – and for good reason.

Should one succeed in this world and fail in the hereafter, as one might consider to be the goal of a materialistic person, albeit unconsciously? Or should one succeed in the hereafter and fail in this life, as one might consider to be the goal of a hermit whose only concern is ritual worship? The key here, as in most issues, is in finding the right balance for the seeker of success, i.e. to succeed both in this world and in the hereafter.

The beautiful selected passage of today closes with the assurance that those who seek success in both this world and the hereafter will be granted their wish. One of the most important keys to success is the establishment of goals. And if the seeker of success establishes the goal of achieving success in this world and in the hereafter, God willing, he will reach it. Moreover, as we learned in an earlier meditation, because there is a direct line of communication between the supplicant and the Creator of all that exists, at all times, the intentions of the seeker of success are instantaneously known to God, the Most Great and the All-aware, and accounted for.

The seeker of success who wishes to reach his goal has absolute faith in God, the Most Great, the First and the Last, and in His beloved messenger, Muhammad. He has the intention of, and works actively towards attaining good in this world and in the hereafter and of being saved from the ultimate failure, i.e. the eternal punishment, equivalent to the torment of being in the fire. He asks his Lord to help him attain his goals.

# Day 14

**They ask you concerning wine
and gambling. Say: "in them is
great sin, and some benefit, for men;
but the sin is greater than the benefit".
And they ask you how much they are to
spend. Say: "that which is beyond your needs".**

(2:219)

# Day 14

The beautiful selected passage of today clarifies two factors that can prevent the seeker of success from reaching his goal: alcohol and gambling, both of which can be prominently identified as key vices in many of the "problem areas" of major metropolitan centers.

The first factor mentioned in today's beautiful selected passage that can prevent the seeker of success from attaining his goal is alcohol, which may result in a transient feeling of pleasure, increased openness, or even improved cardiac function, when taken in a small or moderate amount. However, ingested in larger amounts, alcohol can cause headaches, bloody vomiting, loss of judgment, and the destruction of various organs, including the liver, as well as of the brain and nerves. Even in the most "enlightened" or permissive societies, ingestion of alcohol is not allowed while one is on duty at work. God, the Creator and Sustainer of all that exists has therefore not allowed ingestion of alcohol to man while he is "on duty" on earth to accomplish the tasks he was created for. After one's duty is completed on earth, and if one has been successful in completion of his duty, one's reward will be paradise, where there is no work expected and alcohol will therefore be allowed, as mentioned in the Holy Quran.

With regard to gambling, its benefits are that it may enrich the winner, or appear to improve the economy of a community. However, a closer look reveals that while gambling may produce one winner, it has produced a thousand losers. While improving the economy of a community slightly in the short term, gambling may result in increasing poverty, crime and misery over the long term, and it is not conducive to family development. It is especially damaging towards the youth, whose judgment has not yet been refined and who are the keys to the future.

Today's beautiful selected passage closes with guidance on what one should spend (in the cause of God, the Most Great and the One Who provided to man whatever is in his possession): "what is beyond your needs". This does not require further commentary. The seeker of success is trusted to gauge his needs in good faith and not to breach the trust of the One Who provided him with the resources in his possession.

The seeker of success who wishes to reach his goal has unwavering faith in God, the Most Wise, the Best Guide, and the Most Righteous Teacher, and in His noble messenger, Muhammad. He realizes that there is greater sin and harm than profit in alcohol and gambling, and stays far from them accordingly. He spends whatever is beyond his reasonable needs in the path of his Lord and considers it as the best investment of his resources.

# Day 15

**And make not God's (name) an excuse in your oaths against your doing good and acting piously, and making peace among mankind. And God is the One Who hears and knows all things.**

(2:224)

# Day 15

Today's beautiful selected passage instructs man in the performance of righteous deeds by listing some of them specifically for our benefit. Since performance of righteous deeds is one of the two primary components of success, it is of special concern to the seeker of success. It also instructs man to avoid participating in undesirable activities and especially to avoid invoking the Name of God, the Most Holy, Most Beneficent and Most Merciful, as an excuse for participating in undesirable or harmful activities.

The performance of activities that fall under the category of righteous deeds for the sake of service to God, the Almighty, the All-hearer and All-knower, start with a general category that is labeled "doing good". Here one can refer to one's innate ability to distinguish right from wrong, which man has been equipped with as a gift from God, the Most Wise, the Most Rich and the Enricher. Complete reliance on this ability, without seeking guidance from God, the Best Guide and the Most Righteous Teacher, cannot be in one's best interests in the long run due to the conflict of interest with one's animalistic tendencies for the preference of immediate gratification. Other specific righteous deeds that the seeker of success is instructed to perform include acting piously – praising God, the Most High and the Lord of the worlds, glorifying Him, devoting oneself to His worship, and making peace among mankind.

The main distinguishing feature of the beautiful selected passage of today is the instruction not to make God's name an excuse against doing good, for God is the Doer of Good and commands this to all who hope to succeed, with the performance of righteous deeds being next in importance only to faith in the pursuit of success. We find especially in these days that certain individuals and groups utilize the name of God, the Most Beneficent and Merciful, and the commitment to a life of submission to Him, i.e. Islam, which encourages one to do good, to sometimes do exactly the opposite, i.e. to cause suffering and to sow discord rather than peace among mankind, thus doing things that are contrary to what constitutes glorifying God's Name. These individuals and groups invoke the name of God, the Most Beneficent and Most Merciful without following the path commanded by Him; that is, they do not necessarily follow the religion of Islam, but worship something else, such as an ideology like communism or hedonism, carrying out undesirable activities (as described above), and invoking God's name in vain. Regardless, whoever invokes the Name of God, the Most Kind and Most Loving to work against doing good, preventing others or themselves from increasing their closeness to God and sowing discord among mankind instead of peace, is acting against the instructions of God, the Almighty and the Creator and Sustainer of all, and those who do so, even when invoking His Name, will not succeed. In fact, they will incur his wrath.

The seeker of success who wishes to reach his goal has uncompromising faith in God, the Most Beneficent, Most Merciful, and the Doer of Good, and in His noble messenger, Muhammad. He does not make the Name of his Lord an excuse against doing good. He acts piously and in a pious beneficent way, and attempts to make peace among mankind.

# Day 16

**Guard strictly your (habit) of prayers, especially the middle prayer. And stand before God in a devout (frame of mind).**

(2:238)

# Day 16

One of the key ingredients of success according to God, the Creator and Sustainer of all that exists, has been identified as prayer. As we will learn in more detail in the later passages, man was created for the purpose of worshipping God, the Most Glorious and the Most Great. Therefore, if man is successful in any other endeavor, he would logically be marked a failure if he was not successful in accomplishing the primary reason for his creation, i.e. worshipping and serving the One Who created him and all that exists. As we discussed in the earlier passages, worship and prayer include the methods of praising the Creator and Sustainer of all, as well as personal supplications and other activities. The esteemed reader is referred to the meditation of Day 3 in this collection for a more detailed discussion on worship

Once the importance of the role of prayer is realized, then one can guard one's habit of prayer as one who has precious jewels would likely guard such things in a corresponding manner because he knows their value. The middle prayer of the five obligatory prayers (Asr, the one that usually falls between 3pm and 5pm in the afternoon), has been identified as the one to guard especially - most likely because it is the easiest to neglect, as one is usually busy completing various tasks of the day during this time.

Further instructions in the execution of the important task of prayer or worship are provided in the beautiful selected passage of today for the seeker of success: that he should feel as though he is standing before God, the Creator of the universe, in private audience, having His full attention - for God, the Most Great and the Creator of all that exists, is able to be at all places at all times! For such an important occasion, then, one must be appropriately cognizant of details such as cleanliness, reverence, and above all, intention.

The seeker of success who wishes to reach his goal has complete faith in God, the Almighty, the Best Guide and the Best of those who keep account, and in His beloved messenger, Muhammad. He values immensely the opportunities he has for direct communion with God, the Most Great and the Most Praiseworthy, and stands before his Lord in prayer in a devout frame of mind. Realizing the importance of prayer in helping him to reach his goal, the seeker of success guards strictly his habit of prayer, especially the middle prayer in the afternoon and one which is most susceptible to neglect.

# Day 17

**Who is he that will loan to God
a beautiful loan, which God will
double unto his credit and multiply
many times? It is God that
gives (you) want or plenty, and to
Him shall be your return.**

(2:245)

# Day 17

    The beautiful selected passage of today invites the seeker of success to make an investment with incredible results guaranteed to multiply the initial investment many times over – by providing a beautiful loan to God, the Creator and Sustainer of all that exists. Why is God, the Owner of all and the Most Rich One, asking for a loan from man, who depends on the same Creator for every breath that he takes, and for every beat of his heart? Is it because God, the Supreme Creator of the Universe and all that exists, wants to provide men with an outstanding opportunity to improve others' chances for succeeding as well as improving their own condition? Is it because the Most Generous Creator, Who has given man his faculties of sight, hearing and reasoning for no charge at all, would be pleased that some men would care enough for others' success beyond meeting their own needs? Any opportunity that man has to advance the cause of God, the Most Holy and the Most Great – which includes meeting the needs of those lacking in resources, or making it easier for others to be able to succeed, is an opportunity for man to advance his own condition, as God, the Most rich and the Most Generous, considers these assets as a loan to Him and returns them multiplied manifold, as becoming of His Generosity and Appreciativeness. The honorable reader is referred to the meditation on Day 21 of this collection for a more detailed discussion on the amazing return on investment on the cause of god, the Best of those who keep account and the Most Generous.

    The seeker of success realizes that his situation with regards to abundance or want of resources is ultimately determined by God, the One Who created everything in existence and has power over all that exists, and that He provides rewards or punishments based on one's motives and intentions i.e., whether one seeks to serve the Lord God, the Loving Creator and Sustainer of all that exists.

    The astute seeker of success realizes that he will not be able to take his worldly resources into his grave, and that one day he will meet his Creator, Who will hold him accountable for all the gifts and resources given to man and how he has utilized these resources.

    The seeker of success who wishes to reach his goal has absolute faith in God, the Most Magnificent and the Best Rewarder, and in His noble messenger, Muhammad. He realizes that it is only God, to Whom is the return of all, Who is responsible for whether he experiences want or plenty. He realizes that the best investment of his resources is in the way of his Lord, the One Who is Most Wise, the Most Rich, and the Most Generous.

# Day 18

**God! There is no god but He – the Ever-living, the One Who sustains and protects all that exists. No slumber can seize Him nor sleep. His are all things in the heavens and on earth. Who is there that can intercede in His presence except as He allows? He knows what (appears to his creatures) before or after or behind them. And nor shall they encompass anything from His knowledge except as He wills. His throne does extend over the heavens and the earth, and He feels no fatigue in guarding and preserving them – for He is the Most High, the Supreme (in glory).**

(2:255)

# Day 18

    The incredibly sublime passage of today consists of one relatively long verse from the Holy Quran, which touches on the key points needed for understanding the greatness of God, the Creator and Sustainer of all that exists. Hence, it is one of the most beloved passages of the faithful, and is identified by the noble prophet Muhammad as **the most important verse in the Holy Quran**.

    First, God the Holy Creator informs us in the most beautiful selected passage of today that there is no other creator except Him – the Most Gracious, the Most Merciful One, the Originator of all that exists, and to Whom is the return of all. He informs mankind that He is living, has always lived and that He is eternal. Also, God, the Most Gracious Benefactor of all that exists further clarifies and expounds on His characteristics by informing us that He is not in need of anything or anyone for His subsistence, but that everything and everyone depends on Him for their subsistence. An understanding of this concept is the key to acquisition of faith, the most important component of success

    Second, God, the Most Compassionate One and the Source of all existence, relays to the seeker of success the route to take for achieving success: through Him and Him alone, to Whom belongs all that exists in the heavens and the earth. Moreover, God, the Most Wise and Creator of all that exists, is responsible for guarding His creation, without experiencing fatigue, slumber or sleep for all eternity. Would the seeker of success be considered wise if he were to bypass God, the True Source of all power and guidance, and turn instead to the other things created by the Most Beneficent Source of all that exists, for guiding him towards true success?

    The seeker of success who wishes to reach his goal has unwavering faith in God, the Most Great, Ever-living, Self-subsisting and Eternal One, and in His beloved messenger, Muhammad. He refers often to the beautiful selected passage of today - which is one of the most important set of instructions that will guide him to lasting success, in order to strengthen his faith, the most vital component of success

# Day 19

**Let there be no compulsion in religion – truth stands out clear from error. Whoever rejects evil and believes in God has grasped the Most Trustworthy Handhold that never breaks. And God hears and knows all things.**

(2:256)

# Day 19

The seeker of success is also a seeker of truth – for truth will guide one from darkness to light, while error will lead one from light to darkness. The gracious seeker of success wishes for others the same as for himself, whether it's in this life or the hereafter. Conversely, those mired in ignorance, error, or perversity, wish for others the same. God, the Most Gracious Creator and Sustainer of all that exists, has absolute power to do as He wishes, including turning all His creatures towards His worship. However, God, the Most Wise and the Most Compassionate, sends us guidance on this matter, specifying not to use compulsion even for the purpose of bringing others to His worship. If God, the Most Powerful and the Most Compassionate, does not use compulsion or force others to worship Him, let man also not force others - but instead invite them to God's worship and service in a gracious manner, and lead them towards lasting success .

One yearns for security from different sources at different stages in one's life. A child feels secure in placing his trust in his parents to meet his needs. An adult may feel secure placing trust in material reserves, such as a retirement fund or property, to meet his future needs, or he may trust his boss for his employment, or the police chief to keep order in his city. However, the one who places his trust in God, the Most Powerful, the Most Beneficent and the Most Merciful Creator of all that exists, has indeed grasped the Most Trustworthy Handhold that never breaks – it is a binding promise from God, the Most Benevolent, Who created the universe and all that exists, and sustains it to perfection in the minutest details, the One Who is All-knowing and hears every prayer of every supplicant at all times, in all places.

The seeker of success who wishes to reach his goal has complete faith in God, the Most Holy, the Truth and the Best Friend and Protector, and in His noble messenger, Muhammad. He chooses truth over error, good over evil, and chooses for security the Handhold of God, the Most Great and the Most Powerful, over security provided by any other alternative - by rejecting evil and believing in God, the Creator and Sustainer of all, and in His noble messenger, Muhammad. He invites other to the path of lasting success graciously, and without the use of compulsion.

# Day 20

God is the Protector of those who
have faith; from the depth of darkness,
He will lead them forth into Light.
As for those who reject faith, their
patrons are the evil ones: from Light,
they will lead them forth into
the depths of darkness; those will be
companions of the fire, to dwell
therein (forever).

(2:257)

# Day 20

Unlike any other created entity we know of, man is endowed with the will to choose. A stone cannot choose to move from one city to another; a tree cannot choose to speed up the ripening of its fruit; a rabbit does not choose to clear broken glass from a pathway so that other rabbits or creatures may not harm themselves. Man does share some similarities with other animals in having certain basic instincts. However, only man is able do such things as, when coming across some sumptuous food, and having not eaten for 14 hours, still not partake of the food because he is fasting that day for the pleasure of God, the Most Wise Creator of all that exists.

The seeker of success is awed by the beauty and orderliness in his universe. He realizes that the odds of such beautiful order as we see arising out of disorder is less than one in infinity. He appreciates the Power and Generosity of God, the One Who created order out of disorder and maintains it in perfection. He has faith in God, the One Who has Absolute Power over all that exists. He knows that he will certainly be tested in his faith – but he perseveres patiently and is rewarded by being guided towards the Light from the depths of darkness.

One who fails to appreciate the authority of God, the Possessor of all power and the Creator of order, will be supported by evil and evil beings; he will end up in the depths of darkness. God, the Most Great and the Most Kind One has provided sufficient guidance to man as to how to protect himself from the eternal punishment of the hell-fire as a consequence of rejecting His authority over all that He has created and sustains, and persisting in evil as a result.

The seeker of success who wishes to reach his goal has complete faith in God, the Creator of all, the Most Able Protector and the Best Guide, and in His noble messenger, Muhammad; he chooses the Goodness and Light that emanates from God over the evil and darkness that emanates from all sources other than God, the Most Righteous Teacher and the Source of all good. He understands that evil and darkness is epitomized in the accursed Satan.

# Day 21

**The parable of those who spend their
wealth in the way of God is
that of a grain of corn;
it grows seven ears, and each ear has a
hundred grains. And God gives manifold
increase to whom He pleases. And
God cares for all and He knows all things.**

(2:261)

# Day 21

The beautiful selected passage of today expounds on one of the surest methods of achieving success: spending one's resources for the sake of God, the Most Rich, the Most Generous, and the Creator of all that exists. We spend of our time and resources for a relative, friend, or place of employment at least minimally to maintain satisfactory relationships; when we spend a little more than the minimum, in good faith, such as when we buy a present for a relative or help a neighbor fix his home or stay a few hours extra at the workplace when needed, the recipient will appreciate our sacrifice, and, more than likely, will return the favor by giving back more than was received.

When we give a gift from our resources, such as money, other assets, or time, to the cause of God, the Richest and the Possessor of all Majesty and Honor, He promises to return to us more than what we have spent in His cause. In the beautiful selected passage, an excellent example is given of the return on one's investment in the cause of God, the Most Great and the Source of all good: a grain of corn, having been planted, reaches maturity and produces countless kernels of corn, all from the one grain of corn, under the direction of God, the Most Generous and the Majestic Creator of all that exists. It is indeed a superb investment for the seeker of success.

God, the Provider of all our needs, the Creator and Sustainer of all that exists, the Possessor of all knowledge, and He Who is aware of every action and every thought in every place at all times, is indeed able to enrich beyond any measure anyone he wishes. Indeed, as mentioned in an earlier meditation in this collection, the noble prophet Muhammad explained that if every individual on earth were to ask God, the Owner of all that exists and the Most Generous, for everything they wished, and he were to grant it to all those who asked, it would be as if a drop was removed from an ocean.

The seeker of success who wishes to reach his goal has unwavering faith in God, the Creator and Sustainer of all that exists, and in His noble messenger, Muhammad. He enthusiastically spends from all his available resources in the way of his Lord, as a manifestation of his faith, knowing that it is the best investment he can make, and that it will be reimbursed to him by an unimaginable measure - although the main goal is the pleasure of his Lord.

# Day 22

**Those who spend their wealth in the cause of Allah, and do not follow up their gifts with reminders of their generosity or with injury, their reward is with their Lord.**

**Kind words and covering of faults are better than charity followed by injury. God is free of all wants and He is Most Forbearing.**

(2:262-263)

# Day 22

We learned from the earlier meditations how much charity is pleasing to God, the Most Generous and the Most Appreciative One, as well as how profitable it is to the one who is giving the charity. This concept is again mentioned in the beautiful selected passage of today for reinforcement. In addition, today's beautiful selected passage informs us about particular aspects of charity, or how we can maximize our earnings and reward from giving charity. The first aspect of charity described in the beautiful selected passage of today, has to do with safeguarding the rewards we earned from the giving of charity and which, as we learned earlier, is similar to the output from a kernel of corn which results in harvesting from that kernel of corn, countless other kernels. Suppose there was a disease that afflicted the corn we harvested while it was in storage, and which destroyed 80 percent of the harvest? Certainly, the individual who is more successful would have been able to take appropriate precautions to shield his harvest from being destroyed. Similarly, we are informed in the beautiful selected passage of today that the rewards we accumulate from the giving of charity can be negated by causing subsequent injury such as reminders of our generosity, whether they take the form of words or actions. Although one may not be inclined to such behavior, knowing that it is not in one's best interest to hurt those whom we are attempting to help by giving charity, helps us to be guided toward the optimally beneficial path, and maximize the benefit from the giving of charity. The above factors describe the preferred method of giving charity

The second factor addressed in today's beautiful selected passage describes other methods besides financially supporting a needy person, which have similar merit as, or falling in the category of giving money in charity, and thus being eligible for reward from God, the Most Kind and the Most Generous: Speaking kindly to others and hiding others' faults; these actions are identified as more worthy than charity followed by publicizing one's generosity, with respect to the rewards from the view of God, the All-knowing, the Bestower of all honors and rewards, and the One Who is Most Wealthy. The noble prophet further expounded on this subject and directed that every good action is a form of charity – whether it is something as small in financial worth as giving of half a date to someone, or something that has no financial value, such as smiling at someone. Certainly, we can all afford to give charity, no matter how our financial situation is, and improve our likelihood of attaining success.

If man is discouraged from giving charity by the mistaken perception that charity is helping God, the Most Rich and the Only One Who is free of all wants, because He is not in need of charity, man should realize that when he is giving charity, he is most of all helping himself. And if one has in the past engaged in the unbecoming behavior that is discouraged in the beautiful selected passage of today, i.e., giving charity followed by injury to fellow man or boasting about it, or exposing others' faults, then he should seek the forgiveness of God, and he will find Him Most Forgiving and Most Kind.

The seeker of success who wishes to reach his goal has absolute faith in God, the Most Kind, Most Forbearing and the Only One in existence free of all needs, and in His beloved messenger,

Muhammad. He takes care not to negate the benefits he accrues from giving charity by engaging in acts harmful to others or boasting about his charity. He realizes the importance of kind words and covering of others' faults, and anything else that may help others, such as smiling at someone. He realizes charity consists of non-financial as well as financial matters in his possession that he can give to others to help them.

# Day 23

**O you who believe!
Cancel not your charity by reminders of
your generosity or by injury – like those
who spend their substance to be seen
of men, but neither believe in God
nor on the Last Day. They are in parable
like a hard barren rock, on which is
a little soil; on it falls heavy rain
which leaves it (just) a bare stone. They
will be able to do nothing with what
they have earned. And God guides not
those who reject faith.**

**And the likeness of those who spend their
substance, seeking to please God and to
strengthen their souls, is as a garden, high
and fertile. Heavy rain falls on it and
makes it yield a double increase of harvest;
and if it receives not heavy rain, light
moisture suffices it. God sees well
whatever you do.**

(2:264-265)

# Day 23

    Today's beautiful selected passage touches on the most central and key aspect of life and success according to the Holy Quran, the word of God, the Creator and Sustainer of all that exists and the Most Wise: Faith. The seeker of success should, therefore, consider faith as the prerequisite and essential ingredient for all success, i.e., faith in God, the One Who created everything that exists out of nothing, gave it order and beauty, and sustains it in perfection, and in His noble prophet Mohammed through whom the Holy Quran was relayed to mankind.

    One of the most beautiful parables in the Holy Quran is provided in the profoundly sublime passage of today and discusses what would happen if the key ingredient for success, i.e., faith, were missing, even though some of the other ingredients were present. In the beautiful selected passage of today, is given the example of one of the results of faith, which is giving charity, and which as we reviewed in the earlier meditations, leads to a great return on one's investments

    If a rebel from the authority of God, the Most Beautiful and the Inspiration of faith, were to argue that he would do good deeds and anything else that is virtuous, except having faith in God, the Creator and the Sustainer of the universe and the Hearer and Seer of everything, his good deeds and any other virtues would be like heavy and plentiful rain on a hard, barren rock – it would remain a barren rock. On the other hand, when one who believes in God, the Most Wise One and the Giver of life, spends from his resources for His cause, his good deeds and other virtues are like heavy rain on fertile land – they result in a significant increase in harvest; the most beautiful portion of this parable is that even if heavy rain were not provided to the fertile soil, then light moisture would be sufficient for it.

    The seeker of success who wishes to reach his goal has unwavering faith in God, the Most Great and the Creator and Sustainer of all, and in His beloved messenger, Muhammad; and he knows that it is the most valuable ingredient for attaining lasting success. Consequently, throughout his life, he actively pursues all opportunities daily that can strengthen his faith and lead him closer toward his goal. He realizes that an important opportunity for him to exhibit and strengthen his faith is spending generously in the cause of God, the Most Generous and the Best Rewarder, and does not hurt others by words or actions, nor reminds others of his generosity.

# Day 24

**The evil one threatens you with poverty and bids you to improper conduct. Allah promises you His forgiveness and rewards. And Allah cares for all and He knows all things.**

(2:268)

# Day 24

    The beautiful selected passage of today very effectively compares good and evil, and, more importantly, lists the consequences of following the path man has chosen for himself.

    God, the Most High and the Best Creator, created man in the best of forms – the most beautiful and intelligent of all beings; as a matter of fact, He breathed His Own Spirit into man. Therefore, man is in fact considered the vicegerent of God, the Most Beneficent and Most Merciful, on earth. However, Satan, the arrogant one, has challenged God, the Creator of all that exists and the Most Merciful, saying that he will mislead man, whom God, the Most Beneficent and Most Merciful, has preferred over all other creation, and that he will make man forget the reason for his creation, and will attempt to work against the plan of God, the Most Holy and Most Gracious, i.e., he will attempt to make man go from being the highest in the sight of God the Most Loving and the Most Generous One, to the lowest of the creatures, by misleading man from his mission in life. The accursed Satan can attempt to steer away man from his responsibilities toward God the Most Holy and Most Patient, by making man feel that if he continues to worship and serve God the Creator and Sustainer of all, then he might become poor; and that if he works against God the only Ever-living and Self-subsisting One in existence, then he may attain riches in this life.

    The outcome is clear to see: one who follows the way of Satan or the evil one with acts such as disobeying God, the Most High and Most Great, by lying, stealing, causing mischief and misery to others, or having sexual intercourse without responsibility, will be unsuccessful in both this life and the hereafter. On the other hand, the wise individual who chooses to discard all evil and be close to God, the Most Great and the Source of all goodness, is promised forgiveness for previous sins and also rewards without limits; both in this life and the hereafter, and for all eternity.

    The seeker of success who wishes to reach his goal has absolute faith in God, the Most Great and the Creator of all good as well as evil, and in His noble messenger, Muhammad. He realizes the consequences of choosing good and evil. He knows that, in fact, when he is not selecting good over evil, he is selecting evil and its associated consequences. He consistently selects good over evil, despite the temptation of short-term pleasure and the constant efforts of Satan and his agents.

# Day 25

**If you disclose (acts of) charity, even so it is well; but if you conceal them and make them reach those (really) in need, that is best for you. It will remove from you some of your (stains of) evil. And God is well acquainted with what you do.**

(2:271)

# Day 25

    We have learned from the earlier meditations in this collection that one of the most important methods of earning the pleasure of God, the Lord of all majesty and reward and the Only One deserving of praise, is giving charity. And could there be any higher success for man than earning the good pleasure of God, the Most Kind and the Most Generous? Why is charity so pleasing to God, the Creator and Owner of all that exists? Is it because He created all that exists from nothing, and provided to creation invaluable gifts, such as vision, hearing and reasoning, for no charge or effort, and is pleased when man, the epitome of His creation, in whom He breathed His Own Spirit, behaves most like Himself, the Most Gracious and the Best Provider? And that when man provides to others only for the sake of love for God, with the intention of benefiting others, he not only fulfills his duty as being the vicegerent of God the Most Generous and Most Kind on earth, but also flatters his Lord (and more correctly worships Him), because what can be a higher form of flattery than imitation ?

    Different grades of methods for giving charity are described in the beautiful selected passage of today, with the highest form of charity being anonymous provision to the most destitute and those in real need and the next highest being the provision of charity for its own sake, along with the disclosure of charity. This importance of giving in charity without boasting has been repeated a number of times for our re-inforcement, so we can optimize our rewards from charity and for attaining success

    God, the Most Forgiving and the Most Generous, promises us that just as soap and water remove stains from clothes, so too charity will remove some of the stains of one's evils. God, the Most Kind and the Most Wise, takes careful account of the actions of all His creation, and He is the Best Appraiser and the Most Reliable Keeper of accounts.

    The seeker of success who wishes to reach his goal has unwavering faith in God, the Most Great, the Most Forgiving, and the Most Generous, and in His beloved messenger, Muhammad. He realizes the importance of helping others in helping him to reach his goal - especially those in most need, for no other reason than the love of God, the Most Great and Most Kind, and as a manifestation of his faith.

# Day 26

**(Charity is) for those in need who, in God's cause are restricted (from travel), and cannot move about in the land, seeking (trade or work); the ignorant man thinks, because of their modesty, that they are free from want. You shall know them by their (unfailing) mark: they beg not annoyingly from everyone. And whatever of good you give, be assured God knows it well.**

(2:273)

# Day 26

Today's beautiful selected passage again expounds on fulfilling one of the acts most pleasing in the sight of God, the Almighty and the Sustainer of all and is, therefore, important for achieving success – and second only to His worship in terms of performance of righteous deeds: giving of charity.

One would be overwhelmed if he went out with a sack of money into the marketplace announcing that he is giving away money to those in need; he would instantly be besieged by those professing to be in need, until one's sack of money was quickly exhausted. It is likely that those who were in significant need of assistance might not have been present in the marketplace, and if they were, a certain portion of the people would not want to openly ask for charity and would find it humiliating, on par with begging. The seeker of success would do well to realize that by giving charity, he is benefiting himself more than the recipient of the charity, and therefore it is his responsibility to identify the most deserving recipients: those who are striving to advance the cause of God, the Source of all that exists, the Expander (who expands the resources to enable one to be able to give in charity) and the Constrictor (who constricts the resources to allow one to be dependent on others). The ones most in need of charity are identified, in the beautiful selected passage of today, as the ones least likely to beg or request charity. Similar to a gardener who will not just water the most prominent plants over and over, but who seeks to water the plants also likely to be forgotten - and so benefits from a garden in bloom throughout, the seeker of success should identify as many individuals as possible whom he can help - both in the community and in his relations, and therefore benefit himself (from being rewarded by God, the Most Appreciative and the All-seeing and All-hearing One).

All that one spends in charity is known to God, the Most Reliable Witness and the Best of those who keep account. The immense rewards of charity have been described in the earlier passages as "manifold", and likened to multiple ears of corn resulting from the growth of a single kernel that is planted and harvested.

The seeker of success who wishes to reach his goal has complete faith in God, the Creator and Sustainer of all, and in His noble messenger, Muhammad. He gives regular charity as a manifestation of his faith and makes a sincere effort to identify those who are in need of charity, knowing that some who are in most need of it may also be least likely to ask for it.

# Day 27

**Those who believe, and do deeds of righteousness, and establish regular prayers and regular charity, will have their reward with their Lord; on them shall be no fear, nor shall they grieve.**

(2:277)

# Day 27

    The beautiful selected passage of today begins with the main ingredients needed for success, and which are mentioned most frequently by God, the Most Loving Creator and Sustainer of all that exists, in the Holy Quran: Faith in God, the One Who originated existence, and sustains it - as relayed to us through His noble messenger, Muhammad, and manifestation of that faith by actions that reflect such faith, i.e. by doing righteous deeds.

    In the beautiful selected passage of today, details are provided to us about two of the most important righteous actions, and which will lead one to attainment of success: regular prayers and regular charity. As we will learn in the later passages, the purpose of man's creation is, as with all other creation, to worship God, the Most Magnificent and All-powerful Creator of all that exists. The esteemed reader is referred to the commentary of Day 3 of this collection of meditations on a more detailed discussion of worship. It is logical that one cannot expect to succeed if one is neglectful of his primary task. God, the Most Beneficent One, Who created all that exists out of nothing, and provided invaluable gifts to His creation, such as vision, hearing and the ability to reason, is Alone responsible for nourishing and sustaining it. Man most closely resembles his Creator and acts as His vicegerent, as he is expected to do, when he is able to forgive the mistakes of those accountable to him and to provide, from his resources, to others in need, simply for the sake of the love of God, the Most Beneficent One Who has provided him with all the resources.

    The seeker of success who wishes to reach his goal has absolute faith in God, the Most Supreme One and the Only One worthy of all praise, and in His beloved messenger, Muhammad. He performs righteous deeds as a manifestation of his faith - the most important of which include regular prayers and regular charity, solely for the sake of pleasing his Lord.

# Day 28

**O you who believe! When you deal with each other in transactions involving future obligations in a fixed period of time, reduce them to writing.**

(2:282)

# Day 28

One of the most important reasons that Islam provides one with assurance and peace of mind is that it is not a theoretical concept, with ideals achievable for only a few, but rather provides clear guidance for practical and daily real-life issues; today's beautiful selected passage is one such example.

Many a friendship and relationship has soured and worsened because two close friends, relatives, neighbors, or colleagues initially agreed on a financial transaction, but did not feel a need to write down the terms or time period of the transaction (such as a personal loan), because doing so might question the closeness of their relationship. The fact is that, after several weeks or months have passed, with thousands of other events having been recorded in one's memory, it would not be unusual to find that neither of the two parties has a clear recollection of the details of the transaction to which they had agreed. It is doubtful that the general expectations, and specifically the details, of the two parties' agreements would be remembered by both, and is likely that one party forgets some pre-conditions that were very important to the other party. Writing down a transaction occurring between two parties assures that both parties begin with a clear understanding of the transaction taking place, and that both parties can refer to the written document of the transaction at any time in the future for any questions that may arise up until the obligations by both parties have been met. This ensures that both parties will discharge their business obligations in a professional manner without compromising their personal relationship.

The seeker of success who wishes to reach his goal has uncompromising faith in God, the Most Wise One and the Best Witness, and in His noble messenger, Muhammad. When dealing with others in transactions involving future obligations in a fixed period of time, including his friends and relatives for whom he is not responsible for their maintenance, he has them recorded clearly in writing for future reference, until obligations by both parties have been met.

# Day 29

To God belongs all that is in the heavens and on earth. Whether you disclose what is in your minds or conceal it, God calls you to account for it. He forgives whom He pleases, and punishes whom He pleases - for God has power over all things.

The messenger (prophet Muhammad) believes in what has been revealed to him from his Lord, as do the men of faith. Each one (of them) believes in God, His angels, His books, and His messengers; "We make no distinction (they say), between one and another of His messengers". And they say: "we hear, and we obey; (we seek) your forgiveness, our Lord, and to You is the end of all journeys".

On no soul does God place a burden greater than it can bear. He will be rewarded for that (good) which he has earned, and he will be punished for that (evil) which he has earned. (Pray:) "Our Lord! Condemn us not if we forget or fall in to error; our Lord! Lay not on us a burden like that which you laid on those before us; our Lord! Lay not on us a burden greater than we have strength to bear. Pardon us and grant us forgiveness. Have mercy on us. You are our Protector. Help us against those who stand against faith".

(2:284 – 286)

# Day 29

Selected for today is one of the most sublime passages of the Holy Quran, which begins with the affirmation that all matter everywhere has been created by God, the Creator and Sustainer of all that exists. However, unlike in the case of the trees, stones, water, or even angels, God, the Most Holy and Loving Creator and Sustainer of all that exists, holds man accountable for all his actions, including his hidden thoughts.

Man is reminded in today's beautiful passage not to follow his instincts or passions, but rather to follow the guidance provided by God, the Most Beneficent and Most Merciful through His honorable messengers, including Adam, Noah, Abraham, Moses, Jesus, and His final messenger, the beloved Muhammad, until the Day of Judgment.

Man is additionally reminded that life is not a coincidence where things happen randomly, but in fact is a test - successful completion of which, as determined on the Day of Judgment, **is the highest form of success**. Any teacher or professor, when testing students, would provide the necessary guidance and instruction during his or her teaching, so that the students have a reasonable chance of successfully completing the examination of the course. God, the Best Guide and the Best Teacher, has, through His messengers, provided guidance to mankind as to how to successfully pass the test of life and thus achieve eternal happiness and success. Moreover, God, the Most Merciful and Sublime Creator and Sustainer of all that exists, reassures man that he will not be burdened with a load greater than he is able to carry; in times of seemingly insurmountable hardship, the seeker of success would do well to remember this beautiful safety feature provided by God, the Most Compassionate and Creator of all that exists.

The seeker of success who wishes to reach his goal has unwavering faith in God, the Most Great, the Creator and Sustainer of all that exists, and in His beloved messenger, Muhammad. He knows that he will never be burdened by his Lord, the Most Kind and Compassionate One, with a load greater than he has the capacity to bear in the life of this world.

# Day 30

**He (God) it is Who has sent down to you the Book: in it are verses that are basic or fundamental (of established meaning); they are the foundation of the Book, and others are allegorical. But those in whose heart is perversity, follow the part thereof that is allegorical, seeking discord, and searching for its hidden meanings. But no one knows its hidden meanings except God. And those who are firmly grounded in knowledge say: "We believe in the Book; the whole of it is from our Lord". And none will grasp its message except men of understanding.**

**"Our Lord!" (they say) " Let not our hearts deviate now after you have guided us, but grant us Mercy from Your Own Presence; for You are the Provider of rewards without measure;**

**Our Lord! You are He Who will gather mankind together against a Day about which there is no doubt; for God never fails in His promise".**

(3:6-8)

# Day 30

    The seeker of success is reminded in today's beautiful selected passage to refer to the Holy Quran for guidance on achieving his objective from the life of this world. And when one refers to the Guidance from God, the Most Wise and the Source of all that exists, one is instructed to look for Guidance clearly marked as such. As for those passages in the Holy Quran that are allegorical in nature, these are supportive in nature to the fundamental messages provided in the Holy Quran, whose understanding may be bestowed on a few fortunate souls who are avidly seeking closeness to, and understanding of, God the Most Holy Creator and Sustainer all that exists.

    After attaining the valuable Guidance provided by God, the Most Great and the Most High, the seeker of success should pray that he does not deviate from the path of success leading to his Creator, Who is able to provide rewards "without measure" or limits. Let not the seeker of success short-change himself by opting for transitory material success on earth while disregarding the possibility of unlimited rewards from God, the Creator and Possessor of all that exists. Rather, the aim of the individual sincere in his faith and of the seeker of success, is success both in the life of this world and in the hereafter.

    Let the seeker of success be firm in his conviction and belief that all his actions will be judged on a Day when all mankind will be held accountable for every action and thought, or lack thereof. The seeker of success who followed the Guidance provided by God, the Most Beneficent Creator of all that exists, will be rewarded by God, the Most Great and the Master of the Day Judgment, and will be worthy of a reward from He Who is the Most Generous and the Possessor of all that is in existence.

    The seeker of success who wishes to reach his goal has uncompromising faith in God, the Most Great and the Most Righteous Teacher, and in His noble messenger, Muhammad. He knows that he is accountable for all his actions and that every moment of his life is valuable, which he maximizes for his benefit by seeking the true Guidance from his Lord. He knows that God, the Most Wise and Most Loving, has provided him with the most clear Guidance in the Holy Quran and he does not search for hidden meanings in it. He is ever careful in straying from the path of success and seeks his Lord's help from being disgraced in the future, after having been blessed with the gift of His Guidance earlier.

# Day 31

Fair in the eyes of men is the love of things they covet: women and children, heaped-up hoards of gold and silver, horses branded (for blood and excellence), and (wealth of) cattle and well-tilled land. Such are the possessions of this world's life. <u>But in nearness to God is the best of the goals.</u>

Say: shall I give you glad tidings of things far better than those? For the righteous are gardens in nearness to their Lord, with rivers flowing beneath; therein is their eternal home – with companions pure (and holy) and the good pleasure of God. For in God's sight are (all) his servants;

Those who say: "Our Lord! We have indeed believed; forgive us, then, our sins, and save us from the agony of the fire";

Those who show patience, firmness and self control, who are true (in word and deed), who worship devoutly and who pray for forgiveness in the early hours of the morning.

(3:14-16)

# Day 31

There is no question that every individual desires success. Even an individual who resorts to crime or murder wishes for success – even though in this case it is clear that the success obtained by a murderer upon taking possession of the wealth of the victim is only short-term and may be followed by a long period of incarceration or other punishment. The common perception of success is the accumulation of wealth, including gold and precious metals, property, top-of-the line automobiles, and the quality and quantity of spouses (or girlfriends, for men) and children (the importance of which is somewhat lessened although not entirely, due to the increasing monetary value of material assets in one's wealth) . This perception has not changed significantly during recorded history. However, the seeker of success would do well to remember that **the ultimate measure of success will be how close he will be to God,** the Most Wise and the Most Honorable Creator of all that exists, on the Day of Judgment. A description is provided in the beautiful selected passage of today of the comforts for those who will be nearest to God Most High, in addition to the blessedness of His closeness: gardens with flowing rivers, flowers and fruits along with beautiful and honorable companions .

Additionally, God Almighty and Most Glorious has, through His messengers, kindly provided to mankind clear directions as to how to attain closeness to Him. The important tools of all true seekers of success in order to reach their goal are: a foundation of firm faith in God, the Creator and Sustainer of all that exists, as relayed to us by His noble prophet Muhammad, without associating anything else with Him, and to engage in righteous actions – the most important of which is practice of regular worship, as well as worship at other times (especially in the morning), along with other righteous actions including patience, conviction of purpose, and self control. Truly, God Most High and Most Holy, has been kind to His creation by guiding them so clearly towards Him and towards success. It is well to remember that worship is the reason why man was created by God, the Most Holy and the One deserving of all praise. The esteemed reader is referred to the meditation of Day 3 in this collection for a more detailed discussion of worship.

The seeker of success who wishes to reach his goal has absolute faith in God, the Most Glorious and the Most Trustworthy, and in His beloved messenger, Muhammad. He engages in sincere praise and worship of his Lord, exhibiting patience, firmness, and self-control throughout his life. He knows that no imaginable possession compares to the honor of attaining **nearness to God, the Most Powerful, the Most Rich, and the Eternal One - and which is truly the highest form of success.**

# Day 32

Say: "O God! Lord of Power (and Rule), You give power to whom You please, and You take away power from whom You please; You endow with honor whom You please, and You bring low whom You please; in your hand is all good. Indeed, over all things You have power.

You cause the night to gain on the day, and You cause the day to gain on the night; You bring the dead out of the living, and You give sustenance to whom You please, without measure".

(3:26-27)

# Day 32

    Today's beautiful selected passage begins with the affirmation that the object of our worship is the One Who is the Most Holy Creator of all that exists and the Source of all power, and it ends by affirming the tremendous extent of the power of God, the Most Beneficent Creator of all that exists, including His ability to predictably cause the succession of each day by night; to cause death to things with life (such as occurs in autumn); and to bring life into things that appear without it (such as occurs in spring, when the trees are filled with life after appearing dead during the winter). Surely such a Creator can, on the Day of Judgment, bring back to life the humans who have died, to be held accountable for their actions (unlike the trees, which have no free will).

    The seeker of success is reminded to acknowledge that God, the Most Holy One, Who has control of all power, is able to bestow it on whomever He wills, and to take it away from whomever He wills. The wise seeker of success would therefore do well to remember that the strategy for acquiring success, power or honor is not by acquiring wealth or titles, but by fulfilling the commandments of, and pleasing, God, the True Source and Creator of all power and Possessor of all majesty and honor. And when God, the Most Praiseworthy Source of all power, is pleased, He can provide His fortunate servant with power, honor, or rewards without measure and beyond all expectation.

    The seeker of success who wishes to reach his goal has, with the highest degree of certainty, faith in God, the Most Great Creator of all that exists and the Source of all power, and in His noble messenger, Muhammad. He knows with absolute certainty that all thingss in existence are under the complete control of God, the Most Holy, Most Powerful, and the Source of all that exists. In his quest for power and anything else that he desires, he knows that the Only One Who can grant it to him is God, Who is the Most Majestic, Most Great, and the Exalter as well as the Abaser.

# Day 33

**Say: if you do love God, follow me; God will love you and forgive you your sins: for God is Most Forgiving, Most Merciful.**

(3:31)

# Day 33

Today's beautiful selected passage is short, but it carries profound directives that would serve the seeker of success well on his journey. First of all, the astute seeker of success must have faith in, and love for God, the Most Merciful Creator and Sustainer of all that exists - for countless reasons, including the realization that he has been endowed by God, the Most Magnificent and the Most Generous, with the most invaluable gifts, including sight, hearing, speech, intelligence and mobility. This love for the Most Beneficent and Generous Creator leads the thankful recipient of these gifts to praise and worship Him Who provided these invaluable gifts, and not to associate anything or anyone else in His worship because all other beings and all matter are subservient to the Most Holy and Generous Creator of all that exists.

Second, the thankful recipient of the invaluable gifts provided by God, the Most Holy Creator and Sustainer of all, needs to search for the proper instructions from his Creator, Who is Most Wise and not in the least unjust to anyone. A sign of the Holy Creator's justice and wisdom is that He has sent messengers to guide the seekers of success in their quest. And the seal of the messengers is the beloved prophet Muhammad, after whom there will be no other messengers until the Day of Judgment. For this reason, the intelligent seeker of success will, after the Quran, look to Muhammad, the noble messenger, for further guidance because he has been so instructed by God, the Most Holy Creator and the Most Righteous Teacher.

Because all humans are fallible and prone to sin, we are reassured that the sincere believer in God, the Most Great and the Most Holy, who seeks the guidance of his Lord from the Holy Quran and follows the example of His noble messenger, Muhammad, will earn the love and pleasure of God, the Most Great and Most Glorious, as well as His forgiveness. The best employer may overlook the temporary negligence of his employee (such as carelessness in performing his duties) up to a point, but here we are reminded that God, the Most Loving Creator and Sustainer of all that exists, is also the Most Forgiving and the Most Merciful, and Whose Mercy has no limits. The individual who earns the love and forgiveness of his Lord is the most fortunate one indeed in terms of achieving success.

The seeker of success who wishes to reach his goal has unwavering faith in God, the Most Great and the Most Loving Creator and Sustainer of all that exists, and in His noble messenger, Muhammad. Out of all the things that he loves, including himself, he places the love of God, the Most Great and the Most Forgiving One, at the highest level by far; he follows the example of the beloved prophet Muhammad in how best to express this Love of the most special nature.

# Day 34

**Say: "O people of the book! Come to common terms as between us and you: that we worship none but God; that we associate no partners with Him; that we erect not, from among ourselves, lords and patrons other than God". If then they turn back, say: "Bear witness that we (at least) are Muslims (submitting to God's will)".**

(3:64)

# Day 34

    The beautiful selected passage of today instructs the family of believers who share a common revelation from God, the Most High and the Most Great, i.e. the Old Testament, the New Testament, and the Holy Quran, in the art of civil interaction. The thousands of instructions provided by God, the Most Just and the Most Righteous Teacher, unite the disparate believers under one banner, i.e. all family members (believers) acknowledge God as the Most Supreme and the Only One Worthy of worship. At the same time as the family of believers is united in the cause of God, the Most High and the Most Great, the causes of dissension are identified, and it is recommended that they are dissolved for the benefit of the believers in God, the Most High and the Most Wise, i.e. to not associate any partners in the worship of God Almighty, and the Only One deserving of any praise, as all praise belongs to God Alone. For example, if we wish to praise the intelligence of an individual who scored perfectly on an examination, it would be appropriate to say: "Praise to God Who provided him with superb intelligence", as the individual did not make his own brain nor was any other real or imagined entity such as the god of intelligence responsible for this sign of intelligence. This is the primary injunction to the believers in all three of the monotheistic religions, i.e. to not associate any other being in the worship of God, the Most High. This is the first and the most important of the well-known Ten Commandments from the Old and the New Testaments of the Jewish and the Christian traditions.

    If, in spite of polite invitation, discourse, and attempts at reconciliation, without association of any other being in the worship of God, the Most High and the Most Great, believers of the older two of the three sister monotheistic faiths turn their backs on those who have submitted themselves to God, the Creator and Sustainer of all, then the seeker of success, who wishes for others what he wishes for himself, may politely depart from the unconvinced individuals by identifying himself as one who has surrendered himself to the will of God, the Most High and the Most Praiseworthy, i.e. as a Muslim.

    The seeker of success who wishes to reach his goal has complete faith in God, the Only One Who is deserving of any and all praise and is the Creator and Sustainer of all, and in His noble messenger, Muhammad. He politely invites all towards the path to success, seeking common ground with those who follow the earlier revelations in the Old and the New Testament and also known as the older paths to success. He does so without compromising his faith, which he knows is his most valuable asset.

# Day 35

**By no means shall you attain righteousness unless you give (freely) of that which you love; and whatever you give, truly, God knows it well.**

(3:92)

# Day 35

    The seeker of success is repeatedly instructed by God, the Most High and the Most Great, in the Holy Quran, regarding the two basic requirements for the attainment of success: 1) belief in the existence of God, the Omnipotent and Omniscient Creator and Sustainer of all that exists, and 2) performance of good deeds or righteous actions as a manifestation of #1 above.

    The beautiful selected passage of today expounds on one of the above two requirements for attaining ultimate success, resulting in entrance into everlasting paradise, by attaining righteousness. We are instructed that one of the key ingredients for the attainment of righteousness is to give away that which we love, i.e. charity – and which is second only to worship of God, the Most Holy and the All-Aware

    We know that God, the Most Great, is the Most Beneficent and Most Merciful Provider and Sustainer of all creation. Therefore, all creatures are considered the family of God the Most Great. We also know, as relayed by the noble prophet Muhammad, that because all creatures are considered the family of God, the Most Loving and Most Wise, God is most pleased with any individual who is kind to His family; in this instance, being kind to anyone is considered being kind to a member of the family of God, the Most High and Most Great. One of the best ways of showing kindness to anyone is giving someone in need what he is lacking – whether it is financial support, security, comfort, or happiness.

    Any act of kindness, including giving away whatever one values to another who is in need of those things, is considered the key to righteousness. All such acts are recorded by the All-knowing Creator of everything in existence and will be rewarded many times over in their value. This is a binding promise made by God, the Most Trustworthy One, the Most Generous, and the Creator of all that exists, and is one of the key ingredients for the attainment of success.

    The seeker of success who wishes to reach his goal has absolute faith in God, the Most Loving Creator and Sustainer of all that exists, and in His beloved messenger, Muhammad. He manifests his faith with acts of righteousness and knows that giving freely of the things in his possession he loves, is one of the best acts of righteousness and manifestation of his faith.

# Day 36

**The first house (of worship) appointed for men was that at Bakka (Mecca): Full of blessing and of guidance for all kinds of beings.**

**In it are signs manifest: (For example), the station of Ibrahim – whoever enters it attains security; pilgrimage to there is a duty men owe to God, for those who can afford the journey. But if any deny faith, God stands not in need of any of His creatures.**

(3:96-97)

# Day 36

    The beautiful selected passage of today identifies the Kaaba in Mecca as the first house of worship for mankind. As the first house of worship, it is especially blessed and favored by God, the Most Wise and Most Loving Creator of all that exists. There are signs in Kaaba that facilitate the closeness of an individual to his Creator, even though it was once corrupted by the presence of idols and signs of others being worshipped besides God, the One and the Only One worthy of all praise and worship, prior to its cleansing by the noble prophet Muhammad. One of the signs specifically mentioned as important is the station of Ibrahim, the prototype and ideal of one who left the worship of all false gods and directed his faith, worship, and trust to only God, the Unseen and Most Holy Creator of all that exists, without associating any imagined partners with Him, and was thus credited with the honorable title "friend of God". Just like the noble prophet Ibrahim, who refused to associate anything else with the worship of God the Most High, we should not elevate the prophet Ibrahim as an object of worship, but rather strive to be like him. The prophet Ibrahim left the security of his previous life and was willing to suffer, if necessary, to attain closeness to God, the Most High, the Lord of all that exists, and was rewarded for his efforts with the highest title possible for man, as the "friend of God". One who, like the beloved prophet Ibrahim, sets aside his routine and security and, despite hardships, makes an effort to come closer to God, the Most High and the Most Great, will recreate these steps when he performs the pilgrimage to Mecca; the one who does these things sincerely, like the beloved prophet Ibrahim, is fulfilling one of the requirements for success as instructed by God, the Most High and Most Wise, in the Holy Quran. May the one who fulfills his requirements sincerely have his efforts also rewarded like the noble prophet Ibrahim, as the "friend" of God, the Most Beneficent and Most Merciful.

    The seeker of success who wishes to reach his goal has unwavering faith in God, the Most Great and the Creator and Sustainer of all that exists, and in His noble messenger, Muhammad. He realizes the importance of recreating the steps in Hajj, the great pilgrimage, that the noble prophet Ibrahim took in his search for enlightenment and the attainment of closeness to God, the Most Great, Most Glorious, and the First and the Last. These steps were so pleasing to His Lord, that He has ordained that all of mankind who wishes to attain success shall repeat them at least once in their lifetime

# Day 37

**O you who believe! Fear God, as He should be feared, and die not except in a state of Islam.**

**And hold fast, all together, by the rope which God (stretches out for you), and be not divided among yourselves; and remember with gratitude God's favor on you; for you were enemies and He joined your hearts in love, so that by His Grace, you became brethren; and you were on the brink of the pit of fire, and He saved you from it. Thus does God make His signs clear to you (so) that you may be guided.**

**Let there arise out of you a band of people inviting to all that is good, enjoining what is right, and forbidding what is wrong: <u>they are the ones who attain success.</u>**

(3:102-104)

# Day 37

The beautiful selected passage of today instructs the seeker of success in three methods to facilitate his goal. First, God, the Most Beneficent and Kind, has instructed man to fear Him, even though He is the Most Merciful. Why is it that God is reminding us to fear Him rather than reminding us to love Him? Is it because He loves us so much that He does not want to see us fail? God, the Most Loving and Most Merciful, has created man for a purpose, and that is to worship and serve Him – everything else that man can do is of secondary concern. And if man has not been successful in fulfilling his prescribed primary duty, then he is held accountable for that – the result of which is eternal punishment. And if man has been successful in fulfilling his required duty, then he will be rewarded for that – the result of which is eternal happiness. Why does God, the Most Merciful and Most Kind, punish rather than ignore man's disregard of his prescribed duties? In the vast universes and all of creation and existence, man is known as the only creation whom God, the Most Great and the Most Wise, brought into existence by breathing of His spirit. In fact, man is the deputy of God, the Most High and the Most Great, on earth. If man chooses to ignore the preciousness of his existence and acts in ways contrary to the nature of God, the Most Beneficent and Most Merciful, then he will be punished based on the seriousness of the breach of his responsibility, which is profound. A logical conclusion of this responsibility is the importance of the state of the individual at the time of his death: Does the individual continue to fear his Lord throughout his life, and hence will be counted among the successful? Or would the individual be unfortunate and even though he may have at one time feared his Lord - no longer recognizes his role on earth? This would be extremely unfortunate indeed, as the state of the individual at the time of his death is immensely important, similar to the state of an individual whether he chooses to be among the group that takes precautions and is saved in a storm, or remains in the group that ignores the storm, and does not take the necessary precautions

Second, God, the Most Magnificent and Most Wise, is instructing man in today's beautiful passage that one of the methods for achieving success is to remain united with the other seekers of success in trusting in, worshipping, and serving Him Who created man from nothing. Man is instructed in the benefits of unity and teamwork, which are required for the fulfillment of the mission as instructed by God, the Most Wise and the Most Righteous Teacher. Individual virtuosity is of a naturally selfish nature and even though it is relevant to the virtuosity of a community, what is more important is that the whole group should be engaged in collective betterment of the society. Fulfillment of the mission of God, the Most Holy and Most High, requires collective action on the part of believers, so that their joint effort may result in the victory of Good over Evil throughout.

Third, as we reach the climax of today's beautiful selected passage, we find that if both of the instructions described above are to be followed, i.e. learning the consequences of disregarding the duties of profound nature prescribed to man by God Most Great and Most Kind, and staying united with the other believers in fulfilling the mission of God Most Loving and the Creator and Sustainer of all, then the best method to instill the necessary characteristics of success in as many individuals as possible is to form a group of the faithful for the purpose of inviting others to success as instructed by God, the Source of all good and the Most Righteous Teacher. In the beautiful selected passage of today, the one who invites others to success is indeed promised success by God, the Most Wise, Most Generous and Most Trustworthy.

The seeker of success who wishes to reach his goal has unwavering faith in God, the Most Beneficent and Most Merciful, and in His noble messenger, Muhammad. He has the highest degree of love for God, the Most Compassionate and the Source of all creation, and therefore fears disappointing Him by neglecting the duties of immense value that have been assigned to him. He knows that he is more likely to accomplish his mission in life if he keeps company with those who are on the same mission as himself, and remains united with them. He knows that those who attain the highest degree of success are not content with wishing success for themselves only, but wish for others the same – by inviting all people to that which is good, enjoining that which is right, leading them to success; and forbidding that which is wrong and would lead them towards failure.

# Day 38

**You are the best of peoples evolved for mankind: Enjoining what is right, forbidding what is wrong, and believing in God.**

(3:110)

# Day 38

    Today's beautiful selected passage is short, but its meaning is full of richness, like the richness of a diamond, despite its small size. God, the Most High and Most Great, has instructed us (as described in other meditations in this collection) that man has been created for a purpose: to worship his Creator. The esteemed reader is referred to the commentary of Day 3 of this collection of meditations on a more detailed discussion of worship. Not knowing the reason for one's existence will lead to serious problems both in the short and the long term. The seeker of success will find in today's beautiful selected passage three diamonds that are precious and will serve him well in life and guide him towards his goal: Enjoining what is right, forbidding what is wrong, and believing in God.

    The first requirement for the attainment of success, as per God, the Most Compassionate and Most Merciful, is the belief or faith in God, the Loving Creator and Sustainer of all that exists. One who does not acknowledge the authority of his superior – whether that authority is a parent in the home, the boss in the workplace, the coach training the sports team, or the head of state in the country in which one is living – is not only indicating that he will not act in accordance with what the specific authority figure requires of him, but, more dangerously, that he may act against the requirements of the authority figure and thus hurt not only himself, but others as well. Therefore, the person who believes in God, the Most Loving and the Most Powerful, as the Source of all creation and existence, acknowledges the authority of the One Who created all that exists and the One Who sustains this creation. The belief in God, the Most Great and the Source of all creation, as per the message relayed by the beloved prophet Muhammad, (the absolute requirement and the primary ingredient of success), is the first diamond in the beautiful selected passage of today; when this belief, or faith, is combined with righteous acts or virtuosity, it results in true success, and is repeated many times by God, the Most Wise and the Most Righteous Teacher, in the Holy Quran. The one who calls himself Muslim is recognized as **the best of all people** in creation by God Himself, the Most Beneficent and the Creator of all that exists, and the One Who possesses all honor and glory. This supreme honor is bestowed by God, the Most Holy and the Most Great, for the wise individual who acknowledges the authority of the One Who created and sustains all that exists, follows the Guidance provided by Him through His holy prophet, Muhammad. The second and third diamonds of the beautiful selected passage of today result from following the first diamond, i.e. faith, and lead the individual to 1) performing what is right and required of him, and 2) avoiding that which is wrong. As we have noted previously, and which we will enumerate in the further meditations in this collection, faith and righteous actions are the main ingredients to lasting success. The fortunate individual who is truly successful, does not behave selfishly by keeping the requirements of success, as we discussed above, to himself, but rather wishes for others what he wishes for himself, so that they too may succeed.

    The seeker of success who wishes to reach his goal has complete faith in God, the Most Great and the Most Glorious, and in His beloved messenger, Muhammad. He is honored knowing that he has been placed in the category of the best among mankind by God Himself, the Most Holy Creator and Sustainer of all, for his unwavering faith and for enjoining, both to himself and to others, that which is right, and forbidding that which is evil, as a manifestation of his faith.

# Day 39

O you who believe! Devour not interest, doubled and multiplied; <u>but fear God, that you may really succeed.</u>

Fear the fire, which is prepared for those who reject faith.

And obey God and the messenger – that you may obtain Mercy.

Be quick in the race for forgiveness from your Lord, and for a Garden whose width is that (of the whole) of the heavens and of the earth, prepared for the righteous –

Those who spend (freely) whether in prosperity or in adversity; who restrain anger, and pardon (all) men – for God loves those who do good;

And those who, having done something to be ashamed of, or wronged their own souls, earnestly bring God to mind and ask for forgiveness for their sins (and who can forgive sins except God?), and are never obstinate in persisting knowingly in (the wrong) they have done.

For such, the reward is forgiveness from their Lord, and gardens with rivers following underneath – an eternal dwelling: <u>How excellent a recompense for those who work (and strive)!</u>

(3:130-136)

# Day 39

    The beautiful selected passage of today provides various details of the do's and don'ts for the benefit of the seeker of success to remember during his journey in life. A specific item clearly identified in the list of don'ts to be avoided by the seeker of success, is the benefit obtained by charging interest. Why is the benefit of charging interest specifically mentioned by God, the Most Beneficent and Most Merciful, as one of the factors that the seeker of success should avoid? Is it because when interest is charged on a loan, we are specifically aiming to benefit from the most susceptible members in society – those who are lacking in resources to meet their needs and so they have to borrow money? Is it because when we intend to benefit from the misery of others, we are behaving in a way that is most in opposition to the characteristics of God, the Most Loving, the Most Beneficent and the Most Merciful, Who provides and sustains all that is in existence for no remuneration? Even the praises and worship so deserving of the Creator and Loving Sustainer of all, are not for His benefit at all, but for the benefit of man – so that he may fulfill his required duties and so attain the ultimate success.

    Also clearly identified in today's beautiful selected passage is another item on the list of don'ts, which is the act of rejecting faith. Rejecting belief in God, the One Who created and sustains all that exists, leads one to act contrary to the specific purpose for which man was created, and understandably leads to **the ultimate loss, i.e. eternal punishment in the hell-fire,** about which God, the Most Loving, warns man, so that he may take the alternate route, that leading to paradise, which is the destination God, the Most Kind and Generous, would rather have man achieve.

    As for the list of do's for the seeker of success, the beautiful selected passage of today mentions the requirements in exquisite detail, as expected from the One Who is Most Wise and Most Generous, and Who desires all men to achieve success by entering paradise and avoiding the punishment of hell. The respected seeker of success is referred directly to the text of the beautiful selected passage for the list of do's that will serve him well and help him to reach his goal. Additional commentary from the humble author on these recommendations/commandments provided by God, the All-knowing, the Most Wise and the Most Righteous Teacher, is not necessary.

    The seeker of success who wishes to reach his goal has absolute faith in God, the Most Great and the Most Glorious, and in His beloved messenger, Muhammad. He refrains from knowingly or unknowingly benefiting from the plight of others by charging interest on their loans. He obeys God, the Most Beneficent and Most Merciful, and His noble messenger, Muhammad, performs good deeds regularly as a manifestation of his faith, forgives those who have wronged him, gives regular charity, controls his anger, and seeks forgiveness from God, the Most Forgiving One, to Whom belongs all praise, and Who is the Only One Who can forgive our sins.

# Day 40

**Did you think that you would enter heaven without God testing those of you who fought hard (in His cause) and remained steadfast?**

(3:142)

# Day 40

Any person considered successful will attest to the fact that the attainment of success is not by chance or intuition, but the result of careful planning and persistence in the desire to reach one's goals. God, the Most Loving and the Most Generous One, instructs mankind in the Holy Quran that the **ultimate measure of success for man is the attainment of paradise and avoidance of punishment from the hell-fire.** One is reminded by God, the Most High and the Most Great, that the quest for success for man will require first the understanding of the duties that need to be fulfilled in order to be considered successful by God, the Most High, the Wisest and the Best Judge. After understanding what duties are required from him, the seeker of success will need to remain disciplined and focused on the ultimate prize, i.e. the highest form of success, because the road to success is uphill and difficult, while the road to failure is downhill and easy. God, the Most Beneficent and the Most Merciful, reminds the seeker of success that he will be tested during his journey and that when there are no external threats, he will have to fight hard against himself and the desire to abandon the hardships of the uphill quest for the alternative downhill route and the temporary ease associated with it. When there are external threats, then the seeker of success may indeed have to fight the external threats that are preventing him from reaching his goal and to which is his right.

While the seeker of success is on the uphill journey towards his goal and fighting to overcome the evil within himself and/or externally, he is reassured by God, the Most Powerful and the Most Patient One, to be steadfast during his trials, which are a test from God, the Most Wise and the Most Powerful One, to see who is most befitting to be rewarded with the ultimate measure of success, i.e. eternal paradise.

The seeker of success who wishes to reach his goal has unwavering faith in God, the Most Great and the Most Wise, and in His beloved messenger, Muhammad. He knows that the most precious diamonds have been subjected to the highest degree of stress. He remains steadfast in his journey of life, striving and fighting hard against internal threats, i.e. those of his ego, influenced by instructions from Satan, as well as against external threats, i.e. those of Satan and the enemies of faith, in order to achieve his goal.

# Day 41

**...If any do desire a reward in this life, we shall give it to him; and if any do desire a reward in the hereafter, we shall give it to him. And swiftly shall we reward those that (serve Us with) gratitude.**

(3:145)

# Day 41

The beautiful selected passage of today will serve as reassurance for the seeker of success from God, Who is the Most Rich as well as the Enricher, and explains the reason for preferring long-term benefits, despite suffering hardships in the short-term. And if he strives and is patient, man will indeed attain what he aspires for.

If man desires a reward in the present life as we know it, he can utilize all his resources and strength in the pursuit of the rewards valued in this life: an advanced educational degree, excess capital, the most desirable spouse, etc. God, the Most Excellent and the Source of all power, reassures man that if he desires reward in the hereafter, he shall be so rewarded as well, and which is **the ultimate measure of success**. The impatient individual who desires a reward in this life only shall have what he wished for, but he will be sorely disappointed with his folly, just as a bank robber will be disappointed when he serves his term in prison, even though he enjoyed temporarily his stolen wealth. The wise individual who will succeed, as promised by God, the Most High and the Most Trustworthy, shall have his reward not only in the hereafter, but also in this life as well – and he is the one who prays: "Our Lord! Grant us good in this life and good in the hereafter" (please refer to this collection of meditations, Day# 13).

Therefore, the individual who struggles in this life to please his Lord and suffers hardships throughout his life, yet remains steadfast as he climbs the uphill path leading to his Creator, the Most Holy and the Most Loving One, will be profusely pleased with his outcome, while the individual who spent all his effort in acquiring the benefits of the world at the expense of the hereafter, will come to learn of his utter foolishness. According to the Holy Quran, as documented in another passage (23:112-113), compared to man's existence in eternity to come, the life of this world will appear but a fleeting few hours – hence, the wise individual will spend his life in this world for maximum benefit in the hereafter, not vice versa.

The seeker of success who wishes to reach his goal has complete faith in God, the Most Holy and the One deserving of all praise, and in His noble messenger, Muhammad. He knows the value of being able to postpone the lure of short-term gratification for the love of his Creator, Who is the Truth, the Eternal One, the Most Generous, and the Most Loving One.

# Day 42

**And if you are slain, or die, in the way of God, <u>Forgiveness and Mercy from God are far better than all they could amass.</u>**

**And if you die, or are slain, then indeed it is unto God that you are brought together.**

(3:157-158)

# Day 42

Today's beautiful selected passage helps the seeker of success to understand, cope with, prepare for, and ultimately succeed in life by better understanding the particulars of the one concept that all mortals fear the most: death. The impatient man without a belief in God, the Eternal and the Source of all that exists, may assume that his goal in life is to amass as much material wealth, control, or honor during his lifetime as is possible. And he may be able to achieve his goals and be listed as number one consistently on the list of the 100 richest people alive. However, he will realize that everything he amasses during his lifetime will not avail him in the least if he has not been aware that he will be brought back in the presence of God, the Holy Creator of all that exists, and held accountable for his deeds or oversights, or if he has not prepared for this accountability.

On the other hand, a wise individual attains the most satisfaction when he is serving his Lord Who created him and to Whom will be his final return. If, during the course of his life journey, the seeker of success is killed in the service of God, the Most Loving Creator of all that exists, also known as martyrdom, then he is not afraid to make the ultimate sacrifice for the One Who created him, and the One Who will bring him back to life and shower His Forgiveness and Mercy upon him by granting him **eternal paradise and protection from eternal hell-fire, which indeed is the supreme measure of success**. However, the sincere seeker of success is not greedy or deceptive (to himself or others) and will not create his own definition of terms such as "(killed in) the way of God", but he will investigate and reason intelligently, using the Holy Quran as his guide and the teaching of the noble messenger Muhammad as to what constitutes martyrdom, and which does not include acts such as suicide resulting in death or suffering to other innocent beings.

The seeker of success who wishes to reach his goal has absolute faith in God, the Creator and Sustainer of all, and in His noble messenger, Muhammad. He prepares and acts appropriately to obtain maximum gain both in this life and the hereafter. He knows that if he is slain in the way of his Lord as a manifestation of his faith, i.e. martyred, then Forgiveness and Mercy from his Lord are better than all that he could amass in this world, and that it is his Lord to whom all are brought together.

# Day 43

**If God helps you, none can overcome you; if He forsakes you, who is there, after that, that can help you? In God, then, let the believers put their trust.**

(3:160)

# Day 43

The beautiful selected passage of today is important for the seeker of success to keep in mind as he goes about his daily life, with its complexities and its associated challenges. For man, concepts of trust and security can change during his life: in his infancy, he may view his parents as the ultimate figures who provide security and to trust; in his productive years, he may view the accumulation of material resources as a measure of security for the future. In his declining years, he may put his trust in his employer, state, or children to take care of him. The wise seeker of success realizes that his trust is best placed in God, the One Who created all that exists, the Most Powerful, and the Source of all goodness.

The seeker of success realizes that if he were to expend his energies on convincing one thousand persons to do something for him, he may very well have wasted all his effort if God, the Most Great, the One Who controls the universe, including the exact time for a specific leaf to fall, did not wish for that particular event to happen. The astute seeker of success realizes that if everyone were to join forces to harm him, they would not be able to hurt him in the least if he were to be helped by God, the One Who created all that exists, Who is the Most Reliable Helper, and Who is also responsible for maintaining the entire existence.

The seeker of success who wishes to reach his goal has unwavering faith in God, the Creator of all that exists, the Most Beneficent, Most Merciful and the Most Great, and in His beloved messenger, Muhammad. He knows that if his Lord does help him, there is none that can overcome him; and that if his Lord forsakes him, there is none that can then help him. He puts all his trust in God, the Most Magnificent, the Most Trustworthy, and the Best Helper and Protector.

# Day 44

**Think not of those who are slain in God's way as dead. No! They live, finding their sustenance in the presence of their Lord;**

**They rejoice in the reward provided by God and with regard to those left behind, who have not yet joined them (in their bliss); (the martyrs) glory in the fact that on them is no fear, nor have (they cause) to grieve.**

**They glory in the Grace and the reward from God, and in the fact that God suffers not the reward of the faithful to be lost (in the least).**

(3:169-171)

# Day 44

God, the Most High, Most Loving and the Source of all creation, has created all living and non-living matter for one purpose: to worship and serve Him; no entity except man that we know of, has free will in this regard. However, there is a force, an evil force deriving from Satan, whose aim is to prevent man from attaining success by preventing man from fulfilling his duties towards his Lord, the Most Generous and Most Beneficent One. This evil may be exhibited in variable forms – the simplest of which may be within one's own self, such as by procrastination and neglect of expected duties. In more severe forms, the evil may be manifested by aggressive external measures crafted and assisted by Satan, the accursed one, to prevent the servant of God, the Most Great and Most Loving One, from fulfilling his duties, and may range up to and including death in the way of fulfilling one's duty toward the Creator of all that exists.

However, the beautiful selected passage of today reassures the servant of God, the Most Beneficent and Most Merciful, that whoever is killed in the way of God, the Truth and the Most Wise One, that what may appear to be the death of the martyr, is the beginning of a beautiful existence filled with Grace and Glory from God, the Source of Peace and the Owner of all majesty, matter and honor. Death in the way of God, the Most Beneficent and Merciful, may range from being put to death for believing in God, the Source of all that exists, without assigning partners to him, to being killed while having to physically defend oneself in order to be able to worship the One Who created him. In order to attain the benefits of martyrdom as described in the beautiful selected passage of today, the wise servant of God, the Creator and Sustainer of all that exists, would not resort to a foolish act such as strapping a bomb to himself and killing a number non-believers and believers in God, the Only One Who deserves praise and the Eternal One. This act is more consistent with causing strife, discord, and misery in the community - which entails heavy punishment in the sight of God, the Most Kind and Source of all good, rather than defending one's faith and being killed in the service of God, the Most Beneficent and Merciful.

The seeker of success who wishes to reach his goal has complete faith in God, the Most Great, the Creator and Sustainer of all, and in His noble messenger, Muhammad. He knows that Satan and his agents have as their primary goal the prevention of all seekers of success from reaching their goal. He perseveres in his struggle in life, despite the obstacles, to triumph and reach his goal. He is willing to defend his most valuable asset, i.e. his faith, with all his resources, including his life in the way of his Lord, as a manifestation of his faith.

# Day 45

**Those who purchase unbelief at the price of faith - not the least harm will they do to God, but they will have a grievous punishment.**

(3:177)

# Day 45

    Man is an impatient creature. At his best, he can surpass the angels in virtuosity and nearness to God, the Most Magnificent and Most Powerful and the Creator of all that exists. At his worst, man may become lower than the filthiest animal in his wretchedness and capacity for evil. Man is free to choose either of the two options available and he will be rewarded or punished accordingly.

    When man exhibits his base characteristic of impatience, which is not controlled by his higher faculties or belief in the existence of the One Who so exquisitely and lovingly created him and all that exists, and by divine guidance, he may choose optimal pleasure with the least effort in the present, like a dog when presented with a plate full of meat, satisfies his desire promptly, rather than opting for delayed gratification exhibited by a man of faith, and who engages in fasting or feeding others who are more hungry than himself.

    Taken to the extreme, not only weaker men, but perhaps also the strongest ones, may be tempted by Satan, the accursed and the avowed enemy of man, whose goal is to prevent man from succeeding in the attainment of nearness to God, the Most Sublime and Most Loving Benefactor of all that exists. An example of Satan's strategy is that man may be tempted by being provided with wealth, fame, or honor in the short term, to work against the efforts of others in fulfilling their duties toward the Most Holy Creator of all that exists and preventing others from attaining success. God, the Most Wise and Most Trustworthy One, is warning man in the beautiful selected passage of today that the man who is not able to control his base instincts will end up significantly damaging himself in the long run and will fail miserably. Additionally, God, the Most Magnificent and Most Powerful One, is reassuring those who believe in Him, not to be worried by the efforts of the enemies of God, the Most Loving and Most Kind, because all their efforts against His Holy Existence will not harm Him in the least.

    The seeker of success who wishes to reach his goal has absolute faith in God, the Most Great and the Most Powerful, and His beloved messenger, Muhammad. He knows the true value of faith and is not willing to part with it even if he were to be offered all the riches in the world multiplied thousand fold .

# Day 46

Every soul shall have a taste of death. And only on the Day of Judgment shall you be paid your full recompense. <u>Only he who is saved from the Fire and admitted to the Garden (of Paradise) will have attained the object (of life):</u> for the life of this world is but goods and chattels of deception.

(3:185)

# Day 46

God, the Source of all power and existence, has provided the seeker of success with the beautiful selected passage of today, which is filled with priceless information that is useful to him in his goal of attaining ultimate success without being fooled by craftily placed decoys by the treacherous enemy of man, i.e. the accursed Satan.

The life of this world may seem pleasant, with the acquisition of material wealth, property, increase in children, increase in honor, education, and financial security. However, all the wealth that man accumulates in this world will be of no avail to him the moment he dies. Even the ungrateful one who disbelieves in the existence of God, the One who so lovingly created and sustains all that exists, cannot deny the fact that every mortal shall one day have to die.

God, the Most Compassionate and the Most Trustworthy One, is instructing man in the beautiful selected passage of today that after death, man will be held accountable for his actions or for neglecting his duties, on the Day of Judgment– which all who die shall see. It is at that time that one will know the results of one's test of life in this world. The one who is saved from the eternal fire of hell and admitted to the everlasting Garden of paradise will indeed be termed successful and shall have **attained the true object of life**, while all others will be disappointed and amazed at their foolishness.

The seeker of success who wishes to reach his goal has unwavering faith in God, the Most Great, the Best Teacher, and the Best Guide, and in His Noble messenger, Muhammad. He is not fooled by the glitter and deception of the life of this world and knows that only he will have attained the true objective in life who is saved from the hell-fire and admitted to the eternal Garden of paradise by God, the Most Glorious and the Absolute Truth.

# Day 47

**You shall certainly be tried and tested in your possessions and in your personal selves; and you shall certainly hear much that will grieve you, from those who received the Book before you and from those who worship many gods. But if you persevere patiently, and guard against evil – then that will be a determining factor in all affairs.**

(3:186)

# Day 47

    God, the Creator of order and the Originator and Sustainer of life, informs us in the beautiful selected passage of today that man will be tested in life to see which ones among His creatures are the best in fulfilling the duties for which they were created. The primary duty for which man has been created, according to what we have reviewed in the earlier meditations, is the worship of God, the Most Praiseworthy and Most Holy. When a test is being given, the optimally designed test will contain a degree of challenge so that the results will accurately reflect the mastery of the subject matter. God, the Most Righteous Teacher and the Hearer and Seer of all, informs the seeker of success in the beautiful selected passage of today that this life, which is a test from birth to death, will consist of various challenges, ranging from the loss of personal possessions to injury to one's own physical self. The wise seeker of success will patiently persevere during the life's challenges, knowing that they are an opportunity for him to be able to obtain higher marks when the results are tallied at the end of the wonderful test we call life.

    Because God, the Most Forbearing and the Most Kind, wants all His creation to succeed in this test of life, He is warning the test-takers that they will face challenges, especially from those who worship others besides God, the Holy and the Only One, or those that are confused about the rights due to God, the Highest and the Greatest, i.e. people having faith in the previous scriptures of old and new testament, while denying the truth contained in the Holy Quran.

    God, the Wisest Judge and the Best Guide, not only warns us about the specific challenges in the test of life, but gives mankind the best solution to the challenges: patient perseverance. The one who patiently perseveres during the challenges posed towards him during this life, as instructed by God, the Most Generous and the Best Friend and Protector of mankind, will attain the objective of life, pass the most challenging test, and will be counted among the successful ones when it will count the most.

    The seeker of success who wishes to reach his goal has complete faith in God, the Creator and Sustainer of all that exists, and in His beloved messenger, Muhammad. He knows that he will meet challenges in this test of life and patiently perseveres in all situations, as a manifestation of his faith. He knows that the primary reason for his creation is to worship and serve God, Who is the Lord of all that exists.

# Day 48

**To God belongs the rule of the heavens and the earth; and God has power over all things.**

(3:189)

# Day 48

    The beautiful selected passage of today is short, yet contains concepts of profound significance which will prove useful to the seeker of success in attaining his objective in life and beyond.

    According to the Word of God, the Holy One and Provider and Sustainer of all, the absolute prerequisite and foundation of success is the belief in the existence of God, the One Who created all from nothing, and the Only One deserving of all praise, as relayed to us by His noble prophet Muhammad. On this foundation of belief, if one also performs good deeds based on the love for his Creator, the Most Praised One, then one can be counted among those considered successful by God, the Most Great, the Witness and the Wisest Judge.

    The unfortunate individual who is not able to realize that all authority on earth and in all places and at all times belongs only to God, the Eternal and the Self-existing One, will fail to realize what is required of him by God, the Hearer, the Seer and the Creator of all that exists. Such a foolish individual who rejects the rights due only to the Creator and Sustainer of all that exists will take for worship other entities in addition to God, the Originator and Restorer of life and the Only One.

    The seeker of success who wishes to reach his goal has unwavering faith in God, the Creator and Sustainer of all, and in His noble messenger, Muhammad. He realizes without a trace of hesitation that only God, the Source of all power and the Only One, has power over all things and that He is the One to Whom belongs all praise and Who has absolute control over every affair on earth, heavens, and in all existence at all times.

# Day 49

Behold! In the creation of the heavens and the earth, and the alternation of the night and day, there are indeed signs for men of understanding.

Those who celebrate the praises of God (while) standing, sitting, and lying down on their sides, and contemplate the (wonders of) creation in the heavens and the earth, (saying): "Our Lord! You have not created (all) this without purpose, Glory to You! Give us salvation from the penalty of fire.

"Our Lord! Any whom you admit to the Fire, truly is covered with shame, and never will wrongdoers find any helpers!

"Our Lord! We have heard the call of one calling (us) to faith: "Believe in the Lord!" And we have believed. Our Lord! Forgive us our sins, blot out from us our iniquities and take unto Yourself our souls in the company of the righteous.

"Our Lord! Grant us what You did promise to us through Your messengers, and save us from shame on the Day of Judgment, for You are One Who never breaks His promise".

(3:190-194)

# Day 49

The beautiful selected passage of today includes clear instructions on the most important ingredients necessary for the attainment of ultimate success. First we have been instructed in the Holy Quran by God, the Most Great, the Eternal and Source of all good, that man was created only to worship Him Alone, without ascribing any partners to share in what is due to Him alone, because worshipping anything or anyone else except God, the First and the Last, will prevent man from carrying out his primary duty for which he was created. True worship in its highest form does not came from following a specific formula for recitation or postures, but includes truly praising God, the Source of Peace and the Creator of order, as evidenced by His signs and by His creations, such as the heavens and the earth and the alternation of the night and day. The esteemed reader is referred to the commentary of Day 3 of this collection of meditations on a more detailed discussion of worship.

The seeker of success who is sincere would not have to make an effort to find reasons for praising the One Who created all that exists, gave it order and Who sustains it; he will be able to praise the Loving Creator at all times – sitting, standing or lying down – for His countless gifts, with one example being the precious gift of the air we breathe, and how it supplies oxygen to the lungs, which is then transported to all areas of the body for the generation of energy to carry out the will of the individual. And all this is done without any effort by the individual but under the benevolent guidance of God, the Source of all power and the Best Guide.

The individual who sincerely praises and worships the Loving Creator for His unlimited generosity would be able to fulfill the purpose for which he was created and be rewarded accordingly by **being saved from the punishment of the hell-fire, which is indeed the highest form of success, and being granted entrance to the eternal garden of bliss,** as promised by the messengers of God, the Most Kind and the Most Trustworthy One, Who never breaks His promise.

The seeker of success who wishes to reach his goal has complete faith in God, the Most Great, the Living, and Eternal One, to Whom belongs all praise and worship, and in His noble messenger, Muhammad. Whether he is observing with amazement how an ant crawls, or how the universe is maintained in perfect harmony, he knows Who is responsible for the creation of all that exists and for its sustenance and, to Whom is the return of all. Consequently, he celebrates the praises of his Lord at all times – standing, sitting, or lying down – as a manifestation of his faith and out of sincere appreciation of Him.

# Day 50

**Let not the strutting about of the unbelievers through the land deceive you;**

**Little is it for enjoyment – their ultimate abode is hell: What an evil resting place!**

**But, for those who fear their Lord, are gardens, with rivers flowing beneath; therein are they to dwell (forever) – a gift from the presence of God; <u>and that which is in the presence of God is the best (bliss) for the righteous.</u>**

(3:196-198)

# Day 50

It is characteristic of children to be impatient; if an infant is hungry, he will cry. As the infant proceeds through his development, he gradually learns the benefits of patience. If man encounters another individual with a greater amount of material possessions, higher perception of security in this life, or worldly honor, he may experience jealousy or the desire to emulate him, in order to attain a similar position. In the beautiful selected passage of today, God, the Most Holy and the Possessor of all majesty and honor, is reassuring His believing servants and warning them not to be deceived by the possessions of those who reject His existence or those who prevent others from fulfilling their duties and serving Him. God, the Most High and the Most Trustworthy, has informed us in the Holy Quran that those from mankind who desire the possessions or gains in this life will be provided with what they seek in this life, i.e. wealth and honor in this life. However, these individuals with immature and impatient characteristics, who neglect the duty for which they were created, will indeed be very sorry when they find out that the price of neglecting the duties for which they were created, is the eternal abode of hell-fire.

On the other hand, the wise individual who has faith in the existence of his Creator, based on the observation of the beauty, order, and perfection in nature, and who understands the duties required from him, and fears the consequences of neglecting his duties towards his Creator, the Source of light and the Rewarder of thankfulness, will be provided both in this life and in the hereafter, with the **highest form of success, i.e. eternal happiness in Paradise and nearness to God,** the Most Compassionate and the Best of those who keep account, and which is the best reward and the highest honor for man .

The seeker of success who wishes to reach his goal has absolute faith in God, the Most High, the Creator and Sustainer of all, and in His noble messenger, Muhammad. He is not deceived by the strutting about of the unbelievers and their material possessions, knowing that man's possessions are of no use to him after his death. He realizes that life in this world is transitory and is a preparation for the life after death - which is of much higher significance, and which is permanent.

# Day 51

**O you who believe! Persevere in patience and constancy; vie in such perseverance; strengthen each other; and fear God – <u>so that you may succeed.</u>**

(3:200)

# Day 51

The beautiful selected passage of today guides the seeker of success towards his goal by three specific injunctions that can be considered as major factors required for attaining success both in the earthly life and the after-life. It is addressed specifically to the seeker of success.

One factor identified to reach our goal of success is mentioned by the three related terms in the beautiful selected passage of today, i.e. *patience, perseverance, and constancy*. From learning how to take one's first steps as a child to attempting to reach the moon, an important ingredient for the attainment of one's goal is patience and perseverance, as the end result will not be reached if one gives up after the first unsuccessful attempt.

Another important component of success identified by God, the Most Loving and the Most Compassionate, in the beautiful selected passage of today, is the injunction to *support one another* as each individual strives towards success. One of the most beautiful aspects of the way of life in Islam as instructed by the noble prophet Muhammad, based on revelation from God, the Most Glorious and the Creator and Sustainer of all that exists, is the recommendation to avoid selfishness by performing righteous actions by oneself and attaining success personally, while ignoring how others are doing. A compassionate human being will not only strive to achieve success himself, but also help others to reach the same goal by strengthening and providing support and guidance.

The third component mentioned in the beautiful selected passage of today in order that one may succeed in this life as well as the afterlife is the *fear of God*, the Source of all power and the Best of those who keep account. Although God, the Most Loving and the Most Merciful, loves each creature more than seventy times a mother loves her child, without the presence of fear of God, the Most Magnificent, Most Forgiving One, man is likely to neglect his duties as the deputy on earth of God, the Most Holy Creator and Sustainer of all that exists. The individual who neglects his assigned duties as prescribed by God, the Most Equitable and Most Just, will be held accountable and be punished accordingly – a truly painful punishment, but appropriate for misuse of the most precious treasures entrusted to man (sight, hearing, reasoning, etc.) by his Creator, the Most Wise.

The seeker of success who wishes to reach his goal has unwavering faith in God, the Most Great, Most Patient and Most Righteous Teacher, and in His beloved messenger, Muhammad. He realizes the tremendous responsibilities that he has been assigned by God, the Most Kind and the Most Forbearing One, and fears the consequences of neglecting his duties and disappointing his Lord. He exhibits patient perseverance during the expected and unexpected trials in his earthly life. He helps other seekers of success to also reach their goals and succeed.

## Day 52

O mankind! Revere your Guardian-Lord, Who created you from a single person (Adam), and from him, He created of like nature, his mate [Hawwa (Eve)], and from those two, He scattered (like seeds) countless men and women. Revere your God, through Whom you demand your mutual (rights), and (revere) the wombs (mothers that bore you): for God ever watches over you.

(4:1)

# Day 52

One of the most beautifully written passages in the Holy Quran provided to us by God, the Truth and the Source of all that exists, not only provides the key to the attainment of success on an individual level, but also lays the foundation for guaranteeing security to all members of the human family, and especially to the female sex, which has so often been exploited by the male sex.

The key to success, by which all other methods of attaining success are more easily attained, is the faith in and reverence of the One who created man and all that exists. One who does not revere God, the Originator of life and the Resurrector of man after his death, is not likely to follow any of His recommendations on succeeding in life. Man is also instructed to revere his mother, in whose womb, his physical creation was facilitated.

God, the Glorious and Most Loving Nourisher of all, provides us with the best safeguard in preventing abuse of any one individual by the other, and instructs man in the beautiful selected passage of today, that every human has been created by Him from a single person. Man has been so often exploited by other men simply on the premise that one is inferior to the other because he is "different"; this notion is clearly laid to rest by the most clear language that all humans are derived from a single person. Specific safeguards have been put in place to prevent the exploitation of what is considered the weaker sex, i.e. the female: In the form of the wife, she is not to be treated differently or as an inferior, and in the form of mother, she is to be respected. In any other form as well, she is not to be abused.

The seeker of success who wishes to reach his goal has complete faith in God, the Creator and Sustainer of all, and in His beloved messenger, Muhammad. He reveres the Lord, Who created him and endowed him with invaluable gifts, and respects the mother who bore him with hardship and pain. He knows that all of mankind is of the same family. He does not consider women or any race inferior to himself.

# Day 53

> ...Those who obey God and His messenger will be admitted to gardens with rivers flowing beneath, to abide there in (forever), and <u>that will be the supreme achievement.</u>
>
> (4:13)

# Day 53

Today's beautiful selected passage is concise, clear, and goes directly to the point of concern for the seeker of success in order to reach his goal. In order for one to go from one place to another, one needs a reliable map or guide – otherwise, he would be lost. God, the Most Forgiving and the Best Guide, has provided man with appropriate directions in the Holy Quran and has sent guides to help man in the form of the noble prophets, such as Noah, Moses, Jesus, and Muhammad.

One who studies the Quran for curiosity or to increase his knowledge will have his specific goals met; one who reads the Quran to increase his faith will also have his specific goal met, by being granted an increase in faith. God, the Most Wise and the Eternal, has repeatedly informed us in the Holy Quran that faith, in combination with good actions, will be the determining factor for success on the Day of Judgment, when man will be provided with the results of the test of life. The individual who studies the Holy Quran for increasing his faith, and puts the teachings of the Holy Quran into practice by obeying God, the Most Righteous Teacher and the Source of all good, in the light of Guidance provided by His beloved prophet, Muhammad, will have **the supreme achievement of all: Nearness to God, the Most Beneficent and Most Merciful, in paradise,** with beautiful gardens and rivers flowing in it for all eternity.

Although the Holy Quran is quite comprehensive in providing Guidance to mankind for success, it was revealed through the noble prophet Muhammad, who delivered its good news to the seekers of success, and it is through the beloved prophet Muhammad's explanation that the Holy Quran could be best understood. In the beautiful selected passage of today, God, the Most Wise and the All-aware, instructs mankind to follow His Guidance from the Holy Quran as well the guidance provided by the noble prophet Muhammad. It is for this reason that the seeker of success takes the Holy Quran and the traditions of the noble prophet Muhammad as the best source of Guidance, and which, according to God, the Most Right Teacher and the Best Guide, will lead to supreme success.

The seeker of success who wishes to reach his goal has absolute faith in God, the Most Great and the Creator and Sustainer of all, and in His beloved messenger, Muhammad. He diligently obeys what has been instructed by his Lord and His noble messenger, Muhammad, as a manifestation of his faith.

# Day 54

O you who believe! You are forbidden to inherit women against their will; nor should you treat them with harshness, that you may take away part of the mahr (dower) you have given them, except where they have been guilty of open lewdness. On the contrary, live with them on a footing of kindness and equity. If you take a dislike to them, it may be that you dislike a thing, and God brings about through it a great deal of good.

(4:19)

# Day 54

Man finds it easier to follow his own desires, such as intoxicating himself with drugs or alcohol, rather than following the commandments of God, the Possessor of all strength and the Greatest. Man finds it easier to exploit others for his benefit. Unfortunately, woman has been consistently exploited throughout history and continues to be exploited today, albeit in a more subtle way.

God, the Most Wise and the Best Friend and Protector, has spelled out specific rights for women to prevent their exploitation, in the beautiful selected passage of today. The ancient custom of inheriting of a woman upon death of her husband, by the next of kin male has been outlawed with the beautiful selected passage of today. Demanding return of the gifts provided to the women in the past after souring of the relationship has also been forbidden to prevent the exploitation of women. Less dramatic than the above two injunctions regarding the rights of women, but certainly not less important, is the injunction to treat women as equals rather than as inferiors, and to treat them with kindness. This may be difficult for a man who is larger than the woman physically and not educated, but not difficult for the man who believes in the Wisdom of God, the Most Wise and Most Compassionate.

Today's beautiful selected passage ends with a remarkable analogy that would be of great help in protecting the institution of marriage, which is currently in decline. Man is instructed to be patient in his interactions with his wife and not to dissolve the marriage at the first inclination of disliking his spouse. As an example, one may dislike the taste of a medication, but discarding the medication may bring about significant harm. In the same way, terminating a marriage based on transient perception of dislike may result in greater evils. As instructed by the noble prophet Muhammad, marriage is half of faith. And as has been pointed out to us repeatedly for our benefit in the Holy Quran by God, the Most Beneficent and the Most Righteous Teacher, faith is the most important component of success.

The seeker of success who wishes to reach his goal has unwavering faith in God, the Most Great and the Most Wise, and in His noble messenger, Muhammad. He treats women with kindness and equity. He knows that divorce is one of the least desirable things in the sight of his Lord that has been allowed for man and makes it truly the very last option, exhausting all other options by most sincere means as a result of his faith.

# Day 55

**O you who believe! Eat not up your property among yourselves in vanities, but let there be amongst you traffic and trade by mutual good-will. Nor kill (or destroy) yourselves; for indeed God has been to you Most Merciful.**

(4:29)

# Day 55

The beautiful selected passage of today instructs man to avoid certain behaviors and actions that would be detrimental to achieving success, and encourages the characteristic of moderation, which is a distinctive feature of the way of life known as Islam, or submission of one's baser desires to the will of God, the Most Great, the Eternal, and Source of all that exists.

Man is instructed to avoid the practice of excessive consumption, i.e. not only using resources for what you need, but to exhaust them to satisfy one's vanities. If one wanted to, he might find that spending one billion dollars in one day is not sufficient to adequately satisfy his vanities. If a society takes up the practice of excessive consumption, it would find itself debt-ridden and also would exhaust its resources fairly quickly, leaving the future generations with limited resources. On the other hand, the other extreme to excessive consumption, i.e. miserliness, is also not recommended as an alternative. Traffic and trade by mutual good-will to meet one's needs, as well as to realize one's goals in life, is healthy for the growth and prosperity of an individual as well as society.

The beautiful selected passage of today ends with the instruction not to kill or destroy oneself. There are no extenuating circumstances mentioned that would permit one to kill oneself. God, Most Merciful and Most Wise, is the Creator and Sustainer of everything and everyone; one who desires to kill himself, for whatever reason, has lost faith in God, the Most Reliable Helper and Source of all power to either sustain him or maintain His creation in His control. The individual who has lost faith in God, the Most Great and Most Beneficent and Most Merciful, is missing the key ingredient of success.

The seeker of success who wishes to reach his goal has complete faith in God, the Most Great, the Creator and Sustainer of all that exists, and in His beloved messenger, Muhammad. He is neither extravagant nor miserly with his resources. He does not consider killing or destroying himself as an option – for doing so would mean losing his most valuable asset, i.e. faith in God, the Most Merciful Source of all power, and Creator and Sustainer of all, to sustain him and maintain all His creation at all times and in all circumstances.

# Day 56

**And in no way covet those things in which God has bestowed His gifts more freely on some of you than others. To men is allotted what they earn, and to women what they earn. But ask God from His treasures; surely, God has full knowledge of all things.**

(4:32)

# Day 56

The beautiful selected passage of today instructs man to avoid one of the most negative emotions that can be harmful to the individual and society: jealousy. Jealousy is a negative emotion that may lead one to think less of oneself and to lower one's self-esteem. And without a healthy concept of self, one is unlikely to progress very far in his quest for success. If we see someone possessing something that we desire, we are instructed by God, the Most Wise and the Bestower of all goodness, that instead of harboring the negative emotion, i.e. jealousy, we should attribute the desired object as a reward from God, the Loving Creator of all that exists, for the efforts of the men and women. Instead of the negative reaction of jealousy, we are directed toward the positive aspects of goal-setting, commitment, striving, faith, and perseverance.

The individual who is wise will realize that everything in existence is from God, the Creator of all that exists and the Lord of all majesty and honor. Therefore, if one desires something, one is hoping to receive something which belongs to God, the Holy Creator of all that exists. By setting the goals to acquire what one desires, the wise seeker of success will not demand these things from God, the Supreme and Most Generous, but will ask and pray to receive these objects from their Rightful Possessor, God, the Most Powerful and the Owner of all that exists. The men and women who desire goodness and make an effort to achieve this goodness are promised the reward of being provided with what they wish by God, Who Alone is the Rightful Owner of all that exists and Who is the Most Generous One, the All-aware, in complete control of all existence, at all times.

The seeker of success who wishes to reach his goal has absolute faith in God, the Most Great, the Owner of all and the Most Generous, and in His noble messenger, Muhammad. When he sees someone possessing something he desires, he does not experience the harmful emotion of jealousy, and realizes he also can achieve whatever he desires, with the permission of God, the Creator and Owner of all, with persistence and hard work.

# Day 57

**Serve God and join not any partners with Him; and do good - to parents, kinsfolk, orphans, those in need, neighbors who are near, neighbors who are strangers, the companion by your side, the wayfarer (you meet), and what your right hands possess: For God loves not the arrogant and the boastful.**

(4:36)

# Day 57

The beautiful selected passage of today serves as reminder of the two key aspects for the attainment of success: 1) faith in God, the Most Powerful and the Most Wise, as relayed by His noble prophet Muhammad and 2) performing good deeds as a result of one's faith. The key consideration to judge one's "faith" in God as the Supreme Creator and Sustainer of everything in existence is that the one who has such faith serves only the One Who created everything, and serves no one else.

We are provided with further details to help us to "do good", in case one is not certain what that means, or in case one thinks he will not be able to do good acts due to infrequent exposure to the plight of the very needy and the very poor, or those affected by a catastrophic tragedy. Instead we are reminded of some examples of those to whom we may do good at any time, from morning to night in all situations – parents, family, orphans, the needy, strangers, neighbors, friends, colleagues, and subordinates.

The individual who is arrogant will fail to meet both of the important prerequisites of success, i.e. 1) he will lack faith in God, the Creator of all that exists, and therefore will not perform his primary responsibility of worshipping and serving Him, and 2) he will be self-centered, exhibiting selfishness by wishing only for good things for himself, and being unwilling to be a source of goodness for others less fortunate and more in need. God, the Most Beneficent and Most Merciful, is the Best Guide, Who leads one to success by showing us the details on how to earn His satisfaction and rewards, and how to avoid His anger and punishment.

The seeker of success who wishes to reach his goal has unwavering faith in God, the Most Compassionate and the Best Doer of good deeds, and in His beloved messenger, Muhammad. He finds plentiful occasions to do good every single day and does not wait for catastrophes to manifest his faith and love for his Creator and Sustainer.

## Day 58

**God forgives not that partners should be set up with Him; but He forgives anything else, to whomever He pleases. To set up partners with God is to devise a sin most heinous indeed.**

(4:48)

# Day 58

The most important message in the entire revelation from God, the Most Loving and the Most Wise, recorded in the Holy Quran is that man must not worship anything else except the Only One Who is deserving of worship, God the Eternal, the First and the Last. The beautiful selected passage of today informs us that all sins are forgivable by God, the Most Forgiving and the Most Wise, except the sin of associating partners and consequently serving others besides God the Most Holy and Most Kind, Who created everything in existence.

Instead of asking the question "Why does God, the Most Beneficent and the Most Merciful, disapprove of worship of anything else except Himself more than any other sins that can be committed by man?" it would be more appropriate to ask the question "Why is the worship of anything or anyone else except God, the Most Kind and the Most Forgiving, more harmful to man than any other mistakes he is capable of making?".

Because God, the Eternal and the Self-existing One, cares for all His creation and loves them more than seventy times a mother may love her child, He desires eternal comfort and ease for all of creation. God, the Most Beautiful and the All-knowing, has informed us that all of creation has been made by Him for only one purpose: to worship God, the Most Praiseworthy and the Originator of all existence. God, the most Powerful One, the Originator and the Restorer, also informs us that all of creation is continuously in the worship and service of the Most Wise and Most Glorious Creator. Only man has the free will to choose whether to serve and worship God, the Most Just and Most Generous Creator of all existence, and, as a result, succeed in this life, as well as the hereafter, or man may elect to worship and serve anything or anyone else besides God, the Truth and the Greatest, such as His created objects, like the sun and the moon, money, or powerful animals and men – and consequently fail in his mission in life. The esteemed reader is referred to the commentary of Day 3 of this collection of meditations on a more detailed discussion of worship. God, the Most Generous and the Most Caring, wants all of us to succeed, and guides us by clearly identifying for us the biggest mistake that humans can make that will prevent us from attaining success, and therefore, the commandment of the strongest nature to not associate anything or anyone else in His worship.

The seeker of success who wishes to reach his goal has complete faith in God, the Most Great and the Creator and Sustainer of all, and in His noble messenger, Muhammad. He knows that the most harmful behavior to himself is the setting up of partners in worship, praise, and serving God, the Most Glorious and the Creator and Sustainer of all, to Whom belongs all praise and worship.

# Day 59

**All who obey God and the messenger are in company of those on whom is the Grace of God – of the prophets (who teach), the sincere (lovers of truth), the martyrs and the righteous (who do good). What a beautiful fellowship!**

(4:69)

# Day 59

The beautiful selected passage of today captures the essence of success, and like all communications of the highest caliber, it does so in the simplest terms: if you want to succeed, obey God, the Everlasting and the Owner of all existence, and obey His beloved messenger, Muhammad.

From the moment one wakes up until the moment one falls asleep in the night, one has to make tens of thousands of decisions; all of the decisions can be placed in two categories: either they are pleasing or displeasing to God, the Most Praiseworthy and the Best of those who keep account. We have been provided with clear instructions by God, the Most Pure and the Best Guide, in the Holy Quran, in order to help us on our path to success. We have also been instructed by God, the Most Supreme and the Best Doer of good, in the Holy Quran that the noble prophet Muhammad fulfilled his duty of relaying the message of God, the Most Powerful and the Most Wise, and now it is up to us to utilize this message from the Holy Quran, in conjunction with the teaching of the beloved prophet Muhammad, in order to succeed and avoid failure.

The individual who obeys God, the Source of peace and the Source of all power, and His beloved prophet Muhammad will truly be in the exceptional company of those who are called righteous – martyrs and sincere lovers of truth – and will be placed in the category of the prophets, the highest success that man can aspire to attain. There is no fellowship that can be better than this! What a beautiful fellowship!

The seeker of success who wishes to reach his goal has absolute faith in God, the Most Great and the Most Generous, and in His beloved messenger, Muhammad. He knows that the fortunate individuals who obey God, the Almighty Creator and Sustainer of all, and His noble messenger, Muhammad, will spend eternity in the company of the martyrs, prophets and the most righteous, **attaining the highest degree of success.**

# Day 60

Let those fight in the cause of God, who sell the life of this world for the hereafter. To him who fights in the cause of God – whether he is slain or gets victory – soon shall we give him a reward of great (value).

And why should you not fight in the cause of God and those who, being weak, are ill-treated (and oppressed)? Men, women, and children, whose cry is: "Our Lord! Rescue us from this town, whose people are oppressors; and raise for us one who will protect; and raise for us one who will help!".

Those who believe, fight in the cause of God; and those who reject faith, fight in the cause of Evil. So fight against the friends of Satan; feeble indeed is the cunning of Satan.

(4:74-76)

# Day 60

The beautiful selected passage of today expounds on conflict and struggle, including fighting. Because we don't wish to act contrary to the wishes of God, the Most Wise and the Source of all peace, Who created us all, we lovingly submit to His wishes. Even though we would prefer peace now and always, we know that conflict is part of life, from birth to death, and that only in paradise will we be able to enjoy real peace of a permanent nature.

Of all the possible adversaries with regard to conflict, the greatest adversary is the self. The self prefers to sleep instead of waking up at dawn to praise and worship God, the Most Holy and Most Glorious, Who is the Creator of all that exists; the self prefers to acquire things for free, which may at times be considered stealing, instead of laboring to acquire the same things with effort and hard work; the self prefers to satisfy its desires only, instead of trying to fulfill the needs of those who are unable to meet their needs on their own and may be in much greater need than oneself. Satan, the accursed outcast and enemy of man and God, is not satisfied with inciting man's psyche to prevent him from fulfilling his duties to his Lord, the Most Glorious and the Giver and Taker of life, but is always busy recruiting and inciting others to mislead men from faith and to misguide them, as he has promised to God, the Most Forgiving and the Guardian of faith. And as we have learned from the earlier meditations, faith is the most important ingredient of success. So a man who has lost his faith has indeed lost the most valuable fortune.

The one who succeeds will overcome his base desires for short-term benefits. In order to not only help himself but others as well, one may be called to fight in the way of God, the Most Great and the Most Beneficent and Most Merciful. The one who fights in the way of God, the Light and the Best Guide, against himself, or even others, if the need arises, may seem to a child to be in loss, but in truth, he is the one who earns the highest dividends on his investment, exchanging short-term suffering for the eternal rewards of the hereafter. And whose words can be truer than those of God, the Most Trustworthy, and the Creator of all good, as well as the Creator of harm?

The seeker of success who wishes to reach his goal has unwavering faith in God, the Most Righteous Teacher and the Light, and in His beloved messenger, Muhammad. He knows that the path to destruction is easy, and the path to success entails struggle in proportion to the degree of success he aims for. He fights against his baser self internally, as well as the forces of evil externally – and whose main goal, in congruence with the accursed Satan, is preventing man from attaining success, as a manifestation of his faith and love for God, the Most Great and Most Wise, and for mankind.

# Day 61

**Whatever good, (O man!) happens to you, is from God; but whatever evil happens to you, is from your (own) soul. And we have sent you (Muhammad) as a messenger to (instruct) mankind. And enough is God for a witness.**

(4:79)

# Day 61

God, the Most Equitable and the Most Watchful One, is the Creator of all that is good, as well as the Creator of harm, with full control over all matters at all times. Everything in existence receives its sustenance from the Love and Generosity of God, the Constrictor and the Reliever and Source of all power and all existence. The beautiful selected passage of today helps us to understand an important factor in life, which, if left to the imagination of mortals, may leave one with the residual feelings of emptiness and confusion, as well as keeping one absolved of real accountability for one's actions.

One of the most difficult situations for most people to grasp is when they are touched by an unexpected tragedy. This commonly leads to the question "Why me?". However, on a routine day, when the lungs are extracting the appropriate amount of oxygen from the air, the heart is sufficiently relaying the oxygen to the limbs, organs and the brain, allowing one to be in comfort, one would rarely acknowledge these gifts with the statement "life is good".

An appropriate understanding of today's beautiful selected passage will help the seeker of success to appreciate the countless gifts that he encounters every day as emanating from the All-Comprehending Creator of all order, and to praise and worship Him. In the rare instances when we are afflicted with a misfortune or evil, we are instructed by God, the One Who is Most Wise and Most Merciful, to stop and re-assess ourselves, in order to see what we are doing that may have contributed to the situation, because God, the Most Forbearing and the Most Patient One, loves ease and good things for all his creation, and so rarely afflicts them with misfortune. Based on what we find on our re-assessment, the wise seekers of success will seek forgiveness from the Most Forgiving and Most Wise Creator of all existence. Indeed, no one despairs of the Mercy of God, the Most Merciful and the Responder to all prayer, except one who has no faith. And the wise seeker of success will continue to praise God, the Greatest and the Most Rich One, for all the good things he continues to enjoy, despite the rare misfortune, the source of which has been mentioned above.

The seeker of success who to wishes to reach his goal has complete faith in God, the Most Beneficent and Most Merciful, and in His noble messenger, Muhammad. When he is comfortable and goodness befalls him, which is the vast majority of the time, he is most appreciative and thankful to his Lord. When evil befalls him, which is on rare occasions in his life, he reassesses the actions that may have led to the unfortunate outcome and his role in it, without experiencing despair or losing his faith, knowing that his Lord is Most Forgiving and is He with Whom nothing is impossible.

# Day 62

**He who obeys the messenger, obeys God. But if any turn away, we have not sent you to watch over their (evil deeds).**

(4:80)

# Day 62

    For the seeker of success who prefers instructions, advice, or guidance that is simple yet provides dramatic results, the beautiful selected passage of today would serve well. The wise seeker of success realizes that the rewards given to us in this life are fleeting and astonishingly temporary in nature. The unfortunate individual who prefers the rewards of this world at the expense of the hereafter is no different than the man who prefers to have a penny now instead of having one hundred dollars tomorrow. The intelligent seeker of success realizes that all the rewards in this life, as well as the hereafter, are from God, the Creator of all that exists, the Absolute Ruler of all the creation, and the Owner of all that exists. Even though the rewards in the hereafter are eternal, we are encouraged by God, the Most Generous and the Most Wise, to also seek the rewards in this life – but not at the expense of forfeiting the rewards in the hereafter, for that would be foolish indeed.

    Since God, the Most Beneficent and the Most Merciful, is the Creator, Possessor, and Distributor of all rewards, in this life as well as the hereafter, it is obvious that these rewards are dependent on how well one obeys the wishes of God, the Greatest and the Creator of all that exists, and He informs us in the beautiful selected passage of today that following the instructions of His noble messenger, Muhammad, will be rewarded, as if obeying the instructions of God, the Truth and the Best of those who reward. He who disobeys God, the Most High and Most Kind, and His honorable prophet, Muhammad, would indeed be harming his own soul.

    The seeker of success who wishes to reach his goal has absolute faith in God, the Most Great and the Most Wise, and in His beloved messenger, Muhammad. Having unquestionable faith in the wisdom of his Lord in selecting the noble messenger for relaying, reaffirming, and refining the message of God, the Most Holy and the Best Guide, in the Holy Quran to mankind in attaining lasting success, he obeys the noble messenger Muhammad with enthusiasm and conviction, as instructed by his Lord.

# Day 63

**Do they not consider the Quran (with care)? Had it been from other than God, they would surely have found therein much discrepancy.**

(4:82)

# Day 63

Praise be to the One Who created all that exists from nothing, Who gave perfect order to everything in creation, and Who sustains all His creation – so that it would worship Him, and Who provided mankind with guidance through His messengers and His holy books, and perfected the Guidance for all mankind in his Holy Book of Quran, as a Guide for all mankind to attain everlasting success, perfected the religion for mankind, and chose the most appropriate name for the true seekers of success, naming them Muslims (those who have submitted to the will of God, the Opener and the Finder, and named their religion Islam, indicating submission to God, the Glorious and the Only One).

By turning to the Holy Quran for Guidance, the intelligent seeker of success has grasped the most durable hand-hold which will never break, for it is the Guidance provided from God, the Most Knowledgeable Source, Who created all that exists. And Who better to seek guidance from than the One to Whom all decisions go back, the One Who will judge all mankind for their acts and their performance in this exam we call life, and either reward or punish them accordingly, and provide them with the result on the Day of Judgment to either enjoy their success or suffer their failure for the remainder of their eternal existence? God, the Originator and the Everlasting One, is reassuring man through the beautiful selected passage of today regarding the thorough and sound Guidance in the Holy Quran for attainment of real and lasting success. Man can be reassured of the Divine nature of the Guidance and that there is no discrepancy in the compilation of the profuse and beautiful revelations recorded in the Holy Quran over a course of twenty three years, for the benefit of all mankind.

The seeker of success who wishes to reach his goal has unwavering faith in God, the Most Wise and the Best Guide, and in His noble messenger, Muhammad. He believes with absolute conviction that the Holy Quran contains the best Guidance in this life for all mankind from their Creator and Sustainer, and refers to it often for guidance in his own personal life.

# Day 64

**Whoever recommends and helps a good cause, becomes a partner therein; and whoever recommends and helps an evil cause, shares in its burdens. And God has power over all things.**

(4:85)

# Day 64

Man is by nature a selfish creature; any action that he performs, he does so for his own best interest. Inside his home, man may limit his selfish acts, fearing disapproval from other members in the family. In the community, he may limit his selfish acts, fearing either disapproval from society or punishment, such as imprisonment for gross selfish acts, such as stealing, rape, or murder. However, the highest form of development is that man continues to limit his selfish acts even when he thinks that no one will know of his actions, because he knows that God is the All-seeing, All-hearing, and the All-knowing, and that he will be held accountable for all of his actions.

The beautiful selected passage of today helps the seeker of success by informing him of the opportunity of earning a bonus in addition to the rewards of his good actions, i.e. if he recommends another individual to good actions, then both will be rewarded equally, without diminishing the amount for either on the basis of sharing - for God, the Most Generous, is the Possessor of all that exists and is able to reward without measure or limitations. Similarly, if man will recommend another to an evil cause, then he will be punished accordingly, as well as the one who performs the evil acts. Unfortunate indeed would be that man who is no longer committing evil, but the evil recommended by him continues through the actions of others, and who continues to receive punishment for the evil to which he is an accomplice. Indeed, God, the Most Kind and Most Wise, has power over all things and is the Best Guide to unlimited success.

The seeker of success who wishes to reach his goal has complete faith in God, the Most Great and the Most Generous, and in His beloved messenger, Muhammad. He not only does good acts as a manifestation of his faith, but helps others to do the same as well. And he not only refrains from evil acts as manifestation of his faith, but also discourages others from carrying out evil acts.

# Day 65

**When a greeting is offered to you, meet it with a greeting still more courteous, or (at least) of equal courtesy. God takes careful account of all things.**

(4:86)

# Day 65

    If one contemplates the creation – from subatomic particles, to living organisms, to galaxies and universes – one will be overawed at the level of perfection at which all this has been created and is maintained. That same Source Who created all that exists in perfect order, and is responsible for maintaining that order, wishes for each one of us to succeed, like a parent wishes for his child to succeed and therefore expends considerable effort and resources to ensure that the child should succeed in life rather than fail. The beautiful selected passage of today reflects the thoroughness in guidance and the amazing attention to detail provided by God, the Most Reliable Friend and Protector, as recorded for our benefit in the Holy Quran.

    The fortunate seeker of success will gain from the beautiful selected passage of today the appreciation of building successful relationships, which is an important component to the attainment of success. The reason that a greeting is so important in a relationship is that the first impression you get on initiating a relationship is usually also the lasting impression of that person. Therefore, the wise seeker of success will pay special attention to the greetings in his encounters, as the greeting forms the foundation on which the rest of the relationship is built. And if the other party has already initiated the process of a successful relationship by offering a greeting, then the relationship can be further built upon by returning the greeting with a still greater courtesy, or at least a greeting of equal courtesy. God, the Greatest, the Most Wise, and the Most Righteous Teacher, takes careful account of all things, and wants all individuals to succeed.

    The seeker of success who wishes to reach his goal has absolute faith in God, the Most Great, the Best Guide, and the Most Righteous Teacher, and in His noble messenger, Muhammad. He knows the value of relationships and communication with others, and their importance for one to be able to succeed. He is the first to offer a courteous greeting when meeting someone else. And if a greeting is offered to him first, he replies with a greeting still more courteous, or one at least of equal courtesy.

# Day 66

**God! There is no God but He; of a surety He will gather you together against the Day of Judgment, about which there is no doubt. And whose words can be truer than God's?**

(4:87)

# Day 66

The beautiful selected passage of today is short but filled with two profound messages that are critically important for the seeker of success. The first and the most important message given to us by God, the All-powerful and the Most Generous One, in today's beautiful selected passage, is that one must have an absolute understanding that there is only One God, Who created everything in existence and is responsible for its maintenance, and it is to Him only that we are all accountable. When a person understands this concept of his responsibility towards his Creator, the Most Wise and the Most Powerful, and to nothing or no one else, only then is he able to make any real progress towards the goal of lasting success. Only when he realizes the importance of his accountability and his responsibility, will man be able to distinguish between the two consequences of any decisions that he makes: whether it will lead him towards success or away from it. And whose words can be truer than those of God, the Most Beneficent and the Most Trustworthy?

The second important message that is important for the seeker of success to understand from today's beautiful selected passage is that man has been created for a purpose: for the sole purpose of worshipping God, the Creator and Sustainer of all, the Best Doer of Good, the Most Holy and Most Glorious; we worship no one or nothing else except Him – whether it is our inner desires, or someone who is very virtuous, or someone who has been most successful in serving God, the Hearer and Seer of all, and has himself been created, or something very beautiful and awe-inspiring like the sun, moon, thunder, fire, water or earth, which have all been created so that they may all serve and worship their Creator, the Most Beautiful, Most Powerful and the Only One Who is deserving of any praise. The successful seeker's worship must not be only by verbal praises or postures signifying devotion to God, but must consist of all actions pleasing to, and recommended by Him Who is the Most Magnificent and the Best Rewarder of thankfulness, such as charity, good manners, and all those actions beautifully explained in the Holy Quran. Similarly, those actions which earn the displeasure of God, the Most Great, the Originator and the Gatherer, have been beautifully explained in the Holy Quran, for our benefit. The esteemed reader is referred to the meditation of Day 3 in this collection for a more detailed discussion on worship. Only when man realizes that he will be held accountable on the Day of Judgment for his every action that he performs, or chooses not to perform in this life, does he differ from all other matter, objects or animals in existence; the individual who understands this concept is extremely close to reaching his goal of achieving lasting success.

The seeker of success who wishes to reach his goal has unwavering faith in God, the Creator, Sustainer, Destroyer, and Restorer of all that exists, and in His beloved messenger, Muhammad. He knows with the highest degree of conviction that there is no god but He Alone, Who is the Most Great, Most Wise, the Creator and Sustainer of all, Who will gather all His creation together on the Day of Judgment, holding them accountable for their performance in the exam of this world, and punish or reward them accordingly.

# Day 67

**Not equal are those believers who sit (at home) and receive no hurt, and those who strive and fight in the cause of God with their goods and their persons. God has granted a grade higher to those who strive and fight with their goods and persons, than to those who sit (at home). Unto all (in faith) has God promised good; but those who strive and fight, He has distinguished above those who sit (at home) by a special reward -**

**Ranks especially bestowed by Him and Forgiveness and Mercy, for God is Most Forgiving, Most Merciful.**

(4:95-96)

# Day 67

The beautiful selected passage of today not only helps the seeker of success in attaining his goal, but also helps him to attain the highest level among those considered successful. For the benefit of all, it is clearly identified that faith is the absolute requirement on one's path to success, and when combined with good acts, helps to turn the intent to reality. Lack of faith is truly the biggest hindrance to the attainment of success, for one who lacks faith in God, the Originator of all matter and the Creator of order, is always serving the needs of various other factors – self, employer, ruler, society, etc – rather than serving God, the Almighty and the Creator of all that exists, and for which man was created.

The incredible preciousness of the beautiful selected passage of today is that it instructs one to attain not only success, but to attain **the highest level of success**, by not only having faith in God, the All Comprehending and the Most Loving, but striving in His cause with one's thoughts, actions, property, and person, if necessary – the last of which would be the ultimate sacrifice. Understandably, the greater the sacrifice is, the greater the reward. In this world, we most often see this reward given to fallen soldiers, who are usually given the highest honor by the state. Is it any wonder, then, that the highest level of success granted by God, the Most Wise, Most Rich and Most Generous One, would be reserved for those who paid the highest price, i.e. paid with loss of their worldly life? However, one needs to understand that, just as the state would not honor one who gave his life for a cause which in his mind would benefit the state, but which the state did not recognize as beneficial, he would not be honored by the state. For example, if one gave his life in activities such as suicide attacks on civilians, thinking that one was advancing the cause of God, the Most Kind and Most Forgiving One, when he was actually serving the opposite purpose - by taking innocent lives for one's own selfish purpose, one would instead be deserving of punishment both from the state and God, the Source of peace and the Most Merciful.

The seeker of success who wishes to reach his goal has complete faith in God, the Most Great and the Most Glorious One, and in His noble messenger, Muhammad. He knows that success is directly proportional to the amount of effort he puts in, and strives and fights in the way of his Lord, if needed, with all the resources available to him, including his goods and his person, if necessary.

# Day 68

He who forsakes his home in the cause of God finds in the earth many a refuge, wide and spacious. Should he die as a refugee from home for God and His messenger, his reward becomes due and sure with God; and God is Most Forgiving, Most Merciful.

(4:100)

# Day 68

Throughout history, we find instances when not only individuals, but whole societies have been intoxicated with short-term pleasures and power on earth, believing that they were a result of either chance or of their intelligence and labor, and forgetting that all good things – indeed everything that exists – and all power, come from God Alone, the Source of all power and the Lord of all majesty and honor. When taken to the extreme, these individuals and societies, are so preoccupied with the pleasure and power given to them by God, the Most Kind and Most Rewarding, while forgetting the responsibilities that come with those gifts, that it hurts them to see someone who is trying to fulfill his responsibilities to God, the Most Beneficent and Most Merciful – perhaps because it reminds them of their thanklessness and dereliction of duty.

In certain situations, one who is confident of his faith in God, the Provider of all and the Most Wise, and desires to fulfill his responsibilities to his Creator and Sustainer in order to succeed, may have to forsake the comfort of his home in a society which is hostile to those who would choose to serve God, the Most Magnificent and the Best Protector, and become a refugee. He who continues to suffer as a refugee, even up to his death, for the sake of serving God, the Only Victor and the Guardian of faith, is reassured of attaining sure success by God, the Almighty and the Most Trustworthy, in the beautiful selected passage of today.

The seeker of success who wishes to reach his goal has absolute faith in God, the Most Great, the Creator and Sustainer of all, and in His beloved messenger, Muhammad. He is willing to forsake the comforts of his home and his country for the sake of his Lord, as a manifestation of his faith.

# Day 69

If anyone does evil or wrongs his own soul, but afterwards seeks God's forgiveness, he will find God Most Forgiving, Most Merciful.

And if anyone earns sin, he earns it against his own soul: for God is full of knowledge and wisdom.

(4:110-111)

# Day 69

From the time one wakes up in the day to when he goes to sleep at night, one must make thousands of decisions. Although we would like to make the best possible decision each time, it is not always possible to do so, whether it is due to a lack of knowledge or experience, or because of carelessness or an inadequate control of one's desire for gratification in the short term despite the long-term negative consequences.

The seeker of success realizes that not all of the thousands of decisions he must make every day will be the best decisions; however, he will try to minimize the incorrect decisions. The incorrect decisions can lead to evils of varying intensity. The seeker of success will never knowingly make an incorrect decision or choose evil over good, but is aware that there is a possibility he will realize he has in the immediate or remote past made an incorrect decision and chosen evil over good. The one who will reach his goal among the seekers of success is the one who realizes that any incorrect decision he makes resulting in evil harms his own self the most, and seeks the forgiveness of God, the Greatest, Most Forgiving, the Most Patient, Most Compassionate and the Most Wise, Who wishes for all to succeed and has provided us with instructions such as the beautiful selected passage of today to help us in that regard.

As we have noted above, because man is not perfect, he is apt to have made errors of varying magnitude in his lifetime – both in the short-term and the long-term. Fortunately for mankind, we are informed in the first portion of the beautiful selected passage of today that once man realizes his mistake and seeks forgiveness from God, the Creator and Sustainer of all, he will find God to be Most Forgiving and Most Merciful. There is not any exclusion criterion as to what kinds of evils are pardonable listed in the beautiful selected passage of today, except for the awareness that one has sinned and seeks from God, the Most Beneficent, Most Merciful and the Most Forgiving, and then seeks forgiveness from Him. In the next meditation of this collection, this concept is further clarified, so as to exclude the one unpardonable sin: associating others in the worship of God, the Almighty and the Source of all that exists.

The seeker of success who wishes to reach his goal has unwavering faith in God, the Most Great, Most Forbearing, and Most Wise, and in His noble messenger, Muhammad. He knows that the individual who commits evil is the one who suffers the most as a result of it. When he realizes that he has made a poor decision in the past and has sinned, he sincerely repents and seeks forgiveness from his Lord, and never becomes hopeless about receiving His Mercy and Forgiveness.

# Day 70

**God forgives not (the sin of) joining other gods with Him – but He forgives whom He pleases (all) other sins than this. One who joins other gods with God, has strayed far, far away (from the right).**

(4:116)

# Day 70

The beautiful selected passage of today is short, but the message it conveys is profound and is of utmost importance for one who desires to achieve success: Out of all the possible mistakes that man is capable of making, and the only one that will not be forgiven by God, the Most Generous and the Most Forgiving, is the mistake of associating any other thing or entity with God, the Eternal and the Only One. Like every single entity in existence, man has been created for the purpose of worshipping the One Who created all, i.e. God, the Manifest and the Hidden One; the man who does not realize this would be distracted with other matters than the purpose for which he was created – by serving either his inner desires, imagination, and living or dead individuals who are, or were, famous. The esteemed reader is referred to the meditation of Day 3 in this collection for a more detailed discussion of worship.

God, the Most Beneficent and the Most Merciful One, forgives any mistake or sin that man is capable of committing, for the one who is sincerely repentant, except the sin of associating any partners with God, the Most Magnificent and the Most Glorious One, because man's complete allegiance and service is owed to God Alone, the Originator and the Restorer. One simply cannot be in the service of two individuals, corporations, or entities at the same time effectively. Man's entire existence would be negated if he were to recognize two or more masters, because man was created for the purpose of worshipping God, the Creator and sustainer of all. The man who joins other gods with God, the Alive and the One with none other like Him, has indeed has strayed far, far away from the path of success.

The seeker of success who wishes to reach his goal has complete faith in God, the Most Great, Most Wise, and the Only One, and in His beloved messenger, Muhammad. He knows that the greatest mistake an individual can make – and the only one that will not be forgiven by God, the Most Kind and Most Forgiving – is that of joining others in the worship of God, the Most Great and to Whom Alone belongs all that exists and to Whom Alone belongs all praise and worship.

# Day 71

**But those who believe and do deeds of righteousness, we shall soon admit them to gardens, with rivers flowing beneath – to dwell therein, forever. God's promise is the Truth, and whose word can be truer than God's?**

(4:122)

# Day 71

The beautiful selected passage of today is an amazingly comprehensive one that needs to be thoroughly understood by the seeker of success if he wishes to reach his goal.

The absolute requirement for advancing on the path to success is to start with a firm foundation of faith, i.e. belief in God, the Creator of all that exists and the Creator and Sustainer of order, and in His noble prophet Muhammad - for only with the presence of faith can one truly carry out the duties for which he was created. Man, like all entities in existence, was created for worshipping and serving God, the One Who created everything in existence and the Satisfier of all needs; all other entities in existence are in the constant service and worship of God, the Manifest and the Hidden one. Only man, of the entities known to us, has the free choice to willingly serve and worship God, the Creator and Sustainer of all.

Starting with the strong foundation of faith, we are instructed to add deeds of righteousness to help us reach our goal of success. The seeker of success is referred to the Holy Quran and the recommendations given by the noble prophet Muhammad with regard to deeds of righteousness. These would broadly include such things as worship, charity, fasting, and pilgrimage to Mecca, among others.

The fortunate individual who believes and does deeds of righteousness, as reward for the successful completion of his responsibilities, will be provided with eternal peace and unimaginable delights, such as eternal gardens with rivers flowing beneath, which will not lose their beauty with the coming of the winter, as we see in this life. God, the Most Loving and the Most Generous, provides countless gifts to all creation, even in the present life, such as with the gifts of air, water, food, and sun; how much more beautiful would be his rewards, indeed, for his chosen slaves – those who believe and do deeds of righteousness? God's promise is the Truth, and whose word can be truer than God's? The sincere seeker of success is thankful to God, the Truth and the Most Generous, in providing him with such clear Guidance for true and lasting success.

The seeker of success who wishes to reach his goal has absolute faith in God, the Most Great, Most Generous, and the Best Guide, and in his noble messenger, Muhammad. He does good deeds consistently and enthusiastically as a manifestation of his faith. He has doubts as to whether his employer will pay him his next salary due to him for his work, but he never doubts the rewards that are due to him as promised by God, the Most Great, Most Powerful, and the Most Generous Creator and Sustainer of all that exists.

# Day 72

If any do deeds of righteousness – be they male or female, and have faith – they will enter heaven, and not the least injustice will be done to them.

Who can be better in religion than one who submits his whole self to God, does good, and follows the way of Abraham, the true in faith? For God did take Abraham for a friend.

But to God belong all things in the heavens and on earth: and He it is that encompasses all things.

(4:124-126)

# Day 72

The beautiful selected passage of today reinforces the most important requirements of success mentioned elsewhere in this collection of meditations, and in addition, provides further guidance to help the seeker of success reach his goal. The absolute prerequisites for the attainment of success have so caringly been repeated many times by God, the Most Kind and Most Generous, i.e. to believe in the existence of God, the Greatest and the Creator of all that exists and His noble prophet Muhammad as His messenger, and to have faith in this belief, along with doing deeds of righteousness to manifest this faith. In order to guide man towards success by strengthening his faith and to encourage deeds of righteousness, God, the Most Merciful and the Best Guide, has provided the example of the beloved prophet Abraham as a model of one who went from being ignorant, to intelligently searching for God, the Majestic and the Finder, putting his faith in God, the Possessor of all strength and the Most Trustworthy, and manifesting this faith by doing deeds of righteousness, in good times and in bad: Thus he attained enlightenment, wisdom and **success of the highest degree.**

One who has faith in God, the Originator and the Everlasting One, at all times, and follows the way of the noble prophet Abraham has chosen the sound path to lasting success and will be rewarded in a manner reserved for a faithful friend by God, the Most Rich and Most Generous – for to Him belong all things in the heavens and on earth, and He it is that encompasses all things.

The seeker of success who wishes to reach his goal has unwavering faith in God, the Most Great and the Most Wise, and in His beloved messenger, Muhammad. He submits his whole self to God, the Most Loving Creator and Sustainer of all, and does good deeds as a manifestation of his faith. He takes the beloved prophet Abraham as his model in general, and the noble prophet Muhammad as his model in particular to guide him toward success.

# Day 73

**If anyone desires a reward in this life, (he should know that) in God's (gift) is the reward (both) of this life and the hereafter; for God is He That hears and sees (all things).**

(4:134)

# Day 73

The desire for success is universal among all beings, depending on their capacity – whether we are talking about a fish, a bird, a monkey, a two year old toddler, a ten year old child, a seventeen year old adolescent, a forty year old housewife, or a seventy year old grandfather. Although all beings desire pleasure in the present (or at the earliest time possible), the intelligent being learns from knowledge and experience that things that provide short-term pleasure usually result in long-term pain, and vice versa.

One may take the example of someone who abuses illicit substances so as to experience the short-term pleasures of joy, excitement or calm, even though he knows that after the effects of the illicit substance wears off, he will be in an unpleasurable state for a much longer time. It is not unusual for an addict of materials providing short-term pleasures to resort to various crimes to sustain his addiction. There is no doubt that we have been blessed on earth with magnificent gifts and pleasures from God, the Best Nourisher and the Giver of all: the most sumptuous foods, material wealth and the riches that can be bought with it; the highest educational degree, and the security it implies; and the greatest fame and the pride that comes with achieving it. Through the beautiful selected passage of today, God, the Owner of all majesty and rewards, the One Who hears and sees all, is empowering the seeker of success with the knowledge that if one desires the good things in this life (which is natural), one must know that with God, the Creator and the Sustainer, is the reward both of this life and the hereafter. The one who understands the message of the beautiful selected passage of today will attain happiness both in this life, in the short term, and for eternity in the hereafter, for the long term.

The seeker of success who wishes to reach his goal has complete faith in God, the Most Wise, the Only Truth, and the Richest One, and in His noble messenger, Muhammad. He knows with absolute certainty that with God, the Most Generous and the Most Trustworthy One, is all the good in this life and in the hereafter.

# Day 74

**O you who believe! Stand out firmly for justice – as witnesses to God, even as against yourselves, or your parents or your kin, and whether it be (against) rich or poor: for God can best protect both. Follow not the lusts (of your hearts) lest you swerve, and if you distort (justice) or decline to do justice, indeed God is well-acquainted with all that you do.**

(4:135)

# Day 74

The beautiful selected passage of today is addressed to the seeker of success and begins by calling this group with its interchangeable name, "believer". As described elsewhere in this collection of meditations on success, the critical ingredient and foundation for success is belief or faith in God, the Creator, the Judge, and the Most Just, and in His noble messenger Muhammad.

To the firm foundation of belief, the seeker of success is instructed to add the characteristic of justice in order to turn his aspiration into reality. Everything in existence has been created for a purpose: to worship Him Who created from nothing all that exists and sustains it. For those who fulfill their obligations, will be magnificent rewards, lasting for eternity, given by God, the Truth, the Most Generous, and the Most Just. As for those who neglect their obligations, they will be held accountable – with their fate being the opposite of those who successfully fulfilled their obligation, in a most equitable manner.

Man has been instructed by God, the Most Beneficent and the Most Merciful, to strive to exhibit His characteristics – such as beneficence, charity, forbearance and justice – as His representative an earth. Being just demands not following one's own lusts, which are not beneficial to anyone else except oneself. Being just also entails upholding the truth, even if it appears to be harmful to oneself, one's parents, or friends and relations. And if one distorts justice or declines to do justice, then he should know that God, the All-encompassing and the Most Watchful One, is indeed well-acquainted with all that he does, and one will be rewarded or punished accordingly.

The seeker of success who wishes to reach his goal has absolute faith in God, the Most Great and the Most Just, and in His beloved messenger, Muhammad. As a manifestation of his faith, he is able to decline following those directives meant to satisfy his lusts. He stands out firmly for justice, even if the outcome in this life seems to be against himself and his friends or family, and regardless of the social standing of the parties affected by his judgment.

# Day 75

O you who believe! Take not for friends unbelievers rather than believers. Do you wish to offer God an open proof against yourselves?

The hypocrites will be in the lowest depths of the fire; no helper will you find for them.

(4:144-145)

# Day 75

    The beautiful selected passage of today helps the seeker of success by instructing him in how he can move closer towards success, and how he can move further away from failure. A proper understanding of today's powerful message will also strengthen the seeker of success against possible manipulation by the work of Satan and his agents, as this is one of the often-cited passages utilized by his supporters, who claim that, by submitting oneself to God, the Most Loving Friend and Protector, one is limiting oneself to good relations with only those in society who share one's belief. On the contrary, the proper understanding of today's beautiful passage will help all people by maximizing their chances of attaining lasting success.

    Even though we would prefer that all living creatures would forever be in bliss, we have been instructed by God, the Most Loving and the Most Wise, that the eternal rewards are reserved for those who have earned it, and which involves overcoming significant obstacles in the earthly life. This difficult path we all must tread, can be made easier by those who help us and more difficult by those who hinder us from our goal. Therefore, we are warned by God, the Most Wise and the Most Righteous Teacher, to take for friends those who can help us to reach our goals, rather than hinder us from reaching our goals. God, the Most Wise and the Creator of all good, has instructed the believers that they should be kind and courteous to everyone, including those whose aim is to hinder others from His path. Worse than those who clearly identify themselves as enemies of God, the Most Victorious and the Compeller, are those who outwardly identify themselves as believers, but inwardly work against believers and God, the Knower of all and the Avenger, i.e. hypocrites. Such hypocrites are warned that they will be the recipients of the worst form of punishment. The beautiful selected passage of today helps the seeker of success by warning him to avoid hypocrisy, which leads to the worst form of punishment, and also by instructing him to put his trust in those who are working for the cause of God, the Bestower of all honors and the Most Magnificent, which will help him on the journey to success, instead of putting his trust in those who are openly or secretly working against the cause of God, the Most Forceful One and the Humiliator, which will hinder him on the journey to success.

    The seeker of success who wishes to reach his goal has unwavering faith in God, the Most Wise and the Most Righteous Teacher, and in His noble messenger, Muhammad. He realizes that hypocrisy leads to the worst degree of failure. In attempting to accomplish his mission in life, he places his valuable trust in those who share the same mission and vision as himself, instead of those who oppose his mission and vision. He is kind and courteous to everyone.

# Day 76

**Those who deny God and His messenger, and (those who) wish to separate God from His messenger, saying "we believe in some but reject others", and (those who) wish to take a course midway –**

**They are in truth (equally) unbelievers; and we have prepared for unbelievers a humiliating punishment.**

(4:150-151)

# Day 76

    The beautiful selected passage of today provides clear guidance to the seeker of success as to how to best meet his objectives. The foundation of success is the unwavering belief in God the Originator and the Sustainer of all and in His noble messenger Muhammad. A person who has faith is likely to come to the realization that the beautiful and myriad forms of matter and life in the universe, including one's own self, are not a matter of chance or insignificance - but created for the specific purpose of worshipping and serving their Creator, the Source of Peace, and the Only One. It is easy to get distracted by the immediate pleasures from certain things in this life, unless we realize that there is more to existence than worldly pleasures, just as a child may have difficulty understanding that there is more to life than what he is enjoying when he is in an amusement park.

    God, the Most Kind and the Most Just, has provided guidance to mankind on how to truly succeed both in this life and forever by fulfilling the obligations for which men and women were created. This guidance has been given to us by God, the Most Loving and the Most Wise One, through His messengers – with the last messenger being the beloved prophet Muhammad. The man who is lazy or distracted by the evil of Satan, may rationalize that he will choose whatever seems appropriate to him from the guidance of God, the Greatest and the Most Forgiving and the Best Rewarder of thankfulness. The beautiful selected passage of today instructs the seeker of success to avoid the dangerous folly of selecting from the commandants of God, the Most High and the Most Righteous Teacher, only what he wishes to select from them, while ignoring other commandments, and it also instructs the seeker of success to utilize the wisdom of the holy prophet Muhammad in having a better understanding of what is expected of man in order for him to truly succeed.

    The seeker of success who wishes to reach his goal has complete faith in God, the Most Great, the Most Beneficent and the Most Wise One, and his beloved messenger, Muhammad. He does not challenge the wisdom of God, the Most Wise and the Most Righteous Teacher, by choosing from His commandments only those that he finds suitable, and knows that doing so will result in failure and its associated consequences, which are severe. He utilizes the wisdom of the noble prophet Muhammad in addition to the Holy Quran as his blueprint to success.

# Day 77

...This day, those who disbelieved have given up all hope of your religion; so fear them not but fear Me. <u>This day, I have perfected your religion for you, completed My favor upon you, and have chosen for you Islam as your religion.</u>

(5:3)

# Day 77

    Starting with the foundation and necessary ingredient for success – faith in God, the Creator and the Light and in his beloved messenger Muhammad – one can build further to reach his final goal i.e. everlasting success. The one who follows this path has submitted himself to God, the Giver of Life and the Absolute Ruler, and is known as Muslim. Starting from the foundation of faith, the path to everlasting success has been perfected and clarified in the Holy Quran, which provides guidance and light that is invaluable to the seeker of success as he grapples with the darkness and uncertainties in this life. God, the Most Generous and the Most Glorious, has truly bestowed a great favor upon the seeker of success by providing him with loving guidance and instructions in the Holy Quran through his beloved messenger, Muhammad, as a mercy to mankind and creation - and in this perfected manner, has termed the life of these seekers of success as one of submission to God the Almighty, to Whom all beings must submit if they are to truly succeed, and which has been designated by God the Most Beneficent and Most Merciful, as the religion of Islam.

    The seeker of success is reassured by the beautiful selected passage of today that his path to eternal success has been guided by the One on Whom all existence is dependent – and even though he may encounter evil from the enemies of God, the Most High and Most Kind, he need not fear anyone or anything except the One Who designed all existence, created it, perfected it, sustains it, and has, in the Holy Quran, so generously instructed us on attaining the highest degree of success in this life and forever, through His beloved prophet Muhammad.

    The seeker of success who wishes to reach his goal has unwavering faith in God, the Most Loving Creator and Sustainer of all, and in His noble messenger, Muhammad. He is truly thankful to his Lord for providing him with the most valuable guidance to success in the Holy Quran and the example of the noble prophet Muhammad, and refers to them often for practical use. He does not fear any one at any time except his Lord, Who is the Most Powerful and able to do all He wishes.

# Day 78

**O you who believe! Stand out firmly for God as witnesses to fair-dealing, and let not the hatred of others to you make you swerve to wrong and deviate from justice. Be just; that is next to piety. And fear God, for God is well-acquainted with all that you do.**

(5:8)

# Day 78

    The seeker of success needs to realize that all success begins with the strong foundation of faith in God, the Almighty and the Fashioner of form and beauty for all existence, and His beloved messenger Muhammad. Because faith is the most important ingredient and the foundation of success, it has been cited frequently in the Holy Quran, so that man is appropriately aware of its importance. The beautiful selected passage of today, in addition to identifying faith and piety as the key ingredients of success, also identifies justice as of significant importance; according to today's beautiful selected passage, its importance is next to that of the key ingredients of faith and piety.

    God, the Most Beneficent and Most Merciful, is also the Most Just, not challenging any soul more than what it is able to bear, rewarding it fully for all the good it has earned, and punishing it only to the extent that the soul has wronged itself. Along with the key requirements of faith and piety, man is instructed in today's beautiful selected passage to be just – fully and firmly – as witnesses to God, the Most Beneficent and Most Merciful. Man is specifically instructed to show justice even in the worst case scenario, i.e. when dealing with others who hate him or whom he hates. Indeed, this can be difficult, but this is the command of God, the Most Loving and the Most Equitable. The one who is able to show justice – even to those whom he hates or who hate him – will be rewarded with lasting success. And indeed God, the All-Seeing and the All-Hearing, is well acquainted with all of creation and all that every being does.

    The seeker of success who wishes to reach his goal has complete faith in God, the Most Great, Most Kind and the Most Just, and in His beloved messenger, Muhammad. He fears disappointing his Lord, whom he loves more than anything else, including himself, and stands out firmly for justice and fairness, as a manifestation of his faith. He does not let even the hatred of others toward him or his hatred toward others cause him to deviate from justice and his path to success

# Day 79

...If anyone killed a person unless it be for murder or for spreading mischief in the land, it would be as if he killed the whole mankind. And if anyone saved a life, it would be as if he saved the life of whole mankind.

(5:32)

# Day 79

In order to equip man with faith, the most vital component of success, God, the Most Great and Most Wise, has instructed him to observe the details of the creation of the earth, space, as well as his own body, for signs of His power and existence. Someone who observes the workings of his own body in terms of physiological, anatomic, and neurological details will observe the most remarkable collection of systems, ensuring delivery of nutrition and energy to every component of the body, with an amazing system to enable it to carry out its intentions, and an even more amazing gift, which is unique to man, i.e. the ability to reason.

As we noted, every individual is a collection of the most valuable assets and miracles – including the ability to see, hear, speak and reason. The logical conclusion, upon reflecting on the marvels of the earth and space and the collection of miracles inside the human body, is to praise Him Who created all that exists, and provided order to it. With our knowledge that every individual is a collection of most valuable assets and miracles, whose existence itself reflects the Power, Beneficence and Love of God, it would be an offense not only against the individual, but against God Himself, if one were to kill another person or himself. In the beautiful selected passage of today, we are provided, therefore, with only two justifications by God, the Most Wise and the Best Guide, for the taking of another life – and those are for murder itself and for spreading mischief in the land, thereby preventing others from having a peaceful existence and carrying out the duties for which they were created, i.e. to worship God, the Creator and Sustainer of all. The taking of a life for any reason other than the two designated above has been equated with the killing of the whole of mankind. And the saving of a life has been equated with saving the life of the whole of mankind, reflecting the extremely high worth of every individual in the sight of God, the Most Beneficent and Most Merciful.

The seeker of success who wishes to reach his goal has complete faith in God, the Creator of all, the Most Wise and the Best Guide, and in His beloved messenger, Muhammad. He appreciates the immense value of every individual life, including his own, in the sight of his Lord.

# Day 80

**O you who believe!** *<u>Do your duty to God, seek the means of approach towards Him, and strive hard (as much as you can), in His cause,</u>* **that you may succeed.**

(5:35)

# Day 80

The beautiful selected passage of today is of special interest to the seekers of success as having been addressed directly to them; it has four powerful messages that will be of help to them in reaching their goal, the first of which deals with that component of success which is most important, i.e. faith (in God, the Most Great and the Most Sublime, and His noble messenger, Muhammad); further instructions for the attainment of success are directed to them for their benefit.

Knowledge is of little use unless it is put in action, as specified by the remaining instructions on the attainment of success. Therefore, one must manifest his faith by appropriate action if he is to succeed. The second powerful message in the beautiful selected passage of today specifies how to manifest one's faith, which is by fulfilling one's duty to God, the Creator and Sustainer of all. The Holy Quran instructs us that man was created for the purpose of worshipping God, Who gave him life and nourishes him. The esteemed reader is referred to the commentary of Day 3 of this collection of meditations on a more detailed discussion of worship. Rituals of worship are but one component of worship, and more accurately should include every thought and action of an individual, and which should have God, the Creator and Sustainer of all, as his focus.

The third powerful message in the beautiful selected passage of today to help the seeker of success reach his goal is the instruction to seek the means of approach towards God, the Most Magnificent and the Most Praiseworthy One. A beautiful saying of the beloved prophet Muhammad explains this point well: "(God Said:) The most beloved things with which My slave (man) comes nearer to Me, is by (doing) what I have enjoined upon him, and my slave keeps on coming closer to Me through performing nawafil (praying or performing extra righteous deeds besides what is obligatory) till I love him. Then I become his sense with which he sees, and his hand with which he grasps, and his leg with which he walks".

The fourth powerful message in the beautiful selected passage of today to help the seeker of success reach his goal as instructed by God, the Eternal Owner of Sovereignty and the Lord of all majesty and reward, is to strive as hard as one can, in His cause. The path to lasting success is not easy and one will encounter obstacles and challenges from various sources, including one's own ego, enemies of faith, or the accursed Satan and his agents. Patient perseverance is required while striving and struggling on the steep and righteous path to success.

The seeker of success who wishes to reach his goal has unwavering faith in God, the Most Righteous Teacher and the Best Guide, and in His beloved messenger, Muhammad. He not only does the duties expected of him in relation to his Lord, but seeks additional means to draw closer to Him, and strives hard, as much as he can, with patient perseverance.

# Day 81

**...Fear not men, but fear Me. And sell not My signs for a miserable price.**

(5:44)

# Day 81

    The beautiful selected passage of today is short, but its proper understanding would be invaluable in protecting the seeker of success from two very real, very harmful, and very pervasive dangers that one may succumb to unwillingly, and which are detrimental to reaching one's goal on the journey toward success.

    In order to appreciate the importance of the two priceless pieces of advice for the seeker of success in the beautiful selected passage of today, one needs to return – like in so many other passages in this collection of meditations on success – to the foundation and key ingredient of success: Faith in God, the Most Powerful, the First and the Last, and His beloved messenger, Muhammad.

    The man who is lacking in faith in God, the Most Beneficent and Most Merciful, and the Source of all power, will be overwhelmed with the signs of limited power in things such as thunder, storms, or bombs; or he will be overwhelmed with signs of limited power in others, such as the bully, the boss, the president, or the king. Such a man who is awed by things of truly limited power would certainly have difficulty fulfilling the requirements for which he was created by God, the Truth and the Most Kind, as he would be busy serving others for fear of them, rather than serving God, the Greatest and to Whom belongs all that exists.

    The other real danger of which the seeker of success is warned, occurs if one is not of full conviction that God, the Most Praiseworthy and the Resurrector, has created all matter, including man, with a purpose, and that man will be held accountable for fulfilling or neglecting his duties. Such a man who is lacking an understanding of the purpose of life and its consequences would be in danger of compromising his situation in the eternal afterlife for the relative momentary pleasures in this life – like a drug addict who may sell a precious object at a pawn shop for one percent of its value so he can enjoy a temporary state of pleasure. The worst of these creatures are those who knowingly oppose God, the Eternal and the Most Powerful, and/or oppose those who have faith in Him, for the temporary pleasures and benefits of this life.

    The seeker of success who wishes to reach his goal has absolute faith in God, the Most Great, the Most Glorious and the Source of all power, and in His noble messenger, Muhammad. He does not fear anyone except his Lord. He knows the true value of faith and realizes that the unfortunate individual who would sell his faith in return for everything in this world is not different from the child who would trade a two carat diamond ring for a piece of candy.

# Day 82

**...Life for life, eye for eye, nose for nose, ear for ear, tooth for tooth, and wounds equal for equal. But if anyone remits the retaliation by way of charity, it is an act of atonement for himself.**

(5:45)

# Day 82

    For man, interaction with others is necessary for survival – whether it involves the home setting or the community. We hope that all interactions with others are cordial and mutually beneficial – and the vast majority of them are. However, there are instances when one party has been wronged by another intentionally or unintentionally – and sometimes to a catastrophic degree. When things in life are going as we expect or better, one tends to be in a naturally pleasurable state. When things are going worse than expected, one is less likely to be pleased with the course of events. When one perceives himself as having been wronged, he may feel justified in taking appropriate action to right the wrong that he has experienced. The beautiful selected passage of today is directed at the individual and societal level for the recommended response to the situation in which one has wronged the other.

    For those whose aim is to deny or belittle the message of God, the Most Wise and the Truth, the message of today's beautiful selected passage can be distorted to imply that God, the Most Beneficent and Most Merciful, has decreed that one must punish the other with removal of an eye for an eye lost, or removal of tooth for tooth lost. In reality, the incredibly wise and magnanimous passage of today sets limits on the type of punishment that can be given, so that one does not remove the eye of another for the loss of a tooth. However, the one who is in search of success will learn from today's beautiful selected passage that there are limits to how much punishment one can give to another as a result of suffering from another's actions – and, if he chooses to forgive the transgressor even when he has the right to punish, then God, the Most Merciful and the Most Wise, will be pleased and will ease his journey towards everlasting success.

    The seeker of success who wishes to reach his goal has unwavering faith in God, the Most Great, Most Kind, and Most Forgiving, and in His beloved messenger, Muhammad. He realizes that the most beneficent action for himself, when he has been wronged by another, is to remit the retaliation as a manifestation of his faith. If he chooses to retaliate, he does not inflict damage to the other party greater than what he suffered.

# Day 83

**...But who – for a people whose faith is assured, can give better judgment than God?**

(5:50)

# Day 83

Today's incredibly sublime passage is best understood using the analogy of different stages in a person's life that he or she typically goes through and his or her success in that stage.

As a child, one looks to his parent for guidance – otherwise, the child can succumb to various dangers that exist if the child is left to decide for himself how to utilize his time, energy, and available resources. It is not enough to love the parent, although it may help; success at this stage depends on diligently following the recommendations of the parents, who work on instilling the appropriate characteristics, behaviors and capabilities for the child to succeed in life. The next stage is that of a student. The student looks to his teacher for guidance on how to appropriately master a chosen subject. It's not enough to love the teacher, although it may help; success at this stage depends on diligently working to acquire the knowledge and skills for mastery of the subject for which the teacher is responsible. The next stage is that of a productive member of society; at this stage, one typically looks to one's supervisor or boss for guidance. It is not enough to love the boss, although it may help; success at this stage depends on meeting the expectations and goals that the supervisor or employer has assigned to the worker. Some individuals are self-employed; such individuals usually have a mentor who may be a living individual who actually provides guidance to them, or a historical or current individual whom they respect, and whose life and work inspires and guides the individual

The seeker of success, as he passes through all three stages of a person's life as described above, is aware of the fact that he, along with everything else in existence, is created for a purpose by God, the Owner of all and the Best Guide, and it is to Him that he turns for guidance and any judgment, in order to attain everlasting success. And the seeker of success is confident that no one can provide better judgment than God, the Most Loving and the Most Wise.

The seeker of success who wishes to reach his goal has complete faith in God, the Most Great, the Most Just and the Most Righteous Teacher, and in His noble messenger, Muhammad. He knows that no one can provide better judgment than God, the Most Magnificent, All-encompassing and Most Wise, and seeks His Guidance regularly in all matters of concern to him every day.

## Day 84

Your (real) protectors are (no less than) God, His messenger, and the (fellowship of) believers – those who establish regular prayers and regular charity; and they bow down humbly (in worship).

As to those who turn (for friendship) to God, His messenger, and the (fellowship of) believers – it is the fellowship of God that must certainly triumph.

O you who believe! Take not for friends and protectors those who take your religion for a mockery or sport – whether among those who received the scripture before you or among those who reject faith; but fear God, if you have faith (indeed).

(5:55-57)

# Day 84

Today's beautiful selected passage helps the seeker of success to understand the importance of friendship and support in the realization of fulfillment of one's goals. In order to fully appreciate the wisdom of today's beautiful selected passage, one needs to understand the role of a friend.

A friend is someone who provides you with his companionship, love, trust, and assists you in need. Consequently, being designated as a friend implies significant responsibilities that must be fulfilled. Many times people confuse the term neighbor, colleague, or acquaintance with friend; this kind of confusion can lead to a serious misunderstanding about the relationship between those who have submitted themselves to God, the Creator and Sustainer of all that exists, (i.e. Muslims) and others (i.e. non-Muslims).

Muslims are instructed by God, the Most Refined and the Most Wise, in the Holy Quran to be kind and courteous in their dealings with others, including with those do not share their faith. The beautiful selected passage of today provides sound guidance to the seeker of success by characterizing the sources of support of friends, from the most reliable to the least reliable.

Based on the definition of friend as listed above, the seeker of success realizes that his most valuable friend is indeed God, the Most Trustworthy, Best Friend and Protector, along with His messenger who so faithfully and nobly relayed the beautiful message of God, the Most Beneficent and Most Merciful, as a mercy to His creation. Next in category to those who can fulfill the role of friends are others having the same goal of success – acknowledging the One Who created everyone and everything, understanding the reason in the creation of everything that exists, i.e. to serve their Creator, the Most Glorious and the Most Loving One, by regular worship, regular charity, and fearing the consequences of neglecting their truly profound duties. Lastly, the seeker of success is warned that those who are least likely to be of help to him are those who take his mission as mockery or sport, and would be a hindrance to achieving his goal of attaining everlasting success. The beautiful selected passage of today does not recommend the seeker of success to behave discourteously with those who ridicule his mission; rather, it informs him that the one who ridicules his mission would not be able to help him achieve his goal.

The seeker of success who wishes to reach his goal has absolute faith in God, the Most Great, the Best Friend and Protector, and in His beloved messenger, Muhammad. Although he is courteous with everyone, he knows that putting his trust in those who are hostile to his mission secretly or openly, rather than those who share his vision, is not wise and will prevent him from reaching his goal.

# Day 85

O you who believe! Intoxicants and gambling, (dedication of) stones, and (divination by) arrows, are an abomination – of Satan's handiwork. <u>Eschew such (abomination), (so) that you may succeed</u>.

Satan's plan is (but) to excite enmity and hatred between you with intoxicants and gambling, and hinder you from the remembrance of God and from prayer; will you not then abstain?

Obey God, and obey the apostle (Muhammad), and beware (of evil): If you do turn back, know that it is Our apostle's duty to proclaim (the message) in the clearest manner.

(5:90-92)

# Day 85

The beautiful selected passage of today reinforces the positive factors that will help the seeker of success to attain his goal, and which are also mentioned in other passages from the Holy Quran included in this collection – the factors described in the beautiful selected passage of today include being obedient to God, the Greatest and the Possessor of all strength, and to His beloved prophet, Muhammad. The uniqueness of today's beautiful selected passage among this collection of meditations, in addition to what is mentioned above, lies in the identification of particular negative factors that would prevent the seeker of success from reaching his goal. The most important factor identified as a barrier to success is Satan. The Holy Quran identifies the goal of Satan's existence since his fall from grace as the prevention of as many souls as possible from succeeding and fulfilling their obligations to God, the Greatest and the Most Generous. The seeker of success will pay special attention to the methods with which Satan attempts to hinder man from the remembrance of God, the Most Praiseworthy and the Everlasting One, and from worshipping and serving Him, i.e. the reason for which man was created. The tools which Satan utilizes – intoxicants, gambling, and superstition – to excite enmity and hatred among men, and to hinder them from their duty of prayer and remembrance of God, the Most Beneficent and the Most Merciful, should be eschewed by the one who wishes to succeed and prosper.

The seeker of success who wishes to reach his goal has unwavering faith in God, the Most Great, Most Wise, and the Most Righteous Teacher, and in His noble messenger, Muhammad. He obeys God, the Creator and Sustainer of all, and His noble messenger, Muhammad, and realizes that the greatest hindrance to reaching his goal is Satan. Therefore, he wisely recognizes the traps laid by Satan to hinder him from remembrance of his Lord and from prayer with such diversions as intoxicants, gambling, enmity and hatred among people, and superstitions, and eschews such abominations, so that he may succeed and reach his goal.

# Day 86

**Say: "Not equal are things that are bad and things that are good, even though the abundance of the bad may dazzle you: <u>So fear God, O you who understand, so that you may succeed</u> ".**

(5:100)

# Day 86

The beautiful selected passage of today provides three valuable gems for the seeker of success to increase his worth and to help him to reach his goal - the first of which is the understanding that man must constantly choose between good and bad to varying degrees: When he wakes up in the morning, he must choose whether he will stay in bed a few extra minutes or get up and thank Him Who has provided rest for him, Who sustains the universe, and gives provisions to all for their existence. He can elect during the day to either steal or expend effort to lawfully earn his livelihood. And he must continue making decisions all day, until he goes to sleep at night. From the above examples, we can see that the easier of the two choices we must make during the day, or during the whole of life, is not the better of the choices for the individual in the long term.

The second valuable gem the seeker of success gathers from the beautiful selected passage of today is that one should not be tempted by the perception of immediate benefit to select the easier of the two options. As an example, we will compare two young school children preparing for an exam: one child is expending great effort preparing for his exam, while the other is happily playing in the park. The child who is diligently studying will be pleased with the outcome of his exam, while the child who has been neglectful will fail – even though it appeared before the exam that the child who eventually fails was enjoying himself more than the child who had been diligently studying.

The third valuable gem the seeker of success gathers from the beautiful selected passage of today is that he is accountable to God, the Most Wise and the Best of those who keep account, for every single action he makes; and he makes sure that he selects the good over the bad in each decision, because with every decision he makes, he is either moving towards his goal of lasting success and prosperity (if he chooses the good over the bad), or moving away from his goal (if he chooses the bad over the good) – even though the bad may appear more rewarding in the short term.

The seeker of success who wishes to reach his goal has complete faith in God, the Most Great, Most Wise, and the Best Teacher, and in His beloved messenger, Muhammad. He fears his Lord and the consequences of failing to fulfill his obligations towards Him. He knows that the good and the bad are not equal and consistently selects the good over the bad - not being fooled by what appears to be abundance in the short term, of the bad, compared to the good.

# Day 87

**O you who believe! Guard your own souls – if you follow (right) guidance, no hurt can come to you from those who stray. The goal of you all is to God – it is He Who will show you the truth of all that you do.**

(5:105)

# Day 87

All living creatures, including man, are exposed to external threats of varying degrees in all places – ranging from the jungle to the boardroom of a corporation. Therefore, man takes appropriate measures – individual or collective – in order to adequately protect himself.

The beautiful selected passage of today instructs the seeker of success that the most effective safety measure that one can take is not necessarily the protection of one's body or physical component, but the protection of one's soul, by following the Guidance provided by God, the Most Generous and the Best Guide, through His noble prophet, Muhammad.

The wise seeker of success realizes that no hurt can come to him from anyone, and that nothing can occur except with the permission from the One Who created all that exists and sustains it - including every leaf that falls. Through the comprehensive guidance provided by God, the Truth and the Most Wise, and the life of His beloved prophet, Muhammad, the wise seeker of success realizes that his only fear should be that of neglecting the duties for which he was created by God, the Most Merciful and the Owner of all majesty and rewards, to Whom all must return and be held accountable. It is He Who will show everyone the truth of all that they did and will either reward or punish them accordingly.

The seeker of success who wishes to reach his goal has absolute faith in God, the Almighty and the Source of all power, and in His noble messenger, Muhammad. He realizes that the most effective safety measure he can take in order to succeed is to guard his own soul, and realizes that if he follows the right guidance from his Lord, no hurt can come to him.

## Day 88

**To God does belong the rule of the heavens and the earth, and all that is therein; and it is He Who has power over all things.**

(5:120)

# Day 88

As man passes through the various phases of his life – infancy, childhood, adolescence, young adulthood, adulthood, middle age and the elderly stage – his perception of the authority having the ultimate power tends to change: parents, older siblings and friends, teacher, policeman, professor, governor, president, CEO, or various governing bodies. Therefore, man tends to progress through his various phases as described above by trying his best to win approval from the various authority figures most relevant at a particular point in time.

The beautiful selected passage of today helps the seeker of success to realize that no matter what phase of development he is passing through, the ultimate authority and power always belongs to God, the Owner of all that exists and the Source of all strength and power; only when man realizes this concept can we say that one ceases being a polytheist and truly believes in God, the Self-Existing and the Only One.

And only when man realizes that the ultimate authority in all existence belongs with God, the Truth and the Most Praised One, and that He Alone has power over all things at all times, can man begin to realize why he was created, what is expected of him, and what he can do to attain everlasting success through the Grace and Guidance of God, the Most Generous and the Best Guide. This will save his time and resources from being directed toward things which will not affect him, and more importantly, it is only when he realizes the absolute authority of God, the King and the Source of all power, that man can fulfill the role for which he was created, and succeed

The seeker of success who wishes to reach his goal has unwavering faith in God, the Greatest and to Whom belongs all power, and in His beloved messenger, Muhammad. He realizes that to his Lord belongs the absolute rule of the heavens and earth, and all that is therein – and that He has power over all things.

# Day 89

Say: "Should I take for my protector any other than Allah, the maker of the heavens and the earth? And He it is that feeds, but is not fed". Say: "Indeed! I am commanded to be the first of those who bow to Allah (in Islam), and be not of the company of those who join gods with Allah".

Say: "I would, if I disobeyed my Lord, indeed have fear of the penalty of a mighty day.

**On that day, if the penalty is averted from any, it is due to Allah's Mercy; and that would be the clear Success".**

(6:14-16)

# Day 89

The beautiful selected passage of today is astounding in its comprehensiveness and relevance to the seeker of success in regards to general instructions on how to attain the highest form of success, and which is beautifully reinforced in today's passage. The invaluable message and the treasure to be gathered from the profusely rich passage of today is the realization that man has been created with a purpose by God, the Most Glorious and the Originator: to worship Him only. The esteemed reader is referred to the commentary of Day 3 of this collection of meditations on a more detailed discussion of worship.

Unfortunately, what often happens is that man gets distracted very easily by the gifts that have been provided so freely and graciously by God, the Most Generous and the Most Rich, to the point that man could continue to enjoy God's numerous gifts while neglecting the Source Who has provided them.

The man who is not aware of his mission in life, along with his obligations and responsibilities, will be confused and may serve whatever appears to him to be the most powerful or worthy of adoration, depending on the stage of his development.

However, the man who realizes that there is no protector other than God, the Almighty and the Ultimate Friend and Protector, the Maker of the heavens and the earth, Who is free of all needs while everything else depends on Him for sustenance, is honored to be among the first of those who bows to God, the Most Loving and the Owner of all, in His praise and worship. Moreover, he realizes the tremendousness of his mission in life, i.e. to serve God, the First and the Last, and that if he is serving anything or anyone other than Him, he is in effect disobeying God, the All-aware and the Most Holy. The unfortunate individual who knowingly or unknowingly fails to realize his mission in life and consequently neglects his duties and disobeys God, the Best Judge and the Most Just, has in store a tremendous penalty – to be given on the Day of Judgment– of eternal punishment, in accordance with neglecting the tremendous responsibility that he has been given, associated with His creation. And the one from whom the penalty is averted on the Day of Judgment due to the Grace of God, the Most Loving and the Most Merciful, will indeed have attained the **highest form of success**.

The seeker of success who wishes to reach his goal has complete faith in God, the Best Protector and Sustainer of all that exists, and in His noble messenger, Muhammad. He realizes the reason for which he was created, i.e. to worship and serve God, the Most Holy and the Source of all power. He understands worship as a broad term and includes activities beyond verbal and physical actions signifying greatness and adoration of his Lord, and he truly fears disobeying Him, and the tremendous penalty associated with it.

# Day 90

**And if Allah touches you with affliction, none can remove it but He; if He touches you with happiness, then He has power over all things.**

(6:17)

# Day 90

All living creatures, including man, desire that in their life, they should maximize their pleasurable state and minimize those states causing displeasure. For most living creatures, there is no ethical dilemma when making a decision: they will invariably select that option which will lead to maximal pleasure and/or minimal pain in the shortest time period possible. However, man is unique among the living creatures in that he realizes that those things leading to long-term pleasure require one to be able to tolerate short-term pain, such as studying to pass an examination, or saving enough money to be able to buy a house.

In order to rid himself of a painful situation, or in order to attain a pleasurable state, man may feel that, in addition to his own effort, certain other individuals or entities have to be placated and to reach his goal. The beautiful selected passage of today informs the seeker of success that if he expends his effort and resources to please others in order to attain happiness or pleasure, and to reduce his pain or remove his affliction, then he is wasting his time and effort because all power belongs to God, the Everlasting Creator of all power and the Nourisher of all that exists. Further commentary on this beautiful selected passage is not necessary due to the immense beauty that comes from its exquisite clarity that should be recognizable to all individuals able to read, hear, and understand

The seeker of success who wishes to reach his goal has absolute faith in God, the Most Great and Most Powerful One, and in His beloved messenger, Muhammad. He realizes that not only are his own efforts necessary to achieve happiness, minimize displeasure, and reach his goals - but also that if God touches him with affliction, none can remove it but He; and if God touches him with happiness, none can take it away from him. And he realizes that his Lord has power of over all things at all times.

# Day 91

**Who does more wrong than he who invents a lie against Allah or rejects His signs? But indeed the wrongdoers never shall succeed.**

(6:21)

# Day 91

In order for one to succeed at any task, one needs to know not only the steps to take for succeeding but also the factors that can prevent him from succeeding or mastering the task. Today's beautiful selected passage informs the seeker of success of the two most dangerous factors that can prevent him from reaching his goal. The individual who recognizes the signs of God, the Most Holy and the Most Powerful, in things such as the alternation of the night and the day, the reproduction of life from the sperm and the ovum, the organization required for the billions of cells in the individual, the generation of fresh fruits and grains from the dead earth utilizing the energy and substances in the universe, and the selfless love of the mother for the child, will be more likely to follow the commands of Him Who is responsible for these things, which are a manifestation of His power, Intelligence, and Love. On the other hand, the one who sees the same signs as described above, and instead of seeing the Awesomeness, Perfection, and Beauty of God, the Most Kind and Most Caring, rejects His signs, concluding that these miracles and countless others are a result of random occurrence, is likely to follow his own whims and neglect the duties for which he has been created by God, the All-knowing and Most Wise, and by Whom he will be evaluated and rewarded or punished accordingly. There is another class of more unfortunate individuals who not only neglect the many signs of God, the Manifest and the Hidden One, but also encourage others to neglect their duties to God, the Most Forbearing and the Most Just, by inventing lies against Him.

The two most dangerous factors that can prevent the seeker of success from reaching his goal, are identified in the beautiful selected passage of today, i.e. the rejection of the many apparent and subtle signs of God, the Most Beneficent and Most Merciful, and the encouragement of others to do the same by inventing lies against Him. These are the individuals in clear error and therefore classified as wrongdoers. Indeed, the wrongdoers shall never be able to succeed.

The seeker of success who wishes to reach his goal has unwavering faith in God, the Most Great and the Apparent and the Hidden One, and His noble messenger, Muhammad. He knows that rejecting the many apparent and subtle signs present everywhere of God, the Almighty and Most Powerful one, and inventing lies against Him, are two major negative factors that can prevent him from attaining success.

# Day 92

**What is the life of this world but play and amusement? But best is the home in the hereafter, for those who are righteous. Will you not then understand?**

(6:32)

# Day 92

The beautiful selected passage of today helps the seeker of success to understand the importance of staying focused on his primary goal in spite of the attractiveness of the distractions encountered in life. An appropriate example for understanding the concept of today's beautiful message is that of a student preparing himself to pass an examination. The successful student will realize that he will encounter distractions and various opportunities for amusement, and that if he remains engrossed in the distractions and the amusements, he will not be able to pay the appropriate attention required for the successful completion of his examination. On the other hand, the wise student will appreciate the opportunity of play, amusement, or break from studying, and use it wisely to refresh and rejuvenate himself, so he can more effectively concentrate on his study, without exhausting his mental capacities and neglecting his preparation for the examination.

God, the Most Knowledgeable and Most Kind, informs the seeker of success in the beautiful selected passage of today that the life of this world is play and amusement – and if one is distracted by these things and values the short-term pleasures provided by them, then he will likely harm himself by neglecting the main goal in this life: to fulfill the duties for which man has been created, i.e. worshipping and serving God, the Loving Creator of all that exists, throughout his existence in this life, for which he will be rewarded with happiness in this life and the hereafter. The wise seeker of success realizes that nothing in this life full of play and amusement can be greater than the home he will be rewarded in the eternal hereafter for his effort and hard work in this life.

The seeker of success who wishes to reach his goal has complete faith in God, the Most Wise and the Most Righteous Teacher, and in His beloved messenger, Muhammad. He realizes that the life of this world is only play and amusement and that the highest goal for him is the reward of a comfortable home in the hereafter - a reward which is eternal and requires hard work in this life, including having faith, worshipping his Lord, and doing righteous deeds as a manifestation of his faith.

# Day 93

**Say: Think about this: If God took away your hearing and your sight, and sealed up your hearts, who – a god other than God – could restore them to you? See how We explain the signs by various (symbols); yet they turn aside.**

(6:46)

# Day 93

    The beautiful selected passage of today helps the seeker of success to have confidence in his mission in life. And having confidence in one's mission is an important component of success. The seeker of success is asked to consider the profoundly convincing analogy of today's beautiful selected passage that if his most precious gifts – hearing, sight, and reasoning – were taken away from him by the One Most Powerful and Most Forgiving, Who gave them to him in the first place, who is there that can restore these precious faculties back to him other than God, the Most Generous, the Nourisher and Provider of all that exists, except for Him alone? These lost faculties cannot be restored by oneself, one's wealth, the most capable physicians or scientists, or other men, who cannot even produce a fly on their own except with the permission of God, the Originator and the Resurrector.

    There are innumerable signs of the existence of God, the All-encompassing, the Hearer and Seer of all, and the Best Guide. Today's beautiful selected passage gives some examples of these signs in such a compelling and convincing format that the unfortunate individual who turns away from these signs pointing towards his Creator and Sustainer, the Self-existing and Everlasting One, and his obligations to God, the Most Holy and the Creator of all that exists, is like the one who has eyes but cannot see, or the one who has ears but cannot hear, or the one who has a brain but cannot reason, and therefore is unable to succeed. The seeker of success has his confidence and faith in God, the Most Beneficent and the Most Merciful, reinforced and therefore is primed for success, as a result of a proper understanding of the message from the beautiful selected passage of today.

    The seeker of success who wishes to reach his goal has absolute faith in God, the Almighty and the Source of all that exists, and in His noble messenger, Muhammad. He is ever-thankful to Him Who provided him with the faculties of hearing, seeing, and reasoning, that are priceless -and knows that no one else can provide him with these faculties if it is the wish of God, the Creator and Sustainer of all, to seal these faculties from him.

# Day 94

With Him (God) are the keys of the unseen: the treasures that none knows but He. He knows whatever there is on the earth and in the sea. Not a leaf does fall but with His knowledge: There is not a grain in the darkness (or depths) of the earth, nor anything fresh or dry (green or withered) but is (inscribed) in a record clear (to those who can read).

It is He Who does take your souls by night, and has knowledge of all that you have done by day. By day does He raise you up again – that a term appointed be fulfilled. In the end, unto Him will be your return. Then He will show you the truth of all that you did.

(6:59-60)

# Day 94

The beautiful selected passage of today is amazingly comprehensive in nature and an appropriate understanding of its content will empower the seeker of success by showing him the Light despite being enveloped in darkness, and by showing him the correct Path despite the confusion. The primary message of the beautiful selected passage of today is that there is One Supreme Being: the All-knowing and All-powerful One Who is aware of the entire existence and Who is responsible for every action and everything that happens in the entire existence – even if it appears to be something as mundane as the falling of a leaf. Successful understanding of this concept will prevent the seeker of success from seeking assistance from other real or imagined beings who have no control over anything at all, and instead encourage him to rely on God Alone, Who is responsible for the creation and maintenance of the entire existence.

The second valuable message to obtain from the beautiful selected passage of today is that every action in existence is not only known to God, the Most knowledgeable and the Most Watchful One, but is also recorded in detail. Therefore, the seeker of success will realize that his actions are not futile, and that everything is maintained in a clear record.

The third valuable message to obtain from the beautiful selected passage of today is that not only is the entire existence under control of God, the All-aware and Most Wise, and that every action that one performs is maintained in a clear record, but also that man will be resurrected on the Day of Judgment and held accountable for all his actions. In order for man to understand that resurrection from death back to life is not a difficult matter for God, the Giver of life and the One Who takes it away and will resurrect it again on the Day of Judgment, we are provided with the beautiful analogy of sleeping and awakening from sleep that we encounter every day, and which is not unlike death and resurrection.

The seeker of success who wishes to reach his goal has unwavering faith in God, the Almighty and the Source of all that exists, and in His beloved messenger, Muhammad. He realizes that everything in existence is under the control of God, the Most Beneficent and Most Merciful, and that all his actions are recorded in a clear record, and that he will one day return to God, the Creator and the Resurrector, and the Most Forgiving One, to be held accountable for his actions, i.e. his success or failure to perform what he has been created for.

# Day 95

**Say: Who is it that delivers you from the dark recesses of land and sea, when you call upon Him in humility and in the secrecy of the heart: "If He only delivers us from these (dangers), (we vow) we shall truly show our gratitude"?**

(6:63)

# Day 95

The beautiful selected passage of today conveys in a very ingenious format the awareness that all men and women have of the existence of God, the Most Praiseworthy and the Preventer of all harm. Once man realizes not only subconsciously, but also consciously, the existence of God, the Truth and the Only One, then he can attempt to fulfill the obligations that he has to his Creator, the Most Loving and the Most Powerful. And fulfilling one's obligations to God, the Most Holy Creator of all that exists, is a prerequisite for the seeker of success if he wishes to reach his goal.

In the beautiful selected passage of today, the example given is that of a man who is threatened by impending and emergent danger, such as one may encounter during a storm in the sea. This scenario can be extended to other situations, such as when flying in an airplane in which turbulence is encountered.

In the examples given above, such as possible drowning or an airplane in which control has been lost, then the universal response invariably in these situations is: "God, please help me!". We rarely hear of instinctual messages such as "gods, please help me" or "I hope I'm saved by chance". However, after one has been delivered from these dangers, man has a tendency to forget God, the Most Loving and on Whom all existence relies on for its maintenance, safety and well-being. Having a better understanding of the beautiful selected passage will lead one to be aware of God the Most Trustworthy and All-aware in all situations including when one is feeling safe

The seeker of success who wishes to reach his goal has complete faith in God, the Creator of all (including good and evil), and in His noble messenger, Muhammad. Even though he instinctually remembers God, the Most Beneficent and the Most Merciful when he is in danger and calls on Him for assistance, he continues to show his gratitude to Him even when he is well out of danger and living in peace and security.

## Day 96

**When you see men engaged in vain discourse about Our signs, turn away from them unless they turn to a different theme. If Satan ever makes you forget, then after recollection, sit not in company of those who do wrong.**

(6:68)

# Day 96

For a person who has an assignment to complete in a particular time period, it is important to remain focused on his task. The beautiful selected passage of today helps the seeker of success to remain focused on his goal and to avert the unpleasant consequence of neglecting his responsibilities. For a person to whom life is a chance occurrence arising out of randomness from the physical forces in nature, the meaning of life can be summed up in the doctrine of the survival of the fittest. The goal of life for these individuals is happiness now and in this life as we know it, for there is no knowledge of life beyond death.

The beautiful selected passage of today instructs us to be on guard lest we forget that life is a precious gift provided by God, the Eternal, Self-sustaining Creator of all that exists, the Maker of order, and the Fashioner. The goal of such a person who believes in God, the Giver and Taker of life, is to fulfill the duties for which he has been created by God, the Most Capable Appraiser and the Best of those who keep account.

The seeker of success will attain from the beautiful selected passage of today the advice of immense value: that engaging in useless activities is not only a hindrance to reaching his goal, but will result in unpleasant consequences, and that a specific activity which is not only useless, but completely contradictory to the reason for his existence, is denial of the One Who has created all that exists. This is manifested in vain discourse about God and the signs of God, the Most Holy, the Hearer and Seer of all. If the arch-enemy of man, Satan, whose goal is to prevent man from fulfilling the duties for which man has been created, ever attempts to make him forget, then the seeker of success, after recollection, should not sit in the company of those who do wrong, in order to adequately protect himself.

The seeker of success who wishes to reach his goal has absolute faith in God, the Most Great and the Source of all that exists, and in His beloved messenger, Muhammad. He realizes the importance of remaining focused on one's goal in order to succeed. If he sees others engaged in useless talk about God and the signs of God, the Almighty and the Creator of all, he turns away from them unless they turn to a different topic - and does not sit with such individuals again, in order to protect himself from failure.

# Day 97

Leave alone those who take their religion to be mere play and amusement, and are deceived by the life of this world. But proclaim (to them) this (truth): That every soul (that) delivers itself to ruin, (does so) by its (own) acts — it will find for itself no protector or intercessor except God; if it offered every ransom (or reparation), none will be accepted. Such is (the end of) those who deliver themselves to ruin by their own acts: They will have for drink (only) boiling water, and for punishment, one most grievous; for they persisted in rejecting God.

(6:70)

# Day 97

The seeker of success is referred to the meditation from the previous day for review of an important concept from the recommendation from God, the Most Rich and the Enricher, on attaining success, i.e. avoiding the company of those who would prevent one from fulfilling the responsibilities for which one has been created. Building further onto the concept mentioned above, the seeker of success is further empowered by the beautiful selected passage of today by the description of the responsibilities one has been given and the reason for one's creation and a description of the possible consequence of neglecting to fulfill one's responsibility, i.e. to worship Him Who created all that exists and Who sustains His creation with the most admirable perfection. The esteemed reader is referred to the commentary of Day 3 of this collection of meditations on a more detailed discussion of worship.

Those who enjoy the many good things in life may find them pleasurable and amusing. These people may make significant effort to maximize their pleasure from the innumerable gifts from God, the Most Beneficent Creator and the Nourisher. We can compare these people to workers who come to their place of employment for reasons other than work: passing the time, socializing, enjoying the lunch hour, and obtaining a salary - but neglecting their duties and the responsibilities for which they are expected to be paid.

God, the Most Glorious and the Best Guide, informs the seeker of success in the beautiful selected passage of today to stay away from those who prevent him from fulfilling his responsibilities, for which he has been created, because that would lead to self-ruin. Specific examples of the consequence for neglecting the duties for which one has been created by God, Most Patient and Most Forbearing, are given. The wise individual will heed the clear warnings and grave punishments which God, the Most Merciful and Most Generous, has provided in the beautiful selected passage of today, so as not to be subjected to a tremendous surprise when it's too late (at the time of Judgment by Him Who is the Best Judge and the Best of those who keep account).

The seeker of success who wishes to reach his goal has unwavering faith in God, the Most Great, the Most Righteous Teacher and the Best Guide, and in His noble messenger, Muhammad. He stays away from those who take their religion to be mere play and amusement, and are deceived by the life of this world. He knows the importance of remaining focused on his goal in order to succeed; he understands what is required of him in order to reach his goal. He knows beforehand the dire consequences of failing to fulfill his responsibilities.

# Day 98

Say: "Shall we indeed call on others besides God – things that can do us neither good nor harm – and turn on our heels after receiving guidance from God, like one whom the evil ones have made into a fool, wandering bewildered through the earth – his friends calling: "come to us", (vainly) guiding him to the path?"

Say: "God's guidance is the (only) Guidance, and we have been directed to submit ourselves to the Lord of the Worlds.

And to establish regular prayer and to fear God; for it is to Him that we shall be gathered together".

It is He who created the heavens and the earth in true (proportions); the day He says: "Be", behold! It is. His Word is the truth. His will be the rule the Day the trumpet will be blown. He knows the unseen as well as that which is seen – for He is the Wise, Well-aware of all things.

(6:71-73)

# Day 98

The seeker of success will find in today's beautiful selected passage a precious gift from God, the Most Beneficent Enricher and the Best Guide, and summarized thus: follow the true Guidance from God, the Most Wise and the Absolute Truth, and beware of the corrupting influences of alternate sources, more aptly termed as misguidance. The sincere seeker of success contemplates the marvelous intricacies of all matter in existence, of perfect order from disorder, and the perfection with which this order is maintained by God, the Most Perfect, the Originator and Sustainer of all that exists. Additionally, the seeker of success realizes that there is a purpose behind the creation of everything that exists; he realizes that his life is a precious gift from God, the Most Generous and the Creator of all; and he realizes that he will be held accountable to his Creator when he will be gathered in front of Him, the Most Patient and the Best One Who keeps account, on the Day of Judgment.

The beautiful selected passage of today strengthens the seeker of success by warning him that in order to truly succeed, he must seek guidance only from God, the Most Righteous Teacher and the Best Guide; the seeker of success realizes that all other sources of guidance will lead to failure. When the evil ones attempt to distract the seeker of success from his goal, he says: "God's guidance is the (only) Guidance (for success) and we have been directed to submit ourselves to the Lord of the worlds, to establish regular prayers and to fear God".

The seeker of success who wishes to reach his goal has complete faith in God, the Almighty, Creator and Sustainer of all that exists, and in His beloved messenger, Muhammad. He submits himself entirely to God, the Lord of the worlds, the Most Wise, and He to Whom all shall be gathered in order to give account of their life. He realizes that his Lord's Guidance is the only useful guidance and does not rely on any other besides Him for guidance or help, knowing that they can do him neither any good nor harm.

# Day 99

And (remember) when Abraham said to his father Azar: "Do you take idols for God? For I see you and your people in manifest error".

So also did we show Abraham the power and the laws of the heavens and the earth, that he should be one of those who have faith with certainty.

When the night covered him over, he saw a star, he said: "This is my Lord". But when it set, he said "I love not those that set".

When he saw the moon rising in splendor, he said: "This is my Lord". But when the moon set, he said: "Unless my Lord guides me, I shall surely be among those who go astray".

When he saw the sun rising in splendor he said: "This is my Lord; this is the greatest (of all)". But when the sun set, he said: "O my people! I am indeed free from your (guilt) of giving partners to Allah. (As) for me, I have set my face, firmly and truly, towards Him who created the heavens and the earth, and never shall I join partners with God".

(6:74 – 79)

# Day 99

    Today's beautiful selected passage helps the seeker of success to grasp, and be strengthened by, what is undoubtedly the essential ingredient of success: faith. This primary ingredient is also reinforced in multiple other places in the Holy Quran and is reflected upon in this collection of meditations frequently. However, the grace, beauty, sublimity, and eloquence with which the key ingredient of success in this beautiful passage is presented in the Holy Quran makes it one of its most endearing passages indeed. In order to succeed in life, one needs to understand from whence one came and one's purpose in life. Otherwise, one is likely to drift through life fulfilling one's most immediate needs like an animal, instead of having a plan and purpose for one's life.

    It is not happenstance that the beloved prophet Abraham has been designated with one of the highest titles that can be bestowed on an individual: "intimate friend of God". The noble prophet Abraham has been provided with such honor as so beautifully documented in the beautiful selected passage of today for recognizing, from sincere reflection, that no matter how beautiful or powerful anything might appear – such as the sun or the moon – it is not right to worship anything other than God, the Most Glorious, the Only One, and the Creator of all that exists. In addition to recognizing the Ultimate Source, to Whom belongs all worship and devotion, the beloved prophet Abraham was not selfish and content to benefit his own self on discovery of the key to success, but wished for others to share in the good fortune of the reward of the **<u>ultimate success</u>** of worshipping and serving Only Him to Whom belongs all praise and worship and to Whom is the return of all that exists – by inviting others to share in the good fortune of achieving the highest form of success, starting with the invitation to his father, and then to countless others, including this grateful servant of God, the Most Great and the Most Glorious. And this task was later taken by the noble prophet Muhammad and successfully relayed to mankind, after the beloved prophet Abraham's message was corrupted by intentional and/or un-intentional mechanisms over the course of time.

    The seeker of success who wishes to reach his goal has absolute faith in God, the Almighty, the Creator and Sustainer of all, and in His noble messenger, Muhammad. He devotes his life truly and completely to Him Who created the heavens and the earth, and does not join real or imagined partners to Him. He encourages others to also succeed.

# Day 100

**It is those who believe and confuse not their beliefs with wrong, that are (truly) in security – for they are on (right) guidance.**

(6:82)

# Day 100

For trees, insects, and animals such as monkeys or tigers, life is simple and without significant ethical dilemmas. For example, as far as we know, a cow does not expend much effort considering whether finishing the last stack of grass now in front of her is better than sharing it with her neighboring cow who lives across the pond and has been starving for a week. On the other hand, life can be painfully difficult for a human being: should he get out of bed at sunrise, or continue sleeping to noon? Should he toil physically and/or mentally to acquire the resources to meet his needs or steal the life savings of the elderly lady next door? Should he utilize some of his excess resources to assist the most needy individuals in his community, or take advantage of those most in need by earning interest on loans given to them?

Of the multitude of decisions one must make every day, as described above, the choice is clear for some, and unclear for many others, provided we optimally utilize our logic. The astute seeker of success realizes that God, the Creator of all that exists and the Most Just, has not created in vain all the beautiful things in existence.

The wise seeker of success understands the role of God, the Most Beneficent Friend and Protector to all the creation, and turns to Him for guidance, for he realizes that the One Who can create with such perfection and care would not leave His creations to their own whims without providing them with Divine Guidance. It is those who believe in God, the Most Trustworthy, the Giver and Taker of life, and their duties toward Him, and confuse not their beliefs with wrong, who are truly in security; for they are on right Guidance, fulfilling the duties for which they were created, and on their way to the highest form of success.

The seeker of success who wishes to reach his goal has unwavering faith in God, the Most High, the Best Teacher and the Best Guide, and in His beloved messenger, Muhammad. He knows that Islam, i.e. submission to God, the Creator and Sustainer of all that exists, provides him with the best Guidance, and does not confuse his beliefs with wrong.

# Day 101

It is God Who causes the seed grain and the date stone to split and sprout. He causes the living to issue from the dead, and He is the One to cause the dead to issue from the living. That is God; then how are you deluded away from the Truth?

He it is that cleaves the daybreak (from the dark); He makes the night for rest and tranquility, and the sun and the moon for the measuring (of time): Such is the judgment and ordering of (Him), the Exalted in power, the Omniscient.

(6:95-96)

# Day 101

Contemplation, understanding, and acceptance of the message from the beautiful selected passage of today will lead to mastery of the key ingredient needed for the highest form of success: faith in God, the Creator, Provider and Sustainer of all that exists, as relayed by His noble messenger, Muhammad, and which is the characteristic that is most often mentioned in the Holy Quran for the benefit of mankind and the seeker of success to reach his goal, and which is manifested by performance of good deeds.

An individual who relies completely on objective data may ask: "Since God, the Most Wise and the Most Able, is creator of all that exists, and is able to do anything he wishes, why doesn't He show Himself to us, so that we will not have any doubts regarding Him?" In the beautiful selected passage of today, God, the Most Magnificent, the Manifest and the Hidden One, shows Himself to us in not one way, but in numerous ways: We see Him in the seed grain and the date stone which splits and sprouts and nourishes us; we see Him in the yellowing of leaves in autumn and in their death, as well as their sprouting again in spring and coming to life; we see Him in the maintenance of the sun, moon, and all existence, and in the magnificent way that He cleaves the day from the dark of the night and makes the night for our rest and tranquility. With appropriate understanding of the beautiful selected passage of today, the seeker of success is prevented from being deluded from the truth, and his faith is strengthened in God, the Exalted in Power, the Omniscient. The seeker of success is then prepared to manifest his faith with the appropriate actions which will determine the magnitude of his success.

The seeker of success who wishes to reach his goal has complete faith in God, the Almighty, the Creator of all, the Maker of order, and the Shaper of beauty, and in His noble messenger, Muhammad. He sees the signs of his Lord everywhere: in the daybreak and the sunset, the sprouting of a seed grain, the autumn and the spring. His faith is thus strengthened and he is guided towards the Truth and **everlasting success.**

# Day 102

**Eschew all sin – open or secret; those who earn sin will get due recompense for their "earnings".**

(6:120)

# Day 102

    In order to reach any goal, one has to plan and take positive steps towards it until arrival at the goal. For the goal that the seeker of success has set, God, the Most Kind and Most Generous, has provided him with clear instructions and innumerable constructive steps that he can take to realize his goal, as described elsewhere in this collection of meditations on success from the Holy Quran.

    Besides taking positive steps to reach a set goal, it is also important to remember to avoid things that can keep us from reaching our goal. In the beautiful selected passage of today, God, the Most Wise, the Creator of harm and the Creator of good, is instructing man to utilize his free will that man alone has - unlike any other beings we know of, to avoid selecting the bad over the good, i.e. to avoid sin and to seek virtue.

    There are things that man knows instinctively are wrong, such as murder, stealing, fornication, oppression and deception. The seeker of success is referred to the Holy Quran for a better understanding of those acts considered to be sinful, in addition to what his heart already knows, for man was created pure, endowed with the spirit of God, the Most Pure, the Eternal, and only when he persists in selecting evil over good does he corrupt himself. It is worth mentioning at this point that the greatest sin, and the only one that is not forgiven by God, the Most Beneficent, Most Merciful and the Most Forgiving, is rejecting Him and associating others with Him, and therefore worshipping others than or with Him, because man was created to worship and serve God Alone, the Most Praiseworthy and He to Whom belongs all rule. The seeker of success avoids the biggest sin, as described above regarding rejecting God, the Creator of all and the Most Comprehending One, as well as all other sins, either open or secret. Those who persist in sin, besides not being able to succeed, are forewarned that they will be punished for their rejection of God, the Creator, Nourisher and Sustainer of all, as well as for continuing to choose evil over good and for neglecting the duties for which they were created.

    The seeker of success who wishes to reach his goal has absolute faith in God, the Most Great and the Most Forgiving One, and in His beloved messenger, Muhammad. He stays away from all sin, open or secret.

# Day 103

Those whom God (in his plan) wills to guide, He opens their breast to Islam; those whom He wills to leave straying, He makes their breast close and constricted, as if they had to climb up to the skies. Thus does God (heap) the penalty on those who refuse to believe.

This is the way of your Lord, leading straight; We have detailed the signs for those who receive admonition.

For them will be a home of peace in the presence of their Lord: He will be their Friend, because they practiced (righteousness).

(6:125 – 127)

# Day 103

    The beautiful selected passage of today contains extremely valuable information for the serious seeker of success who is interested not only in transient pleasure, but also in the highest form of success, which is everlasting. The way of God, the Exalter, as well as the Abaser, and the Best guide, is beautifully detailed in the comprehensive and sublime selected passage of today, leading the sincere seeker of success on the straight path to eternal success.

    We are informed in the amazingly comprehensive passage of today that the gift of Guidance from God, the One who is All–aware and the Bestower of honors, as well as the Humiliator, is provided to those who experience His presence in the countless treasures He has provided to us, such as the free oxygen that we breathe, and the free sunlight and water necessary for all life, among countless other signs of His presence. The unfortunate individual who enjoys the numerous benefits of God, the Most Beneficent Nourisher and Sustainer of all existence, but refuses to believe in Him or worship Him, will be left straying, his breast close and constricted, and guidance so far out of his reach that it is as if he would have to climb up to the sky to reach it.

    However, those who appreciate the innumerable benefits provided to all by God, the Creator and Sustainer of all that exists, and who contemplate His greatness and wish to serve Him, will be guided by Him as a reward – and will have their breasts opened to Islam. As a result, they will practice righteousness through the reward of Guidance. For them will be the home of eternal peace in the presence of their Lord, the Most Generous and the Best Rewarder of thankfulness. As a matter of fact, they will be honored with the title of "friend" of God, Who is the Most Trustworthy and the Best Friend and Protector, as the beloved prophet Ibrahim was honored as a result of his desire to serve God, the Inspirer and Guardian of faith and He to Whom belongs all praise and worship.

    The seeker of success who wishes to reach his goal has unwavering faith in God, the Best Guide and the Most Righteous Teacher, and in His noble messenger, Muhammad. He is thankful to his Lord for the numerous treasures provided for the benefit of man and all existence, and turns to Him for Guidance at all times.

# Day 104

Lost are those who slay their children from folly, without knowledge, and forbid the sustenance which God has provided for them, inventing lies against God. They have indeed gone astray and heeded no guidance.

It is He Who produces gardens with trellises and without, and dates, and tilth with produce of all kinds, and olives and pomegranates, similar (in kind) and different (in variety). Eat of their fruit in their season, but render the dues that are proper on the day that the harvest is gathered. But waste not by excess; for God loves not the wasters.

(6:140-141)

# Day 104

Every action that man performs is dependent on his perception of whether it is beneficial for him or not. Although man shares with other animals the reflexive response for preference of immediate gratification, it is precisely this characteristic in inverse proportion that distinguishes him from other animals. Indeed, controlling against the baser instincts of one's self is difficult not only because of man's characteristics he shares with other living creatures for self-gratification, but also because it is the easiest and likely the most effective target of the accursed Satan

Sometimes man behaves so selfishly that he is unwilling to share his resources with anyone, including other fellow beings, neighbors, family, children who have been born, and those not yet born as well. In some cases, the man or the woman may delude himself or herself into thinking that he or she is being practical by killing his or her existing children, or those who have not yet been born, for the fear of lack of resources. The beautiful selected passage of today provides assurance to the seeker of success of the ability of Him Who is responsible for all creation to nourish and sustain His creation, giving the most beautiful examples, and discourages the slaying of beings, especially children who have been born as well as those not yet born, from fear of not being able to provide for them, as this is the responsibility of God, the Nourisher and Sustainer of all his creation.

Marvelous examples are provided in the beautiful selected passage of today: of abundance from gardens of dates, olives, pomegranates, and produce of all kinds. And when the harvest is gathered, man sometimes does not know what to do with the excess. Divine guidance is provided in the beautiful selected passage of today: to avoid waste, to not only enjoy the abundance and thank the Most Kind and Generous One Who provided it – but to share it with others as well.

The seeker of success who wishes to reach his goal has complete faith in God, the Almighty, the Creator and Sustainer of all that exists, and His beloved messenger, Muhammad. Having full conviction that the One Who created everything in existence is also fully capable of sustaining all His creation, he does not forbid the sustenance due to anyone, including his own children – whether already born or not yet born. He shares with others the blessings he has been provided with by God, the Most Great and Most Generous one, and does not waste the resources he has been blessed with.

# Day 105

Say: "Come, I will rehearse what Allah has (really) prohibited you from:

> Join not anything as equal with Him;

> Be good to your parents;

> Kill not your children on a plea of want – We provide sustenance for you and for them;

> Come not near to shameful deeds, whether open or secret;

> Take not life, which Allah has made sacred, except by way of justice and law.

Thus does He command you, that you may learn wisdom.

(6:151)

# Day 105

During a person's life, he or she must make a myriad of decisions on a daily basis. Every decision that one makes tends to be based on whether it is better than the alternative for one's self, family, tribe, race, nation or mankind. The ability to consistently choose the better option will lead one towards lasting success. Indeed, the cumulative effect of selecting right over wrong, in addition to having faith in God, the Creator of all, the Ever-living and the Self-existing One and his beloved prophet Muhammad, will be the basis on which man will be judged regarding whether he has passed the test of life, and whether he will be either rewarded or punished accordingly on the Day of Judgment by God, the Most Forgiving and the Most Wise Judge.

Because God is Most Kind and Most Caring - wishing success for all creation, He has provided clear Guidance in the Holy Quran, with specific commands that are not cumbersome and do not focus on trivialities. The prohibitions given to us in the beautiful selected passage of today, address the major factors that can prevent one from attaining success.

The first and most important prohibition on the path to wisdom and success, listed in the beautiful selected passage of today, is not to join anything as equal to God the Only One, and Who is the First and the Last. This is also the only offense that is not pardonable by God, the Most Forgiving and the Most Kind. Other commandments for the seeker of success outlined in today's beautiful passage full of wisdom and benefit include being good to one's parents, who, after God, the Most Wise Creator, have been most responsible for one's nourishment and well-being during one's most vulnerable phase of life. Along with the above positive factors for the attainment of success, man is instructed to not kill his children, as God, the Provider of all and the Most Loving, is able to sustain all His Creation; to avoid all shameful deeds, which are not listed because they are recognized by one's conscience, which is a manifestation of the Spirit of God, the Most Beneficent and Most Merciful, as it was breathed into man on his creation, distinguishing him from other animals; and not to take life, all of which is sacred, except as necessary, based on justice and law.

The seeker of success who wishes to reach his goal has absolute faith in God, the Most Rich, the Creator and Sustainer of all, and in His noble messenger, Muhammad. He does not negate his conscience when it tells him to refrain from a shameful act, even though it may be beneficial to him in the short term. He knows the position of God, the Source of all power and existence, and does not join anything equal with Him. He is always good to his parents, knowing that they sheltered and sustained him during his most vulnerable stage in life, and kills not his children on a plea of want, knowing that doing so is akin to questioning the ability of God, the Most Great, the Most Loving and the Creator and Sustainer of all, Who is able to sustain his child just as He sustains the entire existence. He knows that all life is sacred, and cannot be taken, except in way of justice and law. He does not take justice and law into his own hands.

## Day 106

...No burden do We place on any soul, but that which it can bear – whenever you speak, speak justly, even if a near relative is concerned. And fulfill the covenant of Allah; thus does He command you, that you may remember.

For sure, this is My Way leading straight – follow it; follow not (other) paths, they will scatter you about from His (great) Path. Thus does He command you, that you may be righteous.

(6:152-153)

# Day 106

    The beautiful selected passage of today empowers the seeker of success by providing him with three precious gifts that would serve him well on his earthly life.

    Life is a challenge for man from birth to death. At times, the challenges in life can appear insurmountable. The first precious gift from the beautiful selected passage of today, will help the seeker to success to withstand any challenge in life is the knowledge that God, the Most Kind, the Most Just, and the One with the ultimate power in all existence, Who is able to do whatever He wishes, will never place on any individual a burden that he cannot bear.

    Because man is the vicegerent of God, the Most Equitable One and the Most Wise, he is instructed to show the characteristics which are attributed in the example as given above of being just, kind, and wise. The second precious gift from the beautiful selected passage of today for the seeker of success is to behave as the vicegerent of God, the Most Beneficent and the Most Merciful, exhibiting His characteristic of Justice - and when he speaks, he should speak justly, even if a near relative is concerned and will incur a loss as a result. This behavior falls under performance of righteous actions, done for the sake of God, the Most Holy and the Most Praiseworthy, will be rewarded by Him, which will increase one's likelihood of attaining success

    The third precious gift from the beautiful selected passage that empowers the seeker of success to meet his goal is the message from God, the Eternal and the Best Guide, that man should stay focused on his mission towards His way, and not be distracted from his mission by following any other path than that of God, the All-knowing and the Most Wise. If one gets distracted from one's goal, one is then less likely to reach it.

    The seeker of success who wishes to reach his goal has unwavering faith in God, the Most Wise, the Best Guide and the Most Righteous Teacher, and in His beloved messenger, Muhammad. He utilizes the precious gifts we reflected on today to remember and follow the commandments of God, the Most Magnificent and the Most Generous, and to stay focused on his mission on the straight Path leading to everlasting success.

# Day 107

Say (O Muhammad): "Truly, my prayer and my service of sacrifice, my life and my death, are (all) for Allah, the Cherisher of the worlds.

No partner has He; this I am commanded, and I am the first of those who bow to His will".

(6:162-163)

# Day 107

From birth onwards, man is in a continuing physical, cognitive and social developmental process - and experiences a similar decline after reaching a peak later in life. After birth, it does not take long for the newborn to realize that his security and well being are dependent on his parent or guardian. As he increases in awareness, the child realizes that he was in error when he attributed to his parent or guardian the control of the entire world. In primitive times, as man progressed in his development, he would eventually shift his thinking to attribute the ultimate source of power to the chief of his tribe or to the head of his village or the king of the country. As man progressed in his intellectual development, we have evidence that he yearned to identify the real source of control of the universe once he realized that his parent, chief, or king was not that source. The evidence of man's quest to identify the source of existence and the universe is the finding of stones and figures to whom the primitive man attributed various powers, and to whom the primitive man offered prayer and sacrifice.

Today's beautiful selected passage empowers the seeker of success by guiding him to the Path which will lead him to acts that are used as criteria for **attainment of the ultimate success**, i.e. on the Day of Judgment. The wise seeker of success realizes that all praise and worship, including his life and death, are all for God, the Cherisher of the worlds and the Ultimate Source of all power. The intelligent seeker of success is no longer lost with primitive thoughts, such as attributing supernatural powers to the kings or leaders, or to a myriad of other imagined beings, but realizes that his life and everything in existence is due to the One Who created everything, sustains it and has no other partners in His Divinity. The intelligent seeker of success is no longer wasting his energy and effort on serving anything or anyone other than God, the Most Holy and the Only One, and wishes to be included among the first of those who bow to His will, and so be the first to succeed as well.

The seeker of success who wishes to reach his goal has complete faith in God, the Creator and Sustainer of all that exists, and the Best Friend and Protector, and in His noble messenger, Muhammad. He knows with certainty that his life and death, and all aspects of his existence in between, are for God, the Source of all power, Who has no other partners whom he needs to serve. He yearns to be the first to bow to His Lord in His praise and worship.

# Day 108

Say "Shall I seek for (my) lord other then Allah, when He is the Lord of all things (that exist)? Every soul draws the consequences of its acts on none but itself; no bearer of burdens can bear the burden of another. Your goal in the end is towards Allah; He will tell you the things wherein you disputed".

It is He who has made you (His) agents, inheritors of the earth; He has raised you in ranks, some above others, that He may try you in the gifts He has given you. For your Lord is quick in punishment, yet He is indeed Most Forgiving, Most merciful.

(6:164-165)

# Day 108

Man tends to look at various predictable figures in different phases of his life for support as we reflected in earlier meditations in this collection: in childhood he puts his trust in his parents; in young adulthood, he relies on the teacher or the mentor; in his productive years, he typically tends to rely on his employer; and in his elderly years, he may rely on his children or the state. However, the intelligent seeker of success will ask himself: "Shall I seek for (my) lord (any) other than He Who is the Lord of all things (that exist)?" Once man realizes Who it is that he can count on for support – and no one else, then he is able to advance to the next step for success: the reason for man's creation. As we noted in the earlier meditations, the reason man was created by God, the Most Beneficent and Most Merciful, was to worship and serve him. We also reviewed that worship is a broad term, with verbal and physical components comprising only part of the process. The esteemed reader is referred to the commentary of Day 3 of this collection of meditations on a more detailed discussion of worship.

After this great realization as discussed above, the seeker of success is quite close to reaching his goal, and what remains for him to realize now is that by his actions man is either helping or harming himself, and no one else. God, the Most Caring and Most Forbearing, is reassuring the seeker of success that he will either succeed or fail depending on his actions. Additionally, having been created with the special honor of being instilled with the Spirit of God, the Most Just and Most Kind, man's behavior must reflect this honored status and the tremendous responsibility he carries as the agent of God, the Most Pure and the Greatest on earth, to act accordingly. With this great responsibility comes not only an opportunity for a great reward, but also punishment, which is real and tremendous, yet God is also reminding the seeker of success that He is also Most Forgiving and Most Merciful, and that He is available always to help every single individual – even if he has been neglectful of his duties in the past, but seeks His forgiveness and assistance in reaching his goal of everlasting success.

The seeker of success who wishes to reach his goal has absolute faith in God, the Creator and Sustainer of all that exists, and the Best Friend and Protector, and in His noble messenger, Muhammad. He seeks only the assistance of God, the Source of all that exists and the Best Friend and Protector, and knows that he is not in need of anyone else's assistance. He realizes that his role on earth is as vicegerent of God, the Most Holy, the Creator and Sustainer of all, and behaves accordingly.

# Day 109

> **O you children of Adam! We have bestowed raiment upon you to cover your shame as well as to be an adornment to you. But the raiment of righteousness – that is the best. Such are among the signs of Allah, that they may receive admonition!**
>
> (7:26)

# Day 109

People do many things that they feel can increase their chance of being liked by others, such as bathing, having a good hairstyle, perfuming themselves, wearing their best clothes, smiling, and speaking in a pleasant manner. The man who contemplates seriously about whom he should concentrate on pleasing for maximal benefit will be faced with a dilemma because he will be unable to serve and please everyone that he has identified as important. The wise individual passes through the contemplative stage regarding whom he should be serving and arrives at the conclusion so beautifully illustrated by the beloved prophet Ibrahim's identical journey mentioned earlier in this collection, i.e. that he will serve only Him Who created all that exists and Who sustains creation, and no one or nothing else. This individual can be said to have grasped the most important ingredient required for the attainment of everlasting success.

The beautiful selected passage of today helps the seeker of success by providing him with useful information as to what would be pleasing to God, the Lord of all majesty and reward, the Most Forceful and the All-seeing One. The profusely sublime passage of today begins with the simplest scenario – that the clothing we wear is used for covering our nakedness as well as being an adornment that others find pleasing. The seeker of success who has identified that the only one he needs to please and serve is the One Who created all and Who is the Satisfier of all needs finds the characteristic of righteousness most pleasing. The fortunate individual who has faith in God, the Truth and the Most Trustworthy, and who acts righteously as a result of his faith, will find himself in the esteemed company of those most favored by God, the Most Glorious and the Best Rewarder, attaining His closeness and achieving the highest order of success.

The seeker of success who wishes to reach his goal has absolute faith in God, the Most Refined and All-Aware, and in His noble messenger, Muhammad. He wears the raiment of righteousness most eagerly, knowing the extent to which it pleases his Lord, the Source of all power and existence and the Most Just.

# Day 110

**Say: "My Lord has commanded justice and that you set your whole selves (to Him) at every time and place of prayer and call upon Him, making your devotion sincere as in His sight. Such as He created you in the beginning, so shall you return".**

(7:29)

# Day 110

There are three valuable points that the seeker of success will obtain from the beautiful selected passage of today that will help him to reach his goal, the first of which leads us to grasp the importance of worship or prayer, including praise with sincere devotion to God, the Most Holy and the Most Praiseworthy, after which, man is able to fulfill the main reason for which he was created. The degree of success man attains will be dependent on how well he has performed the requirements for which he was created, i.e. worshipping sincerely and diligently the One Who created him and to Whom he shall return and by Whom he will be judged. The esteemed reader is referred to the meditation of Day 3 in this collection for a more detailed discussion of worship.

The second valuable point that the seeker of success will obtain from the beautiful selected passage of today is the reinforcement of one's mission in life or reason for existence, which is the basis for all actions that the individual will perform in his life. If one has no mission in life except to go on with life, taking whatever is dealt to him, one's life can be relatively easy – as easy as the non-human beings we share this earth with. If one's mission is to accumulate as much wealth as possible, one can utilize all his energies for this purpose – and many do reach the goals they have set for themselves. The seeker of success is instructed in today's beautiful selected passage to set his whole self to God, the Most Trustworthy and the Most Reliable Friend and Protector. When man is serving others instead of God, the Most Beneficent and Most Merciful, then he is neglecting the main reason why he was created, which is to worship and serve God, the Bestower of all honors, the Exalter and the Humiliator.

The third valuable point that the seeker of success will obtain from the beautiful selected passage of today is to act justly. There will be many opportunities in the test of life when it will be more convenient or beneficial in the short term to not act justly, with one's decision able to be supported by various rationalizations. However, God, the Most Just and the Most Wise, has commanded justice for men, and He is the knower of all, the One Who judges all actions and Who is Most Just, and to Whom is the return of all.

The seeker of success who wishes to reach his goal has unwavering faith in God, the Creator and Sustainer of all and the Most Righteous teacher, and in His noble messenger, Muhammad. He knows his mission in life with certainty, which is to set his whole self to God, the Source of all power and to Whom is the return of all, serving Him diligently, with highest enthusiasm, and praising Him for his immeasurable gifts and Glory. He acts justly at all times, as instructed by God, the Most Glorious, the Most Just and the Best Judge.

# Day 111

**As for those who believe and work righteousness – and no burden do We place on any soul, but that which it
can bear, they will be companions of the Garden, therein to dwell (forever).**

(7:42)

# Day 111

The concepts contained in today's beautiful selected passage should be considered of significant importance, as they have been repeated a number of times in the Holy Quran by God, the Creator of all that exists, the Inspirer of faith, and the Best Teacher, Who wishes for all to succeed. The wise seeker of success will consider these repetitions of key points as important reminders and reinforcements and as identifications of the crucial components of success. The first key point and reinforcement regarding the essential ingredients of success is belief in God, the Most Powerful, the Creator of all power and the Source of all that exists, and man's responsibility to worship Him only and none other, as relayed to us through His noble prophet Muhammad. The man who believes and has faith in God, the Most Supreme and Most Trustworthy, and His noble prophet Muhammad, is then able to work righteousness, and honorably fulfill the duties for which he was created, which is worshipping God, the Most Holy and Most Praiseworthy. The esteemed reader is referred to the commentary of Day 3 of this collection of meditations on a more detailed discussion of worship. The man who attempts to work righteousness without the component of faith will receive the lesser benefit of pleasing himself and others – but not God, the Most Praiseworthy and the Aware, because that was not his intention.

The second key point and reinforcement regarding the essential ingredients of success mentioned in the beautiful selected passage of today is not to despair in life, especially when the trial is toughest, keeping in mind that God, the Most Kind and Most Forbearing, does not place on any soul a burden greater than it can bear. It is when times are toughest, that an individual with faith can mold himself into something more valuable than prior to the cause of his stress, if he has faith - as a goldsmith is able to mold gold into a more beautiful shape exposing it to fire.

The seeker of success who wishes to reach his goal has complete faith in God, the Creator and Sustainer of all that exists, and the Best Friend and Protector, and in His noble messenger, Muhammad. The wise seeker of success thanks God, the Most Loving Originator of all and the Restorer, has faith in Him, working righteousness as a manifestation of his faith, and does not despair during the trials of life, but rather bears them patiently, without weakening his faith. The individual who acquires the key characteristics of success, as described in the beautiful selected passage of today, will have attained the objective of life – to be successful both in this life and in the hereafter - being among the companions of the paradise, therein to dwell forever.

# Day 112

**The most beautiful names belong to Allah; so call on Him by them. But shun such men as use profanity in His names – for what they do, they will soon be repaid.**

(7:180)

# Day 112

    Historical data shows that man has been actively searching for the meaning of life and his relationship as it relates to the world, universe, and the Divine. One thing we commonly see in primitive attempts at finding the meaning of life and man's relationship to the Divine is that many of the primitive cultures arrived at the conclusion that man exists to serve others more powerful than himself, such as parents, ancient relatives and frequently their rulers. As far as man's relationship to the Divine is concerned, man tended to value certain divine characteristics, such as strength, wisdom, compassion, and richness. In many primitive and ancient cultures, such as Greek, Egyptian, and Roman, man would acknowledge and worship the beings considered divine as well as their progeny.

    When man realizes, through the loving guidance of God, the Originator, Eternal, and the Best Guide, that the reason for his creation and existence is none other than to worship God the Creator and Sustainer of All, then he has acquired the most important component needed for success. The esteemed reader is referred to the commentary of Day 3 of this collection of meditations on a more detailed discussion of worship. Man is instructed in the beautiful selected passage of today that all beautiful names belong to God the One, Most Holy, the Most Glorious and the Most Forgiving, and that man should worship, serve, rely on, and praise Him only, Who created all and is Most Wise, and to Whom belongs all praise; His names include He Who is Most Beneficent, Most Merciful, the King, the Pure One, the Victorious, the Most Pure, the Creator of all goodness, the Doer of Good, as well all other beautiful names implying all that is good.

    The seeker of success is encouraged to avoid the company of those who use profanity in reference to God the Most Holy, All-Hearing, and All-Seeing One - for in that case, then he is actually doing the opposite of what he was created for, which is to worship God, the Source of all existence, the All-knowing, and the Hearer and Responder of all supplications.

    The seeker of success who wishes to reach his goal has absolute faith in God the Source of all power, the Abaser and the Exalter, and in His noble messenger Muhammad. He is thankful to God the Greatest, the Creator, the Source of Peace, the Maker of Order, the Shaper of Beauty, the Compeller, the Nourisher of All, the Sustainer, the Opener, and the Knower of All, for empowering him with the valuable knowledge and ability to praise with the most beautiful names, the One who Created all and to Whom everything is to return.

# Day 113

**To such as Allah rejects from His Guidance, there can be no guide; He will leave them in their trespasses, wandering in distraction.**

(7:186)

# Day 113

For the person who wants to achieve his goal, it helps to know not only the factors that can help him to reach his goal, but also those factors that can prevent him from reaching it, so that appropriate precautions can be taken.

Compared to humans, other animals we know of have a relatively easy life as per our understanding: in a typical scenario, they typically wake up in the morning, find nourishment to satisfy themselves or have it provided to them, and go to sleep at night. Although human beings can (and some do) follow the scenario described above, many will find that type of life to be unfulfilling, and most will attempt to find the meaning of life beyond their existence.

The man who reflects on the vastness of the earth and the universe such as the beauty in a flower and in a baby's smile, and the tremendous complexity in the workings of a single cell in an animal (and yet more ingenuity in how billions of cells interact in the same animal as an individual), will not fail to see the Hand of God, the Creator and Owner of all, in His numerous signs everywhere – some of which are described above. This is the fortunate man who sincerely searches for guidance, leading him to the Ultimate Source of guidance and all existence, and therefore achieving the objective of life.

On the other hand, the unfortunate individual who finds it sufficient to rely on his own intelligence, other created beings, or institutions for guidance – without reflecting on or searching for God, the Most Glorious, the Apparent and Hidden, the Most Subtle, and the Sustainer of all – will not receive the blessing of His Guidance, and will be left in his confusion, wandering in distraction, and therefore, will be unable to attain the true objectives of life for which he was created. And for the unfortunate individual whom God, the Light and Source of all Guidance has rejected from His guidance, there can be no guidance, except the guidance of Satan, leading to his destruction – both in this life and in the hereafter, for eternity.

The seeker of success who wishes to reach his goal has unwavering faith in God, the Almighty, the Best Guide and the Most Righteous Teacher, and in His noble messenger, Muhammad. He realizes that the most precious gift he can have is Guidance from his Lord and yearns for it at all times in all stages of his life.

# Day 114

Hold to forgiveness; command what is right, and turn away from the ignorant.

If a suggestion from Satan assails your (mind), seek refuge with Allah; for He hears and knows all things.

Those who fear Allah, when a thought of evil from Satan assaults them, bring Allah to remembrance, and indeed they see (aright)!

But their brethren (the evil ones) plunge them deeper into error, and never relax (their efforts).

(7:199-202)

# Day 114

    Today's beautiful selected passage begins with advice on encouraging activities for the seeker of success that will help him to reach his goal: forgiving others and commanding what is right. The beautifully relayed advice from God, the Creator and Preventer of harm, concentrates on identifying the key threat to the seeker of success, the threat which can prevent him from reaching his goal, and provides practical advice on how to minimize this threat.

    Man has been created and given special standing by God, the Knower of all and the Most Wise, in the finest form – being instilled with His Spirit, even more so than the angels. Even though the angels constantly are in devotion and service to God, the Most High and the Greatest, man has the option to choose whether to serve God, the Most Praiseworthy, Lord of all majesty and bounty, and in this way, he can surpass the angels. Man also has the option to choose to serve himself or others besides God, the Only One and the Creator and Sustainer of all, in which case his standing will be lower than the lowest animal.

    It is out of the extreme jealousy of the special status of man that Satan, the arch-angel until the creation of man, has challenged God, the Most Victorious and the Compeller, that his goal until the Day of Judgment will be to dissuade as many men as possible from worshipping and serving God, the Most Pure, the Creator and Sustainer of all. Most of the beautiful selected passage of today focuses on advice for the seeker of success as to how to avoid those activities that can prevent him from reaching his goal. First, the seeker of success is instructed to avoid the company of the ignorant, so that he minimizes their negative influence on his actions. Second, he is instructed to realize that his main adversary in life is Satan – and that he and his agents, or those influenced by him, never relax their efforts and attempt to plunge man deeper into error in order to meet their objective, which is to prevent as many men as possible from serving God, the Most Beneficent, the Most Merciful, the First and the Last. Third, when a suggestion from Satan, the accursed, does assail the mind of the seeker of success, he is instructed in the beautiful selected passage of today to bring God to remembrance – the Most Magnificent, the One Who hears and knows all things – and seek refuge in Him. And indeed, God, the Most Reliable and Trustworthy, will give him refuge who seeks it, and the seeker of success will then be able to see aright and continue onwards on the path of success.

    The seeker of success who wishes to reach his goal has complete faith in God, the Most Wise, the Best Guide, and the Most Righteous Teacher, and in His beloved messenger, Muhammad. He is quick to forgive others, commands what is right, and turns away from the ignorant. If a suggestion from Satan assails his mind, he brings to his remembrance the Name of God, the Most Reliable, the Best Friend and Protector.

# Day 115

When the Quran is recited, listen to it with attention, and hold your peace, that you may receive Mercy.

And do (O reader!) bring your Lord to remembrance in your (very) soul, with humility and in reverence – without loudness in words, in the mornings and evenings. And be not of those who are unheedful.

Those who are near to your Lord, disdain not to do Him worship; they celebrate His praises, and bow down before Him.

(7:204-206)

# Day 115

No individual is born with the optimal knowledge and skills needed for success, although all individuals have the potential for success. First, one must identify tangible and achievable measures that signify success – wealth, fame, power, respect, etc – and then look for guidance from the appropriate sources to reach the goal one has set for oneself and which signifies success to himself or herself. Interestingly, the definition of success for the same individual will be quite different if he is asked to define it at various stages of his life: At age 4 years, at age 22 years, at age 45 years, or at age 75 years.

The wise seeker of success is observant of the multitude of miracles surrounding him every day: That of the glorious emergence of light from darkness with the sunrise; that of the precious air he breathes – so precious for survival, yet free; and that of his ability to see, hear, think and act. Contemplating the numerous miracles, he sees the signs of God, the Creator, the Nourisher and the Sustainer of all, in the entire existence and resolves to utilize all the resources so magnanimously provided to him to serve the One Whose existence is a sign of these innumerable miracles, and correctly identifies his goal of success as serving, praising, worshipping, and pleasing Him Whose existence is manifested in these daily miracles.

Once the wise seeker of success has identified the correct definition of success, as described above, then he searches for the right guidance from the most knowledgeable source, and finds the most reliable source to be the words of God Himself, the Most Reliable and the Most Trustworthy, Who wishes all mankind to succeed, and therefore, has sent the Quran as a Mercy and Guidance for all mankind, so that mankind may enjoy **the highest form of success, which is complete and everlasting.** And when the Quran is recited, the seeker of success listens to it with attention, in peace and gratefulness at receiving the blessing of Guidance from the Highest Source, as a Mercy. And the seeker of success brings to remembrance in his soul the One responsible for all existence and His loving Guidance in the words of the Holy Quran, reciting them with humility and in reverence, without loudness in words, in the mornings and evenings.

The seeker of success who wishes to reach his goal has absolute faith in God, the Most Holy and the Source of true peace, and in His noble messenger, Muhammad. On receiving the loving guidance towards success from the Holy Quran, the truly wise seeker of success is not one who is heedless of what he receives in guidance from God, the Originator and the most Righteous Teacher, but rather acts upon it, celebrating His praises, bowing down before Him in awe, as those who are near to Him do, and does not disdain to worship Him; thus the seeker of success hopes to be near God, the Most Great, Most Loving, and the Best Friend and Protector. As a sign that the reader understands the importance of the countless benefits, including eternal success, of following the guidance from God, the Truth and the Best Guide, the reader will prostrate at this time, as directed by the Quranic injunction in the beautiful selected passage of today, to the One Who created All, gave it form and sustains it, and will revive him again to reward him for his faithful service, or punish him for neglecting his duties.

# Day 116

**Believers are those who, when God is mentioned, feel a tremor in their hearts, and when they hear His signs rehearsed, find their faith strengthened, and put (all) their trust in their Lord;**

**Who establish regular prayers and spend (freely) out of the gifts we have given them for sustenance;**

**Such in truth are the believers: they have grades of dignity with their Lord - and forgiveness, and generous sustenance.**

(8:2-4)

# Day 116

The seeker of success who has referred to the ultimate Guidance on achieving success in the Holy Quran on his own, or who has referred to the earlier meditations in this collection, will have realized that the key ingredient to reaching his goal of attainment of everlasting success is faith and belief in God, the Creator, Owner and Sustainer of all, as instructed by His beloved messenger, Muhammad. The beautiful selected passage of today will serve an extremely valuable purpose for the seeker of success, helping to strengthen his faith and belief, with details from God, the Most Caring and the Most Righteous Teacher, on how to attain this most valuable requirement of success.

First, an individual must be able to appreciate the presence of God, the Most Glorious and Most Magnificent; the sincere seeker of success will not have to search deeply for His presence, for even though He may appear Hidden, yet He is Manifest everywhere: in the beating of one's heart, in the ability of the bird to fly, and in the feeling of satisfaction from helping another in need. The fortunate individual who is able to appreciate the presence of God, the Eternal and Self-existing One, attains the key ingredient of success: Faith. And the believers are those who, when God is mentioned, feel a tremor in their hearts (from awe and love of Him, yet fear failing to fulfill the duties for which He created them), and, when they hear His signs rehearsed, find their faith strengthened. And as a result of their faith, they put all their trust in their Lord and no one else.

As a manifestation of his faith, the believer establishes regular prayers and uses these opportunities to praise voluntarily Him Who created and sustains all, while the rest of the creation does so involuntarily. Emulating the One Who most lovingly provides the creation with all its needs, the believer spends freely out of the gifts that he himself has received from God, the Most Praiseworthy and the Most Generous, for the benefit of those in need.

The fortunate seekers of success will utilize the comprehensive recommendations from the beautiful selected passage of today to master the key ingredient of success, i.e. faith, and, as a result, they will be rewarded with forgiveness on the Day of Judgment and with generous sustenance, having grades of dignity with their Lord, the Most High and the Best Rewarder, in proportion to their belief and righteous actions, which are a manifestation of their belief. And **the most successful will be he who is the closest to God,** the Most Wise Creator and the Most Reliable Friend and Protector.

The seeker of success who wishes to reach his goal has unwavering faith in God, the Most Great and the Most Forgiving, and in His beloved messenger, Muhammad. When God is mentioned, he feels a tremor in his heart, and when he hears His signs rehearsed, he finds his faith strengthened, and puts (all) his trust in his Lord; he establishes regular prayers and spends (freely) out of the gifts his Lord has provided him, for the benefit of himself, as well as others in need.

# Day 117

**O you who believe! Give your response to God and His apostle, when He calls you to that which will give you life; and know that God comes in between a man and his heart, and that it is He to Whom you shall (all) be gathered.**

( 8:24 )

# Day 117

Certainly it would be simpler if people enthusiastically elected to do whatever was good for them. However, choosing the more beneficial option for the long term frequently requires acceptance of short-term effort and hardship. Take, for example, the typical scenarios applicable to man during his lifetime: whether to enjoy his time in childhood playing games, or to concentrate on his schoolwork and examinations; whether to start working after high school and start earning money, or to attain higher education and a university degree in young adulthood; whether to spend the money that he earns in his early career, or to save the money to buy a house.

In each of the three scenarios described above, the individual who chooses the option best for him in the long run has to forego short-term gratification, but typically reaps much higher dividends in the long run. In today's beautiful selected passage, the seeker of success is instructed in how he can obtain lifetime and eternal rewards – and that is by following the Guidance provided by God, the Most Loving and the Best Guide, and by following Muhammad, the noble apostle of God, the Most Beneficent and Most Merciful, through whom God, the Most Clement and Most Wise, chose to provide His message and Guidance for the benefit of mankind.

And when the situation arises that man is called to action by God, the Almighty, the Originator and the Restorer, and by His apostle, the beloved Muhammad, the fortunate one who believes, and therefore is primed for success, knows that the action he is called for is best for him in the long run, even though it may cause him short-term inconvenience. And the seeker of success is reminded so beautifully in today's sublime message that when he is called to action by the One Who has the most right to him, and by His beloved apostle, then he should train his heart in such a way that there is no intransigence. For, as a believer destined for success, he knows that the action recommend by God, the Greatest and the All-comprehending One, and by His noble apostle leads to closeness to God and to an eternal life of happiness, while rejecting the recommended action leads to damnation and further separation from Him to Whom belongs all existence and its control. And the fortunate seeker of success knows that God comes in between a man and his heart, and records all his thoughts and actions, and that it is He to Whom all shall be gathered, and Who will decide whether one achieves everlasting success or failure.

The seeker of success who wishes to reach his goal has complete faith in God, the All-knowing and the Best Judge, and in His noble messenger, Muhammad. When called for particular action by God, the Most Kind and the Owner of all, or by His beloved messenger, Muhammad, he does so most enthusiastically – knowing that every action in the service of his Lord and His noble messenger is for his own benefit and will provide innumerable benefits in the long term, and that it is to his Lord that all will be gathered in the end.

# Day 118

**O you who believe! Betray not the trust of God and the messenger, nor misappropriate knowingly things entrusted to you.**

**And know that your possessions and your progeny are but a trial; and <u>that it is God with Whom lies your highest reward.</u>**

**O you who believe! If you fear God, He will grant you a criterion (to judge between right and wrong), remove from you (all) evil (that may afflict) you, and forgive you; for God is the Lord of Grace unbounded.**

(8:27-29)

# Day 118

The beautiful selected passage of today begins with a reminder of the key ingredient for success, i.e. belief or faith in God, the Best Judge and the Most Wise, as relayed to us through His noble messenger Muhammad. Additional advice provided from God, the Creator and Sustainer of all, to inculcate success informs us to instill and develop in ourselves the characteristics of trustworthiness and loyalty.

If an individual entrusts his valuables to another, it is a sign of honor for the person who has been trusted by another to return the valuables back on demand. It is a sign of one's faith in God, the Truth and the Bestower of all Honors, as well as the Humiliator, that the one entrusted with another's valuables, return to the one depositing such trust, his property, as the deputy of God, the Highest and the Most Trustworthy. Explained in a most beautiful manner is the remainder of the message, which is the major portion of the blessings and benefits to be derived from today's beautiful passage, and this is explained in beautiful detail, with the summary being that one should also return the valuables that have been entrusted to man from God, the Most Rich One and the Best Enricher, as well as not betraying the trust of His apostle, who has this authority as the noble messenger to all mankind from God, the Most Glorious and Creator of all.

The seeker of success will develop the skills of trustworthiness and never knowingly misappropriate things entrusted to him. From the beautiful selected passage of today, the fortunate seeker of success will realize that all his possessions, including his progeny, have been entrusted to him from God, the Most Beneficent and Owner of all, as a trial, and he sincerely fears that misappropriating the valuables provided to him by God, the Originator and the Restorer, will result in diminishing his status in the view of He Who is Most Holy and the Best in keeping account.

The seeker of success who wishes to reach his goal has absolute faith in God, the Most Merciful and Most Trustworthy, and in His beloved messenger, Muhammad. He is thankful to his Lord for the innumerable blessings provided to him, including his health, intellect, wealth, and progeny, and fears God, the Constrictor as well as the Reliever, of misappropriating the valuables entrusted to him. And the wise seeker of success will then be granted the criterion to judge between right and wrong, from whom all evil will be removed, and who will be forgiven; for God is the Lord of Grace unbounded.

# Day 119

O you who believe! When you meet a force, be firm, <u>and call God in remembrance much (and often); that you may succeed.</u>

And obey God and His messenger; and fall not into disputes, lest you lose heart and your powers depart. And be patient and persevering: for God is with those who patiently persevere.

(8:45-46)

# Day 119

    The beautiful selected passage, like yesterday's, begins with reminder of the key ingredient of success, i.e. belief or faith in God, the Most Forceful and the Best Friend and Protector of those who have faith, as relayed to us through His beloved messenger Muhammad. The seeker of success realizes from information elsewhere in the Holy Quran that the accursed Satan has an ongoing challenge with God, the All-powerful and the Greatest, that he and his evil agents (or those who follow Satan) will try their utmost to prevent man from fulfilling the duties for which man was created, i.e. to worship Him Who created all and is responsible for the sustainment of creation.

    Because of the constant and real danger from Satan and his agents, God, the Almighty and the Best Friend and Protector of those who have faith in Him and Who wishes for them to succeed, has instructed the seekers of success that when they do meet a force dedicated to preventing them from reaching their goal, they must be firm and move onwards to victory, calling God much and often, as a reminder of the support of Him Who is the most Powerful and the Most Victorious, so that they may defeat evil and succeed.

    The other treasures to be obtained from the beautiful selected passage of today to help the seeker of success to reach his goal, besides encouraging the defeat of evil in an effective manner, are: to obey God, the Most Majestic and Most Powerful, as well as His noble messenger, and to avoid falling into disputes with other believers, thereby weakening the overall response from believers to the forces of evil, lest the believers lose heart and their power depart. The final gem in today's collected treasure to enrich the seeker of success is that he should be patient and persevering in the trials of life: for God, the Most Loving and the Most Reliable Friend and Protector, is with those who patiently persevere, to grant them the highest victory as a reward for their belief and the righteous acts resulting from their faith in Him.

    The seeker of success who wishes to reach his goal has unwavering faith in God, the Source of all power and the Most Reliable Friend and Protector, and in His noble messenger, Muhammad. He calls his Lord in remembrance much and often. He is firm when facing his enemy, who wishes to prevent him from fulfilling the duties for which he was created, i.e. to worship Him Who created all that exists and sustains it. The esteemed reader is referred to the commentary of Day 3 of this collection of meditations on a more detailed discussion of worship. He patiently perseveres in all difficulties, knowing that God, the Most Holy, Most Powerful and the Most Patient, is his Help and Support.

# Day 120

**...God will never change the Grace which He has bestowed on a people until they change what is in their (own) souls. And indeed God is He Who hears and knows (all things).**

(8:53)

# Day 120

The seeker of success needs to understand the beautiful selected passage of today in order to appreciate the enormous power he has within himself and to obtain the most brilliant insight into the requirements for effecting change. And change is a necessary component for achievement of success – for no human is perfect and therefore everyone needs to understand the dynamics of change, which the magnificently sublime passage of today explains in the most perfect manner.

As for the person who is lazy, he can hang on to the notion that since God is the Most Powerful and controls every matter in existence, including the falling of every single leaf from every single tree, at a particular time He wishes, then why not accept everything he encounters in life as the will of God, Who is indeed the source of all power and the One Most Wise? In the profound and magnificent passage of today, we are informed that change is something that man should desire when he is not satisfied, and that the key requirement for change is indeed within man himself.

As a result of acquiring the rich treasure from the beautiful selected passage of today, the seeker of success realizes that the first and most important step required for change begins within himself – and only after the first step is taken, can he hope for assistance from God, Who is indeed the All-powerful, the Satisfier of all needs. And indeed God is He Who hears and knows all things and is able to effect all change.

The seeker of success who wishes to reach his goal has complete faith in God, the Source of all power and the Compeller, and in His beloved messenger, Muhammad. When he is not satisfied, he does hope and wish for change, taking concrete steps to effect change, beginning with himself - for he realizes that God will never change the condition of a people until they first change themselves.

# Day 121

**The worst of beasts in the sight of God are those who reject Him: they will not believe.**

(8:55)

# Day 121

The seeker of success who has sincerely searched for guidance from the highest authority in the Holy Quran on his own, or with assistance from someone more knowledgeable than himself, to help him reach his goal, or if he has referred to the earlier meditations in this collection, will have realized that belief or faith in God, the Most Magnificent, the Originator and the Resurrector as relayed to us by the noble prophet Muhammad, is an essential requirement and the foundation on which real success is built. It follows logically, then, that those who are not only lacking in the essential ingredient for the recipe of success, i.e. belief or faith in God, the All-aware and the Only One and His noble messenger Muhammad, but who actively reject it and, even worse, prevent others from acquiring this most valuable possession and right of all individuals, are not only harming others, but harming themselves the most.

Imagine, for example, that one has been invited to a magnificent banquet where the host has arranged for a lavish set-up indicative of his generosity, wealth and beneficence. And not only this, but the host has very caringly utilized the services of some individuals very much like the guest himself to help the guests to get the maximum benefit from the magnificent banquet. And suppose a guest attends this magnificent banquet, but leaves without acknowledging or thanking the host: what will the host think of this ungrateful guest? Life is indeed better than the most magnificent banquet that can be hosted by man, with the countless miracles apparent every single day as signs of the Magnificence, Generosity and Love of the Host, Who is Most Holy, Most Beneficent and Most Generous – such as light, air, water, and the ability to see, hear, think and love. In the beautiful selected passage of today, God, the Most Rich, Most Wise and Most Generous, is helping the seeker of success by informing him of whom He considers to be the worst among His creatures: the ungrateful one who enjoys His Beneficence and Generosity every day, yet rejects Him, and will not believe. The seeker of success is strengthened in his belief from reading today's sublime passage and resolves never to be like the wretched creature that God, the Most Beneficent and Most Merciful, describes as the worst of beasts as noted above.

The seeker of success who wishes to reach his goal has absolute faith in God, the Creator and Sustainer of all and the Most Generous, and in His noble messenger, Muhammad. He is always aware and thankful of the numerous gifts he enjoys every day, such as his sight, hearing, intellect and capacity to love and be loved, among the countless other benefits that are in existence and are provided by God, the Creator and Nourisher of all. As a result, his faith is strengthened and he is led to perform righteous actions consistent with his beliefs.

# Day 122

**O prophet! Sufficient for you is Allah; (for you) and for those who follow you among the believers.**

(8:64)

# Day 122

Man is a weak creature, who tends typically to rely on others in a predictable manner at various stages in his life. In childhood, he relies on his parents to meet all his needs. In adolescence and young adulthood, he relies on his teachers and mentors to equip him with adequate skills to be a productive member of society. In adulthood, he typically relies on his employer to enable him to meet his needs, in exchange for provision of the skills he has acquired. And in old age, he tends to rely on either his children or the state for support - if he hasn't made adequate preparations for it.

In each of the scenarios described above, man is acutely aware that his well-being is dependent on others – depending on his stage in life, a parent, teacher, mentor, employer, child or the state. However, wouldn't it be more appropriate that, instead of relying on the strength of a source who can lift 300 pounds, that he should instead rely on the strength of the One Who gave the individual the ability to lift 300 pounds, as well as supporting all the planets, stars and the entire universes without them falling apart? Wouldn't it be more appropriate that, instead of relying on someone to pay him wages to enable him to buy the things he needs, that he should instead rely on the One Who is responsible for providing all that is needed by anyone in the universes including the sprouting of the seeds into plants that produce the grains and for the development of animals from sperms and eggs? And instead of relying on support from his children or the state in old age, should he not rather rely on He Who protected him in his mother's womb and produced the miracle of life, and Who created all that exists, and also sustains it? As the noble prophet Muhammad was reassured by the message of the beautiful selected passage of today and went onwards to victory, the fortunate seeker of success will also march on to victory, knowing that sufficient for him in all phases of his life is God, the Most Supreme Creator of all, the Nourisher and the Source of all power.

The seeker of success who wishes to reach his goal has unwavering faith in God, the Creator, Provider and Sustainer of all that exists, and in His beloved messenger, Muhammad. He knows that sufficient for him is God, the Almighty, the Source of all power, and the Best Friend and Protector – and that he is not in need of anyone else's help.

# Day 123

**The unbelievers are protectors one of another; unless you do this (protect each other) – there would be tumult and oppression on earth, and great mischief.**

(8: 73)

# Day 123

We learn from the Holy Quran and the Word of God, the Almighty and Most Wise, that the goal of Satan, the accursed and the enemy of man, is to sow discord among men, promote evil, and prevent man from the path of God, the Most Pure and Creator of all, thus preventing him from fulfilling the duties for which he was created: to worship Him Who originated life and sustains it, and to Whom is the return of all. The esteemed reader is referred to the commentary of Day 3 of this collection of meditations on a more detailed discussion of worship.

The accursed Satan expends great effort in his quest to dissuade as many souls as possible from their obligations to Him Who is the Truth, the Most Patient, and Who created all that exists. Those whom Satan succeeds in causing to stray from the righteous path become accomplices in his mission, seeking their inspiration in him, denying the existence of He Who is Most Glorious and Most Forbearing, joining their forces with the accursed Satan and those who follow him, and protecting each other while attempting to dissuade as many individuals as possible from serving their Lord, Who created and sustains all.

The beautiful selected passage of today is a valuable message that can help man in the victory of good over evil. If the ultimate battle of life is between good, as represented by God, the Most Beneficent and Most Merciful, and between evil, as represented by Satan, we know who will win, for God is the Source of all power, the Most Powerful, and the Most Victorious. We also know that life is a battle between evil, as represented by Satan and his followers, and the ability of man to resist evil. The forces of evil are united in their effort to discredit and destroy the righteous souls who wish to serve their Lord, Who created and sustains all; and their united stratagems result in great tumult and oppression on earth, and in great mischief, as is apparent today. From the beautiful selected passage of today, the seekers of success realize that the forces of evil are united, and are protectors of each other, on their assault against those who wish to serve God, the Most Great and the Creator of harm and good, and that unless the seekers of success do this also, i.e. protect each other, unlike what we see today, there will be continued tumult and oppression on earth, and great mischief.

The seeker of success who wishes to reach his goal has complete faith in God, the Most Great, the Best Guide and the Best Friend and Protector, and in His noble messenger, Muhammad. He realizes that unless he coordinates his actions with others who share his mission – as his enemies do, in their attempt to destroy the believers' ability to serve and worship their Lord – there would be continued tumult and oppression on earth, and great mischief.

# Day 124

**Those who believe – and suffer exile and strive with might and main in Allah's cause, with their goods and their persons, have the highest rank in the sight of Allah; they are the people who will achieve (salvation).**

Their Lord does give them glad tidings of a Mercy from Himself: of His good pleasure, and of Gardens for them, wherein are delights that endure;

They will dwell therein forever. **Certainly with Allah is a reward – the greatest (of all).**

(9:20-22)

# Day 124

In the beautiful selected passage of today, the two most important ingredients for everlasting success are reinforced for the seeker of success: Belief or faith in God, the Almighty Creator of all that exists as relayed to us through His noble messenger Muhammad, and performance of righteous acts as a result of this faith. Further details are provided for the benefit of the seeker of success about those righteous acts that will enable the individual to attain the highest ranking in the sight of God, the Most Magnificent and the Most Generous: suffering exile and striving with one's person and resources in the cause of God, the Hearer and the Seer of all.

If an individual suffers by upholding the values revered by the masses, he is accorded the status of a hero by the masses; if an individual suffers in the cause of defense of his country, he is likely to be awarded the highest benefits allowed by the state as a martyr. It is in this context that one can appreciate the significance of suffering for one's belief and faith in God, the Most Supreme and the Absolute Ruler of all that exists, to the point of suffering exile or striving with one's goods and person in His cause.

The one whose actions are appreciated by the masses can be given the adoration of a hero, which is usually of a fleeting nature. The one whose actions are appreciated by his country can be given a special burial or honorable mention by the state, as well as financial reward for him and his family. In today's beautiful selected passage, the One Who rules all universes and to Whom is the return of all, provides a glimpse of what He promises for those who are able attain **the highest success**, as described in the beautiful selected passage of today: they are the people who will achieve salvation, or the highest success. They are given glad tidings of a Mercy from God Himself, of His good pleasure, and of gardens for them, wherein are delights that are not fleeting – they will dwell therein forever.

The seeker of success who wishes to reach his goal has absolute faith in God, the Creator and Sustainer of all, the Most Rich and Most Generous, and in His beloved messenger, Muhammad. He does not aspire for rewards from the masses or the state, but aspires for a reward – the greatest of all – from God, the Eternal, the Most Generous, and the Best Rewarder, while not neglecting his needs in this life.

# Day 125

**O you who believe! What is the matter with you, that when you are asked to go forth in the cause of Allah, you cling heavily to the earth? Do you prefer the life of this world to the hereafter? But little is the comfort of this life, as compared with the hereafter.**

(9:38)

# Day 125

There is no doubt that there is great beauty and comfort in life as we know it. The One who created all that exists, nourishes it and sustains it, has provided everything for the comfort and enjoyment of His creation, and is pleased with their joy and comfort, as a parent is pleased when his child is enjoying the comfort and safety provided by him.

Unfortunately, many people fail to realize that there is more to life than the current situation. In fact, some people unfortunately concentrate on studying how to maximize the pleasures and comfort in this life, erroneously labeling it success. They fail to realize that this life is a preparation for the hereafter and, compared to that, their life on earth is like the duration of less than a day of the time that is reckoned in the afterlife. They also fail to realize that the comfort of this life is very little compared to what God, the Most Great and Creator of all that exists, has prepared for the fortunate souls who are successful in the test of this life.

Like the loving parent who not only gets satisfaction from the enjoyment of his children from his efforts, but is also concerned about their continued success later in life and thus provides them with the necessary skills and information for success in the future, God, the Most Loving and Caring One, wishes that man will have not only transitory success in this life, but also **eternal success** in the hereafter, as exemplified by the beautiful selected passage of today.

The seeker of success who wishes to reach his goal has unwavering faith in God, the Originator and Provider of all, the Most Rich and the Most Generous, and in His noble messenger, Muhammad. When he is asked to go forth in his Lord's cause, he does not cling heavily to the earth, which indicates preference of the life of this world compared to the hereafter, because he knows that the comfort and success in this life is fleeting, while that of the hereafter is lasting and infinitely more important.

# Day 126

**Say: "Nothing will happen to us except what Allah has decreed for us. He is our Protector". And on Allah let the believers put their trust.**

(9:51)

# Day 126

    We see that fear typically takes different forms in various stages of the life of man. In the stage of infancy, as he is learning to stand and walk, he fears falling. In childhood, he fears being abandoned by his parent, whom he sees is responsible for his safety and meeting his essential needs. In adulthood, he fears losing his employment or source of income, as well as the perceived threat from others that results from competition for what appears to be limited resources. In old age, he fears being unable to meet his needs and not having someone to rely on when needed. The fortunate individual who understands the valuable message from the beautiful selected passage of today will have conquered every fear possible in all stages of his life, from the time he is able to think logically. When man is able to realize that all power and glory in every situation, and for all eternity belongs to the One Who created all that exists and sustains His Creation with His unrestricted Power and infinite Justice, and therefore, logically, to Him only belongs all worship and praise, he has taken the first and most important step towards everlasting success.

    The man who understands that all praise and worship belongs only to God, the Most Praiseworthy, the Originator and the Restorer, also realizes that there is no one to fear except God, the Most Powerful and the Reckoner. The wise seeker of success realizes that the beautifully sublime message of today empowers the seeker of success by directing him towards putting his trust only in God, Who is the most Trustworthy and the Protector of all, and also that it does not absolve man from his responsibility towards choosing the right Path and making the most sincere effort to serve Him Who Created all and Whom he is obligated to worship and serve, like all other creation – but in the case of man, with his free will.

    The seeker of success who wishes to reach his goal has complete faith in God, the Most Strong, the Most Trustworthy and the Best Friend and Protector, and in His beloved messenger, Muhammad. He realizes that nothing will happen to him except that which is the will of God, the Greatest and the Most Supreme, and also realizes, as described by Him in the Holy Quran, that God, the Most High and Most Wise, will not change the condition of any person unless the individual first initiates the change by changing what is in his soul and being, and striving towards the change by taking the first step.

# Day 127

**Let not their wealth nor their (following in) sons dazzle you; in reality, Allah's plan is to punish them with these things in this life, and that their souls may perish in their (very) denial of Allah.**

(9:55)

# Day 127

The correct Guidance to achieve success in this life and the hereafter is a precious gift from God, the All-knowing and the Most Generous, and is reserved for special souls who are most deserving of it, based on their sincerity, love and devotion to Him. Success is not a matter of chance or coincidence. One must strive and make an effort to change the probability of a successful outcome from a chance occurrence to an increased likelihood, based on the amount of effort expended. And great success requires tremendous striving and great effort.

The valuable message of the beautiful selected passage of today can be understood with an example of comparing two children's situation. One child is left to his own understanding and as a result acquires the best toys possible, playing and enjoying himself in his free time as much as possible and attracting a multitude of other like-minded individuals who are impressed with the perceived wealth and enjoyment of this child. Another child seeks and receives guidance from his loving and concerned parents, who then direct him to those activities that will maximize his potential for acquiring success in adulthood – minus the multitude of toys and unrestricted play. When both children reach adulthood, one of them will have achieved real success that benefits him for the remainder of his life, while the other one would be a clear failure for the remainder of his life – although he enjoyed himself transiently. In fact, the multitude of toys of the child as described possessing these and his excess enjoyment can, in reality, be considered as contributing to his failure in the long run. One striking difference in the duration of success or failure, when comparing the worldly situations as described above, is that man will experience for eternity either punishment or pleasure, based on the Judgment passed by God, the Most Wise and the Best Judge, on the Day of Judgment.

The seeker of success who wishes to reach his goal has absolute faith in God, the Most Loving, the Best Guide and the Most Righteous Teacher, and in His noble messenger, Muhammad. He knows that the Guidance provided by his Lord will lead him to great success, as a result of his great striving and effort in the present life. He is not dazzled by the wealth or the multitude of others in the group of individuals who are not following the path leading to God, the Originator and the Restorer; and he hopes to guide the others also to the path of real success and warn them that their wealth and their following are actually contributing to their harm, both in this life and in the hereafter, as a result of their denial of God, the Most Glorious and the Best Guide.

# Day 128

**Know they not that for those who oppose Allah and His messenger, is the fire of hell – wherein they shall dwell? <u>That is the supreme disgrace.</u>**

(9:63)

# Day 128

    The goal of the typical aspirant to success is to acquire the knowledge and skills which, when applied in appropriate action, result in the desired outcome or success. Those who aspire to the highest degree of success strive to acquire those skills which have been identified as contributing to that degree of success. The aspirant to success also needs to take note of those factors that can prevent him from reaching his goal, and avoids them accordingly. In the beautiful selected passage of today are identified two characteristics that will lead one to the worst kind of failure: opposing God, the Most Just and Most Forceful, and opposing His noble prophet, Muhammad.

    It is truly sad that there are unfortunate souls who never reach for, and therefore never acquire, the knowledge and skills that can lead them towards success – which all individuals are capable of. It is more unfortunate that there are individuals who are not only careless about their own success, but actively work to undermine others in their pursuit of success by opposing God, the Greatest, the Most Forceful and the Compeller, and attempting to prevent His Mercy and Beneficence from reaching others, and also by opposing His beloved prophet, Muhammad. They are harming no one except themselves, and they are unaware that they are the worst types of failure, for whom is the fire of hell, wherein they shall dwell for eternity. And whose words can be truer than those of Him Who created all that exists and possesses all strength?

    The seeker of success who wishes to reach his goal has unwavering faith in God, the Most Powerful and the Source of all power, and in His beloved messenger, Muhammad. He learns the valuable message from the beautiful selected passage of today of what constitutes the worst failure, and sincerely avoids it, in order to maximize his chances of reaching his goals. He makes sure that he is not one of the most unfortunate ones who oppose God, the Creator and Sustainer of all, and the Avenger, and His noble messenger, Muhammad - knowingly or unknowingly.

# Day 129

**Allah has promised to believers – men and women – gardens under which rivers flow, to dwell therein, and beautiful mansions in Gardens of Adn (Eden) of everlasting bliss. <u>But the greatest bliss is the good pleasure of Allah: That is the Supreme Success.</u>**

(9:72)

# Day 129

The seeker of success will be directed to reflect on the worth of the three valuable treasures to be obtained from the beautiful selected passage of today - the first of which identifies the foundation of lasting success, and this is faith or belief in God, the Most Rich and Most Trustworthy as relayed to us through His noble messenger, Muhammad. Trying to achieve success without its key ingredient, faith, would be like concentrating on the development of various components of an automobile without the formulation of the engine: this automobile would look good, but an automobile with a defective motor would lead one toward disaster.

The second valuable treasure from the beautiful selected passage of today is a description of the benefits of employment, or successful completion of one's assigned duties. When considering the benefits of employment at various companies, people can be impressed by factors including salary, associated benefits, company car, vacation and days off, and bonus. In the beautiful selected passage of today, God, the Everlasting One and the Owner of all, promises to believers – men and women – gardens under which rivers flow, to dwell therein, and beautiful mansions of everlasting bliss. The main difference between the benefits offered by a company or employer and those offered by God, the Most Beneficent and Most Merciful, is that one has to perform services valuable to the employer in order to receive the benefits. As for the services provided by man culminating from his faith in God, the Eternal, the Self-sufficient, and the Best Rewarder, they don't benefit God at all, but benefit only the one performing these actions - both in this life and in the hereafter.

The third and the most valuable treasure from the beautiful selected passage of today is identification of **the best outcome of success, as well as its greatest reward: the good pleasure of God,** the Most Great, the Best Friend and Protector. This is similar to how a typical employee feels when he is called into the office of the CEO/owner of the company, and he is informed that the owner is pleased with his effort and performance, but the pleasure of being informed that God, the Source of all that exists and the Most Generous, is pleased with one's actions in the test of life will be multiplied many times more in comparison. In addition to gardens under which rivers flow, with beautiful mansions to dwell therein, in everlasting bliss, the greatest reward and the sign of the highest form of success will be felt when the believer is informed on the Day of Judgment that he has earned the good pleasure of God, the Lord of all majesty and reward and the Owner of all that exists.

The seeker of success who wishes to reach his goal has complete faith in God, the Truth, the Most Rich and the Enricher, and in His noble messenger, Muhammad. Although aware that he will be provided with mansions in gardens and with everlasting bliss as a result of his effort in this life, he is more interested in earning the good pleasure of his Lord and residing for eternity in nearness to Him, through righteous acts performed as a manifestation of his faith.

## Day 130

**God has purchased of the believers their persons and their goods; for theirs (in return) is the Garden (of paradise); they fight in His cause, and slay and are slain – a promise binding on Him in truth, through the law (of Moses), the Gospel (of Jesus), and the Quran. And who is more faithful to His covenant than God? Then rejoice in the bargain which you have concluded: <u>That is the Supreme Success!</u>**

(9:111)

# Day 130

One of the main objectives of the king, ruler, head of state, or government is to provide peace and security to the citizens, so that they can prosper. The effective leader must be vigilant regarding all potential threats to peace and security. The most effective governments rely on the strength of a strong military force, in order to be able to neutralize potential threats to the peace and security of its citizens. In the instance in which an individual committed to the safety of the government ends up giving his life in the duty of the government, he is rightly accorded the appropriate honor in recognition of his exemplary sacrifice.

In comparing the honor that a government may bestow on individuals who pay the highest price, i.e. their life, in its service, to one's service to God, the owner and Sustainer of all existence, one significant factor must be pointed out: the ruler or the government is in need of the services of the forces or military committed to its protection. However, God, Who is All-powerful and Completely Self-sufficient, is not in the need of the services of anyone to enforce His will.

For the brave individuals who voluntarily, for the love of God, the Best Appraiser, as well the Best Rewarder, and for the love of others (whom they wish to live in peace and prosperity), serve Him with their goods and their persons – including by fighting in His cause if needed – great news is proclaimed in the beautiful selected passage of today from the One Who is Most Generous and Most Trustworthy: That they have concluded the best bargain by their selfless sacrifice for His love and have **attained the highest form of success**. All benevolent rulers and governments would prefer that peace be maintained without fighting. However, the reality is such that, unless backed by strength and force, including having to resort to killing the evil forces or being killed defending the righteous cause, the forces of evil would prevail, threatening the well-being of the upright individuals. It is in this context that God, the Most Just, the Most Compassionate, and the Source of peace, has allowed fighting in His cause. For He knows that without strength and force, peace is elusive, allowing Satan and his allies to prevail. Without adequate security, governments can crumble over short periods and the strongest rulers can lose their power overnight, leaving those who have relied on them disappointed. The seeker of success is reassured that the one with Whom he has concluded his bargain is He Whose Power and Wealth is without limits, and there is none more faithful to his covenant than He – a promise binding on Him in truth as relayed through the law of Moses, the Gospel of Jesus, and the Quran as relayed by Muhammad, peace be on them all.

The seeker of success who wishes to reach his goal has absolute faith in God, the Almighty, the Truth and the Most Generous, and in His beloved messenger, Muhammad. He is pleased to be able to provide in the cause of his Lord, his wealth as well as his life, if needed, as a manifestation of his faith. He is certain that, as a result, he is the one who will profit by a great margin, and knows that it is the **most profitable transaction** he can make.

# Day 131

**Unto Allah belongs the rule of the heavens and the earth. He gives life and He takes it. Except for Him, you have no protector or helper.**

(9:116)

# Day 131

    The seeker of success will find in the beautiful selected passage of today three valuable treasures that he can use to develop or strengthen his faith or belief in God, the Creator, Protector and Restorer as relayed to us through His beloved messenger Muhammad. The first valuable treasure in the beautiful selected passage of today is the knowledge that the heavens and earth and all that exists are under the rule of God, the Most Supreme One and the One Who possesses all strength. Only when he realizes and accepts this reality, will man be able to correctly identify whom he should serve and worship: Whether that would be what his ego demands, parent, employer, king or state, or He in whose Hands is the rule of the heavens and earth. As we learned in the earlier meditations of this collection, faith is the absolute pre-requisite for success.

    Of all the possessions of man, he generally values his life the most. And he fears his loss of life the most. The second valuable treasure in the beautiful selected passage of today is the identification of Him Who is responsible for granting man his most valued possession, i.e. life, as well as the taking of life or death. And although death is most feared by man, it is a certainty for all in this life. The seeker of success who understands that it is God, the Most Generous, the Giver and Taker of life, Who is responsible for everything, including what he values and fears the most, experiences increase in love, devotion and awe of Him – all positive characteristics that will be helpful in reaching his goal.

    Man typically turns for support to various sources, depending on his phase in life. In childhood, he turns to the parents; in adulthood, he typically turns to the employer and others who appear to have power; and in old age, he typically turns to his children or the state for support and protection. The third valuable treasure to be found in the beautiful selected passage of today is the realization by the seeker of success that he has no protector or helper except God, the Most Trustworthy, the Best Friend and Protector. Until this realization occurs, man is liable to place one of his most valuable commodities - his future, into the trust of others, none of whom have his best interest as a priority, except God, the Most Beneficent, Most Kind, Most Generous, and the Most Trustworthy.

    The seeker of success who wishes to reach his goal has unwavering faith in God, the Originator and Giver and Taker of Life, the Originator and the Restorer, and in His noble messenger, Muhammad. He knows that the entire existence is under the control of his Lord at all times and that, except for Him, he has no other protector or helper.

# Day 132

**O you who believe! Fear Allah and be with those who are true (in word and deed).**

(9:119)

# Day 132

Today's beautiful selected passage begins with a reminder of the key ingredient of success, i.e. faith or belief in God, the Owner of all and the Source of all strength, as relayed to us through His beloved prophet Muhammad. In fact, the valuable messages from the beautiful selected passage of today can be considered as instructions in higher mathematics, to those who possess the basic mathematics skills such as the ability to count. For example, instructing someone in Algebra who does not have the basic skills of counting, addition, and subtraction, will not make him a better mathematician.

The other valuable message in the beautiful selected passage of today is also a point reinforced many times throughout the Holy Quran for the benefit of the seeker of success, so that he can appreciate its importance in helping him to reach his goal – and that is the fear of God, Who is the Most Loving, and also is the Avenger and the Most Just. Suppose an individual has been entrusted with the valuable resources of a hundred million dollars – unless he understands the negative repercussions of misappropriating the resources entrusted to him, he is likely to do just that, and may be tempted to spend that on himself for his pleasure. Man has been entrusted with the most valuable resources in the whole of creation, from the anatomic and physiological marvels in his body, to his ability to choose between good and evil (man is the only being in creation we know of who has this ability), and the honor of being the only one we know of in creation filled with the spirit of God Himself, the Eternal and Self-existing One. And unless man is able to understand the negative repercussions of misappropriating the truly enormous and valuable resources entrusted to him by God, the Most Wise and Most Generous, he is certain to waste them in frivolous and transient pleasures.

The final valuable message in the beautiful selected passage of today for the acquisition of success by those who have grasped the essentials of faith in, and fear of, God, the Most Trustworthy and the Best One Who keeps account, is to be with those who are true in word and deed, so that the likelihood of also acquiring those desirable characteristics will be increased and the chances of one's goal becoming a reality will be increased.

The seeker of success who wishes to reach his goal has complete faith in God, the Almighty, the Best Teacher and the Most Reliable Guide, and in His beloved messenger, Muhammad. He fears his Lord as He should be feared, lest he misappropriate the invaluable resources he has been entrusted with. He keeps company with those who are true in word and deed – which, increases the likelihood that he will be able to realize his goal.

## Day 133

Indeed! In the alternation of the night and day, and in all that Allah has created; in the heavens and the earth, are signs for those who fear Him.

Those who rest not their hope on their meeting with Us, but are pleased and satisfied with the life of the present, and those who heed not Our signs –

Their abode is the Fire, because of the (evil) they earned.

(10:6-8)

# Day 133

In the meditation immediately preceding this one (9:119), the importance of the fear of God, the Most Powerful and Most Watchful One, as one of the basic prerequisites for success was discussed, and the example was used of an individual entrusted with a hundred million dollars and how the fear of the negative consequences of misappropriating this trust would be the primary reason preventing him from doing so. We will utilize the same example as above, as well as that of all men (and women), who have been entrusted with the most valuable treasures in the whole creation, including the anatomic and physiological marvels of their bodies. Humans are the only beings we know of who are honored to be able to choose for themselves between good and evil, and the only beings in all creation instilled with the spirit of God, the Eternal and Most Holy One.

So the man endowed with the most valuable treasures, as described above, must come to appreciate the fear of misappropriating them and incurring the wrath of He Who entrusted man with these most valuable treasures – otherwise he is doomed to failure. In the beautiful selected passage of today, two very important concepts are described that can prevent man from misappropriating the valuable treasures with which he has been entrusted. The first is the recognition of Who he is accountable to, i.e. God, the Owner of all and the Gatherer, seeing his signs in the alternation of the night and the day, and in all that He has created in the heavens and the earth. The seeker of success is truly awed by He to Whom he is accountable, and by the beauty and power of His signs, which are evident everywhere, and sincerely strives to prevent misappropriating the valuable treasures he has been entrusted with.

The second valuable concept in the beautiful selected passage of today is the description of what exactly the consequences of misappropriating the valuable treasures man has been endowed with, are: Ignoring the signs of God, the Originator and the Restorer everywhere. If he is satisfied with the life of the present, and pleased with spending the valuable treasures entrusted to him for short-term pleasures, denying the fact that he will meet the One Who entrusted him with the most valuable treasures and be held accountable for them, his abode will be eternal fire: A fitting punishment for misappropriating the treasures of enormous magnitude.

The seeker of success who wishes to reach his goal has absolute faith in God, the Creator of all that exists and the Most Rich, and in His noble messenger, Muhammad. He is strengthened in his resolve, from the knowledge obtained from the beautiful selected passage of today, in being ever-vigilant in utilizing the treasures he has been endowed with, including his vision, hearing, strength and wealth, in the wisest possible manner consistent with his faith.

# Day 134

Those who believe, and work righteousness – their Lord will guide them because of their faith; beneath them will flow rivers in gardens of bliss.

(This will be) their prayer therein: "Glory to you, O Allah!" And "Peace" will be their greeting therein; and the closing of their prayer will be: "Praise be to Allah, the Cherisher and Sustainer of the worlds!"

(10:9-10)

# Day 134

    The beautiful selected passage of today can be divided into two parts in its relevance for the seeker of success. In the first part, which is verse nine of the tenth chapter, we encounter the information that is also provided elsewhere in the Holy Quran numerous times, in order to help man identify the key information that will be helpful to him in successfully passing the test of life: That the key to passing this most important test for man is faith or belief in God, the Most Kind and the Most Righteous Teacher as relayed to us through His noble messenger, Muhammad, and to work righteousness as a result of this faith. The magnificent results of passing this most important test are again also listed, i.e. being admitted to dwell for eternity in gardens of bliss, beneath which will flow rivers, so that the seeker of success will be strengthened in his resolve and will persist in his efforts, despite hardships, for the most worthy results and outcome, as described above.

    In the second portion of the beautiful selected passage of today, we are provided with details about the joy of successfully completing the test of life, receiving the highly anticipated rewards, i.e. being admitted to paradise for eternity. And the believers, who used to glorify and praise their Lord on seeing His many signs on earth, will also glorify Him on seeing His Magnificence and Power in the afterlife in paradise, and also proclaim "Glory to you, O God!", to which God, the Most Loving and Most Trustworthy, will respond with assurance of peace for eternity, as a reward for the constant struggle to succeed in the test of life. And as they used to praise God, the Most Praiseworthy and the Most Generous, in life on partaking of His Generosity, they will close their proclamation on being rewarded with eternal paradise with "Praise be to God, the Cherisher and Sustainer of the worlds!"

    The seeker of success who wishes to reach his goal has unwavering faith in God, the Most Glorious, the Best Guide and the Most Appreciative One, and in His beloved messenger, Muhammad. He consistently engages in acts of righteousness and relies on his Lord for Guidance throughout his life, as a manifestation of his faith. He is able to persist in his mission in life despite hardships, knowing the immense rewards that await him for choosing delayed gratification and for faithful service to Him Who is the Source of all that exists, the Most Rich and the Most Generous.

# Day 135

**When trouble touches man – he cries unto Us (in all postures): lying down on his side, or sitting, or standing. But when We have solved his trouble, he passes on his way as if he had never cried to Us for the trouble that touched him! Thus do the deeds of the transgressors seem fair in their eyes.**

(10:12)

# Day 135

One is more likely to accomplish his mission or achieve success, if he makes constant effort with corresponding positive steps or action to realize his mission, rather than if he were to only concentrate on his mission occasionally - except on rare occasions or under unusual circumstances, and neglects taking appropriate action to realize his mission.

In the beautiful selected passage of today, we are given an example of the unfortunate individuals who are only attentive to their mission when trouble touches them – then they make automatic and profuse supplication to their Creator and Sustainer, God, the Most Magnificent and the Best Friend and Protector, constantly, lying down, or sitting or standing. And when God, the Most Forbearing and Most Merciful, solves their troubles, these unfortunate souls pass on their way as if they had never sought the assistance of Him, in Whose hands is the rule of the heavens and earth. Because these unfortunate individuals only apply the success principles part of the time, i.e. when they are faced with difficulty, and neglect to do so for majority of the time, meaning they do not remember and seek the help and Guidance from God, the Eternal and Self-existing One, except on rare occasion, they are destined to failure.

The seeker of success who wishes to reach his goal has complete faith in God, the Most Merciful, the Creator of harm and the good, and in His noble messenger, Muhammad. He not only remembers God, the Most Powerful and Most Kind, when afflicted with trouble, reflexively, like all individuals, but continues to seek His Guidance and serve Him continuously even when he is out of the dangers and difficult situations in his life, as a manifestation of his faith.

# Day 136

**Who does more wrong than such as forge a lie against Allah, or deny His signs? <u>But never will succeed those who sin.</u>**

(10:17)

# Day 136

One of the key ingredients of success is performance of good acts as a result of faith in God, the Owner of all and the Light with which we see. Performance of good actions other than for the pleasure of God, the Most Beneficent and the Most Merciful, cannot be counted as contributors to lasting success, because they are performed for the pleasure of oneself or others – the reward for which they would already have received on their earthly life - but not worth anything in the afterlife, for they were not performed with the intent of seeking the pleasure of God, the Most Just and the Restorer, who will reward or punish, based on one's performance in the test of life.

As good actions contribute to success, it follows, then, that bad actions or sins lead to failure. Just as the source of the most rewarding good actions is the belief in God, the Most Rich and the Best Rewarder, the source of the most evil acts is the denial of God, the Truth and the One to Whom belongs all that exists. Therefore, one who denies belief in God, the Creator and Sustainer of all, will never succeed – either in this life or, more importantly, the hereafter.

In the beautiful selected passage of today, we are informed that the worst form of wrong action or sin is that of forging a lie against God, the Abaser and the Exalter, and denying His signs. The unfortunate individual who denies the signs of God, the Apparent and the Hidden, will not be inspired to good actions – and if he does do good actions, they will not contribute towards lasting success, because those good actions were not performed for the pleasure of God, the Wisest Judge and the Best Rewarder. And the very unfortunate individual who forges a lie against God, the Most Kind and Most Loving, will not only be harming himself by not being inspired to good acts, but will be led to evil acts and failure – and, worse, he will accrue a future penalty for inciting others to evil acts and preventing them from attaining success.

The seeker of success who wishes to reach his goal has absolute faith in God, the Light, the All-seeing and All-hearing, and in His beloved messenger, Muhammad. He knows that the worst form of wrongful acts – that which will lead him away from his goal and instead into failure – is forging a lie against God, the Truth, the Almighty, and the Wisest Judge.

# Day 137

**Indeed! Allah will not deal unjustly with man in anything. It is man that wrongs his own soul.**

(10:44)

# Day 137

    The examination of life for man is now ongoing. Upon successful completion of the examination, the fortunate ones who pass it, will be rewarded with admittance to gardens with eternal bliss - **this will indeed be lasting success.** And on failure of this examination, the unfortunate ones will be sent for a fitting punishment. The results will be provided on the Day of Judgment when all the examinees, i.e. those provided with the ability to choose between good and evil, will be resurrected by God the Most Wise, the Originator and Restorer - and be judged with absolute fairness, by Him Who is the Best Judge and Most Kind.

    Although it is unusual during the examinations administered by men that any help will be provided during the examination for the examinees, this is not so for God the Most Loving, Most Kind, and Most Patient One, who cares for all mankind so much, wanting them to succeed instead of failing, that He has provided man with clear instructions through his beloved prophets, a clear guidance on attaining success, culminating in the most comprehensive guide provided by Muhammad, the noble messenger and the seal of the prophets. For the examinee with sincerity and desire to succeed, God, the Most Knowledgeable and Most Generous, also provides signs guiding the seekers of success to the correct Guidance – signs such as the alternation of night and day, and the sprouting of the seedling, and creation of new life from two beings.

    God, the Creator of All, and the Maker of Order, desires success for all individuals and provides guidance to the fortunate individuals who turn to Him for guidance; He will not deal unjustly with man in anything. On the contrary, it is man himself that wrongs his own soul by ignoring the signs of God the All-encompassing, the Apparent and the Hidden, in all existence and instead of turning to Him for guidance, being content with transient pleasures in this life, and neglecting the hereafter.

    The seeker of success who wishes to reach his goal has unwavering faith in God, the Most Kind, the Best Guide, and the Most Righteous Teacher, and in His noble messenger Muhammad. He is ever thankful to his Lord, Who takes extraordinary measures to maximize success for all His creation and to minimize failure.

# Day 138

**Behold! Certainly, on the friends of Allah, there is no fear; nor shall they grieve.**

(10:62)

# Day 138

In order to more easily understand the valuable message from the beautiful selected passage of today in terms of its importance in the attainment of success, an example is provided for the reader to consider regarding two groups of people in a particular village in which there was a warning that there will be a catastrophic flood in the coming season. One group takes painstaking safety and precautionary measures in preparation for the flood. The other group doubts that the flood will occur – and deems taking appropriate safety measures to be a waste of time and resources. When the flood arrives as predicted, the group members that have taken appropriate safety measures are calm, collected, and without significant fear. On the other hand, the other group of people, who have enjoyed themselves in the preparatory phase after the warning was provided, but who have failed to take appropriate safety precautions , are in despair, panicking, and with tremendous fear of the consequences of the catastrophic flood.

Man has been created for a purpose: to worship God, the Creator and Sustainer of all that exists and the Most Praiseworthy, and to see which of them is best in fulfilling the duties required of him. The esteemed reader is referred to the commentary of Day 3 of this collection of meditations on a more detailed discussion of worship. Every moment of man's life is valuable and counts either as a positive or negative in the examination of life, the results of which will be provided to him by God, the Resurrector and the Most Just, on the Day of Judgment. Those fortunate individuals who take appropriate safety measures – recognizing the signs of God, the Most Subtle, the Apparent and the Hidden, in all existence – who believe in Him and perform righteous acts as a sign of their faith, accumulating as many positive marks as possible in their examination, and avoiding as many negative marks as possible, will be counted as friends of God, the Most Trustworthy and the Best Friend and Protector. On the Day of Judgment, the natural tendency would be to panic, but those who have adequately prepared for it shall not fear, and nor shall they grieve. **<u>That would indeed be clear success for an individual.</u>**

The seeker of success who wishes to reach his goal has complete faith in God, the Best Friend and Protector, and the Best Reckoner, and in His beloved messenger, Muhammad. He takes appropriate precautionary measures for the impending Day of Judgment – performing as many righteous deeds as possible, as a manifestation of his faith.

# Day 139

And had your Lord willed, those on earth would have believed, all of them together. So, will you (O Muhammad) then compel mankind, until they become believers?

No soul can believe, except by the will of God. And He will place doubt (or obscurity) on those who will not understand.

(10: 99-100)

# Day 139

From a reading of the earlier meditations in this humble collection on the guide to success, the reader is expected to have grasped the valuable concept that the most important ingredient for lasting successes is belief or faith in God, the Most Glorious and Most Pure, as relayed to us through His beloved messenger, Muhammad. On this solid foundation, can be added other components that can help one to achieve success of varying intensity. However, the addition of other components of success to an individual lacking the firm foundation of belief or faith is as futile as placing steel rods on a non-existing foundation, or on a foundation of rotting wood. In terms of its value, therefore, belief or faith is of enormous value to an individual. And, like other things that are also valuable – such as the air we breathe, the water we drink, and the ability to see and hear and understand – it is provided by God, the Most Praiseworthy and the Most Generous, free of charge. However, unlike the air we breathe or the water we drink, the gift of faith is not given to all individuals in a passive manner - it is given to those who are deserving of it, by God, the Most Just and the all-aware.

Even though we may wish for others' success as well – especially for those whom we care for so much – we are informed, along with the noble prophet Muhammad, as example in today's beautiful selected passage, that we should not compel mankind to become believers, as it is a special relationship between an individual and God, the Most Kind and the Most Wise, and it is by God's will alone that one can become a believer and take the first and most important step towards success. As for the unfortunate individual who does not understand, and who ignores the many signs of God, the All-encompassing, the Most Beneficent and the Most Merciful in nature, He will place doubt in their breasts. Therefore, they will not be blessed with the vital ingredient needed for lasting success.

The seeker of success who wishes to reach his goal has absolute faith in God, the Creator and Sustainer of all, the Best Guide and the Most Righteous Teacher, and in His noble messenger, Muhammad. He is ever thankful to his Lord for the gift of belief and faith in Him, which is the foundation for all success, and which is endowed to him only through God's Grace and Beneficence.

# Day 140

**If Allah does touch you with hurt, there is none that can remove it but He; if He does plan some benefit for you, there is none that can keep back His favor; He causes it to reach whomsoever of his servants He pleases. And He is the Most Forgiving, Most Merciful.**

(10:107)

# Day 140

    The beautiful selected passage of today is among the most powerful and sublime method of instructing one in the foundation of success, i.e. belief or faith in God, the Most Magnificent and the One Deserving of all praise, as relayed to us through His noble messenger, Muhammad. When one is able to appreciate the presence of God, the Manifest and the Hidden One, from His innumerable signs in existence, such as the propagation of life and the ability of the universes to exist in an orderly manner, then one will be blessed with the gift of faith, and which is the foundation of all lasting success. And as a result of this wonderful gift, man will be able to move from living a life in which circumstances seem to determine his fate, to living a life filled with purpose – the purpose for which he was created, i.e. worship Him Alone Who is the Source of all creation and Who Alone is Responsible for its sustenance. Faith is best summarized thus: there is no god but God and Muhammad is His messenger; only the man who realizes this will be able to fulfill the purpose for which he was created, i.e. to worship and serve Him Who created man and all in existence and is responsible for its nourishment. The esteemed reader is referred to the commentary of Day 3 of this collection of meditations on a more detailed discussion of worship.

    Man will invariably experience in his lifetime, physical and psychological hurt. The fortunate individual with the gift of faith, will be able understand that the hurt he is experiencing can only be removed by Him Who controls all aspects of the entire existence at all times, and no one else; conversely, he also understands that if God, the Source of all power, and the Best Doer of good, were to wish some good for him, that no one in the world can take it away from him. The unfortunate individual without faith will, when he is hurt, try to get rid of it by all other means except that which is the key: imploring God, the Absolute Ruler and the Most Merciful; conversely, if he desires something good, he will seek it from all means except That Which is the key: God, the Most Holy and the Best Provider.

    The knowledge gained from today's beautiful selected passage will be of great help for one to cope in a healthy and productive manner with any negative events that befall in an individual's life, and/or if an individual is hoping for any positive events to happen in his life.

    The seeker of success who wishes to reach his goal has complete faith in God, the Source of all existence, the Best Guide and the Most Righteous Teacher, and in His beloved messenger, Muhammad. He realizes that there is no god but God the Most Powerful, Most Forgiving and Most Merciful – and that if He does touch man with hurt, there is none that can remove it but He; and that if He does plan some benefit for him, there is none that can keep back His favor.

# Day 141

**Say: "O you men! Now truth has reached to you from your Lord! Those who receive Guidance, do so for the good of their own souls. Those who stray, do so at their own loss. And I am not (set) over you to arrange your affairs".**

(10:108)

# Day 141

    The beautiful selected passage of today is addressed to all men and women, and invites them all to success – informing them all that the true message from God, the Most Wise and the Truth, has been relayed to mankind through His noble prophet, Muhammad, and recorded in the Holy Quran as the ultimate source of Guidance forever.

    Next we are informed that if anyone turns to the Truth from God the Most Beneficent and the Most Trustworthy for Guidance, he is helping no one but himself, by being guided towards lasting success. And if anyone either does not receive this precious gift of Guidance, or turns away from it, he is harming no one but his own self.

    Man is endowed with the ability to select for himself between good and evil, and this is what sets him apart from all other creatures. That is why no other creatures besides man, that we are aware of, are accountable to God, the Most Kind and the Originator and Restorer, for their actions. In the final portion of the beautiful selected passage of today, the ability to let man choose for himself between good and evil or between success and failure is reinforced, as well as the message that one cannot impose his will on another and choose for him good instead of evil – for this is the choice of every individual, as part of his performance in the test of life. No cheating is allowed.

    The seeker of success who wishes to reach his goal has complete faith in God, the Best Guide and the Most Wise, and in His noble messenger, Muhammad. He knows that the Quran is the Truth and the Word of God, the Most Trustworthy and the Truth - as revealed to the beloved prophet Muhammad, for his benefit as a mercy, guiding him to success, and as a mercy to the worlds; he turns to it for Guidance in all situations, and knows that if he follows it, that it benefits him only – and that if he chooses not to do so, it is only he that incurs a loss.

# Day 142

**There is no moving creature on earth, but its sustenance depends on Allah; He knows the time and place of its definite abode and its temporary deposit: All is in a clear Record.**

(11:6)

# Day 142

A child typically relies on his parent to meet his needs. After the child becomes an adult, he usually spends considerable energy and effort in securing his needs; in old age, he may turn to relatives, his employer, the state or friends to help him meet his needs. In the beautiful selected passage of today, man is reminded that his sustenance, along with that of all creatures is, in actuality, dependent on God, the Creator and Sustainer of all that exists. It is God, the Most Beneficent and Most Generous Provider Who provides the air, water, sun, power and order in the universes and Who is responsible for the maintenance of all creation; and their sustenance is binding on Him Who created them in the first place.

All sustenance, as well as all control at all times, is dependent on God, the Most Wise, the Source of all power and the Creator and Sustainer of all that exists; He knows the time and the place and the exact state of all creation, at all times – all is maintained in a clear record.

If the seeker of success was in the past concerned about his sustenance in the present or the future, or about the state of events which did not previously make sense to him, he is strengthened by the powerful message from the beautiful selected passage of today, and reassured that his sustenance, and that of all others, is dependent on no one else except God, the Most Kind and Most Powerful, and that all events at all times are under the control of God, the Creator and Sustainer of all that exists. And as a result of having acquired the above knowledge, the seeker of success will be less inclined to worship others and more inclined to worship God Only, the Most Beneficent and Most Worthy of all praise, and will be guided towards lasting success. The esteemed reader is referred to the commentary of Day 3 of this collection of meditations on a more detailed discussion of worship.

The seeker of success who wishes to reach his goal has absolute faith in God, the Creator of all that exists and the All-aware, and in His beloved messenger, Muhammad. He knows that the sustenance of himself and every creature, as well as the outcome of all events, is under the complete control of God, blessed be His name, at all times.

# Day 143

If we give man a taste of Mercy from Ourselves, and then withdraw it from him, behold! He is in despair and (falls into) blasphemy;

But if we give him a taste of (Our) favors after adversity has touched him, he is sure to say: "All evil has departed from me". Behold! He falls into exultation and pride.

But not those who show patience and constancy, and (they) work righteousness. For them is forgiveness (of sins) and a great reward.

(11:9-11)

# Day 143

In the beautiful selected passage of today, the seeker of success is provided with valuable counsel in helping him to reach his goal – that in all circumstances, both good and bad, he should exhibit patience and constancy, continuing to work righteousness, as a result of faith in God, the Creator of life and death and the Resurrector -  for this is the only currency that is valid for use in the hereafter. For the individuals who acquire this main characteristic of success as relayed to us through the noble prophet Muhammad, will be forgiveness of sins and a great reward – both in this life and the hereafter.

When faced with hardship during times of difficulty, and God, Most Wise and Most Forgiving, chooses it to be in the best interest of man to withdraw His Mercy and blessings from him, the seeker of success, fortified with the knowledge gained from the beautiful selected passage of today, does not fall into despair, but exhibits patience and constancy, continuing to perform righteous acts, knowing that this is a trial period from which he will emerge stronger than before, if he continues to trust in the judgment of God, the Most Wise and the All-aware.

And when blessed with the favors of God, the Most Rich, the Only Enricher, and the Best Rewarder of thankfulness, the seeker of success, after having been afflicted with adversity, and with the knowledge gained from the beautiful selected passage of today, does not fall into exultation and pride, but continues to exhibit patience and constancy, continuing to work righteousness onward to lasting success.

The seeker of success who wishes to reach his goal has unwavering faith in God, the Most Wise, the Creator of all harm and good, and in His noble messenger, Muhammad. He realizes that all pain and pleasure in this life is transitory and from his Lord; and that it is precisely during these fluctuating periods that his test of life is hardest, and that he will emerge successfully from these periods if he continues to show patience and constancy and works righteousness.

# Day 144

Those who desire the life of the present and its glitter – to them We shall pay (the price of) their deeds therein, without diminution.

They are those for whom there is nothing in the hereafter but the fire; vain are the designs they frame therein and of no effect are the deeds that they do!

(11:15-16)

# Day 144

Success is not a matter of chance; it requires hard work. But even before work is started on the path to success, there needs to be a clearly identified vision of what one wishes to achieve, a sincere intention to reach the vision, and tireless work on one's mission to achieve the vision or success as planned. The loftier the vision is, the greater the effort that is required to make it a reality.

In current terminology, suppose an individual takes out a loan for one hundred thousand dollars at twenty one percent interest: Can we be justified in calling this individual an example of success, despite what can appear to others who don't have the all the details about this individual, as if he is the most successful individual they have seen, at least on the day that he takes out the hundred thousand dollar loan? On closer examination, we see that this individual will have to pay dearly for his short-term pleasure, with twenty one percent extra payment, in addition to the principal, during the first year alone. In reality, this individual is a total failure, having mortgaged his future for some short-term pleasure.

Keeping the above example in mind, we can understand the valuable message from the beautiful selected passage of today: That those who desire the life of this world and its glitter, even though they receive what they desire immediately – like the individual above who desired and attained the hundred thousand dollar loan for immediate gratification – are the real failures in the long run.

The seeker of success is aware that his entire stay on earth is less than a day of his current life in comparison to the afterlife and his entire existence. Accordingly, he plans for success not only for today, but for the rest of his life as well. And he realizes that if all his efforts were for success for today only, he would have nothing left for tomorrow; as a matter of fact he would be foolish to choose short-term pleasure for long-term pain. And because he had no concern for what would benefit him in the long run, i.e. righteous deeds performed for the sake of God, the Most Beneficent and Most Merciful, all his deeds in the present life would be wasted and he would have nothing to look forward to in the hereafter.

The seeker of success who wishes to reach his goal has complete faith in God, the All-knowing and the Best Guide, and in His beloved messenger, Muhammad. He plans earnestly for success both for today and for the remainder of his life, and for his earthly sojourn - which is transient, as well as for the hereafter - which is permanent.

# Day 145

Those who would hinder (men) from the path of God and would seek in it something crooked – these were they who denied the hereafter!

They will in no way frustrate (God's design) on earth, nor have they protectors besides God! Their penalty will be doubled!

They lost the power to hear and they did not see! They are the ones who have lost their own souls; and the (fancies) they invented have left them in the lurch!

<u>Without a doubt, these are the very ones who will lose the most in the hereafter!</u>

But those who believe and work righteousness, and humble themselves before their Lord – they will be companions of the garden, to dwell therein forever!

The likeness of these two parties is as the blind and the deaf compared to the seer and the hearer. Are they equal when compared? Will you not then take heed?

(11:19-24)

# Day 145

From the earlier meditations in this humble collection, we have learned that for those who believe in God, the Almighty and the Best Guide as relayed to us through His noble messenger Muhammad, and, as a result of their faith, work righteousness for His pleasure and humble themselves before their Lord in awe, praise, and worship, will be companions - also pure and righteous, in gardens of everlasting bliss, to dwell therein forever.

In contrast to the above example are those unfortunate individuals who are not only lost themselves, but have worked to prevent others from attaining success; these are they who would hinder men from the path of God, the Inspirer and the Guardian of faith. These are the unfortunate individuals who seek in the path of Righteousness something crooked – hoping to divert others from the Righteous Path; and these are they who deny the hereafter, hoping to also prevent others from their preparation for the hereafter, by enticing them with short-term pleasures in this life, not unlike the drug dealers who would like to have people addicted to their heroin and cocaine, satisfied with the brief pleasures, even though their lives are in chaos. In the beautiful selected passage of today, these unfortunate individuals are informed of the awful consequences of their harmful behavior, perchance they will stop their harmful behavior and stop harming themselves. First, their attempts to hinder men from the path of God, the Possessor of all strength and the Most Victorious, will in no way frustrate His design on earth. Nor does one have any protector except God, the Most Powerful and the Best Protector. Second, these unfortunate individuals are considered as the worst among the losers, having incurred double the penalty, having lost their own souls and having been left in the lurch by the fancies they have invented. And without a doubt these are the unfortunate individuals who have lost the most, for they have lost the hereafter, which is the bulk of man's existence.

All individuals except the most cognitively impaired will be able to recognize that a man who can see and hear is not equal to the man who is deaf and blind. From the beautiful selected passage of today, the unfortunate individuals who have been hindering others from the path of God, the Compeller and the Subduer, will recognize their futility, and that they are harming no one but themselves, and that they stand to lose most in the hereafter. With this realization, they too can begin the march toward lasting success by desisting from their severely harmful behavior and seeking God's forgiveness, for God is Ever-forgiving and Most Merciful.

The seeker of success who wishes to reach his goal has absolute faith in God, the Most Great, the Best Friend and Protector, and in His noble messenger, Muhammad. He knows that those hindering others from the path of God, the Creator and Sustainer of all that exists, are the **worst form of losers or failures**. He performs righteous deeds as a result of his faith, and humbles himself before his Lord.

# Day 146

**(Noah said:) "Of no profit will be my counsel to you, much as I desire to give you (good) counsel, if it be that God wills to leave you astray; He is your Lord! And to Him will you return".**

(11:34)

# Day 146

    We have learned from the previous meditations in this humble collection that the key ingredient of success is faith or belief in God, the Most Beneficent and the Most Merciful as relayed to us through His noble messenger Muhammad. We have also learned that no one can acquire this most precious characteristic of success except by the will of God, the Almighty and the All-aware. We have also learned that God, the Most Great and the Most Wise, will not change the condition of people unless they desire a change and first change what is in themselves. Therefore, for an individual to be blessed with the vital ingredient of success, the individual must initiate a sincere desire to search for the Truth, and he will find it everywhere he turns – pointing to Him Who created and sustains all that exists, without anyone's assistance. And when the individual takes the first step toward his Creator, he will find God, blessed be His name, coming to him with speed, and he will be blessed with the most vital ingredient of success.

    Without the sincere desire to search for truth, the counsel of any well-wisher will be of no profit – even though it is his desire to give good counsel (such as the noble prophet Noah's warning to those who ridiculed him) – if it be that God, the Most Just and Most Kind, wishes to lead him astray because he has not shown himself to be worthy of the gifts of faith and guidance to lasting success. These gifts are destined for those who search for their Creator Lord, the Most Kind and Most Beneficent, and therefore, wish to praise, thank, worship and serve Him – knowing that it is to Him that is the return of all.

    The seeker of success who wishes to reach his goal has absolute faith in God, the Source of all that exists, the Best Guide and the Most Righteous Teacher, and in His noble messenger, Muhammad. He realizes that acquiring this most vital ingredient of success, i.e. faith, is due to the Grace of his Lord Alone and not to any mortal's intervention. Thus, he takes the first step to acquiring it, knowing that God, the Most Generous and Most Wise, helps those who help themselves. He attempts to instill in those he wishes to give good counsel, the characteristics which will help them to take that first step.

# Day 147

**I put my trust in Allah, my Lord and your Lord! There is not a moving creature but He has the grasp on its forelock. Indeed! It is my Lord Who is on a straight Path.**

(11:56)

# Day 147

Today's beautiful selected passage instructs the seeker of success in three special ways that will help him to reach his goal. The first valuable message in the beautiful selected passage of today for the seeker of success is that he should put all his trust in God, the Greatest and the Most Reliable Trustee and the Lord of all that exists. People typically place their trust in the following ascending order: their enemies, strangers, acquaintances, the state, friends and then family. But the seeker of success who wishes to reach his goal, based on the knowledge acquired from the beautiful selected passage of today, will only put his trust in God, Who is the Most Trustworthy, the Best Friend and Protector.

The second valuable message in the beautiful selected passage of today for the seeker of success is that God, the Almighty and the All-powerful, has complete control over all of His creation, including every single living being, at all times. If one needs something done in a large organization, one will find that there will be a greater probability of having one's request fulfilled the higher one reaches into the hierarchy of the organization. Because God is Most Caring and Most Powerful, He is not in need of any intermediaries; all living beings have full access to Him at all times, for He is All-seeing, All-hearing and All-aware. Therefore, when the seeker of success is in need of anything in the largest organization in all existence, i.e. the entire creation itself, he does not waste his time with members of the lower hierarchy of the organization, but utilizes his special access to the CEO and the Highest Authority in the organization itself, i.e. God, the Creator and Sustainer of all, and takes his request to Him directly.

The third valuable message in the beautiful selected passage of today for the seeker of success is the realization that every being in the entire creation has its own agenda with regard to what it expects from another member in the creation, whether it is Satan, an employer, a close relation, a close friend, a neighbor, or a colleague – each would like to have a certain need met. But only God, the Most Loving and the Doer of all good, has one agenda only for His creation: that they all succeed in this life and the hereafter.

The seeker of success who wishes to reach his goal has complete faith in God, the Most Trustworthy and the Most Powerful, and in His noble messenger, Muhammad. He puts all his trust in his Lord and knows that He has complete control over the entire existence at all times. He knows that his Lord's is the only Straight Path leading to success, and that all other paths lead to failure.

# Day 148

**(Shuaib said:) "And O my people! Give just measure and weight. Nor withhold from the people the things that are their due; and commit not evil in the land with intent to do mischief".**

(11:85)

# Day 148

The seeker of success will find in the beautiful selected passage of today three valuable instructions in helping him to achieve his goal the first of which is that man should give just measure and weight when he is responsible for dispensing anything by measure, and by extension, dispensing any other responsibilities. As the representative on earth of God, the Most Just and the Most Wise, man is expected to provide just measure and weight when he is charged with that duty, or similar ones. Thus, satisfactorily discharging one's assigned duty will lead to success, and not doing so (especially maliciously), will lead to failure.

The second valuable instruction in the beautiful selected passage of today to help the seeker of success reach his goal is that he should not withhold from the people the things that are their due. As a member of society with so many people having rights over him, it is possible to neglect this obligation. But the seeker of success, as a result of the knowledge gained from the beautiful selected passage of today, will not withhold from the people the things that are their due – whether it is the parents, spouse, child, sibling, relative, neighbor, acquaintance, friend, colleague, fellow believer, guest, stranger, teacher, student, employer, employee, state, king or the governing head, or even himself.

The third valuable instruction in the beautiful selected passage of today to help the seeker of success reach his goal is that he should not commit evil in the land with intent to do mischief – for in that case he is acting as a representative of Satan, who delights in such acts, causing misery and pain to people. As a representative on earth of God, the Most Beneficent and Most Merciful, the seeker of success who wishes to reach his goal will be a source of comfort, joy and progress in the land, encouraging as many of the people as possible to join him in success now and in the hereafter, which is a right of all.

The seeker of success who wishes to reach his goal has absolute faith in God, the Most Just and the Best Doer of good, and in His beloved messenger, Muhammad. He discharges all his responsibilities honorably, giving just measure when dispensing, and gives everyone the due that he or she is deserving of. He is a source of pride in the community in which he lives, and does not do mischief in his community or anywhere else.

# Day 149

"But ask forgiveness of your Lord, and turn to Him (in repentance); for my Lord is indeed full of Mercy and loving Kindness".

(11:90)

# Day 149

Being endowed with the ability to think, choose, and act is certainly an honor for man. However, there is a tremendous risk of choosing the bad over the good, as choosing the bad usually results in instant gratification and choosing the good usually means delaying the gratification. And with Satan enticing and encouraging man to choose the bad over the good, the matter becomes even more difficult, and man faces an uphill battle in his quest to choose goodness over evil and achieve success.

Fortunately for man, God, the One Who created him, gave him form, and gave him the ability to think, choose and act, is Most Kind – indeed, is full of Mercy and Loving Kindness; and because of this fact, God, the Most Beneficent and the Most Merciful, instructs the seeker of success not to give up on his uphill battle and the quest for lasting success; He acknowledges that man may experience setbacks during this uphill battle, but also lovingly informs us that man should not give up, and, when he has experienced setbacks or indulged in sin, should ask for forgiveness from his Lord, the Creator of all and Most Forgiving. The child who errs and comes to his parent seeking forgiveness and guidance will indeed find not only forgiveness, but also sincere guidance and help from the parent regarding the alleviation of the child's hardship; the child who errs and continues in his errors without seeking forgiveness and guidance and help from his parent will not find that and will continue on his self-destructive path.

The seeker of success who wishes to reach his goal has unwavering faith in God, the Most Merciful and Most Forgiving, and in His noble messenger, Muhammad. He realizes that he is not perfect, and that when he does err, he can ask for sincere forgiveness from His Lord, the Most Wise and Most Clement, and turns to Him in sincere repentance – for he knows that his Lord is indeed full of Mercy and Loving Kindness, providing him with all that he asks for and more - for He is Most Forgiving, capable of doing all that He wishes, and infinitely more loving and caring than any parent could be towards his child, and multiplied manifold

# Day 150

And incline not to those who do wrong, or the fire will seize you – and you have no protectors other than Allah; nor shall you be helped.

And establish regular prayers at the two ends of the day and the approaches of the night; for those things that are good remove those that are evil: That is a reminder (an advice) for the mindful (those who remember their Lord).

And be steadfast in patience. For certainly, Allah will not suffer the reward of the righteous to perish.

(11:113 – 115)

# Day 150

  The beautiful selected passage of today provides the seeker of success with three valuable instructions in helping him to reach his goal - the first of which is the recommendation to avoid the company of those who do wrong, and especially to avoid giving them preference over those who do good. When one associates with others who do wrong, one is likely also to pick up the tendency to do wrong, without even realizing it. On a personal level, every individual has a duty to select good over evil. On a collective level, each individual should also make an effort to be part of a group which prefers good over evil – in this respect, he cannot incline to those who do wrong, or he will be contributing to evil, the consequence of which is failure in this life, and being consumed by fire in the hereafter. If one considers inclining to those who do wrong, based on being impressed with their perceived strength in the present life, one should keep in mind that one has no protectors other than God, the Source of all power and the Best Friend and Protector, and nor can anyone be helped except by Him.

  The second valuable instruction in the beautiful selected passage of today to help the seeker of success to reach his goal is to establish regular prayers at the beginning, middle and end of the day (being symbolic for the entire day) – and those things that are good, of which prayer is an excellent example, remove those things that are evil, similar to how soap removes the dirt. This is a caring reminder and most helpful advice for the mindful, who remember their Lord, the Most High and the Most Praised One, and wish to succeed. Indeed, worship of God, the Most Holy and Most Gracious, is the reason for which man was created, of which the regularly established prayers are an important component. The esteemed reader is referred to the commentary of Day 3 of this collection of meditations for a more detailed discussion of worship.

  The third valuable instruction in the beautiful selected passage of today to help the seeker of success to reach his goal, is to be steadfast in patience. Every individual in this life will be challenged with varying degrees of hardship at certain points in his life. Just like the brightest student who cannot be distinguished except by the most challenging portion of the examination, or the most precious diamond, which cannot be formed without the highest application of stress, the one who succeeds will withstand the most challenging periods of his life with patience and faith in God, the Most Kind and the Best One Who keeps His promise - for certainly, He will not suffer the reward of the righteous to perish, as He has promised. Therefore, the periods of high stress are necessary as an opportunity for individuals to grow even stronger - in order to distinguish the rubbish from the diamond, and the mediocre from the gifted.

  The seeker of success who wishes to reach his goal has complete faith in God, the Best Guide and the Best Rewarder, and in His beloved messenger, Muhammad. He chooses good acts over evil, and keeps company with good, rather than evil individuals or groups. He establishes regular worship to his Lord daily, and is steadfast in patience at all times – especially when things seem most difficult.

# Day 151

**To Allah do belong the unseen (secrets) of the heavens and the earth, and to Him goes back every affair (for decision). Then worship Him – and your Lord is not unmindful of anything that you do.**

(11:123)

# Day 151

    The beautiful selected passage of today provides the seeker of success with three powerful messages that will help him to reach his goal - the first of which is that God, the Most Great, the Manifest and the Hidden One, is He to Whom belong the unseen secrets of the heavens and the earth. Certainly, man is not being discouraged from being inquisitive. On the contrary, his attempt at observations in nature, from the microscopic level of individual cells down to the atom itself, or at the macroscopic level, up to the study of the universes, should be counted as praise and worship of the One Who created and sustains all with breath-taking precision and awe. However, unless man keeps in mind that God, the Most Wise and the All-knowing, is He to Whom belong the ultimate secrets of the heavens and the earth (that are visible as well as invisible), then he is unlikely to receive Guidance from God the All-knowing and the Best Guide, leading to frustration and disbelief, and the worship of himself or other than the One Who created all that exists.

    The second powerful message in the beautiful selected passage of today to help the seeker of success to reach his goal is the understanding that it is God, the Supreme One and the Owner of all, to Whom goes back every affair for decision – down to the decision of when a particular leaf will fall from a particular tree, and where it will end up. This does not absolve man from his responsibilities, even though all decisions are ultimately made by God, the All-Seeing, All-Hearing and the All-Aware, for the following reasons: 1) man has the ability to choose between good and evil and is in actuality being tested on how well he utilizes this ability, and 2) unless man desires a particular thing and takes the first step toward achieving it, God, the Most Wise and Most Powerful, will not provide it for him, as we reviewed in the meditation of Day 120 in this collection. The seeker of success takes the first step to achieve what he hopes for, and knows that the rest is up to God, the Most Kind and Most Able, and that to Him goes back every decision, and he trusts completely in His decisions.

    The third powerful message in the beautiful selected passage of today to help the seeker of success to reach his goal is the logical extension of the above two powerful messages, i.e. that since God, the Most Pure and Most Glorious, controls the entire existence of the heavens and the earth, and that it is to Him that every affair returns for decision, then it is logical that to Him Only belongs all worship and praise. It is precisely for this reason itself that He created all existence, and our Lord is aware of all activity of everything in existence at all times, as supported by the beautiful selected passage of today. The esteemed reader is referred to the commentary of Day 3 of this collection of meditations on a more detailed discussion of worship.

    The seeker of success who wishes to reach his goal has absolute faith in God, the Source of all that exists, the Manifest and the Hidden, and in His noble messenger, Muhammad. He knows with complete conviction that it is to his Lord that belongs the awesome secrets of the entire existence; that every decision is dependent on Him; and that He is aware of everything and everyone in existence, at all times. This leads the seeker of success to praise and worship his Lord with sincere devotion.

# Day 152

**...The (human) soul is certainly prone to evil, unless my Lord do bestow His Mercy. But surely, my Lord is Oft-forgiving, Most Merciful.**

(12:53)

# Day 152

All of creation glorifies and worships its Creator in a correspondingly befitting manner consistent with its ability. In fact, the angels are in constant worship of God, the Creator and Sustainer of all. However, there is one group of creation that we are aware of that glorifies and worships its Lord as a matter of choice, and that is man. Endowed with the ability to think, to choose between good and evil, and to act according to its wishes, instilled with the spirit of God Himself, the Most Holy One and the Source of peace, and assigned the task of the vicegerent on earth of God Himself, the Most Great and Source of all power, mankind has indeed been given a special status among creation. The arrogant and accursed Satan, who up until the creation of man was the head angel, questioned the Wisdom of God, the Most Wise and the Most Great, and vowed to encourage man to choose evil over good, until the Day of Judgment. However, those who sincerely turn to God, the Most Beneficent and Most Merciful, will God cover with his All-encompassing Mercy, and prevent them from being under the control of Satan, the accursed, who delights in the failure of men.

The beautiful selected passage of today strengthens the seeker of success by pointing out his inherent limitation, i.e. tendency to evil, compounded by the effort of the accursed Satan. In the short-term, evil is more enticing than good – but it leads to long-term failure. Further, the beautiful selected passage of today strengthens the seeker of success by instructing him on how to minimize his inherent limitations, i.e. by turning to God, the Best Guide and the Best Friend and Protector, for Guidance and Strength to overcome evil by His Mercy, before having committed evil. And even if he has been less then exemplary in the past, the seeker of success still hopes for Mercy from His Lord, for He is Most Kind and Most Forgiving, and forgives again and again, and is ever-willing to guide and assist all those who wish, towards lasting success.

The seeker of success who wishes to reach his goal has unwavering faith in God, the Oft-forgiving and Most Merciful, and in His beloved messenger, Muhammad. He realizes that he is prone to evil, and therefore turns to his Lord for Guidance on all matters and for his Forgiveness and Mercy, so that he may be guided to the Right Path and saved from evil and destruction.

# Day 153

**...Truly, no one despairs of Allah's Mercy, except those who have no faith.**

(12:87)

# Day 153

We know that children generally cannot resist candy. With time, training, and experience, the child will have to learn how to resist candy for his own good. In the process of maturing, it would be expected that most children will have had poor judgment initially and eaten candy when they were not supposed to do so. Is there any parent who would not forgive the child who realizes that he has made a mistake, asks for forgiveness, and seeks help from his parent as to how to prevent such mistakes in the future? It is not the child who seeks forgiveness and help, but the one who does not even realize his shortcomings, the one who persists in the wrongdoing ways despite the consequences, and, worse still, the child who not only harms himself, but encourages others on the destructive path, who will earn the anger and wrath of his parent.

In the Holy Quran, we find that out of the ninety-nine known names of God known to us, that the names He most often prefers to identify Himself with, is as the Most Merciful, along with the Most Beneficent, and the Most Forgiving – all of which signify the common attributes of the relationship between a parent and child at a lower level, with the highest intensity of all good attributes, designated with the prefix "Most", only attributable to God, the Most Great, the Most Loving and the Lord of all majesty and possessions.

With the knowledge known to us that God, the Most Loving and Most Kind, loves man many times more than his own parents love him, and that, like children, humans are prone to error, the seeker of success who wishes to reach his goal must realize that God, the Most Beneficent and Most Merciful, is willing to forgive all of man's errors out of His infinite love for him, except only one: worshipping anyone other than or including anyone or anything in the worship of God, the Almighty and the One deserving of all praise. It is only those who insist on persisting in error, without seeking forgiveness, and, worse still, encourage others toward evil, that are not worthy of God's Generosity and Forgiveness. Truly, no one despairs of the Mercy of God, the Most Forgiving and Most Merciful, except those lacking the primary ingredient of success, i.e. faith.

The seeker of success who wishes to reach his goal has complete faith in God, the Most Kind, Most Forgiving, and Most Merciful, and in His noble messenger, Muhammad. He never despairs of Mercy and Forgiveness from his Lord.

# Day 154

...Indeed! Never will Allah change the condition of a people until they change it themselves (with their own souls).

(13:11)

# Day 154

The seeker of success who has progressed thus far in his readings of this collection of meditations is expected to have grasped the concept that the primary ingredient of success is belief or faith in God, the Most Supreme and the Possessor of all Strength, as relayed to us through His beloved prophet, Muhammad. We also reviewed that 1) God is He on Whom all creation is dependent for its sustenance, and Who is not in need of anything from anyone; and 2) God is He Who is able to enforce His will at all times in all places, for He is the Absolute Ruler, the All-powerful, and Owner of all.

However, one must realize that life is not for the show of the strength, power and beneficence of God, the Most Beneficent, the Most Powerful and the Source of all strength, but for testing the ability of man to think, realize his mission in life, and to worship God, Who created and sustains not only him, but all that exists, to choose good over evil, and perform righteous actions as a result of faith. The esteemed reader is referred to the commentary of Day 3 of this collection of meditations on a more detailed discussion of worship. Therefore, even though God, the Most Praiseworthy and Most Great, is able to do as He wills, without restrictions, it is man's ability to act, or at least initiate the right action, that is being tested in life. Because positive change is an important component of success, it is repeated in several places in the Holy Quran for our benefit to highlight its importance by God, the Most Wise and the Best Teacher. This concept was reviewed earlier in this collection in the meditation of Day 120, i.e. change requires initial action from man before God's help.

We all would like that whatever we wish, would happen - and that is what is in store for us in the future if we succeed the test of this life, i.e. in heaven. However, while we are on earth, having whatever we wish to happen can still occur, but it is going to require our effort and struggle, according to the beautiful selected passage of today. In fact, the first step for the change is going to have to occur at the individual level, starting with a person's intention, i.e. which causes a change in his soul, which then utilizes the energy form the individual as well as the collective energy from others, and the change will occur with the permission of God, the source of all energy and the One without Whose permission, not even a leaf can fall from a tree.

The seeker of success who wishes to reach his goal has absolute faith in God, the Most Wise and Most Powerful, and in his beloved messenger, Muhammad. He realizes from the beautiful selected passage of today that the most vital part of all change that he wishes and hopes for is within himself, and that God, the Most Glorious and Who is Able to do what He wills, will never change the condition of any one or any group until they change what is in themselves first, desiring the change and taking the first step towards it.

# Day 155

**Allah does enlarge, or grant by (strict) measure, the sustenance (which He gives) to whomsoever He pleases. (The worldly) rejoice in the life of this world – but the life of this world is little comfort in the hereafter.**

(13:26)

# Day 155

God is the Creator of all that exists and the Sustainer of all His creation. He does enlarge, or restrict and grant by strict measure, the sustenance which He gives to whomsoever He pleases. A person who is wise will plan for optimal comfort for the present as well as the future. A person who is impulsive will opt for optimal pleasure in the present at the expense of his future, and end up paying with long-term misery for the short-term pleasure that he opted for.

From other references in the Holy Quran, we know that the life span on earth for man is comparable to less than one day in his life of the hereafter. Therefore, the wise person will strive for comfort not only in the present but also, and in fact, especially, in the hereafter. And if he must choose, the wise person will opt for greater comfort in the hereafter rather than the present, with the respective duration of each period in mind. However, the impulsive person, who is not so wise, rejoices in the life of this world, gets the maximum pleasure out of the present moment, and does not make any preparation for the future or the hereafter; he will find that the transient pleasures he experienced in the present life are of little comfort to him in the hereafter.

Someone who was considered extremely successful in the life of this world, such as being listed as number one in the entire world in terms of material wealth for twenty years, but who neglected to prepare for the hereafter, will find little comfort, if any, in the hereafter for eternity. This same individual, when compared with another, who was homeless, but lived his life worshipping God, the Most Rich and the Most Generous arising from his Faith and the love of his Creator, which causes him to perform other righteous activities, as described in the Holy Quran, will see a complete role reversal. On the other hand, the individual possessing material wealth in his worldly life, if he also was devoid of faith in God the Truth and the Wisest Judge, as relayed to us through His noble messenger Muhammad, and therefore, did not perform any righteous actions arising from his faith, would be placed in hell, where the suffering will be intense. Therefore, choosing intense suffering for eternity, for a few hours' pleasure comparatively would be considered a fool's bargain indeed.

The seeker of success who wishes to reach his goal has unwavering faith in God, the Most Great, the Most Trustworthy and Best Rewarder, and in His noble messenger, Muhammad. He learns from the beautiful selected passage of today to plan for optimal comfort both in this life and in the hereafter; if he must choose, the wise seeker of success will opt for greater comfort in the hereafter rather than in the present, for he knows the present life is for him only less than one day of the afterlife.

# Day 156

The unbelievers say: "Why is not a sign sent down to him from His Lord?" Say: "Truly, Allah leaves to stray whom He will; but He guides to Himself those who turn to Him in penitence –

"Those who believe, and whose hearts find satisfaction in the remembrance of Allah – for <u>without doubt, in the remembrance of Allah do hearts find satisfaction-</u>

"For those who believe and work righteousness, is (every) blessedness and a beautiful place of (final) return".

(13:27-29)

# Day 156

The seeker of success is being prepared by God, the Most Kind and Most Merciful, in the beautiful selected passage of today, to also assist others towards the path to success. A description is given of a most eloquent response to the mocking of an ill-wisher: "Why is not a sign sent down to him from His Lord?". In actuality, the signs of the presence of God, the Most Magnificent and the Almighty, are everywhere – from the predictable sunrise, to the sprouting of a seedling, to the beating of the heart. In the truly sublime response befitting the All-encompassing wisdom of God, the Most Great, He directs the search for His signs to the heart of each individual, including the ungrateful critic, i.e. that in the remembrance of their Creator, all will find satisfaction.

With the recognition of the innumerable signs of God, the Most Great and the Most Glorious, everywhere, including in his own heart, and with a sincere desire to praise, worship and serve Him, the unfortunate soul can be transformed from being astray in darkness, to being guided towards Him Who created all that exists and sustains and nourishes it. Transformed from darkness into light, now in possession of the first and most important step to lasting success, finding satisfaction in the remembrance of Him who created all and sustains it, and working righteousness as a sign of his faith – for him will be every blessedness in this life and the hereafter, and a beautiful place of final return. This is the soul that knows the true worth of things, the highest of which is being guided towards God, the Best Appraiser and the Best Guide, Who finds this individual's life satisfactory. This is the soul that finds in the world its highest satisfaction in the remembrance of God, the Most Glorious and the Source of peace.

The seeker of success who wishes to reach his goal has complete faith in God, the Manifest and the Hidden, and the Most Righteous Teacher, and in His beloved messenger, Muhammad. From the moment he wakes up until he goes to sleep, he appreciates signs of his Lord's work, and the events throughout the day as well. He finds the greatest satisfaction in the remembrance of God, the Most Loving, the Most Reliable and the Source of all that is in existence. He performs righteous deeds as a result of his faith.

# Day 157

**Those who love the life of this world more than the hereafter, who hinder (men) from the path of Allah and seek therein something crooked – they are astray by a long distance.**

(14:3)

# Day 157

In addition to gaining knowledge about those factors that will help him in his pursuit, the wise seeker of success will also pay attention to factors that can prevent him from reaching his goal. Three significant negative factors that can prevent the seeker of success from reaching his goal are identified in the beautiful selected passage of today - the first of which is identified as the love of the life of this world being more than the hereafter. With the life of this world comparable to less than one day of that of the hereafter, we can see that if an individual prefers to enjoy today in luxury, and to suffer the rest of his life in destitution, this individual is not exhibiting wise judgment and would be considered an utter failure, no matter how much be enjoyed himself throughout his worldly life.

The second negative factor that can prevent the seeker of success from reaching his goal that is identified in the beautiful selected passage of today is that, instead of seeking all that is good and beneficial, he should seek crookedness and evil. One who seeks the good will incline toward good, while one who seeks crookedness and evil, will be inclined towards crookedness and evil. One needs to stay away from crookedness and evil - because even though it provides an opportunity for instant gratification, it results in a penalty that will be manifested both in this life, and more importantly, in the hereafter. Because God, the Most loving and the Most Kind, loves us much more than our biological parents, He warns us about the sources of evil as well as all things that can harm us in the Holy Quran, through His beloved prophet Muhammad.

The third negative factor that can prevent the seeker of success from reaching his goal that is identified in the beautiful selected passage of today is hindering others from the path of God, the Most Beneficent and the Most Merciful. A life lived in the service of God, Most High and Most Generous, is exemplary and successful. A life lived for maximizing one's comfort in this life is mediocre. But a life lived in which the individual hinders men from the path of God, the Hearer and Seer of all and the Most Beneficent One, is an utter failure, indeed, since the negative consequences of one's actions in this situation will continue to accrue through others' actions, even after one's death.

The seeker of success who wishes to reach his goal has complete faith in God, the Best Guide and the Most Righteous Teacher, and in His noble messenger, Muhammad. He does not prefer the life of this world to the hereafter; he refrains from evil and crookedness, which may incline him towards performing such actions. More importantly, he does not prevent others from the path of Allah, the Source of all creations and the Sustainer of all. He knows that engaging in these three activities means he will stray from his goal by a long distance.

# Day 158

**The parable of those who reject their Lord is that their works are as ashes, on which the wind blows furiously on a tempestuous day: no power have they over anything that they have earned; that is the straying far, far (from the goal).**

(14:18)

# Day 158

The seeker of success is often referred back to the first step, and the most vital ingredient of, success, as named in the Holy Quran and also in this collection of meditations on success, and which is the belief or faith in God, the Most Wise and the Most Righteous Teacher as relayed to us through His beloved messenger Muhammad .

Life is a test to see who is best in his deeds or actions, choosing goodness over evil, and the best of these being worshipping God, the Creator of all, the Sustainer and the Resurrector. The esteemed reader is referred to the meditation on Day for a more detailed review on worship. The path to success begins with the recognition of God, the Most Great, the Manifest and the Hidden One, to Whom all existence points: the light, life in all its forms, the love of a parent for the child, and the voice of his own inner heart, among others. Once man is able to recognize God, the Most Beneficent and the Most Merciful, which is a process involving both the effort of man and the gift of God, the Most Kind and Most Generous, for man's effort and sincerity, he can progress to the next step of success, which is serving and worshipping his Lord God, the Creator and Sustainer of all that exists, and performance of righteous acts. Man will then be judged on how well he fulfills the duties for which he was created - as a result of his faith and love for his Creator.

In the beautiful selected passage of today, the folly of rejecting the existence of God, the Originator, Sustainer and Restorer, or of failing to recognize or acknowledge Him, is described. The unfortunate individual who lacks the most basic prerequisite, and the most vital one, to success, i.e. faith, will be unable to progress higher on the ladder of success, and will be doomed to failure. His actions satisfy his own self, another individual, or even Satan himself – for which he will have already received what is due to him, from the identified sources. Because the work of the unfortunate individuals who reject their Lord God, the Most Magnificent and the Satisfier of all needs, was not for Him, and because they already attained their pleasure for the work they performed, i.e. self-gratification or gratification of and from others, instead of God, the Creator and Sustainer of all, it will not be acknowledged in the hereafter. Their works are as ashes, on which the wind blows furiously on a tempestuous day, leaving behind nothing; therefore, on the Day of Judgment, their actions in this life will not earn them anything from God, the Creator and the Most Wise - for the actions were not meant to serve and please Him, and thus they stray far, far from the goal of success.

The seeker of success who wishes to reach his goal has absolute faith in God, the Creator of all and the Maker of order, and in His noble messenger, Muhammad. He performs righteous acts as a result of his faith and love of His Creator, Who in turn rewards him both with success in this life and with everlasting success in the hereafter.

# Day 159

Do you not see how Allah sets forth a parable? A goodly word like a goodly tree, whose root is firmly fixed, and its branches (reach) to the heavens –

It brings forth its fruit at all times by the leave of its Lord. So Allah sets forth parables for men, in order that they may receive admonition.

And the parable of an evil word is that of an evil tree; it is torn up by the root from the surface of the earth – it has no stability.

(14: 24-26)

# Day 159

    God, the Most Wise and the Most Righteous Teacher, uses parables in various portions of the Holy Quran, in order to help us to understand certain particularly important concepts better, and thus to help us in the pursuit of lasting success. In the parable used in the beautiful selected passage of today, comparison is made between a goodly and evil word and its associated consequences.

    As for the goodly word, its best example is the word of God himself, as given in the Holy Quran, and the clear recommendations and instructions for man to follow, which will result in the attainment of success in this life and in the hereafter. Another example of a goodly word would be that of Muhammad, the beloved prophet of God - for God, the Most High and Most Wise, instructed man in the Holy Quran to obey His word and that of His beloved prophet, Muhammad. And the goodly word is like a goodly tree, whose root is firmly fixed, and its branches reach high to the heavens, bringing forth its fruit or success at all times, both in this life and the hereafter.

    As for the evil word, an example of that would be the opposite of what is recommended and instructed by God Himself in the Holy Quran, and the opposite of what is recommended by His beloved prophet, Muhammad. The evil word in its most clear example would that be of the chief proponent of evil, Satan himself, and its conduit could be one's own mind or the enemies of those who believe in God, the Greatest and the Creator of harm and good. The evil word can be recognized by its complete rejection of, or casting of doubt on, the words of God, the Almighty and the Most Pure. And the evil word is like an evil tree, defective in its foundation, torn up by its roots from the surface of the earth, offering no stability either in the life of this world or in the hereafter, and leading to ruin and hell.

    The seeker of success who wishes to reaches his goal has unwavering faith in God, the Most Trustworthy and the Creator of all harm and good, and in His beloved messenger, Muhammad. He chooses to follow the good Word of God, the Most Wise and the Best Guide, and that of His noble prophet, Muhammad, rather than the evil word of Satan, his own mind, or that of the enemies of faith. He realizes that the good word offers stability, and bears fruit both in this life and at all times, i.e. success, including in the hereafter; and that the evil word offers no stability, and leads to failure - both in this life and the hereafter.

# Day 160

"O my Lord! Make me one who establishes regular prayer, and also (raise such) among my offspring O our Lord! And accept my prayer.

O our Lord! Cover (us) with Your forgiveness – me, my parents, and (all) believers, on the day that the reckoning will be established".

(14:40-41)

# Day 160

In the beautiful selected passage of today, we find an exemplary supplication from the beloved prophet Ibrahim, a model of success – the one who sincerely searched for God, the Creator and Sustainer of all, and was blessed with the gift of faith by God, the Most Generous and the Best Guide, and who performed righteous acts to serve his Lord, the Most Beneficent and Most Merciful, as result of his faith, and wished for success for others as well, starting from training his offspring in the methods of attaining lasting success. In the first part of the exemplary supplication of the beloved prophet Ibrahim from the beautiful selected passage of today, he requests assistance from his Lord, the Most Great and the Most Generous, in establishing regular prayer not only for himself, but also for his offspring, who can continue his work after him, inviting all to shun the worship and serving of all others except God, the Truth, the Creator of all, and the Only One. The individual who is thus directed away from useless acts, towards the worship of Him Who created and sustains all, and towards serving Him, will be fulfilling what he was created for, and will therefore achieve lasting success. And like the child who knows that his parent loves him, and is capable of fulfilling his request, Ibrahim, the beloved prophet of God, the Most Great and the Responder to all prayer, and also the one honored with the title of "friend of God", requested that his supplication be accepted.

In the second part of the exemplary supplication of the beloved prophet Ibrahim from the beautiful selected passage of today, he unselfishly requests, not only for himself and his family, but for all believers, forgiveness on the Day of Judgment, on which the ultimate reckoning will be established. Because man is not perfect and in fact is prone to error and sin, the outcome of the reckoning is a foregone conclusion unless there is intervention due to the Mercy and Forgiveness of God, the Most Great, Most Forgiving, and Most Merciful.

The seeker of success who wishes to reach his goal has complete faith in God, the Most Generous and Most Forgiving, and in His noble messenger, Muhammad. He performs righteous acts as a result of his faith, with worship of his Lord as the most apparent manifestation of his faith. He prays to his Lord that he, as well as his offspring, are consistent in performing worship and prayer- and seeks forgiveness from His Lord for himself, his parents and all believers – like a model believer and seeker of success, Ibrahim, the beloved prophet and friend of God, the Most Great and the Best Guide.

# Day 161

**Ibrahim said: "Who despairs of the Mercy of his Lord, but such as go astray?"**

(15:56)

# Day 161

    The teacher who repeats certain important points to the students does not do so as a matter of redundancy, but as a matter of reinforcing the key points that are necessary for the group studying the subject matter, and as a concern and sign of benevolence and caring, so that as many students as possible will be able to pass the examination. In the beautiful selected passage of today, is therefore, repeated such a topic as an example for mankind from the conversation of the noble prophet Ibrahim - recorded for our benefit in the Holy Quran by God, the Most Righteous Teacher and the Best Guide, for succeeding in this life and the hereafter, and which is a sign of His Mercy.

    There are at least two important considerations regarding the importance of the Mercy of God the Most Beneficent, and the Most Merciful in terms of man's ability to achieve lasting success - the first of which is that no one will be able to attain the first step of success and its most vital component, i.e. faith or belief in God, the Most Pure and Most Powerful, except by God's will and as a Mercy for the man with sincerity who is struggling to search for his Creator and find out about what is expected from him in this life – therefore being guided to the righteous path that leads to everlasting success.

    The second important consideration regarding the importance of the Mercy of God, the Most Beneficent and Most Merciful, in terms of man's ability to achieve lasting success is the point that man is imperfect. With the ability to choose between good and evil – that being his primary weakness, compounded by the unrelenting effort of Satan, the accursed, and his agents – no man could hope to pass through life without having erred, unlike an angel. But the ability of man to recognize his limitations and imperfection, and to strive to serve his Lord, the Creator and Sustainer of all, just as a child strives to please his parent - not only seeking, but expecting, pardon for errors committed in good faith as an expectation a child has from his parent - despite having committed errors, is what will determine whether one will be covered with the All-encompassing Mercy of God, the Most Loving and Most Kind, or whether one will be among the doubters of the Love and Magnanimity of God, the Most Magnificent and the Most Loving, and be among those doomed to failure, for God has for man Love of infinite capacity compared to what his parent has for him.

    The seeker of success who wishes to reach his goal has unwavering faith in God, the Most Forgiving and Most Kind, and in His beloved messenger, Muhammad. **He never despairs of the Mercy of his Lord, the Most Beneficent and Most Merciful, under any circumstance.**

## Day 162

**To the righteous (when) it is said: "What is it that your Lord has revealed?" They say: "All that is good". To those who do good, there is good in this world, and the home of the hereafter is even better. And excellent indeed is the home of the righteous:**

**Gardens of eternity which they will enter; beneath them flowing (pleasant) rivers – they will have therein all that they wish; thus does Allah reward the righteous.**

(16:30-31)

# Day 162

The righteous are those who have belief or faith in God, the Creator and Sustainer of all that exists, as revealed to us through His noble messenger, Muhammad. They recognize His presence in all of existence, as a result of which they are happy to praise and worship Him, wish to serve Him, turn to Him for Guidance, and perform righteous acts as a manifestation of their faith; these are they who will attain lasting success, and the beautiful selected passage of today is addressed to them regarding the way they will find their reward on the Day of Judgment, and the fruits of their labor and struggle in this life.

When the righteous are given their reward on the Day of Judgment, it will be asked of them: "What is it that your Lord has revealed?". And they will be awed by the Magnificence and Glory of their Lord, even more than by their earthly life, and reply: "All that is good". And they will reply thus, as a result of the revelation and Guidance from their Lord, the Best Guide and the Possessor of all strength: that they were guided from darkness into light, attaining good in their earthly life, and, as they witness with great awe, that their abode in the hereafter will be even better.

Like the student who struggles with strenuous studies to successfully complete the rigors that correspond to the intensity and level of his education – and even more so – the righteous, or the seekers of success who reach their goal, will find excellent indeed their home: gardens of eternity, beneath which flow pleasant rivers, and wherein they will have all that they wish. Thus does God reward the righteous – for He is the Most Rich, the Most Generous and the Best Rewarder.

The seeker of success who wishes to reach his goal has complete faith in God, the Truth and the Most Trustworthy, and in His noble messenger, Muhammad. He is ever thankful to God, the Almighty and the Best of those who keep their promises, for guiding him from darkness into the light, and for attaining all that is good in this life, and that which is better awaiting for him in the hereafter.

# Day 163

**To those who leave their homes in the cause of Allah, after suffering oppression – We will assuredly give a goodly home in this world; but truly the hereafter will be greater if they only realized (this)!**

**(They are) those who persevere in patience, and put their trust in their Lord.**

(16:41-42)

# Day 163

For man, few things evoke greater attachment than his home: it is what he has struggled to build and maintain throughout his life. It is where he feels safe. It is where he has forged lasting relationships – with relatives, neighbors, friends, and acquaintances. For the rich or the poor, young or old, there is no place like home. However, the seeker of success who wishes to reach his goal will have cultivated his faith in God, the Greatest and the Most Praised One, such that nothing is more important to him than his Lord – the One Who created him, sustains him, and to Whom he will return – including his self, his family, his possessions and his home.

Therefore, if a situation arises in which the enemies of God, the Most Victorious and the Subduer, cause unbearable oppression for the believers and the faithful, making it difficult for them to serve their Lord, the Most Great, the Hearer and Seer of all, then the beautiful selected passage of today advises the believers to put their trust in their Lord, the Best Friend and Protector and the Most Trustworthy One, and to persevere in patience, leaving their homes in the cause of Him Whom they love more than anything else, including their selves and their homes.

And in return for the love of serving their Lord, the Almighty and Most Holy, those who leave their homes in His cause, after suffering oppression, are promised in return a goodly home in this world, and a much better home in the hereafter - for eternity, by the One Who rules the heavens and the earth, and the Best of those who keep their promises.

The seeker of success who wishes to reach his goal has absolute faith in God, the Most Praiseworthy and Most Generous, and in His beloved messenger, Muhammad. If necessary, he is willing to leave his home in the cause of his Lord, Whom he loves more than anything else, including his own self, his family, his home, and all that is in his possession.

# Day 164

And you have no good thing but is from Allah – and moreover, when you are touched by distress, unto Him you cry with groans.

Yet, when He removes the distress from you, behold! Some of you turn to other gods, to join with their Lord.

(16:53-54)

# Day 164

A considerable portion of the Holy Quran is devoted to guiding man from darkness into light, from a life of aimlessness to one devoted to worshipping and serving the One Who created and sustains all that exists – the reason for which man was created – and with helping him to acquire belief and faith in God, the Lord of all and the Most Wise as relayed to us through His beloved messenger, which is the first step towards, and the most important ingredient of lasting success.

The intelligent individual possessing faith in God, the Almighty and Most Glorious, contemplates about all the things that he enjoys and need not purchase as a norm, such as his vision, hearing, reasoning, and the capacity to love and be loved, and realizes all his good things are from God, the Source of all good, and the best Provider. The intelligent and logical individual knows that when he is in distress and is really in need of help, it is only logical that the One Who has provided him with all that is good, is the One he needs to call, to relieve him from his distress.

The unfortunate individual who has not yet been blessed with belief and faith in God, the best Doer of good and the Preventer of harm, is reminded that all of the good things he has acquired and continues to receive are from God only – and, moreover, that his innermost heart is certainly aware of Him, for, when touched by distress, he automatically turns to none other than God, blessed be His name, and with cries and groans. Unfortunately, when the distress is removed from men, many of them forget to Whom they cried for assistance, and continue in their arrogance and disbelief, turning for guidance to, and serving and worshipping others instead of God, the Most Supreme and the Only One. As a result of the excellent parable provided in the beautiful selected passage of today, one previously devoid of faith, should be guided from darkness towards light, and make further progress toward success; and both (those with and without faith), will remember that calling God, the All-Hearing and the Responder to all prayers, during the times of distress is appropriate – but they should continue to remember Him after they have been relieved of their distress

The seeker of success who wishes to reach his goal has unwavering faith in God, the Most Great, the Creator and Sustainer of all, and in His noble messenger, Muhammad. He realizes that all good things in existence are from the Beneficence and Generosity of his Lord; if he has not yet been blessed with belief and faith, the first step and the most vital ingredient of success, he listens to his innermost voice pointing towards God when touched with distress, and does not turn to others besides Him for guidance and worship after the distress has been mercifully removed from him. If He has been already blessed with faith, he continues to remember his Lord after he has been relieved of his distress

# Day 165

**And Allah sends down rain from the skies, and gives with it life to the earth after its death. Certainly, in this is a sign for those who listen.**

(16:65)

# Day 165

Today's beautiful selected passage is again aimed at the unfortunate individual who has not yet been blessed with the necessary prerequisite and the most important ingredient of lasting success – belief and faith in God, the Most Great, the Creator of all and the Restorer, as relayed to us through His beloved prophet Muhammad. Additionally, the beautiful selected passage of today contains a message of immense value that can transform a purposeless life into one that is lived with a clear purpose – a life dedicated to achieving for oneself lasting success. And for the fortunate individual who has already been blessed with belief in God, the Almighty and the Most Generous, the message of the beautiful selected passage of today will strengthen his faith and intensify his resolve and purpose in life, maximizing his chances of attaining lasting success.

First, the beautiful selected passage of today states in an incredibly brilliant way what the heart already knows, but which arrogance, assisted by the effort of Satan, the accursed, can prevent one from acknowledging: that God, the Most Magnificent and the Source of all power, is in control of everything, at every place, and at all times. The actual example given in the beautiful selected passage of today is that it is God, the Most Beneficent and Most Merciful, who sends down rain from the skies – every individual in his heart knows that. If man, in his arrogance, tries to invoke the scientific principles down to the atom, he will be confounded with the remaining question still: who controls the subatomic particles, then, that man is not even aware of? And why is there such perfection and order in universe, when the natural state of all matter is tendency toward disorder?

Man has a tendency for disbelief in the afterlife, especially if he has not been blessed with the gift of faith in God, the Most Holy, the Giver and the Taker of life, and therefore, unfortunately, may not prepare for it. However, the fortunate man, on contemplation of the beautiful selected passage of today, reflects on the yearly resurrection, when the earth is revived, from death in autumn, to greenery and life in spring. This fortunate man is then led to the acquisition of, or strengthening of, faith in God, the Creator and Sustainer of all – and which is the key ingredient of success. He realizes that the One who can bring the leaves on a tree back to life in spring after their death in the autumn, can certainly bring the man who has experienced earthly death back to life on the Day of Judgment. This is indeed a tremendously brilliant method of relaying to the most ardent skeptic the reality of the afterlife.

The seeker of success who wishes to reach his goal has complete faith in God, the Originator of all existence, the Creator of life and death and the Resurrector, and in His beloved messenger, Muhammad. He acknowledges openly and with conviction that God, the Most Great and Most Holy is in Control of everything in life at all times. He is certain of being resurrected on the Day of Judgment – which he does not find any more outlandish than the concept of a plant that is revived in the spring – and that he will be held accountable for all his actions, to be rewarded or punished accordingly in the afterlife. As such, he makes a diligent effort in preparation for the afterlife – every day of his earthly life, to ensure a favorable outcome, and **lasting success.**

# Day 166

**And Allah brought you forth from the wombs of your mothers when you knew nothing; and He gave you hearing, sight, and affection: that you may give thanks (to Allah).**

**Do they not look at the birds, held poised in the midst of (the air and) the sky? Nothing holds them up but (the Power of) Allah. Certainly in this are signs for those who believe.**

(16:78-79)

# Day 166

The beautiful selected passage of today contains superb descriptions of daily life that might otherwise be ignored by the unfortunate soul – but as a result of the Mercy and Generosity of God, the Most Beneficent and Most Merciful, the most ardent skeptic, enveloped in darkness and living a life of futility, while enjoying the innumerable benefits of God, the Most Kind and the Most Generous, without ever acknowledging or thanking Him, should be able to acquire the fundamental and most vital ingredient of lasting success, i.e. belief or faith in God, the Creator and Sustainer of all that exists.

The addressee is referred back to his embryonic development– from a microscopic mixture of contents, from his mother and father, out of which an individual with perfect form and shape is formed. And to this individual are provided the precious gifts of hearing, sight and emotion. The addressee is beautifully guided to reflect on the source of these precious gifts, which can be none other than God, the Creator of all and the Shaper of beauty. Now that the addressee has been guided to the most vital ingredient of success, i.e. belief and faith in God, the Most Beneficent and Most Merciful, he is then instructed to act as a result of his faith, giving thanks to Him Who is the Source of all that is good and the Source of Guidance.

Additionally, the addressee is referred to another common scenario which, on reflection, contains marvels of immense proportions in nature, pointing to Him Who is responsible for that and everything else in existence: the bird, held poised in the sky; who is holding this bird in mid-air? Gravity is an impulsive and shallow answer to the above question. Further analysis by any individual, as well as the combined effort of all the most brilliant minds, will point to the power of none other than God, the Greatest and the Most Magnificent.

The seeker of success who wishes to reach his goal has absolute faith in God, the Creator of all and the Source of all that is good, and in His noble messenger, Muhammad. He is thankful to his Creator for all the wonderful gifts given to him, including his hearing, sight and affection. Additionally, he is able to recognize the existence of God, the Most Beneficent and Most Generous in all of existence, including the ability of a bird to be held poised in air, without falling.

# Day 167

Abraham was indeed a model; devoutly obedient to Allah, (and) true in faith, and he joined not gods with Allah.

He showed his gratitude for the favors of Allah, Who chose him and guided him to a straight way.

And We gave him good in this world, and he will be, in the hereafter, in the ranks of the righteous.

(16:120-122)

#  Day 167

    The beautiful selected passage of today is addressed specifically to the seeker of success and is an excellent synopsis of the various stages of success. Because success is not a passive process that one may happen to stumble across, the beautiful selected passage of today is extremely useful for identifying the specific actions one should take to turn one's vision of success into a reality.

    Ibrahim, the noble messenger of God, the Most Beneficent and the Most Merciful, who is honored with the title of "friend of God", is recommended as a model to follow for the seekers of success, in the beautiful selected passage of today. Subsequently, the beloved prophet Muhammad himself became the model for success, having gradually perfected faith, through the revelations of God, the Almighty and the Best Guide – for all believers and all seekers of success. The first portion of the beautiful selected passage of today is appropriately focused on the initial stage of success, which is also the most important stage and the foundation of success, i.e. belief and faith in God, the Most Perfect and the Most Wise. Ibrahim, the noble prophet of God, the Almighty and All-aware, was himself born into a family practicing idolatry. The beautiful story is described elsewhere in the Holy Quran, and in this collection of meditations, of how the noble prophet Ibrahim, with sincerity, searched for and recognized the Oneness and All-encompassing Power of God as the source of all power and realized that He is the Only One deserving of worship. As a result, prophet Ibrahim was awarded with the most valuable ingredient and the foundation of success, i.e. belief and faith in God, to Whom belongs all praise, and dissociated himself from serving idols or paying service to anyone or anything except God Alone, Who created all and sustains it, and was devoutly obedient to Him.

    And as is promised to those who have faith in God, the Greatest, and Most Trustworthy, and who perform righteous acts as a result of their faith, the beloved prophet Ibrahim was awarded, as will the others who meet these criteria of lasting success, with good in this world and being placed in the ranks of the righteous and successful in the hereafter. One who desires success in this world and the hereafter should study and follow the path of the noble prophet Ibrahim, as was recommended by his descendant and conscious follower, the beloved prophet Muhammad.

    The seeker of success who wishes to reach his goal has unwavering faith in God, the Creator of all that exists and the Only One deserving of praise and worship, and in His beloved messenger, Muhammad. He utilizes the noble prophet Ibrahim's life as a model of success - a model which was later supplanted by that of the life of the honorable prophet Muhammad, through whom the religion of God, the Most Wise and Most Holy, was perfected.

# Day 168

**Invite (all) to the way of your Lord with wisdom and beautiful preaching; and argue with them in ways that are best and most gracious – for your Lord knows best who has strayed from His Path and He is best aware of those who are guided.**

**And if you punish (your enemy), then punish them with the like of that with which you were afflicted; but if you show patience, that is indeed the best (course) for those who are patient.**

**And do be patient – for your patience is but from Allah. Nor grieve over them, and distress not yourself because of their plots;**

**For Allah is with those who restrain themselves, and those who do good.**

(16:125-128)

# Day 168

The beautiful selected passage of today instructs the seeker of success in three valuable methods to help him reach his goal during his struggles in this life - the first of which is that, as the representative on earth of God, the Most Beneficent and Most Merciful, man cannot be selfish and contented with his own success, but wish for good things and success for all. In this respect, man is instructed to invite all to the way of the Lord of all that exists, with beautiful preaching. During his invitation to success and preaching, if the seeker of success is forced to argue, he is instructed to argue in ways that are best and most gracious. And the Lord Almighty knows best who has strayed from His Path, and He is best aware of those who are guided.

The second valuable method instructed in the beautiful selected passage of today to help the seeker for success reach his goal during his struggles in this life is that if one is faced with a situation in which one can punish his enemy, then the maximum punishment one is instructed to inflict is the amount comparable to that which was inflicted by the enemy – but if one is able to show patience and forgive, that is recommended as the best course: A magnanimous recommendation from the One Who is Most Magnificent and Most Forgiving.

The third valuable method instructed in the beautiful selected passage of today to help the seeker of success reach his goal during his struggles in this life is to exhibit patience – not only in the instances described above, but at all times. And the seeker of success is recommended not to grieve and distress himself on account of the nefarious plots of the enemies of faith, but to be patient and continue serving his Lord, the Most Holy and the Best Friend and Protector – for God is with those who patiently restrain themselves and do good.

The seeker of success who wishes to reach his goal has complete faith in God, the Most Just and the Most Wise, and in His noble messenger, Muhammad. He wishes for success for others as well as for himself, and therefore invites others to the service of God, the Creator and Sustainer of all, in a polite and gracious way. When afforded the opportunity to punish those who have wronged him, he strives for patience and forgiving the wrongdoer, as charity and as a manifestation of his faith; but if he is unable - or chooses not to do that, then he does not inflict punishment greater than what was inflicted on him.

# Day 169

**Who receives guidance, receives it for his own benefit. Who goes astray, does so to his own loss. No bearer of burdens can bear the burdens of another. Nor would We visit our wrath until We had sent a messenger (to give warning).**

(17:15)

# Day 169

Today's beautiful selected passage contains three valuable messages that will help the seeker of success to achieve his goal - the first of which is the realization that, if an individual receives Guidance from God, the Most Great and the Best Guide, and then acts righteously as a result of the Guidance, he benefits no one else except himself. And if an individual rejects the Guidance from God the Most Beneficent and the Most Merciful, he does so to his own loss.

The second important message in the beautiful selected passage of today that will help the seeker of success to achieve his goal is that no bearer of burdens can bear the burden of another. Achievement of lasting success takes significant effort and considerable struggle in this life. Those who fall into the trap of Satan, who is ever on the lookout for distracting gullible souls from the right Guidance, and from lasting success, offering quick routes to success with no effort from the participant, and offering to bear his burdens on the Day of Judgment instead of being held accountable for their actions, will be sorely disappointed on the Day of Judgment.

The third important message in the beautiful selected passage of today that will help the seeker of success to achieve his goal is that, because God is Most Compassionate and Most Patient, He does not punish a people until they have been warned. We have in the Holy Quran many examples of populations that were destroyed after they rejected the warnings of the many messengers of God, the Most Beneficent and Most Merciful. The noble prophet Muhammad is the last prophet of God, the Most Praiseworthy One and the Witness over all, who very courageously and beautifully conveyed the message of God, the Most Pure and Most Wise, for all mankind until the Day of Judgment, and all seekers of success who wish to reach their goal will heed his warning and prepare themselves accordingly for the Day of Judgment.

The seeker of success who wishes to reach his goal has absolute faith in God, the Best Guide and the Most Righteous Teacher, and in His beloved messenger, Muhammad. He realizes his responsibilities on this earth and knows that no one can bear the burden of his responsibilities other than himself. He knows that his existence is not meaningless . He knows that his faith, and the righteous acts it leads him to perform, benefit no one more than they benefit himself.

# Day 170

Your Lord has decreed that you worship none but Him, and that you be kind to parents – whether one or both of them attain old age in your life, say not to them a word of contempt; nor repel them, but address them in terms of honor.

And, out of kindness, lower to them the wing of humility, and say: "My Lord! Bestow on them your Mercy even as they cherished me in childhood".

Your Lord knows best what is in your hearts; if you do deeds of righteousness, indeed He is most forgiving to those who turn to Him again and again (in true penitence).

And render to the relatives their due rights, as (also) to those in want, and to the wayfarer; but squander not (your wealth) in the manner of a spendthrift.

Certainly, spendthrifts are brothers of the evil ones and the evil one is to his Lord (himself) ungrateful.

And even if you have to turn away from them in pursuit of the Mercy from your Lord which you do expect (later), yet speak to them a word of easy kindness.

And make not your hand tied (like a miser's) to your neck, nor stretch it forth to its utmost reach, so that you become blameworthy and destitute.

(17: 23-29)

# Day 170

The beautiful selected passage of today and the one for tomorrow are a continuum of a portion of the same chapter in the Holy Quran, split in this collection of meditations into two sections, for the seeker of success to reflect on the great number of highly valuable instructions to help him reach his goal, with three important instructions in today's portion of the beautiful selected passage.

The first important instruction in the beautiful selected passage of today to help the seeker of success reach his goal, after the reminder of the basic prerequisite of all success, i.e. that one should not worship or serve anyone other than God, the Most High and the Only One, is that one should be kind to his parents. And one should remember how his parents cared for him when he was helpless – and, whether one or both parents attain old age in his life, to say not to them a word of contempt, nor repel them. If one is not able to remember how one's parents so lovingly cared for him in his infancy and childhood, then he should look at the typical behavior of a parent towards the newborn, infant and at various stages of the child's growth. Just as they loved and cared for him in his childhood, the child should return the favor toward his parents, and address them in terms of honor always, and especially when the parents reach a stage where they are the ones now requiring love, assistance and care from the child.

The second important instruction in the beautiful selected passage of today to help the seeker of success reach his goal is the reminder that besides one's obligations to God, the Most Beneficent and Most Merciful and toward his parents, one should remember that he has obligations toward others that are also to be honored, and that due rights should be given to others as well – to other relatives besides the parents, to those in need, and to those who have no resources, such as the wayfarer or the homeless.

The third important instruction in the beautiful selected passage of today to help the seeker of success reach his goal is to exercise good judgment and having the right balance while fulfilling one's obligations to others as described above – neither being stingy like a miser, nor being extravagant and exceeding one's capacity, such that one may himself become destitute. And if one is not able to meet the needs of others until a later date, when he expects to receive the Mercy of his Lord, Most Kind and Most Generous, then at least to speak to them a word of easy kindness interim.

The seeker of success who wishes to reach his goal has unwavering faith in God, the Most Wise and the Most Righteous Teacher, and in His noble messenger, Muhammad. He feels a special love for his parents, who nurtured him and protected him from the time of his conception to when he was capable of caring for himself. He feels a special obligation to be able to care for his parents throughout their life, and especially in their vulnerable stage in later life, when the role is typically reversed and it's the elderly parents who need nurturing and protection, which he feels honored to provide. He is kind also to relatives and others in need. He is neither miserly nor so extravagant while fulfilling the above duties, that he may himself become destitute as a result.

# Day 171

Certainly your Lord does provide sustenance in abundance for whom He pleases, and He provides in a just measure – indeed He is the All-knower and All-seer of His slaves.

And kill not your children for fear of poverty; We shall provide sustenance for them as well as for you. Surely, the killing of them is great sin.

And come not near to unlawful sex – for it is a shameful (deed) and an evil, opening the road (to other evils).

Nor take life – which Allah has made sacred, except for just cause. And if anyone is slain wrongfully, we have given his heir authority (to demand Qisas – law of equality in punishment, or to forgive, or to take Diyah (blood-money); but let him not exceed bounds in the matter of taking life – for he is helped (by the Islamic Law).

And come not near to the orphan's property except to improve it, until he attains the age of full strength; and fulfill (every) engagement - for (every) engagement will be enquired into (on the Day of Reckoning).

And give full measure when you measure; and weigh with a balance that is straight – that is the most fitting and the most advantageous in the final determination.
And follow not that of which you have no knowledge; for every act of hearing, of seeing, or of (feeling in) the heart will be enquired into (on the Day of Reckoning). Nor walk on the earth with insolence; for you cannot rend the earth asunder, nor reach the mountains in height. The evil of all such things (mentioned above) is hateful in the sight of your Lord.

These are among the (precepts of) wisdom which your Lord has revealed to you. Take not with Allah another object of worship, unless you should be thrown into hell, blameworthy and rejected.

(17:30-39)

# Day 171

The beautiful selected passage of today is continuous from yesterday's, which has been split into two sections, for the seeker of success to reflect on the great number of highly valuable instructions to help him reach his goal. The instructions in the beautiful selected passage of today are greater in number and more specific than those of yesterday; they are listed below in summary form for the benefit and quick reference for the seeker of success:

God is the Creator of all that exists, Most powerful, All-knowing and All-Seeing. He Alone is responsible for providing sustenance for all that He created – providing it in abundance, in a just measure, and for whom He pleases. Therefore, if one fears he will be unable to provide sustenance for his children, he should not kill them for fear of poverty – because the One Who created all is responsible Alone for providing the sustenance to His creation.

Consider unlawful sex as anathema to success – for it is a shameful, evil deed, which strikes at the root of trust between individuals and the community, and opens the road to other evils.

Do not take life – except for a just cause, for God, the Most Beneficent and Most Merciful, has made it sacred. And if anyone is slain wrongfully, his family is entitled to take one of three options recommended by God, the Most Just and Most Wise: equality in punishment for the guilty, i.e. death, financial compensation, or forgiveness.

If one is in charge of an orphan's property, one should not use it for any purpose except for the benefit of the orphan until the orphan becomes able to manage his own affairs.

To weigh with an accurate balance and give just measure is most fitting of a righteous individual, and most advantageous in the final outcome.

Follow not that of which one has no knowledge, i.e. saying "I have seen" when in fact one has not seen, or saying "I have heard" when one has not heard.

Don't behave in an arrogant manner, but acquire the characteristic of humbleness instead.

Take not with God, the Most Holy and the Only One, another object of worship. This is the **most important factor that will determine whether one achieves lasting success or will be a failure,** being thrown into the punishment of hell, blameworthy and rejected, for serving and worshipping others than He Whom one was created to worship and serve.

The seeker of success who wishes to reach his goal has complete faith in God, the Most Wise, the Best Guide and the Best Judge, and in His beloved messenger, Muhammad. He pays careful attention to the recommendations from the Lord of all that exists, as listed above, to help him follow the right path for the attainment of sure and lasting success.

# Day 172

**The seven heavens and the earth and all beings therein declare His Glory; there is not a thing but celebrates His praise. And yet you understand not how they declare His Glory. Indeed, He is Most Forbearing, Most Forgiving.**

(17:44)

# Day 172

All that is on earth and the seven heavens and everything in existence has been created by God, the Creator of all, the Maker of order, the Source of all Power, and the Shaper of beauty. We find in all of creation, everywhere we turn, breathtaking beauty, perfect order, and awesome power – all pointing towards God and His Greatness.

All creation, therefore, declares the Glory, and celebrates the praises of and worships, the One Who gave everything its form and shape and Who brought it into existence. As humans with certain limitations, we are not able to understand how, but we do know from the beautiful selected passage of today, that there is not a thing in the entire existence – the seven heavens and the earth and all beings therein – that does not declare God's Glory and celebrate His praises. An important consideration at this point is that man is given the freedom to choose whether he worships and serves his Lord. We can try to guess how each thing or being in existence declares the glory and celebrates the praise of its Creator – God, the Most Pure and the Almighty – but the seeker of success need not know that, to understand the message of the beautiful selected passage of today.

Out of all creation, it is only man that we know of, who has the privilege of choosing between good and evil; everything else fulfills what it was created for without choice, declaring the glory and celebrating the praises of God Who created all and sustains it. It is this ability to choose good over evil that resulted in man being placed above angels in the hierarchy of creation. Satan arrogantly disagreed with this, and it resulted in his downfall and his perpetual enmity towards man until the Day of Judgment.

The seeker of success who wishes to reach his goal has absolute faith in God, the Most Holy, the Only One, the One deserving of all praise, and in His noble messenger, Muhammad. He realizes that all beings in existence celebrate the praises of their Lord in their unique fashion; he also celebrates in praising and worshipping God, the Creator, Sustainer, and Owner of all – voluntarily, devoutly and diligently. The esteemed reader is referred to the commentary of Day 3 of this collection of meditations on a more detailed discussion of worship. And if he has been in the past deficient in fulfilling what he was created for, due to lack of faith, the vital ingredient of success, then he will find that God is Most Forgiving and Most Forbearing, if he seeks His forgiveness and guidance from Him.

# Day 173

Say to my servants that they should (only) say those things that are best – because Satan indeed sows a state of conflict and disagreements among them. Truly, Satan is to man an avowed enemy.

(17:53)

# Day 173

Knowledge of factors that can contribute to meeting one's objective, as well as knowledge of those factors that can impede one from meeting one's objective, is important for accomplishing one's mission. In the beautiful selected passage of today, one of the major impediments to man's ability to succeed is identified: the avowed enemy of man – the accursed Satan, as well as instructions on how to neutralize Satan's treacherous strategies.

Satan is truly an avowed enemy of man. His primary mission is to distract as many men as possible from the straight path of success. Among the many strategies that the accursed Satan employs in distracting men from the straight Path of God, the Most Beneficent and Most Merciful, and from the Path of success, is that of sowing a state of conflict and disagreements among men – so that they will utilize their energies and resources on those conflicts and disagreements, preventing them from utilizing those energies and resources in the cause of God, the Most Holy, the Source of peace and the Source of all power. In the beautiful selected passage of today, man is instructed to say only those things that are best, which will increase the love and co-operation among men, and minimize conflict and disagreements among them.

The seeker of success who wishes to reach his goal has unwavering faith in God, the Most Wise, Most Patient, and the Source of all good, and in His beloved messenger, Muhammad. He recognizes the accursed Satan as one of the primary impediments to reaching his goal, as well as the methods he uses, as the avowed enemy of man, of sowing a state of conflict and disagreement among men. Additionally, he says from his mouth only things that are best, with sincerity, from his heart – which, upon reaching the heart of his fellow beings, increases love and co-operation among them, and minimizes conflicts and disagreements. Thus, instead of utilizing his energies and resources to address conflicts and disagreements with others, man will be able to utilize them in the service of God, the Most Loving and the Most Patient, and increase his likelihood of attaining success.

# Day 174

**That which is on earth We have made but as a glittering show for the earth, in order that We may test them – as to which of them are best in conduct.**

(18:7)

# Day 174

    To understand the truly important message from the beautiful selected passage of today, we will utilize an example of a vast and powerful organization and the relationship of its employees to its proportionally powerful CEO. In a different era, we may have used the example of a truly rich and powerful kingdom and the relationship of its subjects to its proportionally powerful king. Suppose that in a large organization there is a group of employees who are thoroughly impressed with the power, richness and capabilities of the organization they are a part of, and have no regard for the effort, capabilities and contribution of the CEO in having the organization run smoothly for the benefit of all, and have no regard for fulfilling the roles they were hired for, but are interested only in enjoying the benefits of being a part of the organization. Suppose also, that in the same organization, there is a group of employees who, although impressed with the power, richness and capabilities of the organization, have a sincere admiration for the effort, capabilities and contribution of the CEO in having the organization run smoothly for the benefit of all. And, moreover, they wish to not only express their admiration, but serve the CEO in their best capacity, to perform what is expected of them as employees in the organization. Out of the two groups used in the example above, which group would incur the pleasure of the CEO, and which one would be likely to incur his wrath?

    Seen from another aspect, we are reminded of the reason for our existence. We have reviewed in the earlier meditations that man was created to worship and serve God, the Creator and Sustainer of all that exists. The esteemed reader is referred to the Day 3 meditation of this collection on more details about what constitutes worship. An individual who recognizes and worships God, the Most Wise and Provider of all, as relayed to us through His noble messenger Muhammad, is said to possess faith, which we have reviewed number of times, is the key requirement for success. An individual who possesses faith, is able to distinguish consistently right from wrong and display good conduct, despite having to forego the pleasures and the glitter of this life, if necessary.

    The seeker of success who wishes to reach his goal has absolute faith in God, the Creator of all that exists, the Nourisher and the Sustainer, and in His beloved messenger, Muhammad. He realizes the vastness, beauty and perfection of the largest organization, i.e. the entire existence, of which he is a part. Moreover, he appreciates the unlimited power, ultimate wisdom, all-encompassing knowledge, the highest form of Beneficence and Love, and the highest form of Magnificence and Justice in God, the CEO of this vast organization of existence, to Whom belongs complete control of the entire existence. And further, the seeker of success who wishes to reach his goal realizes that, even though he is impressed with the glittering show of the earth, it is more important for him to fulfill his assigned duties in this vast organization, with sincere admiration and praise of the One Who Created it and Who Alone Sustains it, wishing to serve Him. He knows the reason for his existence in this magnificent organization, and his special relationship with its CEO.

# Day 175

**Nor say of anything, "I shall be sure to do so and so tomorrow",**

**Without adding, "If Allah wills!". And call your Lord to mind when you forget, and say, "I hope that my Lord will guide me ever closer (even) than this to the right way".**

(18:23-24)

# Day 175

Although certain of the components of success can be considered vital elements and foundations of success, such as faith in God, the Most Supreme and the Most Praiseworthy, and performing righteous acts as a result of faith (both of which are discussed from various perspectives in this collection of meditations), there are other components of success, which, while not being its vital components, can make the difference between mere success and **astounding success.** Attention to fine details can make the difference between a building that is strong with solid foundations, and one that is not only strong and beautiful with solid foundations, but also exhibiting the passion and care of the builder. In today's beautiful selected passage, instructions are provided on two finer details, attention to which can make the difference between achieving mere success and a higher degree of success.

Having been blessed with the absolute prerequisite and the most vital ingredient of lasting success, i.e. faith in God, the Creator and Sustainer of all, as relayed to us through His noble messenger, Muhammad, the seeker of success manifests his faith in all his actions. For example, the individual blessed with faith, realizes that nothing in existence can occur without God's approval. Therefore, the seeker of success who aspires to reach its highest degree, will manifest his faith with righteousness in all his actions, and if he intends or promises to do certain things in the future, he always adds to his intention and promise "If God wills", recognizing God's will as the absolute requirement for any occurrence at all times in the entire existence.

Additionally, the seeker of success should realize that even though Satan, the avowed enemy of man, and the primary impediment to his success, is busy planning various strategies to undermine his success (such as by causing him to forget his Creator and the duties required of him), he knows that God is the Most Powerful, Most Merciful and Most Generous, and calls his Lord to mind when he forgets, saying "I hope that my Lord will guide me closer even than this (situation) to the right path".

The seeker of success who wishes to reach his goal has unwavering faith in God, the Source of all power and the Best Guide, and in His noble messenger, Muhammad. In addition to acquiring the vital components of success, i.e. faith, resulting in worship of God and the performance of righteous acts as a result of faith, he acquires additional characteristics which endears him to God, the Creator of life and Death, the Restorer and the Reckoner, such as believing, and manifesting the belief that all events are under control of his Lord at all times. Therefore, whenever he intends to do something, he always adds, both verbally and non-verbally, "If Allah wills", and when he forgets something, he brings his Lord to mind and asks God to bring him closer to the right path.

# Day 176

**And keep your soul content with those who call on their Lord morning and evening, seeking His Face; and let not your eyes pass beyond them, seeking the pomp and glitter of this life. Nor obey any whose heart We have permitted to neglect the remembrance of Us - one who follows his own desires, and whose affair (deeds) has been lost.**

(18:28)

# Day 176

The beautiful selected passage of today instructs the seeker of success in two valuable methods to help him to achieve his goal - the first of which instructs him to seek the company of others who are also in search of success, especially those who are in search of reaching the highest level of success, calling on their Lord morning and evening, seeking Him, i.e. His Face, Who is the Most Loving, the Creator of all, and the Shaper of beauty. Following the instructions of He Who is Most Wise and the Most Righteous Teacher, the seeker of success who keeps company with those who are dearly in love with their Lord, seeking His company, and aspiring to the highest levels of success, instead of seeking the artificial and transient pomp and glitter of this life, will be more likely to acquire the characteristics that will help him to achieve his goal, whereas the alternate route of solely following the pomp and glitter of this life will result in increased likelihood of taking him further away from his goal of lasting success.

The second valuable method the seeker of success is instructed in to help him achieve his goal in the beautiful selected passage of today is not to obey any whose heart has been permitted to neglect the remembrance of Him Who created all that exists in the first place and Who sustains it – this type of individual follows his own desires, and whose deeds are without any merit, for only those deeds have merit that are done for the pleasure of God, Who is the Absolute Ruler, the Creator of all, the Best Appraiser and the Most Generous.

The seeker of success who wishes to reach his goal has complete faith in God, the All-knowing, the Best Guide, and the Best Rewarder, and in His beloved messenger, Muhammad. He keeps company with the highest aspirants of success, so that he too will acquire their favorable characteristics, and he does not follow his own desires if they are in conflict with the Guidance of his Lord, the Most Great and the Most Wise. And he does not follow the unfortunate individual who has forgotten his Lord and instead follows his own desires, and who is an example of clear failure.

# Day 177

As to those who believe and work righteousness, certainly We shall not suffer to perish the reward of any who does a (single) righteous deed.

For them will be gardens of eternity; beneath them rivers will flow – they will be adorned therein with bracelets of gold, and they will wear green garments of fine silk and heavy brocade; they will recline therein on raised thrones. How good the recompense! How beautiful a resting place!

(18:30-31)

# Day 177

The beautiful selected passage of today reinforces the fundamentals of lasting success, i.e. belief and faith in God, the Lord of all that Exists, the Most Rich, and the Best Rewarder, as relayed to us through His beloved messenger, Muhammad, and the importance of righteous acts as a result of the faith. Success will be cumulative, depending on the extent to which the individual's faith is manifested by righteous deeds done for the purpose of serving Him Who has absolute control of all that is in existence, with the reward of not even a single righteous deed being overlooked – for God is the Best of those who keep account, and the Most Generous.

The beauty and richness of detail in today's beautiful selected passage is striking, and serves to link the cause and effect in an unforgettable way, contributing to not only reminding the seekers of success of the most fundamental components required to reach their goal, but also introducing in them enthusiasm, which is an important component of being able to successfully accomplish one's mission.

Success does not come easily, and requires continuous hard work, but the seekers of success who have in their sight the recompense of being successful in their mission, and who will gather the necessary resources, fired with enthusiasm and the certainty of attaining it as result of their worthy struggle, will be rewarded by Him Who is the Creator of all, the Most Rich and the Enricher. For them will be gardens of eternity. Rivers will flow beneath the gardens, and the inhabitants of the gardens will be adorned with bracelets of gold, and will wear green garments of fine silk and heavy brocade, and will recline on raised thrones. How excellent a recompense! How beautiful a resting place!

The seeker of success who wishes to reach his goal has absolute faith in God, the Creator and Sustainer of all, the Owner of all that exists and the Most Generous, and in His noble messenger Muhammad, and works deeds of righteousness as a result of his faith. He realizes these characteristics constitute the key to lasting success. Envisioning the end result of success, as noted in the earlier paragraphs of today's meditation, the seeker of success has his enthusiasm increased, resulting in further strengthening of his faith and the performance of righteous deeds.

# Day 178

**Set forth to them the similitude of the life of this world: it is like the rain which we send down from the skies; the earth's vegetation absorbs it, but soon it becomes dry stubble, which the winds do scatter. It is only Allah who prevails over all things.**

(18:45)

# Day 178

A proper understanding of the powerful message of the beautiful selected passage of today is essential for the seeker of success to be able to reach his goal – and it can make the difference between someone who is only concerned about his condition for today, neglecting the future, and someone who is concerned about his condition not only today, but also about the future.

In relative terms, we know that the life of this world is like a day or less out of an individual's current life compared with the reckoning of the hereafter. An excellent example is given by God, the Most Magnificent and the Most Righteous Teacher, in today's beautiful selected passage, describing the transient nature of this life and comparing it to the rain which is sent from the skies: although the rain is beautiful, welcomed, and appreciated by all, the earth's vegetation absorbs it, and the vegetation soon disappears in the fall. In fact, everything in this life – wealth, power, children, and everything one finds comfort in – will disappear. The Only One and Only thing that is not transient and prevails is God, the Eternal and the Self-existing, Who will gather all mankind on the Day of Judgment and take a detailed account of each individual's performance in this life, and will reward one based on his performance. The unfortunate individual who was only concerned about his condition in the life of this world will be very sorry indeed for his foolishness and impulsiveness.

The seeker of success who wishes to reach his goal has unwavering faith in God and in His beloved messenger, Muhammad. He realizes the transient nature of this life. He makes appropriate preparations for his comfort both in this life and in the hereafter - for today and for the rest of his life. And if he must choose, he prefers greater success in the afterlife compared to the life of this world, knowing the relative duration of this life compared to the hereafter.

# Day 179

Wealth and children are allurements of the life of this world – but the things that endure, good deeds, are best in the sight of your Lord as reward, and best as (the foundation for) hopes.

(18:46)

# Day 179

If a child is asked what he considers success, he will likely answer that success is having a hoard of candy, parents who listen to all his wishes, being allowed to play in the park or with his toys as much as possible, being allowed to stay up past midnight watching television or surfing the internet, and freedom from having to go to school or doing any chores in the house. If an individual who is lacking in faith in God, the Creator of all and the Source of all power, as relayed to us through His noble prophet Muhammad, is asked what he considers success, he will likely answer that success is having a hoard of wealth which can be manifested in a multitude of ways, such as in property, currency, precious metals, etc. Although children are no longer considered an immediate source of wealth in our society as compared to other possessions listed above, they are nevertheless allurements, and a source of immense satisfaction for many.

Like the child who grows up and changes his perception of success as a result, the individual who is blessed with faith in God, the Most Magnificent and the Satisfier of all needs, and His beloved messenger, Muhammad, will have changed his perception of success compared with what it was before having acquired faith. Now the individual with the gift of faith, the most vital ingredient of success, realizes the futility and the transient nature of the things that used to previously give him pleasure; now he realizes his true mission – Who created him, why He created him, and what is expected of him. Now, as a result of his faith, he praises and worships God, the Almighty and the Most Generous, and performs righteous deeds, which pleases his Lord, Who is able to dispense rewards without measure or limitations.

The seeker of success who wishes to reach his goal has complete faith in God, the Source of all that exists, the Distresser and the Reliever, and in His noble messenger, Muhammad. He realizes that the best route to reach his goal is to build a solid foundation of sincere faith in God, the Creator of all, the Most Beneficent and the Most Merciful, and which is manifested by performing righteous deeds as a manifestation of his faith. In this context, he understands that wealth and children are an allurement in this life, but not his end goal.

# Day 180

Say: "Shall we tell you of those who lose most in respect of their deeds?"

"Those whose efforts have been wasted in this life, while they thought that they were acquiring good by their works;

"They are those who deny the signs of their Lord and the fact of their having to meet Him (in the hereafter): Vain will be their works, nor shall We, on the Day Judgment, give them any weight.

"That is their reward, hell - because they rejected faith, and took My signs and My messengers by way of jest.

"As for those who believe and work righteous deeds, they have, for their entertainment, the gardens of paradise,

"Wherein they shall dwell (forever): no change will they wish for themselves".

(18:103-108)

# Day 180

Knowing what one needs to do to successfully accomplish one's mission is important. Equally important is the knowledge of what one needs to avoid in order to successfully accomplish his mission. In the beautiful selected passage of today, the seeker of success will find an excellent summary of what needs to be done and what needs to be avoided to be able to reach his goal.

The characteristics of the worst failures in this life are listed in detail: these are they who deny the signs of their Lord, although they witness them throughout the day – from their ability to arise from the relative death, i.e. arising from sleep every morning, to the predictability of the daily sunrise, to their ability to think, hear and see – all thanks to God, Who is the Creator of all that exists, and the source of all power and goodness. Therefore, those who are ungrateful – denying all the gifts they receive from their Lord – are classified as the worst losers; all the work that they do, whether to satisfy themselves or others (including Satan), they will have received their rewards from those sources, so their actions in this life will count for nothing in the hereafter. Indeed, these are the worst losers, and they will have a fitting reward such as those who receive punishment for treason in this life. They shall be punished with hell, because in their arrogance and treachery they rejected faith, and took the numerous and apparent signs of their Lord and His messengers by way of ridicule. They will wish that they never had existed.

Also mentioned in the beautiful selected passage of today are those characteristics of people who are successful – both in this life and the hereafter: These are they who acknowledge the Beneficence, Generosity, and Awesome Power of God, based on His signs everywhere in existence, praising Him sincerely, and performing righteous deeds as a result of their faith and their desire to worship and serve their Lord. Because their righteous deeds were for Him Who is the Creator of all and Master of the Day of Judgment, it is these deeds that shall have merit on the Day of Judgment – and for those who have attained lasting success, there will be a fitting reward – all that they shall desire for entertainment in gardens of paradise, wherein they shall dwell forever, amply pleased with their reward for their struggle in life and for faithfully serving Him Who is the Creator of all and the Most Praiseworthy; they will wish no change for themselves.

The seeker of success who wishes to reach his goal has absolute faith in God, the Most Righteous Teacher, the Most Generous, and the Best Rewarder of thankfulness, and in His beloved messenger, Muhammad. He is grateful to his Lord for His countless blessings, which he appreciates from the time he wakes up to the time he goes to sleep daily. He praises and worships his Lord as a result of his appreciation and awe of Him, and performs righteous deeds as a result of his faith.

# Day 181

**Say: "If the ocean were ink (wherewith to write out) the words of my Lord – sooner would the ocean be exhausted than would the words of my Lord, even if We added another ocean like it, for its aid".**

(18:109)

# Day 181

    Although short, the beautiful selected passage of today is yet quite comprehensive in addressing the characteristics of God, the Most Supreme and the Only One, to whom Belongs all praise and worship, to Whom is the return of all, and Who is Most Just and Most Wise.

    No matter how many, or how intense the praises, they are not enough to adequately address the Greatness, Benevolence, and the Majesty of He Who created all that exists, gave it order, and sustains and nourishes His creation. In terms of vocabulary, all languages are lacking, due to having a finite number of words and adjectives to address God's greatness. In terms of attempting to describe God Who is the Almighty, the Creator of all that exists, and the Only One, even if we were to utilize words, despite the limitations posed by vocabulary, and even if the ocean were ink (for the pen or the electronic printer) and we were to utilize it to write out the words describing and praising God, the Most Praiseworthy and Most Holy, sooner would the ocean be exhausted than would the words of God, the Most Magnificent and the Source of all that exists, even if another ocean like it were added for its aid.

    The seeker of success who wishes to reach his goal has unwavering faith in God, the Most Great, the Creator and Sustainer of all and the Most Praiseworthy, and in His noble messenger, Muhammad. He appreciates the Magnificence of his Lord in all of existence, seeing His Perfection, Love, Wisdom, and Power in the entire existence – and as a result of his faith, praises and worships Him, performing righteous deeds as a manifestation of his faith and for the desire to please Him, knowing that he is limited by language, resources, and intelligence in fully praising God Who is the Creator of all and the Most Great, and yet he is not hindered in praising, worshipping and serving Him - Who is also the Most Glorious, the Eternal, and the Only One to Whom belongs all praise, to the best of his capability, and does so profusely.

# Day 182

**Say: "I am but a man like yourselves, (but) the inspiration has come to me, that your God is One God. Whoever expects to meet his Lord, let him work righteousness, and, in the worship of his Lord, admit no one as partner".**

(18:110)

# Day 182

    The beautiful selected passage of today contains two valuable messages reinforcing the basic essentials and foundations of lasting success for the benefit of the seeker of success to help him reach his goal. The first valuable message that is one of the basic essentials and the foundation of lasting success mentioned in the beautiful selected passage of today for the benefit of the seeker of success is the realization and faith that God, the Most Beneficent and Most Merciful, is One; in addition to the countless signs of God's presence to explain this assertion - including the creation and control of the planets and matter, the production of the grains and fruits from the dead earth to nourish us, and the intricate coordination of the billions of cells in our bodies, we are relying on the acceptance of the message of an individual who was in his life extremely trustworthy, honorable and upright, even before being selected for prophethood: The beloved prophet Muhammad. God, the Most Great and Most Wise, selected the noble and upright Muhammad to relay His message to mankind, as He had done with the prophets of older times, which is recorded in the Holy Quran, with the noble prophet Muhammad being designated as the seal of prophethood, through whom God, the Most Wise and Most Powerful, has perfected the religion of man and given it the most appropriate name of Islam, i.e. submission (to God, Most Great and the Creator of all), and has completed His favor on mankind by providing them with the Best Guidance to be able to succeed. This is the leap of faith that the seeker of success who wishes to reach his goal is proud to take, and that he is certain of – as certain as the fact that he expects the sun to rise from the east the following day and to set in the west, as long God wills it, Who Created All and is the Most Reliable One.

    The second valuable message that is one of the basic essentials and foundations of lasting success in the beautiful selected passage of today for the benefit of the seeker of success is that, as a result of his faith as described above, he should manifest his faith with corresponding action, including praise and worship of God, the Almighty and the Source of all creation, and performance of righteous deeds, expecting to meet his Lord, the Almighty, the Originator and the Restorer, and to be held accountable for his actions, and hoping for the Mercy and forgiveness from his Lord, the Most Merciful and the Most Generous- for he is aware that, despite his best effort, man is short of perfection.

    The seeker of success who wishes to reach his goal has complete faith in God, the Only One, the One deserving of all praise and worship, and Eternal, and in His beloved messenger, Muhammad. He realizes that worshipping and serving anyone other than God, the Most Pure and the Only One, including his own ego, is counterproductive to his goal of lasting success. And in the worship of his Lord, he admits no one as partner. He works righteous deeds as a manifestation of his faith.

# Day 183

**And Allah does advance in Guidance those who seek guidance. And the things that endure – good deeds, are best in the sight of your Lord, as rewards, and best in respect of (their) eventual returns.**

(19:76)

# Day 183

    The beautiful selected passage of today contains two powerful messages that the seeker of success needs to understand to help him to be able to reach his goal. The first is the knowledge that the source of all advancement and change is within man himself, and that the first step must be taken by him for any change to occur. The specific example given in the beautiful selected passage of today is the gift of guidance from God, the All-aware, the Most Wise and the Best Guide. For those who take the first step and seek guidance, they will be rewarded with increase in guidance from God, the Most Magnificent and the Best Rewarder. And the increase in guidance will strengthen the seeker of success, transforming his aspirations into reality – of achieving maximal success, now and forever.

    The second powerful message in the beautiful selected passage of today that the seeker of success needs to understand to help him reach his goal can be understood in terms of sound investment advice for optimal returns – provided for everyone's benefit, from God, the Almighty, the Best Appraiser, and the Most Righteous Teacher. Man is advised in the beautiful selected passage of today about concentrating on accumulating things that endure. Of the things that man values, there is no mention of wealth, fame, power, family, or other things that are markers of success for those who value the life of this world. Man is instructed by God, the Most Great, and the All-comprehending One, that good deeds are the things that endure, and are best in God's view as worthy of being rewarded, and best in respect to their eventual returns.

    The seeker of success who wishes to reach his goal has absolute faith in God, the Most Great, the Best Guide and the Most Righteous Teacher, and in His noble messenger, Muhammad. He understands that wisdom is not automatically instilled in him, and he must take the first step towards attaining it. He realizes that good deeds that are performed for the pleasure of one's ego, or the pleasure of someone else other than God, the All-hearing and the All-seeing and the Most Appreciative One, one would already have been recompensed in the worldly life – and only those good deeds done as a result of faith in God, the Most Beneficent and Most Generous, and to serve Him are worthy of being rewarded by Him in the hereafter, and which yield optimal returns.

# Day 184

**Allah: there is no god but He!**
**To Him belong the most beautiful names.**

(20:8)

# Day 184

The beautiful selected passage of today is an excellent example that the most important information is best summarized in the shortest form, is more eloquent than the longer discourses, and is best retained by the greatest numbers of people, with the greatest effect.

The powerful message of the beautiful selected passage of today is, in the humble opinion of the author, the most important message of the entire Holy Quran; it is also the most vital component of faith and belief in God, the Living and the Eternal One, which is the first step and the essential foundation of all lasting success. With the correct understanding of the powerful message of the beautiful selected passage of today, one will be able to fulfill what he was created for, i.e. to worship and serve Him Who created all that exists and sustains it. Without an understanding or knowledge of this most vital information, one is restricted to serving the short-term interests of either oneself or others, and therefore doomed for failure. One must understand that everything in existence depends entirely on God, Who is the All-powerful and the Only Self-sustaining One in existence. The esteemed reader is referred to the commentary of Day 3 of this collection of meditations for a more detailed discussion of worship.

The beginning portion of the beautiful selected passage of today, as described above, is reinforcement of the knowledge essential for the seeker of success, and which is repeated elsewhere in the Holy Quran for maximal benefit. However, the latter portion of the beautiful selected passage of today gives it unmatched eloquence and beauty – to dispel all the misconceptions and doubts of any sincere heart that is confused and has not yet been blessed with the gift of faith, the most vital ingredient of lasting success. In it, we find the reason why all that exists praises and worships God: for He is the source of all that exists and the source of all that is good. Therefore, the most beautiful names belong to God Alone, Who has brilliantly informed us in the Holy Quran, of His beautiful ninety nine names, which help us in providing him with the degree of praise he is most deserving of.

The seeker of success who wishes to reach his goal has unwavering faith in God, the Source of all creation and the Only One deserving of praise, and in His beloved messenger, Muhammad. He praises, worships, and performs righteous deeds as a manifestation of his faith and love for God, and Whose most beautiful names are listed below.

## The Ultimate Guide to Success

| | | | |
|---|---|---|---|
| 1. **Allah:** the Greatest Name of all | 26. The Humiliator | 51. The Witness | 76. The Manifest |
| 2. The Most Beneficent | 27. The All-hearing | 52. The Truth | 77. The Hidden |
| 3. The Most Merciful | 28. The All-seeing | 53. The Tustee | 78. The Governor |
| 4. The King | 29. The Judge | 54. The Possessor of all strength | 79. The Supreme One |
| 5. The Holy | 30. The Most Just | 55. The Most Forceful One | 80. The Best Doer of good |
| 6. The Source of Peace | 31. The Most Gracious | 56. The Protecting Friend | 81. The Most Relenting |
| 7. The Guardian of Faith | 32. The All-aware | 57. The Most Praiseworthy | 82. The Avenger |
| 8. The Protector | 33. The Most Forbearing | 58. The Best Appraiser | 83. The Forgiver |
| 9. The Almighty | 34. The Most Magnificent | 59. The Originator | 84. The Clement |
| 10. The Compeller | 35. The Forgiver and Hider of faults | 60. The Restorer | 85. The Owner of all sovereignty |
| 11. The Greatest | 36. The Most Appreciative | 61. The Giver of life | 86. The Lord of all majesty and honor |
| 12. The Creator | 37. The Most High | 62. The Taker of life | 87. The Equitable |
| 13. The Maker of order | 38. The Greatest | 63. The Living | 88. The Gatherer |
| 14. The Shaper of beauty | 39. The Preserver | 64. The Self-Existing | 89. The Rich One |
| 15. The Forgiving | 40. The Nourisher | 65. The Finder | 90. The Enricher |
| 16. The Subduer | 41. The Best of those who keep account | 66. The Most Glorious | 91. The Preventer of harm |
| 17. The Giver of all | 42. The Majestic | 67. The Only One | 92. The Distressor |
| 18. The Provider | 43. The Most Generous | 68. The Indivisible | 93. The Creator of good |
| 19. The Giver of Victory | 44. The Watchful | 69. The Eternal | 94. The Light |
| 20. The All-knowing | 45. The Responder to prayer | 70. The All-powerful | 95. The Guide |
| 21. The Constrictor | 46. The Omnipresent | 71. The Creator of all power | 96. The Incomparable One |
| 22. The Reliever | 47. The Most Wise | 72. The Expediter | 97. The Everlasting One |
| 23. The Abaser | 48. The Most Loving | 73. The Delayer | 98. The Inheritor of all |
| 24. The Exalter | 49. The Most Majestic | 74. The First | 99. The Most Righteous Teacher |
| 25. The Bestower of honor | 50. The Resurrector | 75. The Last | 100. The Most Patient One |

# Day 185

Certainly, he who comes to his Lord as a sinner (at Judgment) – for him is hell; therein shall he neither die nor live.

But as for those who come to Him as believers who have worked righteous deeds – for them are ranks exalted:

Gardens of eternity, beneath which flow rivers; they will dwell therein forever – such is the reward of those who purify themselves (from evil).

(20:74-76)

# Day 185

    Repetition of key points serves to reinforce the essential information the teacher considers is needed by the student for a better grasp of the subject matter for successful outcome on the examination, and is a sign of the concern of the teacher in helping the student with the above goal in mind. God, the Most Kind, the Most Righteous Teacher and the Best Guide, reinforces for man the details about the possible two outcomes for each individual in the beautiful selected passage of today, to guide him toward the better outcome.

    Of the two available options for men, one is to live a life of aimlessness, concerned about the greatest amount of pleasure in the shortest time possible, without a concern for the future, ignoring one's responsibility in relation to God, Who created all and sustains it, and denying the signs present everywhere that point towards Him – for fear of the loss of short-term pleasures. The actions of this group of individuals reflect their lack of faith in God, the Apparent, the Hidden and the All-encompassing One, such that their actions are aimed at maximizing short-term pleasure without regard to long-term consequences, similar to that of a drug addict or a thief. These are the individuals who come to their Lord, the Creator, Restorer and Gatherer, as sinners – for them is hell, a place for suffering long-term pain for their sins, which were committed while they were preoccupied with the short-term pleasures in life. Therein they shall neither die nor live, but continue to suffer. If one is concerned with the severity of punishment described above, he should consider the severity of offenses and sins. Even in the life of this world, with the limited intelligence and sense of justice or wisdom in man, there are severe penalties for crimes committed to finance one's addiction to drugs, dereliction of duty, and treason. God, in His infinite Wisdom, Mercy, and Justice, has decreed that those guilty of the highest offenses – refusing to carry out their duties for which they were created, working against the One Who created and nourishes them, and refusing to recognize His Authority – shall have a special place set aside for a fitting punishment consistent with the severity of offenses. This place is known as hell. And God is Most Wise, Most Merciful and Most Just. The other option available for men – and much better for them – is to recognize the Power and Greatness of God, manifested in the beauty and perfection in the entire existence, as well as in their own bodies, and to submit to Him and not oppose Him, leading them to praise His greatness and glory out of sincerity, worshipping Him and performing righteous deeds to show their love and faith in God, the Most Glorious and the Most Loving. And for them will be ranks exalted, gardens beneath which flow rivers, to dwell therein forever. Such is the reward of those who purify themselves from evil. The esteemed reader is referred to the commentary of Day 3 of this collection of meditations on a more detailed discussion of worship.

    The seeker of success who wishes to reach his goal has complete faith in God, the Source of all that exists, the Best of those who keep account, the Most Just, the Avenger and the Best Rewarder, and in His noble messenger, Muhammad. He knows the consequences of the two general options for all actions (good versus bad), does his best to avoid the group who are sinners, refusing to be enticed with their short-term pleasures, and does his best to be of that group which is promised the highest rewards from He Who is Almighty, Most Generous and the Most Trustworthy. He knows that God is the Most Merciful and the Best Guide, and seeks guidance and forgiveness from his Lord.

# Day 186

**And without doubt, I am indeed forgiving – to he who repents, believes, and does righteous deeds, and then remains constant in doing them.**

(20:82)

# Day 186

We encounter in the beautiful selected passage of today a concept that is repeated in the Holy Quran for reinforcement, with concern for guiding as many individuals as possible towards success: the infinite Mercy of God, the Almighty and the Most Pure, which is one of the characteristics He most often chooses to describe Himself with in the Holy Quran, and logically, as a result of which, He is also the Most Forgiving.

Suppose that we take the example of a typical individual with any sort of authority in this world, such as a parent, teacher, employer, or a judge, even with the characteristics of selfishness of varying degrees typical of human nature. What is the response of a typical parent to his child when the child knows that he has erred, and asks for forgiveness? What is the response of a typical teacher when the student asks pardon for his limitations and seeks help? What is the response of a typical employer when the employee recognizes that his performance has been suboptimal, but he sincerely desires to do better in the future? What is the response of a typical judge to a criminal who realizes his error and begs for pardon, or at least leniency?

A typical parent knows that it is normal for children to make mistakes and is most willing to forgive; it is usually the child who does not realize his mistakes or seek forgiveness on whom descends the wrath of the parent. A typical teacher knows that the student has inherent limitations in knowledge and is most willing to guide the student who asks. A typical employer knows that no employee is perfect, but that the one who realizes he can perform better and is sincere in his desire is an asset for the organization. A typical judge knows that he is dealing with human beings – and as such, they are prone to imperfections. There are certain crimes that are not pardonable by any judge with the highest degree of mercy – but for the criminal who realizes he has erred and feels sincere remorse and then asks for forgiveness, a typical judge is willing to grant some degree of leniency.

Infinitely more loving than the most loving parent, possessing infinitely more information than the most knowledgeable teacher, infinitely more rich and powerful than any employer, in fact the Most Benevolent Employer of all beings, and Infinitely More Wise and More Just than any judge, God, the Most Beneficent and Most Merciful, instructs the seeker of success who wishes to reach his goal, in the beautiful selected passage of today, to not be despondent over his shortcomings and errors, but to realize that errors have been made, to seek forgiveness from God, the Most Forgiving and the Most Merciful, to repent for the sinful behavior of the past, and to not repeat such behavior again, to continue to have faith in God, the Only One Who is perfect and Who is the Most Forgiving, as relayed to us through His beloved messenger, and to perform righteous deeds as a manifestation of his faith, remaining constant in doing them. Such an individual will find the forgiveness he seeks, the knowledge he requires, and the guidance he needs, to attain lasting success.

The seeker of success who wishes to reach his goal has absolute faith in God, the Creator and Sustainer of all, the Best Guide and the Most Forgiving One, and in His beloved messenger, Muhammad. He does his best to avoid evil, but when he recognizes he has done such, he seeks sincere forgiveness of his Lord, does not repeat such evil again and performs righteous deeds, remaining constant in doing them.

# Day 187

Therefore, be patient with what they say, and celebrate (constantly) the praises of your Lord - before the rising of the sun, and before its setting, and during some hours of the night, and at the sides of the day, that you may be pleased.

And strain not your eyes in longing for the things We have given for enjoyment to various parties of them (disbelievers) - the splendor of the life of this world, through which We test them; but the provision of your Lord is better and more enduring.

Enjoin prayer on your people, and be constant therein - We ask you not to provide sustenance; We provide it for you. But the (fruit of) the hereafter is for the Muttaqun (the pious and righteous persons).

(20:130-132)

# Day 187

The beautiful selected passage of today provides the seeker of success with three valuable methods to help him to achieve his goal - the first of which is to be patient with the disbelievers in God, the Most Great and Most Patient, and what they say. The disbelievers are expected to say things hurtful to the believers who have faith in God, the Most Pure and the Guardian of faith. However, the response of the believers and seekers of success should be that of patience and they should not be incited to discord as the disbelievers hope for.

The second valuable method instructed for the seeker of success by God, the Most Magnificent and the Best Guide, is to celebrate with constancy the praises of God, the Most Glorious and the One deserving of all praise. Specific time periods are prescribed and staggered throughout the day and night for work, socialization, and rest – corresponding with the five obligatory prayers daily. With the sustenance that one needs being provided for by God, the Creator, Nourisher and Sustainer – such as a large variety of grains, fruits, vegetables and meats – man would be ungrateful indeed if he did not praise and thank Him who provides all that he needs. Also, one will be pleased with the regular prayers, both in terms of spiritual joy in this life and with a most handsome reward in the hereafter. Man is encouraged to wish success for others and encouraged to enjoin prayer on others as well.

The third valuable method instructed for the seeker of success by God, the Most Rich and the Most Wise, is not to covet the possessions of others – especially of those lacking faith in God, the Most Beneficent and Most Merciful. The disbelievers, focusing on the enjoyment in the life of this world, will be given what they desire, at the expense of their suffering in the hereafter, and they will be taken further away from the Light and Mercy of Him Who is the Creator and Sustainer of all - which is indeed an unfortunate situation.

The seeker of success who wishes to reach his goal has unwavering faith in God, the Most Exalted, the Source of all goodness, and the Best Guide, and in His noble messenger, Muhammad. He is reassured that what is awaiting the pious and righteous individuals in the hereafter and eternity is better and more enduring than what the enemies of faith are proud to be enjoying in the transient life of this world. He understands the importance of delayed gratification. He hopes to attain good both in this life and in the hereafter, and understands the folly of choosing pleasure in the short term at the expense of pain in the hereafter. He celebrates the praises of his Lord throughout the day, at specified periods, and does not find it more cumbersome than feeding his body at specified periods for its daily nutritional needs.

# Day 188

**My Lord knows (every) word (spoken) in the heavens and on earth; He is One Who hears and knows (all things).**

(21:4)

# Day 188

An appropriate understanding of the beautiful selected passage of today – albeit short, will provide valuable insights into several aspects of success that will help the seeker of success to reach his goal. It also is an excellent example that profound concepts are best understood in simple terms

From a proper understanding of the beautiful selected passage of today, the seeker of success will have his faith strengthened in God, the Most Great, Most Beneficent and Most Merciful, knowing that He Who is the Creator and Sustainer of all, is completely aware of the entire existence and in complete control of it at all times. And with strengthened faith in God, Who is the Most Majestic and Most Glorious, the seeker of success will manifest it with greater devotion by praising and worshipping Him, an increase in desire to serve Him and an increase in performance of righteous deeds as a result - all of which facilitate his likelihood of attaining **lasting success.**

Second, with the knowledge that God, the Most Supreme and the Almighty, is aware of every word spoken in heavens and earth - hearing, seeing and knowing all things that are occurring in the entire existence at all times, one will have a better understanding of how all his actions have relevance at all times, as they are able to be recorded by He Who is the Most Praiseworthy, All-comprehending and the Best of those who keep account, and how one will be held accountable for all his actions on the Day of Judgment. As a result, the seeker of success who wishes to reach his goal again performs an increase in righteous deeds, knowing that every moment of his life is valuable.

Finally, with the knowledge that God, the Possessor of all strength and the Source of all power, is aware of the entire existence at all times, the seeker of success who wishes to reach his goal realizes that he does not need an intermediary, such as a priest, to inform about his needs to God, the Creator of all, Most Wise and the All-aware, and that if he wishes for any change in his life or this world, that he should initiate the change starting with himself first.

The seeker of success who wishes to reach his goal has complete faith in God, the All-Hearing, All-Seeing and All-Aware, and in His beloved messenger, Muhammad. He knows that every moment of his life is of importance, and his words and actions at every moment of his life are heard and seen by God, and will either help him to achieve his goal – which is being saved from hell-fire and living in peace and security for eternity – or will take him further away from his goal, by being punished with the hell-fire for eternity.

# Day 189

**Not for idle sport did We create the heavens and the earth and all that is in between!**

**If it had been Our wish to take (just) a pastime, We should surely have taken it from the things nearest to Us, if We would do (such a thing).**

(21:16-17)

# Day 189

    Aimlessness, lack of purpose in one's life, and unawareness of what is required from one during his life in this world are common reasons that not only prevent individuals from attainment of lasting success, but often lead to deviance, hedonism and self-destructive behavior. And being unaware of the rule of law in one's physical domain does not absolve one from the penalty of not following the rule of law, unless it is that one is impaired in his mental faculties.

    In the beautiful selected passage of today, man is informed by God, the Most Great, the Most Wise and the Most Righteous Teacher, that the creation of the heavens and the earth and the entire existence is not meaningless or only a coincidence. Although the reason for the creation of man and all that exists by God, the Creator and Sustainer of all, is discussed elsewhere in the Holy Quran (including what role he is expected to play and what he can do to succeed), the individual who acquires the knowledge from the beautiful selected passage of today that there is a purpose behind the creation of the entire existence, including that of his own creation, will have gained valuable information that will serve him well. In case an unfortunate individual believes that the creation of all existence is a meaningless pastime of God, the Creator of all, the Almighty and the Most Wise, then he is instructed that if God, the Sublime and the Most Magnificent wished to take a pastime, it would not involve things that man is most familiar with, but something nearest to Him, which we are presently unaware of, with our limited senses. **<u>Those who are fortunate to have achieved the highest degree of success will be most pleased to find themselves nearest to God, the Truth and the Best Rewarder, for eternity.</u>**

    The seeker of success who wishes to reach his goal has absolute faith in God, the Unique, the Self-sufficient and the Everlasting, and in His noble messenger, Muhammad. He realizes that there is a reason behind all of creation, including himself; knowing that all his time in this world is valuable, he lives every moment attempting to fulfill the duties he was created to perform by God, the Creator of all that exists, the Maker of order, the Bestower of honors, and the Humiliator. The esteemed reader is advised to refer to other meditations in this collection to review further details on the reason man was created by God, the Most Holy and the Most praiseworthy - which includes to praise and worship Him, and specifically to the commentary of Day 3 of this collection for a more detailed discussion of worship.

# Day 190

**Do not the unbelievers see that the heavens and the earth were joined together (as one unit of creation), before We clove them asunder? We made from water every living thing – will they not believe?**

(21:30)

# Day 190

    Directed at the unfortunate individuals lacking the most important prerequisite for attaining success, i.e. faith and belief in God, the Originator and the Creator of all that exists, there is an intensity and depth of power, beauty, truth and eloquence in the beautiful selected passage of today, that will be effective in guiding the most obstinate critic and skeptic to shed his ignorance and arrogance – guiding him from darkness into light, and setting him on the path to success. For the fortunate individual who already possesses the gift of faith, the beautiful selected passage of today will serve to increase its intensity and increase his enthusiasm, which will greatly help him on his journey to success.

    Two of the most advanced observations in science on the origins of the earth, planets, space and the origins of life – and only accepted relatively recently are 1) that all planets and entire existence as we know it in our universe occurred from a single origin, termed as the big bang theory, and 2) that water is an absolute requirement for the origin of life. To expect an illiterate resident of the desert fourteen hundred years ago – however noble and upright, such as the beloved prophet Muhammad, to have knowledge of what is only known to us recently, would be impossible except under the revelation of Himself, Who is the Creator of all, the Giver and Taker of life, and the Restorer.

    The seeker of success who wishes to reach his goal has unwavering faith in God, the Originator, the First and the Last, and in His beloved messenger, Muhammad. He marvels at the entire existence and the heavens and the earth that were joined together at one time before being cloven asunder by God, the Source of all power, and the Creator of all that exists, and at the beauty and miracle in every living thing – made by water. And in his awe of the Magnificence and Perfection of He Who clove asunder the heavens and earth to precision, and made all living things from water, he offers throughout his existence, sincere praise and worship as a result of his faith, performing righteous deeds.

# Day 191

**Every soul shall have a taste of death – and We test you by evil and by good by way of trial; to Us you must return.**

(21:35)

# Day 191

The beautiful selected passage of today is short but contains concepts that are vital and are foundations of lasting success; in it, the seeker of success will find three valuable messages that will help him to reach his goal - the first of which is the knowledge that every individual will have a taste of death; this knowledge is important for the proper understanding of the remaining portion of the beautiful selected passage of today. In fact, everything in existence is to perish – and only He will remain Who created all and sustains it.

The second valuable message in the beautiful selected passage of today that will help the seeker of success to reach his goal is the knowledge that his life in this world is a trial or test, and that he will be tested by good and evil. At various stages in one's life, man expends varying degrees of effort in passing various tests in life for increasing benefits in this world. The individual who aspires for success expends proportionate effort in all his tests – the successful individual realizes that his most important test is life itself, and his ability to consistently choose good over evil.

The third valuable message in the beautiful selected passage of today that will help the seeker of success to reach his goal is the knowledge that, having experienced death at the end of his test in life, man is to return to God, the Restorer and the Reckoner, Who will inform him about his performance in the test of life and reward or punish him accordingly. With this knowledge, the seeker of success will be able to utilize his time on earth most wisely for optimal gains from his actions and how he chooses to spend his life.

The seeker of success who wishes to reach his goal has complete faith in God, the Originator, the Giver and Taker of life, and the Best Judge, and in His noble messenger, Muhammad. He lives every moment of his life knowing its cumulative importance. He prepares and performs in the exam of life to the best of his ability, always keeping in mind the instructions and the preferences of his Evaluator, Who will evaluate his performance in life. He knows that life is a test in which he must not fail, and expends the proportionate effort in passing this most important test.

# Day 192

**We shall set up scales of justice for the Day of Judgment, so that not a soul shall be dealt with unjustly in the least. And if there be (no more than) the weight of a mustard seed, we will bring it (to account). And enough are We to take account.**

(21:47)

# Day 192

The topic of reflection for today's meditation on success is best considered as continuous from yesterday's topic, where we reviewed the importance of the realization of life as a test. Having made the appropriate choices in the examination of life to the best of one's knowledge, effort, and ability, one anxiously awaits the result of his examination, and hopes to have passed or succeeded.

Even with considerable effort in man-made examinations, there are usually some limitations that render the scoring to be disadvantageous and unfair, at least to some of the examinees. However, in regards to the most important examination that all individuals take, i.e. the examination of life itself, we are reassured of the utmost fairness of the grading and tallying of the results on the Day of Judgment, when the scales of justice shall be set up by He Who is All-knowing, All-aware, All-seeing, All-hearing, Most Forbearing, Best of those who keep account, and Most Just, so that not a soul shall be dealt with unjustly in the least. And if there be no more than the weight of a mustard seed (of good or evil performed by an individual), then it will be brought to account. And God is the Best Witness, Most Equitable, able to do all He wishes – without any limitations in keeping the most accurate account.

The seeker of success who wishes to reach his goal has absolute faith in God, the Most Holy and the Most Equitable, and in His beloved messenger, Muhammad. He realizes that in his test of life, every action at every moment is important – either contributing to his success or preventing him from reaching it, depending on his response. He knows that persistent effort, hard work, and attention to detail distinguish between a satisfactory and exemplary performance on all examinations, including the examination of life. He is reassured that his evaluation will be a most fair reflection of his performance in life, by Him Who is Most Merciful, the Best of those who keep account, and Who is the Most Just.

# Day 193

And remember Dhu al Nun (Jonah), when he departed in wrath; he imagined that We had no power over him! But he cried through the depths of darkness, "There is no god but You; glory to You; I was indeed wrong!"

So We listened to him and delivered him from distress. And thus do We deliver those who have faith.

(21:87-88)

# Day 193

A proper understanding of the powerful message of the beautiful selected passage of today will lead to that component of success that has been mentioned several times in this collection of meditations, and many times in the Holy Quran: the capacity to realize one's error and to seek forgiveness from Him Who is the Creator of all, the Most Merciful and the Most Forgiving One. Therefore, we will consider this characteristic of realizing one's error and seeking forgiveness for it, as one of the foundations of lasting success – for the one who has erred, realized his error with sincere repentance, sought and received forgiveness for his error, will not only be freed from punishment for that error on the Day of Judgment, but also be less likely to repeat that error in future, compared to the unfortunate individual who errs, without realizing his error – who will be held accountable for that error on the Day of Judgment, and will continue repeating such errors throughout life.

The example used in the beautiful selected passage of today is that of the noble prophet Jonah, who, in his anger at his people for not accepting his message, wishing for the wrath of God, the Most Beneficent and Most Merciful, left his prophetic duties without the permission of his Lord, imagining in error that God, the Most Powerful and the Most Magnificent, was limited in His power. For this, he was punished by being swallowed in whole by a large fish, finding himself in the darkness of the fish's belly. He would have remained in the fish's belly until the Day of Judgment had he not realized his error, crying through the depths of darkness to God, the Most Beneficent and Most Merciful: "There is no god but you: Glory to you. I was indeed wrong!". And it was because of the noble prophet Jonah's faith, in realizing his error, and seeking forgiveness from the Most Forgiving One, that he was forgiven and delivered from distress.

The seeker of success who wishes to reach his goal has unwavering faith in God, the Most Compassionate and Most Forgiving One, and in His noble messenger, Muhammad. He realizes that he is not perfect; he does his best to avoid error - but if an error has been made, he realizes his error, feeling sincere remorse, and asks forgiveness for it from his Lord, and remains vigilant in not repeating such errors in the future.

# Day 194

**Indeed! This brotherhood of yours is a single brotherhood, and I am your Lord and Cherisher. Therefore, serve Me (and no others).**

(21:92)

# Day 194

    The beautiful selected passage of today is directed at both the individual and collective level, and its importance and strength lies in associating the most important component of success, i.e. faith and belief in God, the Creator and Nourisher of all, as relayed to us through His beloved messenger, Muhammad, at both the individual and collective level. There are two important messages in the beautiful selected passage of today to help the seeker of success to reach his goal - the first of which is directed at the collective level. Clearly, the collective effort of a group benefits every single member of the group, with significantly greater outcome for each member compared to the situation where each individual expends individual effort rather than as a member of a group. Those individuals desiring lasting success, starting with the most important common denominator for each member of the group and also its most important component, i.e. faith and belief in God, the Creator of all and the Most Supreme, as relayed to mankind through His honorable prophets Abraham, David, Solomon, John, Jesus, and ending with Muhammad (the seal of prophethood), are instructed to consider themselves as a single brotherhood, with the outcome for each member being significantly greater, compared to his individual effort. Therefore, minor variations of different members need to be accommodated for the greater benefit of the entire group, as long as the basic premise of faith and the greatest asset of the seeker of success, is not compromised.

    The second important message in the beautiful selected passage of today to help the seeker of success to reach his goal is directed both at the individual and collective level (of the brotherhood of believers): The manifestation of one's faith, with all of one's actions being for the sole purpose of serving Him Alone Who is the Creator of all, and the Only One to Whom belongs all praise and worship. Actions performed for any other reason than to serve God, the All-hearing and All-seeing, will not be considered for reward on the Day of Judgment, as their reward would already have been attained in the life of this world, depending on whose pleasure it was performed for.

    The seeker of success who wishes to reach his goal has complete faith in God, the Almighty, the Best Guide, and the Most Generous, and in His beloved messenger, Muhammad. He knows he is a part of the brotherhood united by faith - and from which he is strengthened as well as being a source of strength for others. He serves none other than God, the Most Holy, and He to Whom belongs all praise.

# Day 195

**Whoever works any act of righteousness and has faith – his endeavor will not be rejected; We shall record it in his favor.**

(21:94)

# Day 195

The seeker of success who has been reviewing the earlier meditations in this collection, will recognize that the beautiful selected passage of today contains concepts that have been reviewed earlier. However, as previously mentioned, repetition of key points by a teacher is appreciated by the students who hope to pass their examination, and repetition of key points in the Holy Quran by God, the Almighty, the Best Guide and the Most Righteous Teacher, is sincerely appreciated by the seekers of lasting success who wish to reach their goal.

The first key point of success reinforced in the beautiful selected passage of today is the importance of having faith in God, the Creator and Sustainer of all, recognizing His presence, power, and benevolence in the entire existence, and everywhere he turns, and, as a manifestation of one's faith, performing acts of righteousness, recognizing that to be one's duty, together with praising and worshipping God and expressing one's love for Him. If the seeker of success takes away this one point from this collection of meditations, the humble author will be pleased with his effort by the Grace of God, the Most Beneficent, the Most Merciful and the Only One Deserving of all praise.

The second key point of success reinforced in the beautiful selected passage of today is the awareness that the process of acquiring, manifesting, and sustaining faith – with performance of righteous deeds as described above – is an endeavor requiring continuous effort and struggle, in the face of opposition from forces as varied as one's ego, the enemies of faith and their patron, the accursed Satan, who is the avowed enemy of men, and of particularly those on the path of success.

The third key point of success reinforced in the beautiful selected passage of today is that every moment of one's life in this world is valuable and must not be wasted, as one's entire life is an examination, with every action being recorded as either in one's favor or against him by God, the All-aware and the Best of those who keep account, with the results to be announced on the Day of Judgment – the consequence of which is lasting success for those who have passed, and long-term pain and suffering for those who have failed, in the most important examination of life.

The seeker of success who wishes to reach his goal has unwavering faith in God, the Most Great, the All-knowing, the Reckoner and the Most Generous One, and in His noble messenger, Muhammad. He performs righteous deeds as a manifestation of his faith throughout his life. He is certain of the Day of Judgment and prepares for it accordingly.

# Day 196

**We sent you (O Muhammad) not, but as a mercy for all creatures.**

(21:107)

# Day 196

As we noted earlier, concepts of varying intensity, especially those of extreme importance, are best relayed in the simplest terms, so as to be understood and retained by as many as possible, rather than in complex terms, which can be understood by few and retained by even fewer individuals. The ability to relay complex ideas into simple terms is the sign of an effective teacher. The beautiful selected passage of today is an example of one of the most important ingredients for attainment of success being relayed to us by God, the Most Wise and the Most Righteous Teacher, and explaining the importance of the noble prophet Muhammad, for the benefit of the seeker of success; being directed, in effect, from a life of pointless existence, to one which is lived for the sake of God, the Creator and Sustainer of all that exists, and thus being directed to long-term success from impending failure, by submitting oneself to God, by living a life of submission to Him Who gave him life and nourishes him. The medium through which this most important foundation of success is laid, i.e. faith, is delivered to us through the noble prophet Muhammad, and who is thus rightly designated as a mercy to the worlds

In fact, recognition of the honorable prophet Muhammad as the messenger of God, the One and the Only One, through whom God selected to convey the much needed Guidance for mankind, is a requirement for the attainment of faith, the primary component of success, and which then confers on the fortunate individual the esteemed title of one who submits himself to the service of God, the Creator and Sustainer of all that exists, i.e. Muslim. The fortunate individual so endowed with faith will manifest it with praise and worship of his Lord, along with performance of other good deeds, which are not done for any selfish motives - except for the love of God, the Most Loving and the Most Appreciative One, which is the currency in the afterlife and is the primary basis on which an individual's degree of success will be gauged

The seeker of success who wishes to reach his goal has unwavering faith in God, the Most Pure One and the Ruler with absolute authority, and in His beloved messenger, Muhammad, who was sent from God as a mercy to guide all creatures to praise, worship, and serve God, the Creator of all that exists, Who gave everything in existence its form and order, and Who is the Most Righteous Guide and Teacher, so that we can all attain the highest form of everlasting success.

# Day 197

**Allah will admit those who believe and work righteous deeds, to gardens beneath which rivers flow - they shall be adorned therein with bracelets of gold and pearls; and their garments there will be of silk.**

(22:23)

# Day 197

An effective communication is one in which the important concepts will not only be presented - but repeated, to make sure the audience grasps the message, as well as understands its importance. Because God is Most Kind and Most Caring and wants man to succeed, He has provided clear guidance to all men through the noble prophet Muhammad in the Holy Quran, and has repeated the important concepts, as can be gauged by their repetition both in the Holy Quran and in this collection of meditations, albeit in varying format, so that they could be understood as being important, and so that all individuals can succeed.

As the Best Communicator of all, God, the Best Guide and the Best Teacher, has repeated many times and in many ways the key ingredients for success in the Holy Quran: faith in God, the Bestower of all honors and the Humiliator, as relayed to us through His noble messenger, Muhammad. The man who lacks faith can be compared to a fish or the bird, for whom the goals for each day will be mostly predictable: eat as much as possible of whatever is found, stay safe, and choose the option that provides immediate pleasure instead of pain, whenever possible. However, the man who has faith in God, the Originator, Sustainer, and Resurrector, recognizes the reason for his existence and, as a result, manifests his faith with sincere praise, thankfulness and worship of his Creator, the Maker of order and the Owner of all, along with other good acts, as a result of his faith. The man who has faith and does good deeds has mastered the key to success and will be rewarded with the best rewards by God, the Truth and the Best Enricher, for his efforts in life by being admitted to eternal paradise, with gardens beneath which rivers flow, and being adorned therein with garments of silk and bracelets of gold and pearls: a beautiful resting place indeed and an appropriate reward for fulfilling one's duties for which he was created.

The seeker of success who wishes to reach his goal has faith in God, the Creator of all that exists, the Most Compassionate, the Most Rich and the Most Generous, and in His noble messenger, Muhammad. He praises and worships his Lord with humility and awe, along with performance of righteous acts, as a manifestation of his faith.

# Day 198

...And your god is One God. Submit then your wills to Him (in Islam). And give the good news to those who humble themselves –

To those whose hearts, when Allah is mentioned, are filled with fear, who show patient perseverance over their afflictions, keep up regular prayer, and spend (in charity) out of what We have bestowed upon them.

(22:34 -35)

# Day 198

Most of the actions of animals are reflexive in nature: sleeping, waking up, escaping from predators, attacking prey, reproducing, protecting family members, and being hostile or indifferent to others outside the family, or from whom the individual will not benefit. Conversely, most of the actions of humans require forethought, having a purpose behind them – although some reflexive patterns can also be seen. The purpose behind most actions in man is most often to benefit himself, and to a lesser extent, to benefit one's family, race, employer, community, city or country. The beautiful selected passage of today empowers the seeker of success by guiding him to the key to success, i.e. belief in God, Who created everything in existence and sustains it, and submitting one's will to Him, as relayed to us through His noble messenger, Muhammad - so that all his actions are thenceforth primarily for the pleasure of God, the Best of those who keep account and He Who will reward or punish one's actions accordingly.

Specific actions arising from faith and submission of One's will to God, Who created all and to Whom everyone will return for judgment, are listed below to further empower the seeker of success to be able to reach his goals, after having attained faith, the key to success:

- ✓ To have knowledge that one is accountable for all his actions to God, the Most Beneficent and Most Merciful, so that when He is mentioned, his heart is filled with fear.

- ✓ To be patient during afflictions and persevere during these times on the path to success.

- ✓ To keep up regular prayer, which is the highest on the list of good actions one can perform, and key to continuously reminding oneself of God, the Most Holy and Most Kind, so that all actions are for His pleasure.

- ✓ To spend in charity out of what God, the Most Generous and Most Caring, has bestowed upon man – because as the vicegerent of God, the Most Loving and the Most Appreciative One, man is closely exhibiting God's characteristics when he is providing to others for no reason other than to help them, and thereby is increased in standing and closeness to Him Who created all that exists and sustains it.

The seeker of success who wishes to reach his goal has absolute faith in God, the Most Glorious and the Most Generous, and in His beloved messenger, Muhammad. He submits his will to his Lord with earnestness and humility, with his heart filled with fear when the name of God, the Most Majestic and the Almighty is mentioned, shows patient perseverance during hardships throughout his life, keeps up regular prayer, and spends in charity from what is bestowed on him by his Lord, Who is the Best Provider and the Most Generous One.

# Day 199

**It is not their (sacrificial animals') meat, nor their blood, that reaches Allah: it is your piety that reaches Him; He has made them subject to you, that you may glorify Allah for His Guidance to you and proclaim the good news to all who do right.**

(22:37)

# Day 199

In the history of man pertaining to religion, spirituality, and his quest for establishing a connection with the Divine, we find that the rite of animal sacrifice has played a prominent role in most religions and cultures. These days, if we want to please someone, we may invite them to a nice meal or offer them other things that are pleasing to them. As evidenced by a wide variety of similar practices, man has also attempted to please the Divine Source, whom man frequently acknowledged as separate beings rather than different characteristics of the One Indivisible Divine Source, with the primary offering being blood or meat of sacrificial animals.

The beautiful selected passage of today clears the primitive misconceptions and provides the seeker of success with valuable information about what we can offer to please God, the Creator of all that exists and He to Whom belongs all worship and praise. What can be more pleasing to God, the Richest One and Source of all power, than offerings such as fruits, sweets, flowers, money gold, incense, or the meat and blood of sacrificial animals? God, the Most Wise, and the One who is All-aware, is informing the seeker of success what man can do to gain His favor: offer Him something more valuable than any of the things mentioned above, including the meat and blood of the sacrificial animals - something which requires significantly more effort than providing the above-mentioned things, and which involves having to say no to one's ego and baser instructs, foregoing instant or short-term gratification for the love, consciousness, and fear of God, the Lord of all majesty and goodness and the Most Appreciative One, i.e. ***piety.*** We are informed in the beautiful selected passage of today from God Himself, the Most Glorious and the Source of all that exists, that of all the things man can offer Him, that **it is man's piety which reaches Him and which is important to Him.** Good news is proclaimed to the seeker of success who understands the valuable message and gift from the beautiful selected passage of today and glorifies God, the Most Trustworthy and Most Generous for His guidance and innumerable gifts, including the very valuable message of today.

The seeker of success who wishes to reach his goal has unwavering faith in God the Most Holy and the Master of the Day of Judgment, and in His noble messenger, Muhammad. He realizes that things like blood, meat, or other things valuable to humans, are not what pleases God, the Most High and the Source of all that exists, but rather man's piety or love, consciousness, and fear of Him - and on which his actions are based; and he Glorifies his Lord with utmost sincerity and awe.

# Day 200

**Certainly, Allah will defend (from ill) those who believe; certainly, Allah loves not any who is a traitor to faith, or shows ingratitude.**

(22:38)

# Day 200

There are many types of beliefs – both past and present. One of the most prevalent beliefs, from pre-historic times to the present, is that the amount of strength one has, determines one's success and happiness. Another belief is that the presence of matter, orderliness, existence, and life, is a coincidence. Another belief is that since man is the most intelligent creature known to us, then he is capable of designing and maintaining the best rules on earth. Another belief is that the accumulation of most wealth is the object of life. And yet another belief is that one should do whatever makes him feel good, and this should be the objective of life.

In contrast to the many beliefs mentioned above, there is a belief that the world, universe, and life is not a matter of chance, but designed to perfection by God, the One Who is Perfect, Most Generous, and Most Loving, for the purpose of praising, worshipping, and serving Him. And further, this belief holds that God, the Most Beneficent and the Best Guide, would not revel in the failure of His creatures to fulfill their duties, but sent His guidance through various prophets, based on need, and perfecting it through the prophethood of His noble servant and messenger, Muhammad. Those who hold this belief or faith have submitted themselves to the will of God, the Most Magnificent and Creator of all that exists, and not to their baser self or to any others except Him, and call themselves Muslim: This is the most important ingredient needed for the ultimate success.

Those who continue to enjoy the countless blessings of God, the Most Praiseworthy and the Most Generous, such as light, air, water, and their own bodies and minds, without acknowledging, praising, or thanking Him, can be considered to be exhibiting the characteristic of ingratitude, and can be considered traitors for serving others than the One who so lovingly and generously created them and everything else in existence and sustains them. This is mentioned so that, perchance, these unfortunate individuals can be empowered also with faith - for God, the Most Kind and Most Generous, wants all to succeed.

Historically, we see that even though there are many different beliefs as described above, many individuals and groups feel threatened by those who believe in God, the Most Loving and Eternal, and His Guidance through the noble prophet Muhammad, while others have made it difficult for the believers to practice their faith - from Islam's earliest days to the present. The beautiful selected passage of today provides reassurance to the seeker of success to hold onto his most important possession, i.e. faith, for God Himself promises to defend him. And who can be more reliable than the One Who created all that exists, and without Whose permission nothing can occur, including the falling of a single leaf.

The seeker of success who wishes to reach his goal has complete faith in God, the Most Great, the Best Friend and Protector, and the Best Guide, and in His beloved messenger, Muhammad. He is thankful to his Lord for his faith and the countless blessings provided to him, including that of sight, hearing, feelings, Guidance from Him, and the faculty of distinguishing right from wrong. He exhibits gratitude, love and loyalty to his Lord, not ingratitude; and nor is he a traitor to Him, by refusing to acknowledge and worship and serve Him – and worse, by engaging in acts to prevent others from worshipping and serving God, the Source of peace and the Guardian of faith.

# Day 201

Those who believe and work righteousness – for them
is forgiveness and a sustenance most generous.

But those who strive against Our signs, to
frustrate them – they will be companions of the fire.

(22:50-51)

# Day 201

Parents, naturally concerned for their children, are quite used to repeating over and over again the information they feel is necessary to help their children. The teacher who naturally wants the students to learn the material and pass the examination will reinforce the important points in multiple ways. The manager who wants his employees to succeed will find creative ways to reinforce the important points that will lead his employees towards a positive outcome.

Because God is Most Just, Most Loving and wants all to succeed, He has reinforced the key ingredients of success in numerous ways: Having faith in Him who created everything and sustains His creations, as relayed to us through His noble messenger, Muhammad, and manifesting this belief with praise, worship and work of righteousness. The fortunate individuals who benefit from the ample reinforcement and identification of these important ingredients of success – faith, worship and good deeds – will be rewarded by God, the Most Caring, Most Forgiving, and the Best Teacher, with forgiveness and a sustenance most generous, both in this life and for eternity.

Those individuals who fail to grasp the importance of the key to success of faith, worship and other good acts, as reinforced in many ways by God, the Most Patient and Most Generous, are unfortunate indeed. However, the most unfortunate individuals are not those who fail to grasp the key ingredients of success, i.e. faith and good acts, but those who want to prevent others from succeeding as well by striving against the signs of God, the Compeller and the Most Victorious – for they will be companions of the fire for eternity. The one who has been on the path of error and destruction to now and who has been preventing others from attaining success will recognize himself from the beautiful selected passage of today, desist from such activity in the future, and himself acquire the essential keys to success – faith, worship and righteous acts – by serving Him Who Created all that exists and is the Sustainer of all.

The seeker of success who wishes to reach his goal has absolute faith in God, the Most Forgiving and the Most Generous, and in His noble messenger, Muhammad. He praises his Lord often and worships Him regularly, and performs other righteous acts as a result of his faith. He encourages others to succeed, and realizes the seriousness of preventing others from the path of success by actions such as striving against God, the Source of all that exists, the All-aware, and the Most Strong.

# Day 202

**It is He (Allah) Who gave you life, will cause you to die, and will again give you life. Truly man is a most ungrateful creature.**

(22:66)

# Day 202

We encounter again an example in the beautiful selected passage of today that the most important messages should be relayed in the shortest and simplest form for practicality and maximal benefit. In it, we find four powerful messages that are fundamental components of lasting success - the first of which is an answer to one of the first questions that man should ask himself if he is to live a meaningful life, unlike the other life forms in creation: "Who am I?" and "How did I get here?". The answer is clearly provided in the beginning portion of the beautiful selected passage of today: man has been created by God, the Most Great and the Creator of all. Having this knowledge, man is less likely to lead a life of aimlessness, and begin to have a basic understanding of what he needs to do to succeed.

The second powerful message in the beautiful selected passage of today and one of the fundamental components of success is an answer to one of the most important concerns of all living creatures, and especially man: his death. Man typically desires to live as long as possible, fearing death more than anything else; if given the option of eternal life, he will pay any price to attain it. Man is informed in the beautiful selected passage of today by God, the Almighty and the Most Wise, that it is He Alone Who causes man to die. Having this knowledge, man is freed from fear of anything else in the world, so that he will not waste his energy on unnecessary fears of other things that may cause his death besides God, the Giver and Taker of life, and would be able to concentrate on attaining success.

The third powerful message in the beautiful selected passage of today and one of the fundamental components of success is the knowledge that man will be resurrected on the Day of Judgment by God, the Creator and the Resurrector. Two important ways this particular knowledge will help man in attaining success is knowing that he is to be resurrected and held accountable for his actions; he will perform righteous acts worthy of reward in the hereafter and avoid the evils that will lead to punishment. Also, man will be able to realize one of his primary wishes – that of attaining eternal life. He will strive to make sure that the eternal life he will have will be that of comfort, as promised to those who are successful, and not that of pain, as promised to those who fail in the test of life.

All of the three concepts that are discussed above – although they are fundamental components of success, cannot be helpful to man unless he understands the fourth powerful message of the beautiful selected passage of today: That in realization of the greatness of God, the Almighty, the Creator of all, Giver of life and Death, and the Restorer, man should be grateful to his Lord, in awe of His Power, Beneficence, and Love for all His Creation, and manifest this gratefulness with praising, worshipping and serving Him, along with performing righteous acts as a result of his faith and gratefulness.

Truly ungrateful is the unfortunate individual who has received the above knowledge, and continues to enjoy all the gifts of God, the Most Beneficent and Most Merciful, but without being moved to action – the actions of praise, worship, love, and righteous acts to serve Him.

The seeker of success who wishes to reach his goal has unwavering faith in God, the Eternal, the Owner of sovereignty, the Giver of life and the Creator of death, and in His beloved messenger, Muhammad. He knows that life is created and death occurs only with the permission of God, the Most Great, the Alive and Everlasting, and he is grateful to his Lord and praises and worships his Lord profusely and performs righteous deeds as a manifestation of his faith.

# Day 203

**Are you not aware that Allah knows all that is in heaven and on earth? Indeed, it is all in a record, and that is easy for Allah.**

(22:70)

# Day 203

We encounter again in the beautiful selected passage of today concepts that have previously been reviewed in the Holy Quran and the earlier portions of this collection of meditations, as keys to success. And we are thankful to God, the Most Wise and the Most Righteous Teacher, for reinforcing for us the key points we need to understand and that which will help us to succeed and to pass our examination of this life.

The first reinforced key point in the beautiful selected passage of today to help the seeker of success to reach his goal is that God, the Almighty, the All-hearing and All-seeing, is completely aware of all that happens on earth and in all of existence at all times. A proper understanding of this valuable message is important for the seeker of success, so that he is appropriately aware of the proper rules of examination of the life of this world – that every moment of his life is valuable for his success; he is not being judged once a week, or on special days only, by his Creator, so that he may act however he pleases for the rest of the week. Besides serving to enhance the performance of man in the examination of life, the knowledge obtained about this reinforced key point also serves to re-affirm the absolute power of God, the Almighty and Most Magnificent, over all of existence at all times, strengthening one's faith in Him, which is the most valuable component of lasting success.

The second reinforced key point in the beautiful selected passage of today to help the seeker of success reach his goal is knowledge about another rule about his examination of the life of this world that he needs to know for maximizing the chances of successful outcome: that not only is every moment of his life valuable, but his performance at all times is being recorded, and the results of the exam will be provided to him on the Day of Judgment, when he will learn whether he has succeeded (by being saved from the punishment of the hell-fire) or failed (by being placed in the hell-fire for eternity).

The seeker of success who wishes to reach his goal has unwavering faith in God, the All-aware, All-seeing and All-hearing, and in His beloved messenger, Muhammad. He knows the value of every moment of his life in this world, and knows how best to utilize it to his advantage.

## Day 204

**O men! Here is a parable set forth! Listen to it! Those on whom besides Allah you call, cannot create (even) a fly – if they all met together for the purpose! And if the fly should snatch anything from them, they would have no power to release it from the fly. So feeble are those who petition and those to whom they petition.**

(22:73)

# Day 204

    The beautiful selected passage of today gently and brilliantly guides man to the absolute prerequisite and the most important component of lasting success: faith and belief in God, the Almighty, the Most Wise and the Most Refined, as relayed to us through His noble prophet, Muhammad. The powerful message of today has been reinforced in the Holy Quran and in this collection of meditations with the frequency relative to its importance, for the benefit of the seekers of success. Out of all the parables provided in the Holy Quran by God, the Most Righteous Teacher and the Best Guide, for the benefit of the seekers of success, the beautiful selected passage of today is the personal favorite of the humble author, exhibiting the degree of eloquence, wisdom, benevolence, patience, and reassurance that cannot be surpassed by any except He Who is Most Perfect and the Source of all power and knowledge.

    Let us review the details of today's most wonderful parable provided by God, the Most Beneficent and the Most Wise, for the benefit of man. Let us picture the creation of life. If man is so impressed with his own intelligence and ability, can all the best minds in existence create something as simple as a fly, out of nothing, as the God Almighty has created all that exists – from nothing? If man is so impressed with his power, can he use it to release something the fly has snatched away from him? Can man call anyone else except God, the Creator and Sustainer of all, to help him in creating anything, such as even a fly, or to help him reclaim what the fly has snatched away from him?

    In response to the above questions, even the most ardent doubter will be able to realize the futility of calling anyone or any being to assist him, with something as simple as reclaiming an object snatched by the fly, and the futility of claiming that life is a matter of coincidence, when the most intelligent minds or any other imaginary beings cannot even create something as simple as a fly from nothing.

    The seeker of success who wishes to reach his goal has absolute faith in God, the Most Powerful, the Creator of all, and the Only One Who is self-existing, and in His beloved messenger, Muhammad. He realizes that everything in existence has been created by God, the Creator and Sustainer of all, that He has absolute control at all times over all existence, and that everything is to return to Him. He lives his life praising, worshipping, and serving God - to Whom belongs all power, praise, and worship, along with performing other righteous deeds.

## Day 205

**O you who believe! Bow down, prostrate yourselves, and worship your Lord; and do good <u>so that you may succeed.</u>**

**And strive in His cause as you ought to strive, (with sincerity and under discipline). He has chosen you, and has imposed no difficulties on you in religion; it is the religion of your father Abraham; It is He who has named you Muslims, both before and in this (revelation) – that the messenger may be a witness for you, and you be witness for mankind! So establish regular prayer, give regular charity, and hold fast to Allah! He is your Protector – (and Who is) the Best Protector and the Best Helper!**

(22:77-78)

# Day 205

The beautiful selected passage of today consists of three closely related portions that deal with the key prerequisite and the most fundamental component of success: Faith in God, the Creator, the Nourisher and the Sustainer, as relayed to us through His noble messenger, Muhammad, along with useful details about specific actions that are recommended for turning one's goal of success into reality.

The first portion of the beautiful selected passage of today is clear, concise, and will be recognized from earlier references in this collection of meditations regarding the relationship between faith, worship and performance of righteous deeds, to the realization of success. And in the beginning portion, we see details emerging that better clarify the role of faith and action: Success is unequivocally linked to faith, which the seeker of success is instructed to demonstrate by the acts of bowing down, prostrating before and worshipping God, the Creator of all that exists and the Source of all power, and by the performance of righteous acts or good deeds to serve Him; and this the seeker of success will perform most sincerely throughout his life. Demonstrating his faith and sincerity, the sincere seeker of success is instructed to begin on his path of success, starting at this moment, with a prostration to his Lord, to Whom belongs all praise, and to continue this process with the regular worship of his Lord, along with performing other righteous deeds.

The second portion of the beautiful selected passage of today instructs in further detail about what are considered righteous deeds resulting from faith, and which will result in the attainment of success: establishing regular prayer, giving charity, holding fast to one's faith, relying on God, Who is the Most Trustworthy and the Best Friend and Protector for help and protection - and no one else, and striving in His cause despite obstacles, with sincerity, discipline and conviction.

The third portion of the beautiful selected passage of today reminds man about the favor of God, the Most Righteous Teacher and the Best Guide, to mankind, for guiding them from darkness to light, from self-destructive behaviors to those that will lead them towards lasting success, through His messengers, instructing man on how he can worship and serve God, the Most Beneficent and Most Merciful – the reason for which he was created. Specific mention is made in the beautiful selected passage of today of the beloved prophet Abraham, acknowledging him as the patriarch of those seeking the path to lasting success, for transmitting the revelation from the Mercy of God, the Most Beneficent and Merciful, guiding man to success, and thus designated with the honorable title of "One who submits (to God, the Almighty and the Most Glorious)", or "Muslim".

The seeker of success who wishes to reach his goal has unwavering faith in God, the Most Holy and the Most Praiseworthy, and in His noble messenger, Muhammad. He strives to reach closer to his Lord, as did his patriarch Abraham. He realizes that the Guidance and Love of God, the Most Great and Most Kind, for mankind, continued through other prophets, ending with the beloved prophet Muhammad, the seal of the prophethood. Additionally, he is most honored to be known as "One who submits (to His Lord)", or "Muslim", knowing it is the surest path to success. As a manifestation of his faith, he praises and worships his Lord regularly, and performs other righteous deeds, including giving regular charity, and holding fast to God, the Most Trustworthy and the Best Friend and Protector.

# Day 206

Indeed, those who live in awe for fear of their Lord;

Those who believe in the signs of their Lord;

Those who join not (in worship) partners with their Lord;

And those who dispense their charity with their hearts full of fear, because they will return to their Lord –

It is these who hasten in every good work, and these who are foremost in them.

On no soul do We place a burden greater than it can bear; with Us is a record which clearly shows the truth. They will never be wronged.

(23:57-62)

# Day 206

The beautiful selected passage of today will be divided into three parts for the ease of analysis of the relationship to a specific characteristic of success; two of the three parts are repeated often in the Holy Quran, as well as in this collection of meditations, and will be considered as reinforcing the fundamentals of success. The first portion we will review in the beautiful selected passage of today consists of examples of righteous deeds, as instructed by God, the Most Wise and the Most Righteous Teacher:

1. Living in awe for fear of God, the Almighty and the All-aware. This is not the type of fear one may have of someone who is dangerous, but the fear of disappointing someone who has entrusted us with things of tremendous value. The individual who realizes the role of God, the Most Great and Most Kind, in the entire creation, including himself – with the priceless gifts of reasoning, sight and hearing – will indeed fear disappointing the One who has entrusted him with these things of tremendous value.

2. Believing in the signs of God, the Creator and Sustainer of all, one will see these signs everywhere he turns, for nothing could have been created except by His will and also is sustained only through Him. This is the most fundamental concept of success, and without it, progress to any degree of success is not possible - for all righteous deeds require the acceptance of this fundamental principle.

3. Giving of charity – as a sign of their faith, requiring one to provide for those in need, as the vicegerent of God, the Most Kind and Most Generous.

4. Not joining any others in the worship of God, the Only One and the One worthy of all praise. This is a fundamental component of faith and indistinguishable from it, for it is not possible to have faith in God, the Most Beneficent and Most Merciful, without recognizing that nothing else is deserving of praise or worship.

The second portion of the beautiful selected passage of today is not the one that is reinforced as frequently as the other concepts have been, but it is important for the seeker of success to be aware that God is Most Kind, Most Loving and Most Just. Like a parent who will not assign a chore to a child that he knows the child is not capable of performing, and like an ethical employer who will not place an unreasonable demand on his employee, God, the Most Beneficent and Most Merciful, informs us that he will not place on any soul a burden greater than it can bear, and He is infinitely more loving and compassionate than the most loving and compassionate parent or employer.

The third portion of the beautiful selected passage of today discusses the return of every individual to his Lord, the Most Great and Most Just, to be held accountable for all his actions in the life of this world – all his actions clearly recorded, and not being wronged in the least. This is a reinforced point and also one of the fundamental components of success.

The seeker of success who wishes to reach his goal has complete faith in God, the Most Holy, the Source of all power, and the Best of those who keep account, and in His beloved messenger, Muhammad. He sincerely hopes to fulfill the duties he was created for by his Lord, praising and worshipping Him with enthusiasm, and performing righteous deeds as a manifestation of his faith. He knows that he will not be challenged beyond his capacity by God, the Most Kind, Most Forgiving and Most Wise.

# Day 207

Repel evil with that which is best: We are well-acquainted with the things they say.

And say: "O my Lord! I seek refuge in You from the suggestions of the evil ones.

"And I seek refuge with you, my Lord! Lest they should come near me".

(23:96-98)

# Day 207

Success of any degree is not an easy endeavor, and neither is it a coincidence. In addition to the inherent struggle associated with any degree of success, the seeker of lasting success has his difficulties compounded due to the incessant efforts of Satan, the avowed enemy of the seekers of success, and those that take him as their patron, i.e. the enemies of faith. Today's beautiful selected passage instructs the seeker of success in valuable strategies to help him when faced with various impediments, or various evils, to overcome them and reach his goal,

The first scenario of the types of evils one may encounter, discussed in the beautiful selected passage of today, is that posed by the enemies of faith and their evil acts to frustrate the efforts of the seekers of success. In this instance, God, the Most Wise and Most Great, instructs the seeker of success to respond with the opposite of what is utilized by the enemies of faith, like the effect of water on fire. Therefore, if the enemy of faith will shun the seeker of faith, he will respond with a warm greeting. And God is Most Wise, All-knowing.

The second scenario of the types of evil one may encounter, discussed in the beautiful selected passage of today, is that of the incessant effort against the seekers of success by their avowed enemy, the accursed Satan. More often than using others to help him, Satan and his agents will directly attempt to influence the mind of the seeker of success, whispering various evil suggestions to hamper his efforts at attaining success, so that his faith will be undermined, and he will incline to evil acts instead of righteous acts. In this instance, the besieged seeker of success is instructed to seek the protection of his Lord, requesting: "O my Lord! I seek refuge in You from the suggestions of the evil ones". And God is Most Powerful, the Best Friend and Protector. One who seeks refuge in God, the Most Strong and the best Protector, will find the protection he desires from the evil of Satan and his agents, who will be unable to influence or harm him while he is under the protection of God, the Source of all power and the Protector from harm

The seeker of success who wishes to reach his goal has absolute faith in God, the Most Great, the Subduer and the Best Friend and Protector, and in His noble messenger, Muhammad. He repels the evil from others with that which is better, and seeks refuge in his Lord – from the evil both in himself and in others that the accursed Satan seeks to utilize to his optimal advantage.

# Day 208

Then when the trumpet is blown, there will be no more relationships between them that day, nor will one ask after another!

**Then those whose balance (of good deeds) is heavy – they will attain success;**

But those whose balance is light, will be those who have lost their own selves; in hell will they abide.

(23:101–103)

# Day 208

The beautiful selected passage of today provides three valuable messages that are closely related, and that will help the seeker of success to reach his goal. - the first of which is the reminder to man that he is being examined at all times during his life on earth. Due to the Benevolence and Generosity of God, we can consider this examination to be an open-book format, with guidance available to us if we desire. The examination of an individual will end with his death, but the collective end of examination for all men is to come to an end at a certain point in time, described as heralded by a trumpet being blown. At that point, we can figuratively say that the examination session is over, and that is the Day of Judgment. The seeker of success must be aware that every moment of his life is important and is being recorded in detail, with respective credits for righteous deeds done as a result of one's faith in God, the Most High and the Creator of all that exists, as relayed to us through His beloved messenger, Muhammad, and penalties for evil deeds as well as neglecting the duties for which man was created. On the Day of Judgment will be set up scales, most accurate, to determine the performance of each individual.

The second valuable message in the beautiful selected passage of today is that, when judged with the most accurate scales by God, the Most Holy and the Most Just, those whose balance of good deeds is greater than evil deeds will have passed the examination of life and will be saved from hell-fire, **the ultimate desire of all those who are in pursuit of lasting success.** The seeker of success is directed to the Holy Quran and other meditations in this collection for further guidance on how to increase his balance of good deeds and minimize the evil deeds, so as to optimize his chances for a successful outcome.

The third valuable message in the beautiful selected passage of today is the logical conclusion of the above scenario: that the unfortunate individual whose balance on the Day of Judgment comes out to be light will indeed be a failure, having lost his own self, through his own choice and his own neglect in the life of this world. There are two ways one can be found to have an end balance that is light – one is by the lack of having accumulated good deeds worthy of reward or not performing the duties for which one was created, and the other is by doing evil deeds, worthy of penalty, and both resulting from a lack of faith in God, the Almighty and the Most Just, as relayed to us through His noble messenger, Muhammad. For these unfortunate individuals, there is a fitting punishment reserved in a place for them – hell, which would indeed be an awful resting place for eternity.

The seeker of success who wishes to reach his goal has unwavering faith in God, the Best Guide, the Best of those who keep accounts and the Most Just, and in His beloved messenger, Muhammad. He knows that every moment of his life is important, and is an opportunity to either help or harm himself, and that a successful outcome of his exam of his life in this world is of utmost important to him. He knows what he needs to do to have the balance showing heaviness (of his good deeds) on the Day of Judgment, and which is **the key sign of attaining the ultimate success.**

# Day 209

**Did you think that We had created you in play (without purpose), and that you would not be brought back to Us (for account)?**

(23:115)

# Day 209

We reviewed earlier in this collection of meditations on success, that one of the first questions an intelligent being enquires into is "Who am I?" and "How did I get here?". The beautiful selected passage of today addresses two other questions that an intelligent being needs to ask himself as he contemplates life and his role in it, for he is able to think and reason, unlike other forms of life we know of: "Why am I here?" and "Where am I going?' or "What's there after this (the end of the life of this world)?".

In response to the logical question all men of reason should ask themselves – "Why am I here?" – man is asked to contemplate the possibility of being in the world for play or amusement, without purpose. Consider the possibility of a human being, whose body is composed of billions of individual cells (each one of the cells a miracle in itself), contributing to things of immense value to the individual, working in coordination with all other cells, in providing nourishment, sight, hearing and reasoning, with the individual having final control over his body – at his service. The individual who sees in his own amazing body the signs of the Power, Intelligence, and Love of God, Who created all that exists, will have taken the first and the most important step to lasting success, and he should logically conclude that the reason he exists is to praise and serve his Lord, i.e. to worship Him. The esteemed reader is referred to the commentary of Day 3 of this collection of meditations for a more detailed discussion of worship.

In response to the other questions that all intelligent beings should ask themselves, i.e. "Where am I going?" or "What is there after this (the end of the life of this world)?", man is asked to consider the possibility that having been provided with the truly amazing treasures described above (starting with his possession of his body, along with all other things with which he has been provided, including oxygen, water, shelter, etc), that he will not be called to account by Him who provided those things to man. The unfortunate individual who has wasted the treasures he has been entrusted with, as described above, has indeed done a great disservice to his Creator, as well as to himself – for he **will be held accountable** for all the treasures he has been entrusted with, on the Day of Judgment.

The seeker of success who wishes to reach his goal has complete faith in God, the Creator and Sustainer of all, and the Best Guide, and in His noble messenger, Muhammad. He knows that he was created for a purpose in life – to worship God, the Originator, the Resurrector and the Gatherer, and he knows that he will be called to give a detailed account on the Day of Judgment about his performance of duties in the life of this world, and that he will be rewarded or punished accordingly. He realizes that worship consists of more than verbal and physical actions.

# Day 210

Allah is the Light of the heavens and the earth. The parable of His Light is as (if there were) a niche, and within it a lamp – the lamp is in a glass; the glass as it were a brilliant star: lit from a blessed tree – an olive, neither of the east, nor of the west, whose oil would almost glow forth (of itself), though no fire touched it. Light upon Light! Allah guides to His Light whom He wills. And Allah sets forth parables for mankind; and Allah is All-knower of everything.

(Lit is such a Light) in houses, which Allah has permitted to be raised to honor – for the celebration, in them, of His name; in them is He Glorified, in the mornings and in the evenings, (again and again) –

By men whom neither trade nor business diverts from the remembrance of Allah, nor from regular prayer, nor from the practice of regular charity; their (only) fear is for the Day when the hearts and eyes will be transformed (in a world wholly new) –

That Allah may reward them according to the best of their deeds, and add even more for them out of His Grace; for Allah does provide for those whom He wills, without measure.

But the unbelievers – their deeds are like a mirage in sandy desert, which the man parched with thirst mistakes for water – until when he comes to it; he finds it to be nothing; but he finds Allah (ever) with him, and Allah will pay him his account. And Allah is swift in taking account.

Or (the unbelievers' state) is like the depths of darkness in a vast deep ocean overwhelmed with waves topped by waves, topped by dark clouds; layers of darkness upon darkness: if a man stretches out his hand, he can hardly see it! And he for whom Allah has not appointed Light, for him there is no Light!

(24: 35-40)

# Day 210

Today's beautiful selected passage is filled with the highest degree of beauty, eloquence, breadth and depth of knowledge sought by the seekers of lasting success. Indeed it is one of the most treasured passages of those who profess an intense degree of love of God, the Most Great, the Light, and the Creator and Sustainer of all. We can find in the beautiful selected passage of today, many valuable messages that will help the seeker of success who wishes to reach his goal - out of which four that are most important in the humble opinion of the author, are presented below.

The first valuable and powerful message that is presented in the beautiful selected passage of today to help the seeker of success reach his goal, is the description of God, the Creator of all, the Most Beneficent and Most Merciful, Who is described as being the Light of the Heavens and the Earth. Therefore, if someone is a doubter or denier of faith and will not believe in the Existence or Power of God, the Source of all power, and the Living One, he can be directed to find Him wherever he sees light. Although additional details about the description of the Light of God, the Most Beneficent, Most Merciful, and to Whom belongs all praise, are beautifully provided in the treasured passage of today, referring to the highest degree of purity and intensity, further discussion about these topics is beyond the scope of this collection of meditations. The seeker of success has his faith in God, the Light and the Best Guide, as relayed to us through His beloved messenger, Muhammad, increased manifold degrees from the knowledge gained in the beautiful selected passage of today, and which is the most important component of success.

The second valuable and powerful message that is presented in the beautiful selected passage of today that will help the seeker of success to reach his goal, is the knowledge about what can be done by man to facilitate access to his Lord and where we will find Him in order to celebrate His praises and glorify His Name. Although such a place can be anywhere that God's Name is glorified, the most likely places that fit this criteria are designated houses for worshiping or praising Him, or mosques. As per our earlier discussions, God, the All-Encompassing and most Glorious, is everywhere, the beautiful selected passage informs us that His presence is felt more keenly, where His name is glorified, such as the places where he is worshipped

The third valuable and powerful message that is provided in the beautiful selected passage of today, and that will help the seeker of success to reach his goal is that those who desire the Presence of God, by invoking His Name and celebrating His praises, and who are not diverted by worldly affairs (such as business), and who perform other righteous deeds (such as regular and additional prayers along with regular charity) and fear of having failed on the Day of Judgment– those are the fortunate individuals who will attain **lasting success**, and who are rewarded by God, the Most Rich and the Most Generous – for He provides to whom He wills and deems worthy, without measure.

The fourth valuable and powerful message that is provided in the beautiful selected passage of today to help the seeker of success reach his goal is the knowledge that for those who have no faith in God, the Creator of all and the Light, is intense darkness, such as one might find deep in a vast ocean, and a meaningless life without any purpose or guidance. All their acts that they perform in such a state will be designated as meaningless on the Day of Judgment, for they were not performed as a result of faith in God, Who is the Creator of all and the Restorer; and they will be taken to account for all their evil acts and the failure to fulfill the duties for which they were created. Indeed, God, the Most Great and Most Powerful, is the Best of those who keep account, and is swift in doing so. As for the most unfortunate individual whom He has deemed not worthy to receive the Light, for him, indeed, there is no Light (Guidance)!

The seeker of success who wishes to reach his goal has absolute faith in God, the Light, the Source of all that exists, the Best Guide, and the Most Righteous Teacher, and in His noble messenger, Muhammad. He performs righteous deeds as a result of his faith and celebrates the praises of his Lord often – letting neither trade nor business divert him from the remembrance of his Lord, or from regular prayer or charity, as a result of intense love of his Lord. He has an intense fear of failing to fulfill the duties for which he was created and of how he would be affected by such failure on the Day of Judgment.

# Day 211

**Do you not see that it is Allah Whose praises all beings in the heavens and on earth do celebrate, and the birds (of the air) with wings outspread? Each one knows its own (mode of) prayer and praise. And Allah knows well all that they do.
And to Allah belongs the dominion of the heavens and the earth; and to Allah is the final goal (of all).**

(24:41-42)

# Day 211

The beautiful selected passage of today is divided into two portions, containing information on three components of success that are considered among its foundations, and thus have been reinforced elsewhere in the Holy Quran and also in this collection, for the benefit of the seeker of success.

Verse 41 of the beautiful selected passage of today helps an individual to acquire, in a most brilliant and intelligent manner, that which he needs more than anything else for the attainment of lasting success: Faith in God, the All-knowing and the Most Righteous Teacher, as relayed to us through His noble messenger, Muhammad. The example of a bird with wings outspread is used brilliantly with two powerful effects: 1) nothing else is able to explain it other than God, the Creator and Sustainer of all (gravity falls short by a long distance in explaining this scenario, not the least of it being that gravity is unable to create the bird), and 2) the next step after the acquisition of faith, i.e. action, and more specifically, righteous actions, is introduced. God, Most Wise and Most Magnificent, has informed us elsewhere in the Holy Quran that all of creation is made for the purpose of worshipping Him and does so automatically. Only man, of all creation that we know of, has free will to praise, worship and serve his Creator, and he is to be judged on that basis. Therefore, all of creation has its own way of praising and worshipping its Creator, including the bird with its wings outspread in air.

Verse 42 of the beautiful selected passage of today serves to reinforce two other key points that are to be considered foundations of success, and are presented for reinforcement: 1) that the control of the earth, heavens and existence belongs to God, the Creator and Sustainer of all, and every individual has access to his Creator at all times (therefore, if one been instructed to deal directly with the CEO and has direct access to him, but selects to submit his request to the junior manager, one is indeed not being optimally resourceful in the business sense, but in the relationship between God and man, there can be no intermediary, because each individual is responsible for his own actions, and 2) that the return of all that exists , including man, is back to God, the One Who created all from nothing. However, no other beings in creation that we know of, will be held accountable for their actions, as they have no free will and only do what they were created for. Man, though, will be called for a detailed account, for the life of this world is a test for him.

The seeker of success who wishes to reach his goal has unwavering faith in God, the Eternal, Owner of all sovereignty, and the Only One to Whom belongs all praise, and in His noble messenger, Muhammad. He truly feels awe of the Creator - Who made him and everything else, Who is the Gatherer, and to Whom is the return of all, and lives his life praising, worshipping and serving Him, including the performance of other righteous deeds.

# Day 212

The answer of the believers, when summoned to Allah and His messenger, in order that He may judge between them, is no other than this – they say: "We hear and we obey". <u>It is such as these that will attain success.</u>

<u>It is such as obey Allah and His messenger and fear Allah and do right, who will be successful.</u>

(24:51-52)

# Day 212

The beautiful selected passage of today specifically refers to success in both of its verses – which is the focus of this collection of meditations. Therefore, the seekers of success should pay careful attention to the powerful messages contained in the beautifully selected passage of today, addressed openly to them.

As mentioned elsewhere in the Holy Quran and also in this collection, we will begin with the component of success which is an absolute prerequisite, without which further progress toward the attainment of it is not possible, i.e. belief or faith in God, the Most Beneficent, the Most Merciful, and the Creator of all, as relayed to us through His noble messenger, Muhammad. Hence, it is to the believers and those having faith that further directives are provided, guiding them further on the path to success.

The specific instructions and details about the valuable message of the beautiful selected passage of today include obeying God, the Creator and Sustainer of all, (as instructed in the Holy Quran) and obeying His messenger, the beloved prophet Muhammad, which according to God, the Most Trustworthy and the Most Wise, leads to success. Imagine a child who is instructed by his parent to perform specific tasks and to listen to the teacher he has hired for him; suppose the child responds by saying: "Let me think it over and if it makes sense to me, I'll do it". This child will not go very far in earning the love and reward from his parent for completing the required tasks, or in growing up and helping himself. Similarly, an individual having faith in God, the Most Glorious and the Most Praiseworthy - as relayed to us through His noble messenger, Muhammad, when presented with the instructions from God, blessed be His name, and His messenger, wastes no time in putting these instructions into practice, without a need to mull it over.

The seeker of success who wishes to reach his goal has complete faith in God, the Most Beneficent and Source of all power, and the message relayed by His beloved prophet, Muhammad, fears being deficient in performing the duties for which he was created, which includes praising, worshipping, and serving his Lord - including performing other righteous deeds as a result of his faith, and realizes the immense value of the resources which he has been endowed with from his Creator, such as his hearing, sight and reasoning. Upon finding a particular directive aimed at him from God, the Most Great and the Best Guide, and from His beloved messenger, Muhammad, he has no second thoughts, and his response is quick and decisive: "I hear and I obey". It is he – and those like him, who shall attain lasting success.

# Day 213

Blessed is He who made constellations in the skies, and placed therein a lamp (sun) and a moon giving light;

And it is He who made the night and the day to follow each other: for such as have the will to celebrate His praises or to show their gratitude.

And the servants of (Allah) Most Gracious are those who walk on the earth in humility, and when the ignorant address them, say "Peace!".

Those who spend the night in adoration of their Lord prostrate and standing;

Those who say: "Our Lord! Avert from us the wrath of hell, for its wrath is indeed an affliction grievous –

"Evil indeed is it as an abode, and as a place to rest in";

Those who, when they spend, are not extravagant and not miserly, but hold a just (balance) between those (extremes);

Those who invoke not with Allah, any other god, nor slay such life as Allah has made sacred, except for just cause, nor commit fornication – and any that does this (not only) meets punishment, But the penalty on the Day of Judgment will be doubled for him, and he will dwell therein in ignominy –

Unless he repents, believes, and works righteous deeds, for Allah will change the evil of such persons into good, and Allah is Most Forgiving, Most Merciful.

# Day 213

References have been extensively made, both in the Holy Quran and in this collection of meditations, to the most important characteristics necessary for the attainment of lasting success: belief and faith in God, the Creator and Sustainer of all, as relayed to us by His beloved messenger, Muhammad, along with worshipping God Almighty and performing righteous deeds as a result of the faith. The beautiful selected passage of today, although quite extensive in comparison to the other selections, has nevertheless been selected for the benefit of the seeker of success in view of grasping a valuable opportunity to provide details about what constitutes righteous deeds, so as to increase the likelihood of attaining a higher degree of success. The beautiful selected passage of today begins with references to the many signs in existence pointing to God, the Most Holy and the Most Praiseworthy One, such as the constellations, sun, moon, light, night and day. Having referred to the absolute prerequisite for success, i.e. faith, further details are provided specifying particular actions one should take, or righteous deeds that can lead to the success of the highest degree, as summarized below:

1. As a result of having attained faith, celebrate the praises of God, Most Great and Most Generous, to show one's gratitude. Praise and worship of God is indeed the highest form of righteous actions
2. Have a sense of humility, and avoid the ignorant or being provoked by them.
3. Spend extra time and effort in sincere devotion to God, the Source of peace and the Source of all goodness (such as during the night, considering it more valuable and satisfying than sleep).
4. Desiring the love and reward from God the Most Loving and the Most Generous One, and fearing His Punishment and the wrath of hell, resulting from negligence in carrying out the duties for which one was created
5. To spend of one's resources without the extremes of miserliness or extravagance.
6. Not invoking any other in the worship of God, to Whom belongs all praise and worship.
7. Not taking a life- which is sacred, and is only the right of God, the Giver and Taker of life, to take, except with just cause.
8. Not committing adultery – one of the root causes of evils, leading to many other evils. The penalty for these wicked transgressors is to be doubled on the Day of Judgment with respect to the seriousness of the crime, unless one has sought forgiveness from one's Lord and has been righteous afterwards
9. Sincerely seeking forgiveness from God, the Most Forgiving and Most Merciful, for having committed any evils, and afterwards practice righteousness, with constancy.
10. Not bearing false witness.
11. Avoiding ignorant fools and their futile acts, in an honorable manner.
12. When presented with signs of God, the Most Great and Most Glorious, feeling an increase in faith, love and awe of Him, and not ignoring His signs, such as the deaf or the blind, who cannot hear or see.

And whoever repents and does good has truly turned to Allah with an (acceptable) conversion:

Those who witness no falsehood and, if they pass by futility, they pass by it with honorable (avoidance);

Those who, when they are admonished with the signs of their Lord, droop not down at them as if they are deaf or blind;

And those who pray: "Our Lord! Grant unto us wives and offspring who will be the comfort of our eyes, and give us (the Grace) to lead the righteous";

<u>Those are the ones who will be rewarded with the highest place in heaven because of their patient constancy;</u> therein shall they be met with salutations and peace,

Dwelling therein - how beautiful an abode and place of rest!

Say to the rejecters: "My Lord is not uneasy because of you if you call not on Him; but you have indeed rejected (Him), and soon will come the inevitable (punishment)".

(25:61 – 77)

13. Wish for good things, such as a loving spouse and children, not only in this life, but also for the ability to act righteously, and for the attainment of good things both in this life as well as the hereafter.

The beautiful selected passage of today ends with reference to the unfortunate rejecters of faith in which God, Most Great and Most Magnificent mentions that He has no need for their worship, and that the loss is only to those who reject Him and His Guidance.

The seeker of success who wishes to reach his goal has absolute faith in God, the Most Caring, the Best Guide and the Most Righteous Teacher, and in His noble messenger, Muhammad. He has his faith strengthened after the reading of the beautiful selected passage of today, and refers to it often to guide him to specific righteous acts.

# Day 214

And recite to them the story of Ibrahim,

When he said to his father and his people:

"What do you worship?"

They said: "We worship idols, and to them we are ever devoted".

He said: "Do they hear you, when you call on (them)?"

"Or do they benefit you or do they harm (you)?"

They said: "(No) but we found our fathers doing so".

He said: "Do you observe that which you have been worshipping –

You and your forefathers?"

"Truly they are enemies to me, save the Lord of the Alamin (mankind, Jinn, and all that exists),
Who has created me, and it is He who guides me.

And it is He who feeds me and gives me to drink.

And when I am ill, it is He who cures me.
And Who will cause me to die, and then will bring me to life (again),

And Who, I hope, will forgive me my faults on the Day of Judgment".

(26:69 -82)

# Day 214

    The beautiful selected passage of today is a portion of the story of the beloved prophet Ibrahim – to be continued in the discussion of tomorrow's selection, God-willing. The contiguous beautiful passage of the story of the prophet Ibrahim selected for today and tomorrow has been split into two, so as to highlight particular concepts with greater ease for the seeker of success.

    The story of the beloved prophet Ibrahim is a landmark event for the seekers of success -for it was he who, with the will of God, the Most Great and Kind, was the one to crack the code for attainment of success – for the benefit of all mankind: The necessity of faith in God, the Most Beneficent, Most Merciful, and the Only One, and this message was later perfected with the seal of the prophets, the beloved prophet Muhammad . Therefore, it is to the honorable prophet Ibrahim that all seekers of success, i.e. those who submit willingly to the service of God, the Almighty and Most Glorious, i.e. Muslims, refer as their spiritual patriarch. Although bloodline is of no significance to the seekers of success, it was the beloved prophet Muhammad who relayed the complete message to mankind from God, the Most Beneficent and Most Merciful, and both prophets do have a bloodline link – with the beloved prophet Muhammad expressing great admiration and love for the honorable prophet Ibrahim in a collegial, as well as familial sense.

    The first portion of this two-part story of the beloved prophet Ibrahim is related to his acquisition of faith, the most important component of lasting success – from which all can benefit in their own quest of success. The seeker of success is referred to how the beloved prophet Ibrahim observed the signs of God in all of existence – the One Who created, sustains, and has complete power over all of existence at all times, and to Whom all must return – and he recognized that worshipping idols or anything else except God, to Whom belongs all praise and worship, was not only futile, but a detriment to success.

    The seeker of success who wishes to reach his goal has absolute faith in God, the Eternal, the Self-sustaining and the Nourisher of all, and in His beloved prophet, Muhammad. He realizes the importance of faith as the primary ingredient of lasting success and finds inspiration in the story of the beloved prophet Ibrahim, who struggled over his own ego, as well as over significant external barriers, to acquire this most precious asset, and passed on to all others in future an example of how they, too, could acquire it. If God, the Most Great and Most Merciful, wills, the second part of this story will follow next.

# Day 215

"O my Lord! Bestow wisdom on me, and join me with the righteous;

"Grant me honorable mention on the tongue of truth among the latest generations";

"Make me one of the inheritors of the garden of bliss.

And forgive my father, for he is of the erring.

And let me not be in disgrace on the Day when (men) will be raised up -

"The day when neither wealth nor sons will avail,

"<u>But only he (will succeed) who brings to Allah a sound heart;</u>

"To the righteous, the garden will be brought near,

And to those straying in evil, the fire will be placed in full view".

(26:83-91)

# Day 215

The beautiful selected passage of today is a continuation of the story dealing with the beloved prophet Ibrahim. In the first portion of the noble prophet Ibrahim's story in yesterday's meditation, we reviewed the admirable story of the honorable prophet Ibrahim's acquisition of faith, the most important ingredient of lasting success, despite significant impediments – and how he subsequently took appropriate action to manifest his faith and worked to make sure that others would not have to struggle as hard as he did for acquiring it. For this, he is designated our hero, and the spiritual patriarch of all seekers of success, later supplanted by the honorable prophet Muhammad as the desired individual to emulate for all seekers of success, as mentioned by God Himself, the Most Wise and All-aware, in the Holy Quran.

The beautiful selected passage of today reviews how the noble prophet Ibrahim manifested his faith after acquiring it, combining the two most important ingredients of success: faith and righteous deeds as a manifestation of the faith. The text of the beautiful selected passage of today is the beloved prophet Ibrahim's prayer after having acquired faith; his supplication indicates his intention for corresponding action with the acquisition of faith, which he took subsequently, and with the help of God, the Inspirer and Guardian of faith; his intentions for success in this life were realized, and those for success in the hereafter are likely to have been realized, for success of the highest degree, as per indication in the Holy Quran, based on his standing in the sight of God, the Best Friend and Protector and the Best Rewarder of thankfulness, was awarded to him with the title of "friend of God".

The summary of the beloved prophet Ibrahim's supplication and indication of righteous actions manifesting his faith are described below, for the benefit of the seekers of success who wish to reach their goal, to emulate:

1. Desire for wisdom and Guidance from God, the Most Beneficent and Most Merciful.

2. Desire for performing righteous seeds as a manifestation of faith and love of his Lord.

3. Desire for assisting one's family, as well as others, to succeed.

4. Desire for paradise in the afterlife.

5. Love of family, specifically parents, under all circumstances – even if they are on the erring path.

6. Desire for averting failure on the Day of Judgment (going to hell).

7. Awareness that faith is the most important component of lasting success and desire to strengthen it.

8. Awareness that righteous deeds as a result of faith are deserving of reward in the hereafter, and desire to increase performance of righteous deeds.

9. Awareness that evil, the opposite of righteous acts, is condemnable and deserving of punishment in the hereafter, and desire for protection from sources of evil and evil acts.

The seeker of success who wishes to reach his goal has absolute faith in God, the Best Guide, the Inspirer of faith and the Most Righteous Teacher, and in His beloved prophet, Muhammad. He pays special attention to the details listed above which formed the supplication of the noble prophet Ibrahim, and makes a concerted effort to incorporate them into his life as a manifestation of his faith.

# Day 216

The people of Lot (in Sodom) denied the messengers,

When their brother Lot said to them: "Will you not fear (Allah)?

I am to you a messenger worthy of all trust,

So fear Allah and obey me;

"No reward do I ask of you for it – my reward is only from the Lord of the worlds.

"Of all the creatures in the world, will you approach males,

"And leave those whom Allah has created for you to be your mates? You are a people transgressing (all limits)".

(26:160-166)

# Day 216

The beautiful selected passage of today is the story of one of the honorable prophets of God, the Most Great and Most Kind, and is provided for guidance of mankind to the path of success. It is noteworthy that all of the messengers of God, the Most Beneficent and Most Merciful, faced stiff opposition from the people to whom they delivered the message of Guidance and Righteous path, up to the last one – the beloved prophet Muhammad – suffering ridicule, harassment, and even death in some cases.

The opposition to the honorable prophets of God, the Creator and Sustainer of all, and their warnings to abandon the self-destructive path and substitute it with the right Guidance from the Mercy of God, the All-Knowing, All-Hearing and All-Seeing, to enable man to succeed in this life and the hereafter, typically arose from being asked to abandon specific behaviors in those populations that, although providing short-term pleasure, were preventing them from achieving long-term success (such as prostitution, fornication, homosexuality, gambling, cheating, and idolatry, or the worship, praise and serving others than God, Who Alone is the Creator and Sustainer of all, and to Whom belongs all praise and worship).

Characteristic of the stories of other messengers cited in the Holy Quran, the honorable prophet Lot identifies himself as carrying to his population a message to them from God, Who created all that exists and is Most Great. He also warned the people to fear the consequences of their evil actions, not only in this world but, more importantly, in the hereafter, and recommends it best for people to obey God, the Most Kind and the Best Guide, so that they can be successful and avoid the terrible penalties of disobedience and failure in this life and the hereafter. The prophets were indeed admirable – for having suffered severely in fulfilling their task of conveying divine Guidance to mankind, with no reward expected except for earning the pleasure of God, the Most Great and the Most Generous.

The specific behavior that the honorable prophet Lot instructed his people to abandon on the instructions of God, the Most Great and Most Wise, was a practice prevalent in that population: homosexuality. The admirable prophet Lot gave specific details why homosexuality was wrong: God, the Most Wise and Most Great, has made for man mates of the opposite sex, through whom he shall reproduce, with His will. Man is instructed by God, the Most Wise and the Most Righteous Teacher, that He has created for males, females, with whom he is instructed to dwell with tranquility as mates. The righteous individual listens and follows what has been commanded to him by His Creator. Having free choice, the man who succeeds, selects good over evil. He desires to follow the commandments from God, the Almighty and the Most Wise, and fears the punishment of not following the commandments of his Lord. He desires to do what he was created for, i.e. praising, worshipping and serving his Creator.

The seeker of success who wishes to reach his goal has unwavering faith in God, the Most Wise, the Most Just and the Most Righteous Teacher, and in His noble messenger, Muhammad. He realizes that his Lord has made for him mates of the opposite sex to fulfill his sexual needs; and he realizes that obtaining short-term pleasure from any action that has been identified by God, the Best Guide, the Resurrector and the Avenger, as harmful, including homosexuality, leading to long-term suffering, should be avoided, as it will prevent him from attaining his goal.

# Day 217

The dwellers of Al-Aikah (near Midian) denied the messengers,

When Shuaib said to them: "Will you not fear Allah?

"I am to you a messenger worthy of all trust,

"So fear Allah and obey me;

"No reward do I ask of you for it – my reward is only from the Lord of the worlds,

"Give just measure, and cause no loss (to others by fraud),

"And weigh with scales true and upright;

"And withhold not things justly due to men, nor do evil in the land, working mischief.

"And fear Him Who created you and (Who created) the generations before (you)."

(26:176-184)

# Day 217

As a continuation of the same chapter in the Holy Quran that we reviewed in yesterday's meditation, the beautiful selected passage of today reviews the story of Shuaib, the honorable prophet of God the Most Beneficent and Most Merciful, who was sent for guidance to a particular people of Al-Aikan (near Midian).

Characteristic of the prophets, Shuaib the righteous prophet, identifies himself as a prophet with a message to his people from God the Most Great and Creator of All, that they should obey Him – and that there is no reward in this duty for himself to be expected from the people, but only that from the Lord of the worlds and All that exists. Pleased with the short term pleasures of various evils - including prostitution, homosexuality, fornication, gambling, cheating and idolatry or the act of worshipping and serving others than God the Creator to All and to whom belongs all praise, various people to whom messengers were sent by God the Most Beneficent and Most Merciful, faced stiff opposition up to last prophet, the beloved Mohammed, including threats, harassment, and up to death for some prophets.

The honorable prophet Shuaib, then proceeds to deliver his message, starting with recommending his people to fear the consequences of their (evil) actions from their Lord, not only in this world but more importantly in the hereafter. The specific behaviors that the honorable prophet Shuaib instructed his people to abandon were dishonesty, injustice, and oppression; they were instructed to give to others what is their right, to weigh with accurate balance when dispensing; to not practice fraud, and not to do evil or make mischief on earth. As the representative of God, the Most Beneficent and Most Just on earth, none of the actions listed above, is becoming of an individual with the honorable task of representing God, the Most Great and Most Pure. These are the evil acts that the people to whom the honorable prophet Shuaib was sent, were practicing - contrary to their expected duties, that, even though were providing them with short term benefits, were harmful for them in the long run - both in this world, and especially the hereafter.

The seeker of success who wishes to reach his goal has complete faith in God, the Most Just and the Most Glorious, and in His beloved messenger Muhammad. He realizes from the beautiful selected passage of today the tremendous responsibility he carries along with the honor of being representative of God, the Most Glorious and the Most Majestic One during his life on earth – and he fulfills that responsibility with utmost care. He realizes that dishonesty, injustice, fraud, oppression and working mischief on earth and similar evils are unbecoming of someone in an honorable position as himself, for which there are severe consequences, from the One Who created him and assigned him the task of praising, worshipping and serving Him.

# Day 218

Ta Sin.

These are verses of the Quran – a Book that makes (things) clear;

A guide and glad tidings for the believers–

Those who establish regular prayers and give in regular charity, and also have (full) assurance of the hereafter.

As to those who believe not in the hereafter, we have made their deeds pleasing in their eyes – and so they wander about in distraction;

Such are they for whom a grievous penalty (is waiting). <u>And in the hereafter they will be the greatest losers.</u>

(27:1-5)

# Day 218

The beautiful selected passage of today begins with two Arabic alphabets (Ta, Sin), which have no apparent meaning by themselves, but which are likely to have mystical significance, with consensus being that only God Alone, Who is All-knowing and Most Wise, knows their exact meaning. The passage is of special significance for providing clear descriptions of success and failure – which are of special interest to the seekers of success.

The beautiful selected passage of today begins with clear instructions regarding what one should expect to find in the Holy Quran (the final revelation and Guidance to mankind from God, the Most Beneficent and Most Merciful, through His beloved messenger, Muhammad): Clear instructions with good news for those who follow His Guidance and impending disaster for those who ignore it.

In the first part of the beautiful selected passage of today, we find the factors identified as contributing to success. The first and the most important factor identified is belief and faith in God, the Creator and Sustainer of all, and in His messenger, the beloved prophet Muhammad. Other contributing factors identified, which are a product of faith include: establishing regular prayers and giving of regular charity. For the fortunate individuals who meet the above requirements, good news is given with glad tidings of success and full assurance in the hereafter, by Him Who is Most Trustworthy, and is the Best of those who reward.

In the second part of the beautiful selected passage of today, we correspondingly find factors that contribute to failure: not believing in the hereafter (due to lack of faith), and doing whatever seems best in one's mind as to what one should do, wandering about in distraction, with no clear purpose in life except maximizing one's pleasure and comfort in it, and being pleased with whatever one is doing and believing that to be the best action, based on the increase in worldly possessions. These are they who, in fact, are identified as those for whom a grievous penalty is waiting. And in the hereafter they will be the greatest losers.

The seeker of success who wishes to reach his goal has absolute faith in God, the Most Glorious and the Lord of all majesty and wealth, and in His noble messenger, Muhammad. He performs righteous deeds as a manifestation of his faith, including regular prayer and regular charity, and knows he will be held accountable for his performance in the life of this world by his Lord, and is certain of the hereafter.

# Day 219

**But if any have done wrong and have thereafter substituted good to take the place of evil – truly, I am Most Forgiving, Most Merciful.**

(27:11)

# Day 219

Considering that human beings are not perfect - and are unlike angels who don't have free will; and also considering that man is subject to the unrelenting efforts of the accursed Satan, the avowed enemy of man, and his agents, to thwart the efforts of man in his pursuit of attaining lasting success, man truly is in need of forgiveness from his Lord, the Creator and Sustainer of all, if he is to have any real chance of attaining his goal of success. The beautiful selected passage of today summarizes the concept of forgiveness in an elegant and comprehensive manner.

The first step on the path to forgiveness is the realization that one has made a mistake. The unfortunate individual who does not realize that he has made a mistake will persist in his error, continuing to undermine his chances of attaining success. The fortunate individual who realizes that he has made an error is ready to take the next step, such as removing the weeds from a garden, to speak figuratively. The individual who has not noticed the weeds in his garden cannot take the next step of removing the weeds, and they will continue to multiply.

After recognition that an error has been made, one needs to feel sincere remorse, seeking forgiveness from God, Who is Most Forgiving and Most Merciful, and thereafter making a concerted effort to not repeat the error in future, and substituting good actions for the errors of the past. Fortunately for man, God describes His characteristic of Mercy as being greater than His Anger, and has love for man greater than manifold times than that of the love of a mother towards her child; therefore, He forgives again and again, to those who ask.

The seeker of success who wishes to reach his goal has absolute faith in God, Who is the Most Forgiving and the Most Merciful, and in His beloved messenger, Muhammad. He realizes that he is not perfect. He recognizes the errors he has made, seeking forgiveness from his Lord, and substituting good actions in the future for the errors of the past.

# Day 220

...And who is more astray than one who follows his own lusts, devoid of guidance from Allah? Indeed, Allah guides not people given to wrongdoing.

(28:50)

# Day 220

Imagine a scenario where a group of four year old children are placed on an island with everything they need for survival, but with no further instructions. What kind of systems will they develop to ensure fairness, harmony, safety, and code of behavior and action for success on a short-term, as well as long-term, basis?

Keeping the above scenario in mind, we can understand the significance of the question posed in the beautiful selected passage of today by God, the Best Guide and the Most Righteous Teacher, because the answer itself is found in the way the question has been brilliantly posed. Would any reasonable person expect that the Creator and Sustainer of man and all that exists, leave it up to man to do as he pleases, like leaving it up to four year old children to decide for themselves? As regards the entire creation (living and nonliving), no significant problem is posed in regard to guidance, except man alone, of the creatures we are aware of, due to being endowed with the ability to choose between good and evil; in fact his whole life is a trial to judge his performance in the examination of life. If left to his own resources, the best that man can conclude with his limited reasoning is: 1) do whatever makes you feel good, and 2) in life, survival is for the fittest. In both conclusions, man would be off by a magnitude of a very great degree – for without the Guidance from God, the Most Loving and the Best Guide, man is doomed to failure - both in this life and, more importantly, in the hereafter. In regard to the concept of survival of the fittest, man has been created in the best form – out of nothing – and sustained by Him Who created all and is the Source of all power; if he is not performing what he was created for, i.e. worshipping and serving his Creator with good actions, then he has the potential of becoming the worst of creation. As the representative on earth of God, the Most Kind and Most Great, the man who is promised **lasting success** is he who best fulfills his duties on earth, which include, besides worshipping and serving Him, exhibiting towards other creatures (including fellow men) the characteristics of goodness, such as benevolence, generosity, fairness, and kindness, with the highest form of all good characteristics found in God Alone. The truth is that real survival is not for the most aggressive or physically strong, but, on the contrary, for those who are humble, benevolent, and generous, as a result of their faith, and who will be living contentedly in eternity. The last part of the beautiful selected passage of today informs man that for those who are pleased with whatever their minds tell them is good - by following their lusts and wrongdoing, will not be deemed worthy of guidance from their Lord, and therefore, they will remain misguided, which is indeed a terrible handicap for an individual.

The seeker of success who wishes to reach his goal has complete faith in God, the Greatest One, the Best Guide, and the Most Righteous Teacher, and in His noble messenger, Muhammad. He realizes that if man is left to follow his own lusts without the Guidance of God, the Creator of all and the Most Wise, that it would lead to the worst kind of failure. He earnestly seeks the Guidance from his Lord, to help him on his path to success.

# Day 221

**And when they (believers) hear al-Laghw (dirty, false, and useless talk), they turn away from there and say: "To us our deeds and to you yours; peace be unto you – we seek not the (way of) the ignorant".**

(28:55)

# Day 221

In order to successfully accomplish one's mission, it is important not only to be aware of factors that will contribute to succeeding, but those that can also prevent one from succeeding as well. In the beautiful selected passage of today is identified one such factor that can prevent the seeker of success from reaching his goal and is therefore presented for our benefit.

Before discussing the danger one should avoid as discussed above, it is noteworthy that the importance of faith (in God, the Most Great and Most Merciful and in His messenger, the beloved Muhammad) is first reinforced - as it is to them that the beautifully selected passage of today is addressed, as an advanced measure. Those desirous of attaining lasting success (or believers) are instructed to avoid Al-Laghw ( Arabic for dirty, false, and useless talk) and to stay away from those participating in such activity. The ability to see, speak, hear and reason are truly valuable gifts from God, the Most Beneficent, Most Merciful and the Most Generous one, and, therefore, their best use is for praising, worshipping and serving Him. If an individual can be diverted from remembrance of his Creator, this would be pleasing to the accursed Satan – for that is his goal. But what pleases the accursed Satan even more is sowing discord and hostilities among men – and Al-Laghw (dirty, false, and useless talk) is an excellent source of meeting his objectives, leading to the failure of many - for it spreads in a rapid manner and in a vicious cycle. Another problem with Al-Laghw, similar to slander and backbiting, is that with each new transmitter of the "story" about someone else, it tends to get embellished - sometimes so much that the person who started the rumor or slander may not recognize it himself that what has come back to him is the account that he initially gave.

The seeker of success who wishes to reach his goal has complete faith in God, the All-Seeing, All-Hearing, and Most Wise, and in His noble messenger, Muhammad. He sincerely praises and thanks his Lord for all the valuable resources He has provided to him and knows that their best use is to praise, worship and serve Him; when he hears dirty, false, and useless talk, he turns away from it and says: "To us our deeds, and to you yours, peace be to you – we seek not the way of the ignorant".

# Day 222

**The (material) things which you are given are but the conveniences of this life and the glitter thereof; but that which is with Allah is better and more enduring – will you not then be wise?**

(28:60)

# Day 222

The powerful message of the beautiful selected passage of today is one of the fundamental components of success. As such, it has been repeated a number of times in the Holy Quran, as well as in this collection of meditations, in varying format, for reinforcement and for the benefit of the seeker of success.

We will utilize again the scenario of a child in relation to his parent, because truly – with respect to the relationship between man and God, the Creator and Sustainer of all – there are striking parallels, including benevolence and reliance for meeting basic needs, such as nourishment, safety, guidance and love.

Let us imagine a scenario where the parent has lovingly provided for the child, who is at the age of three years, all that he needs and desires, including a beautiful home, safety, toys and candies. The three year old is truly pleased with all that has been provided for him. Now let us imagine that the loving parent instructs the child that he should start waking up earlier in the mornings, limiting his playing time, and doing some household chores, and that he should be courteous to others instead of having conflicts, and start learning alphabets and numbers. Suppose the three year old child does not want to limit the pleasure he is currently enjoying, even though the parent says that if he follows what he is being instructed in at this time, that his future will be better?

Similar to the scenario described above, man is being reminded by God, the Most Loving and the Best Guide, that even though the life of this world is filled with conveniences (provided by Him) and it appears appealing, like glitter, that which is in store for him in the afterlife, with God, the Most Rich, Most Generous, and the Truth (if he follows His Guidance), is better and more enduring.

The seeker of success who wishes to reach his goal has absolute faith in God, the Best Guide, the Most Loving and the Most Trustworthy, and in His beloved messenger, Muhammad. He trusts his Lord completely and knows that, if he follows the loving Guidance of God, the Most Merciful and the Most Glorious, he will attain lasting success. He realizes the value of delayed gratification, without being distracted or overwhelmed by the transient glitter of the life of this world.

# Day 223

...Exult not, for Allah loves not those who exult (in riches);

But seek, with (the wealth) which Allah has bestowed on you, the home of the hereafter, nor forget your portion in this world – but do good, as Allah has been good to you, and seek not (occasions for) mischief in the land – for Allah loves not those who make mischief.

(28:76-77)

**Day 223**

The beautiful selected passage of today contains two powerful messages that can help the seeker of success who possesses the necessary foundation, i.e. belief and faith in God, the Most Beneficent, the Most Merciful, and Creator of all, and His beloved messenger Muhammad, in helping him to reach his goal.

The powerful message in the beautiful selected passage of today, for the benefit of the seeker of success, is Guidance on resource management, specifically in regard to the individual who has been blessed with material wealth during his life, keeping in mind that everything in existence has been created by God, the Creator and Sustainer of all, and that He appoints whatever portion to whomsoever He pleases, and also that that his life in this world is a test of his performance, which includes how he utilizes the gifts that have been provided to him by his Creator. Specific Guidance on the use of one's wealth for optimal benefit in terms of lasting success is provided:

1. First, do not exult – for that is a sign of lack of faith and lack of acknowledgement that the wealth, like everything else, is provided by God, the Most Generous and the Enricher. One who exults, does so believing that he is responsible for his wealth – which is therefore a sign of denial of God, the Creator and Nourisher of all. Although the wealth should be enjoyed in this world (with appropriate thanks to its Provider and the Provider of all that exists), man is encouraged to invest the wealth for optimal long term gains by doing good – as God, the Most Wise and the Best Guide, has been good to him - by providing charity and spending in His cause, Who Bestowed the wealth and everything also that is of use to him. With this method of investment, the wise seeker of success will have improved his overall long-term returns significantly.

2. Second, do not seek occasions for mischief in the world, which includes hurting others as well as oneself - for God, the Most Great and the Source of Peace, loves not those who make mischief; and those that He does not love will not be guided towards the right path and indeed will be deprived of joy and success.

The seeker of success who wishes to reach his goal has unwavering faith in God, the Creator, Provider and Sustainer of all and the Source of all goodness, and in His noble messenger, Muhammad. He realizes that all which exists, and his wealth, is from the Beneficence and Generosity of God and he does not exult in his wealth. He invests his wealth for optimal gains by doing good deeds with it, including spending it in the cause of Him Who provided him with the wealth and everything else. He does not make mischief. Nor is he a source of pain in this world – but rather is anxious to do good, as his Lord has been good to him.

# Day 224

So he (Qarun) went forth among his people in the (pride of his worldly) glitter. Those whose aim is the life of this world said: "Oh! That we had the like of what Qarun had got! For he is truly a lord of mighty good fortune!".

But those who had been granted (true) knowledge said: "Alas for you! <u>The reward of Allah (in the hereafter) is best for those who believe and work righteousness</u> – but none shall attain this, save those who steadfastly persevere (in good)".

So, we caused the earth to swallow him and his dwelling place. Then he had no group or party to help him against God, nor was he one of those who could save themselves.

And those who had desired (for a position like) his position the day before, began to say: "Know you not that it is God Who enlarges the provision or restricts it to whomsoever He pleases of His slaves. Had it not been that God was gracious to us, he could have caused the earth to swallow us up (also)! <u>Know you not that the disbelievers will never be successful</u> "

That the home of the hereafter (paradise), We shall assign to those who rebel not against the truth with pride and oppression in the land nor do mischief by committing crimes. <u>And the good end is for the pious.</u>

(28:79-83)

# Day 224

The beautiful selected passage of today narrates the story of Qarun, who lived in the time of the honorable prophet Moses and who was given great wealth in his time; it is a continuation of the same chapter reviewed yesterday, related to wealth and the Guidance for its best use. We will review three powerful messages from the story of Qarun, for the benefit of the seeker of success.

The first powerful message for the benefit of the seeker of success from today's beautiful selected passage and the story of Qarun is that when one has been blessed with wealth from God, the Most Beneficent and the Most Rich One, one should exhibit thankfulness to God, Who provided him with the wealth, spending it wisely, as discussed in yesterday's passage, without exulting and without exhibiting arrogance. And it was because of Qarun's exultation and arrogance - that the One who provided him with wealth, then also caused his destruction, referring to an earthquake; and neither Qarun's wealth nor arrogance was useful to him.

The second powerful message for the benefit of the seeker of success from today's beautiful selected passage and the story of Qarun is that when one sees someone else who has been provided with excess material wealth, one should not feel envy, but realize that it is God, the Most Wise and the Most Rich, who enlarges or restricts the provision of whomsoever He pleases, and one should be satisfied with whatever has been given to him. Being provided with excess wealth carries with it excess responsibilities, and if one does not discharge them appropriately, one's wealth could be a cause of destruction for himself, as it was for Qarun.

The third powerful message for the benefit of the seeker of success from today's beautiful selected passage and the story of Qarun is that no matter how much wealth one might see with someone else, or no matter how many alluring things in this world, he should also know that whatever one can receive from God, the Most Great and the Truth, in the hereafter, is better – due reward for faith and working righteousness, and requires effort and striving. And only those who steadfastly persevere in their struggle for good will be able to achieve it.

The seeker of success who wishes to reach his goal has complete faith in God, the Most Rich, Most Appreciative and the Most Generous One, and in His beloved messenger, Muhammad. He realizes that the good end is for the pious – those who have faith, persevere, and struggle in righteousness. He knows that lacking faith, rebelling against God, the Most Great and the Truth, with pride and oppression, and making mischief in the world by committing crimes, will prevent him from reaching his goal.

# Day 225

**And call not, besides Allah, on another god. There is no god but He. Everything (that exists) will perish except His Own Face. To Him belongs the command, and to Him will you (all) be brought back.**

(28:88)

# Day 225

    Two fundamental components of success are repeated in the beautiful selected passage of today; they are found in the Holy Quran, and this collection of meditations, with the frequency which relays to us their importance for the seeker of success. The first powerful message and one of the fundamental components of success reinforced in the beautiful selected passage of today goes to the heart of faith, i.e. belief in God as the Sole Creator and Sustainer of all that exists - as relayed to us through His noble messenger, Muhammad, which is the primary and most essential component of success. As a result of having acquired faith, the fortunate individual realizes that he exists for no other reason than praising, worshipping, and serving the One Who created him and everything else. He realizes that worshipping or serving anything or anyone besides God, the One to Whom belongs all praise and worship, is an error of the highest degree, preventing him from fulfilling what he was created for, and preventing him from the attainment of lasting success.

    The second powerful message and one of the fundamental components of success reinforced in the beautiful selected passage of today is the realization that everything that exists will perish except God, the Eternal and the Only Self-sufficient One, and when He commands it, to Him will be the return of all. With this realization, man will be able to understand the importance of every moment of his life in this world, and how it can be of either help or hindrance to him when he will be brought back to his Lord for a full accounting of how well he fulfilled the duties for which he was created, and will be rewarded or punished accordingly. Without the knowledge of accountability and the Day of Judgment, man will follow and serve his own lusts and reasoning, leading to whatever benefits him temporarily in the life of this world, and only one possible outcome on the Day of Judgment: Clear failure and lasting punishment.

    The seeker of success who wishes to reach his goal has complete faith in God, the Creator and Sustainer of all that exists, and in His beloved messenger, Muhammad. He worships and serves no one except God, the Most Holy and the One deserving of all praise, and knows that everything will perish one day except Him to Whom is the return of all, and he or she will be rewarded or punished accordingly on the Day of Judgment, based on his performance in the life of this world. He makes the best effort for a successful outcome, by consistently praising and worshipping his Lord and performing other righteous deeds as a manifestation of his faith.

# Day 226

**Do men think that they will be left alone on saying "we believe", and that they will not be tested?**

(29:2)

# Day 226

Although relatively short in length, the beautiful selected passage of today relays the most fundamental components of lasting success in a most brilliant and effective manner. The seeker of success who has reviewed the earlier meditations in this collection will have realized the value of belief or faith in God, the Creator and Sustainer of all, and His messenger, the beloved Muhammad, as being the absolute prerequisite and the most important component of lasting success. God, the Most Wise and the Most Righteous Teacher, guides the seeker of success in the beautiful selected passage of today to the most effective understanding of this most vital concept, which is more than verbalization of his faith, or saying " I believe".

First, the fortunate individual who has been blessed with faith, as noted above, and in His messenger, the beloved Muhammad, experiences it in his entire being and is infused with enthusiasm to serve the rest of his life in His praise, worship, and service, of God, the Most Wise and the Only One deserving of praise, performing righteous deeds as a manifestation of his faith and love of his Creator. If we use the similitude of an automobile, we can say that an automobile's engine is like the heart and mind of an individual, filling its tank with fuel is like verbalizing faith - and resolving to live the rest of his life in the praise, worship and service of the Creator and Sustainer of all, is like turning on the automobile. One can then have some hope of utilizing the automobile to reach his destination - or an individual regarding achieving success.

Second, the fortunate individual who has been blessed with faith should realize from the beautiful selected passage of today that, after verbalization of his faith, he is expected to encounter things in his life that will test his faith. He will therefore acquire increased resolve and strength to preserve his most valuable asset - his faith, during such trials. If we continue to use the similitude of an automobile, we can say that, after filling the automobile with fuel, and turning on the ignition, one is expected to encounter occasionally difficult terrain during one's trip.

The seeker of success who wishes to reach his goal has complete faith in God, the Most Righteous Teacher and the Best Guide, and in His noble messenger, Muhammad. He realizes that even though faith is central to his quest for success, it is not sufficient for him to say "I believe". He manifests his faith with praise and worship of his Lord and performing other righteous actions, knowing that he will be tested in his faith during his life on earth. He takes adequate preparations beforehand, strengthening his faith, and shows resolve and patience during the periods that he is being tested, knowing that the worth of a diamond is in proportion to the amount of stress that has been applied to it.

# Day 227

**And if any strive (with might and main), they do so for their own souls; Indeed! God stands not in need of any of the creation.**

(29:6)

# Day 227

The beautiful selected passage of today can benefit a wide range of people besides those who are firm in their pursuit of success and have acquired the primary prerequisite for lasting success, i.e. faith, or belief in God, the Most Beneficent and Most Merciful, and His beloved messenger, Muhammad. It can also benefit those who have faith but are not yet firm in it, those who are interested in success but have not yet acquired its primary prerequisite, i.e. faith, those who are not interested in success, as well as those who actively work to prevent others from attaining success. It has a certain special power, truth and beauty in it that can convince the firmest of hearts.

The powerful message in the beautiful selected passage of today that will benefit all, including the seekers of success, is the knowledge that if any individual strives with whatever resources are available to him, with praise, worship, and performance of righteous actions, for the purpose of serving God, the Creator and Sustainer of all, then the one who benefits from those righteous acts is himself, when he will be judged on the Day of Judgment for his performance in the life of this world, with a detailed account, and rewarded by his Lord, the Most Rich and the Most Generous. The unfortunate individual who believes that all actions are for selfish reasons, and is unable to understand the characteristics of beneficence and love in anyone, with the highest degree of such characteristics in God Alone, might even consider God, Who is the Most Beneficent and Merciful, to have selfish characteristics, questioning why He requires men to worship Him and perform righteous acts, asking "How does that benefit God?". Such an individual has three possible options:

1) remain in his unfortunate state, concerned about maximizing his pleasure in the present, without regard for the future,
2) with continued effort and the Grace of God, the Most Beneficent and Most Merciful, be blessed with faith, with the realization that God created all that exists from nothing, and sustains His creation, and that to Him is the return of all, and that, as a thankful beneficiary of His Grace, it is his desire, as well as his duty, to serve his Creator; with this realization, he will realize the powerful message from the beautiful selected passage of today, i.e. if any strives to perform righteous deeds for the pleasure of his Creator, he does so for his own benefit, and that God, the Most Great, the Source of all power and the Creator of all, is not in need of anything from his creation, and
3) as a result of the understanding of the powerful message of today, that he takes the next most logical step, i.e. believing in God, the Creator and Sustainer, the Most Beneficent and the Source of all power, as relayed to us through His noble messenger, Muhammad, and attains faith - after which he strives for the rest of his life in praise, worship and service his Creator, and taking the first step to helping himself and to succeed.

The seeker of success who wishes to reach his goal has absolute faith in God, the Creator and Sustainer of all and the Eternal and Self-subsisting One, and in His beloved messenger, Muhammad. He knows that God is not in need of his worship or righteous deeds, or that of any of His creation, but continues to strive - doing so with might and main, from his love and sense of obligation towards Him, and knows that the greatest beneficiary of his efforts is himself.

# Day 228

**The parable of those who take protectors other than Allah is that of the spider, who builds (to itself) a house; but truly, the flimsiest of houses is the spider's house – if they but knew.**

(29:41)

# Day 228

The beautiful selected passage of today reinforces again the most important component of success, i.e. faith and belief in God, the Most Beneficent and Most Merciful, using one of the most profound and effective parables. It will be of great help to the widest range of persons on their journey to success – from those who are enemies of faith (by helping them to acquire it), to those possessing the highest degree of faith (by further strengthening it).

Throughout various stages of his life, man craves safety – from the parent as a child; perhaps from his peers as an adolescent; as a young adult, from acquiring education and skills of value to his employer; and in his older life, from the support of his children or the state.

In terms of meeting his temporary needs, man does obtain a certain degree of safety and sense of well-being from the corresponding stage of life as described above. Man also has other needs for which he may look to others, e.g. guidance, knowledge, love, justice, etc. However, without further information, man would have obligations to many sources for meeting his many needs – this is the essential premise of polytheism. With his own observation of the perfection and harmony in the universe, up to and including the marvels of his own being, all pointing to a Single Creator, as well as from the revelations in the Holy Quran, he who develops an understanding of how God, the Originator, Creator and Sustainer of all, created the entire existence from nothing and sustains it, and how it is to Him that everything must return – is fortunate and has been blessed with faith, the most important component of success. He is then able to realize the fallacy of his previous reliance on others to meet his needs – how the parent would not be sufficient for the child, if the parent did not receive sustenance from his Sustainer; and how the employer would not be enough to provide him with his daily needs if the employer was not himself enriched by God, the Most Rich One and the Enricher.

The seeker of success who wishes to reach his goal has unwavering faith in God, the Most Forceful and the Best Friend and Protector, and in His noble messenger, Muhammad. He realizes that the source of all that exists is God, and Who Alone is responsible for sustaining His creation. He realizes the fallacy of relying on anyone or anything except God, the Creator and Sustainer of all - for anything, including protection, as similar to that of a spider which builds itself a house, thinking it will provide protection, when in fact it is the flimsiest of houses.

# Day 229

**Recite what is sent of the book by inspiration to you and establish regular prayer; for prayer restrains from shameful and unjust deeds. <u>And remembrance of Allah is the greatest (thing in life), without doubt.</u> And Allah knows the deeds that you do.**

**(29: 45)**

# Day 229

    The beautiful selected passage of today is addressed in the first person by God, the All-knowing Creator and Sustainer of all, to His beloved messenger, Muhammad, so that once the message is relayed, it is the same as if it were personally addressed to the other individuals receiving the message. It contains three valuable advices for the benefit of all, and is of special interest to the seeker of success for the identification of a specific action that an individual can perform that is best in terms of leading him to his goal. The first valuable advice in the beautiful selected passage of today is the instruction to recite the inspiration from God, the Most Great and Most Wise – the message to the worlds, conveyed through His messenger, the beloved Muhammad, which has been recorded in Holy Quran. Recitation of Holy Quran by the believer has a number of benefits, the most obvious being access to guidance on all matters from God, the Highest Authority on all matters, the Most Wise and the Best Guide. Other benefits of reciting the Holy Quran include spiritual reward for the performance of a highly virtuous deed, and it is reported that jinns who are also beings having free will, and angels (who are existing with continuous praise of their Creator, without having free will), both of whom we are not able to discern with our limited capabilities, also listen to the recitation when the Holy Quran is audibly recited. As a result, the jinns receive the benefits of Divine Guidance for which they are grateful; and the angels implore their Lord to increase the blessing and reward for the reciter and his virtuous action.

    The second valuable advice in the beautiful selected passage of today is the instruction to establish regular prayer. Prayer, as instructed by the noble prophet Muhammad, contains verbal praises of God, the Creator and Sustainer of all, recitation of passages of Holy Quran, and physical postures that acknowledge the greatness of the Holy Creator. It is also the best of the righteous deeds arising from faith, and is the reason for man's creation, i.e., we will be held accountable on the Day of Judgment, by God, the Best of those who keep account and the Most Just, for succeeding in fulfilling our duties, or failing to do so. Regular prayer also restrains one from shameful and unjust deeds, with one's preoccupation being praising and serving the Creator of all, Who is Most Pure and the Source of all that is good, so the individual would then not be focused on serving others than his Lord – including one's ego, other individuals, imaginary beings, or the accursed Satan, who makes a continuous effort to lead man to shameful and unjust deeds. And **remembrance of God is the greatest thing in life - without doubt**, giving not only spiritual joy and satisfaction, but also most worthy of reward in the hereafter, from Him Who is Most Generous and is the Best Rewarder. The third powerful message in the beautiful selected passage of today is the reinforcement of another fundamental component of success: that man is to return to his Creator and be held accountable on the Day of Judgment for his performance in the life of this world, and that God, the All-aware, and the Best of those who keep account, knows the actions all individuals are performing at all times, maintaining the data in a most accurate record, to be utilized on the Day of Judgment to reach a just verdict.

The seeker of success who wishes to reach his goal has complete faith in God, the All-Knowing, the Most Wise and the Most Appreciative One, and in His beloved messenger, Muhammad. He recites the Holy Quran for personal guidance as well as spiritual satisfaction and reward, establishes regular prayer, performs other righteous actions, and knows that the greatest thing in life for both short-term and long-term satisfaction is the remembrance of his Lord, who is the Creator of all and the Source of all power and strength.

# Day 230

And dispute not with the people of the book, except with means better (than mere disputation), unless it be with those of them who inflict wrong (and injury), but say: "We believe in the revelation which came down to you; our God and your God is One – and it is to Him we have submitted (in Islam)".

(29:46)

# Day 230

    Effectiveness in interpersonal skills and communication are important components of success. The guidance provided in the beautiful selected passage of today will, therefore, be helpful to the seeker of success in optimizing these important skills.

    The fortunate seeker of success who has acquired faith or belief in God, the Creator and Sustainer of all, and His messenger, the beloved Muhammad, will be expected to have discussions about his faith either when he invites others also to the path of success, or out of satisfying the curiosity of others, or when he happens to interact with those who are the enemies of faith. We are informed elsewhere in the Holy Quran that God, the Most Wise and the Best Guide, has sent many messengers to the entire mankind with the same message, and which was completed and perfected with the prophethood of beloved Muhammad. Some of the other messengers' stories are also relayed in Holy Quran. Of the revelations received by earlier prophets are two that have been recorded and followed by their people, the Torah of the honorable prophet Moses and the Gospel of the beloved prophet Jesus; these people are referred to as "people of the book" in Holy Quran. Of the people of the book, there were many who were living at the time that the beloved prophet Muhammad received his revelations and preached the message from God, the Best Guide and the Best Teacher, who recognized the source of the revelations of the Holy Quran and the Holy Torah and the Holy Gospel as One, who attained and strengthened their faith (the most important component of success), and others who questioned and argued, and, at the other extreme, some declared hostility and persecuted the believers.

    The seeker of success is instructed in the beautiful selected passage in the proper form of interaction and communication, specifically with people who claim faith in the earlier revelations from God the Most Great and Most Wise than the Holy Quran, and that such interaction should be pleasant. Acknowledging that man is not an angel, God the Most Wise and the Most Patient, allows that only individuals who have been wronged or injured are allowed to have interactions that may be considered as disputation. If logical persuasion, pleasantness and cordiality are unsuccessful, the seeker of success is advised to invite the individuals with faith in the earlier revelations by relaying to them the information that his source and their source of worship in unadulterated faith is the same: God the Most Praiseworthy and the Most Holy, and it is to Him he has submitted himself and dedicated his life. This will count towards manifestation of one's faith with righteous action, i.e. inviting others to good action and success through acquisition of faith, the primary ingredient of success

    The seeker of success who wishes to reach his goal has absolute faith in God, the Most Pure and the Only One, and in His noble messenger, Muhammad, who provided, as the final messenger, the revelations from God, the Creator and Sustainer of all, which are recorded in the Holy Quran. He also believes in the earlier revelations, i.e. the Holy Torah and Holy Gospel - before having been altered. When he interacts with people who profess belief in only one or two of the three revelations as being from God, the Most Great and the Most Kind, and who have not caused any harm to the believers, the seeker of success will take care and will be gentle and polite in his discussion, saying : "We believe in the revelation which has come down to us and in that which came down to you; our God and your God is One, and it is to Him we have submitted in Islam".

# Day 231

**What is the life of this world but amusement and play? But certainly the home in the hereafter – that is life indeed; if they only knew.**

(29:64)

# Day 231

The powerful message in the beautiful selected passage of today is repeated in the Holy Quran, and also in this collection of meditations, for reinforcement, as one of the fundamental components of success, and therefore, presented for the benefit of the seeker of success.

There are undeniably many things in the life of this world, starting from our own faculties, such as hearing, sight, and reasoning, along with external beauty in the world, such as trees, birds, and other life forms, and more remote factors of awe, such as the sun, moon, sky, the planets and the perfect harmony and order in our universe – indeed in the entire existence, which all point to the Greatness and Power of God, Who created all from nothing, Who sustains it, and to Whom will be the return of all.

In one's worldly life, there are also many other things from which one can attain pleasure: wealth and possessions, mansions and comfortable homes, fine automobiles, comfort in relationships with parents, mates, progeny, friends etc. If one is not careful, it is possible for man to be so impressed and preoccupied with attaining further pleasures in the life of this world, that one concentrates all his energies and efforts in maximizing the pleasure and comforts of this life. Based on the information provided to us in the beautiful selected passage of today by God, the Most Powerful and the Truth, the life in the hereafter is many times better than the life of this world, in all aspects, for those who succeed in the test of this life as we have noted in the previous meditations. Therefore, one pays careful attention not only to one's life on earth – but also, and indeed, more importantly, the life of the hereafter. In summarizing the above concepts for a better understanding, the life of this world can be considered as trivial as transient amusement and play.

The seeker of success who wishes to reach his goal has unwavering faith in God, the Best Guide and the Most Trustworthy One, and in His beloved messenger, Muhammad. He knows the difference in the degree of unimaginable magnitude between the hereafter and the life of this world, and realizes the foolishness of expending all of his efforts for attainment of what the life of this world can offer him and neglecting the hereafter.

# Day 232

**And those who strive in our (cause) – We will certainly guide them to Our paths; for indeed, Allah is with those who do right.**

(29:69)

# Day 232

The beautiful selected passage of today contains a very valuable message for the benefit of the seeker of success, which provides helpful information on Guidance – which we all need if we are to succeed. If a child wants to minimize unnecessary losses and disappointments, he needs to understand the importance of asking for guidance on a regular basis, instead of relying on his own reasoning – especially in the early stages of his life. If a student wants to minimize unnecessary frustration and failure, he needs to understand the importance of asking for guidance from the teacher, especially when he is confused – and he will find the teacher to be most willing in providing the appropriate guidance for a successful outcome. Similarly, man is in need of guidance from his Lord, the Creator and Sustainer of all, to minimize unnecessary losses, disappointment, frustration and failure. Man will only be able to realize the need for guidance when he acquires faith in God as the Source of all power and creation, as relayed to us through His noble messenger, Muhammad – as a result of which he lives a life committed to praising, worshipping and serving God with righteous acts, the path to which is not easy and requires striving, combined with patience and perseverance.

Now having done his part, i.e. acquiring faith and striving in the cause of serving his Lord, man is ready for the next step to acquiring the guidance that he needs, as we are instructed in the beautiful selected passage of today, which ends with the reassurance that in relation to above, as well as all other matters, that God, the Most Powerful and the Best Protector, is indeed with those who do right, i.e. to support them in their needs.

The seeker of success who wishes to reach his goal has complete faith in God, the Most Great, the Best Guide and the Most Righteous Teacher, and in His noble messenger, Muhammad. He realizes the need for guidance from God, the Most Wise and the Most Patient, in his life; he strives with patience amid adversity in serving God, knowing that His Lord is most pleased to provide him with guidance if he only asks. And he knows with full conviction that God, the Almighty and Best Friend and Protector is always with those who do right.

# Day 233

Do they not see that God enlarges the provision for whom He wills and straitens (it for whom He wills). Indeed, in that are signs for a people who believe.

So, give to the relative his due, and to the poor and to the wayfarer. That is best for those who seek God's countenance; <u>and it is they who will be successful.</u>

And that which you give in gift (to others), in order that it may increase (your wealth by expecting to get a better one in return) from other people's property, has no increase with God; but that which you give in Zakat (charity), seeking God's countenance, then they will have manifold increase.

(30:37-39)

#  Day 233

    We find in the beautiful selected passage of today, a point that has been repeated a number of times in the Holy Quran and also in this collection of meditations for reinforcement and, therefore, is considered one of the key components of success. The seeker of success is instructed to pay special attention to the clear link between one's actions and success. We begin with the component of faith, the absolute prerequisite for success, which is then manifested by righteous action. Those who believe in God, the Creator and Nourisher of all, and the Constrictor and the Reliever, we are reminded, notice His signs – which include enlarging and straitening the provision of whomever He wills. Having been blessed with the gift of faith, the logical next step, if one is sincere, is action, and more specifically, righteous action – that which is done for the love of the One Whom one has developed faith as the Creator, Sustainer and Lord of all that exists. The believer progresses next to the level where he realizes that the reason for his creation, along with praising and worshipping his Creator, is to serve Him - which is also a component of worship, and that he fulfills the role on earth of having the distinct honor of being the representative of God, the Most Beneficent and Most Merciful. As the One Who provides for the needs of the entire existence, one of His characteristics that God uses most often to describe Himself is as that of Beneficence. Hence we can see the importance for man in terms of providing for and giving to others in the world. The esteemed reader is referred to the commentary of Day 3 of this collection of meditations for a more detailed discussion of worship.

    The beautiful selected passage of today provides further details and guidance about giving: the righteous act that is so pleasing to God, the Most Generous and the Best Provider, that those who give to others, seeking His countenance and not for selfish reasons - to relatives, the poor, and the needy, not expecting anything in return from them except the pleasure of their Lord, shall have manifold increase of what they give, and will be rewarded with **lasting success**.

    The seeker of success who wishes to reach his goal has absolute faith in God, the Most Generous and the Most Appreciative One, and in His noble messenger, Muhammad. He feels pleasure in giving to others from what his Lord has provided him - not expecting anything in return, except the pleasure of God, the Most Rich, the Enricher and the Most Trustworthy.

# Day 234

**Then contemplate (O man!) the memorials of Allah's Mercy! How He gives life to the earth after its death; indeed the Same will give life to the men who are dead – for He has power over all things.**

(30:50)

# Day 234

    The beautiful selected passage of today contains a very powerful message that can help the unfortunate individual lacking faith in God, the Creator and Sustainer of all, as relayed to us through His noble messenger, Muhammad, and which is the most important component of success. It can also help the fortunate individual already possessing faith - to strengthen it. At the same time, it also sheds light on another important component of lasting success: the relationship between life, death and resurrection.

    Let us contemplate the example provided to us by God, the Most Great and Most Merciful, the example of how the earth is revived in spring with greenery after its relative death in autumn. If the trees could think, and they had never experienced the cycle of life and death, would the trees be able to believe that after their death in autumn, they would be revived in spring? Although the parallel between men and trees as put forth by the humble author is not entirely applicable because the trees cannot think as far as we know, and they don't have free choice for acting like men do, still the vital message is able to be relayed, i.e. that for the one who knows and has seen the cycle repeated, it is not unbelievable at all.

    The more important point from the example provided by God, the Most Wise and the Creator and the Restorer, is that He is the One Who gave life to the earth, causes it to "die" on a yearly basis, and then to be revived again in spring – for He has power over all things. What else can explain this phenomenon except the Knowledge, Power, and Benevolence of the Holy Creator? Now the fortunate individual who has been able to understand the above example has acquired faith and it remains that he shall manifest it by appropriate action.

    The seeker of success who wishes to reach his goal has absolute faith in God, the Creator of life and death, and in His beloved messenger, Muhammad. He has no difficulty understanding that it is his Lord Who gave him life, causes him to die, and will give him life again. He lives his life in such a manner that, when he is given life again for eternity, that it will be one in which he will find rest and satisfaction - and not pain and misery, which he knows depends on his own choice and actions in this life.

# Day 235

**Alif Lam Mim**

**These are verses of the wise book –**

**A Guide and a Mercy to the *muhsinun* (doers of good – for the sake of God);**

**Those who establish regular prayer, and give regular charity, and have (in their hearts) the assurance of the hereafter;**

**These are on (true) guidance from their Lord – and <u>these are the ones who will succeed.</u>**

(31:1-5)

# Day 235

The beautiful selected passage of today begins with three Arabic alphabets, characteristic of some other chapters in Holy Quran, with the consensus being that they may have mystical significance, but that only God Alone, the Apparent and Hidden One, knows their true significance. It has special importance for the seekers of success, being addressed directly to them, with clear instructions outlining the path to success.

The beginning and the ending of the beautiful selected passage of today contains reassurances about the worth and source of the instructions outlining the path to success – from the Lord of all that exists, through His messenger, the beloved Muhammad, recorded in the wise book, the Holy Quran, on true Guidance from their Lord, the Most Wise and the Knower of all.

The path outlined by God, the One Who created all, to Whom all must return, and the One Who will judge every individual and determine which ones will attain lasting success or failure, begins with the most important component of success: Faith. It is addressed to *muhsinun*, or those who are doers of good for the sake of God only, the Most Magnificent and the One Who is the source of all good, and not for the sake of anything else.

The next step is outlined for the fortunate individual who has taken the first and most important step on the path to success, i.e. faith, which is manifesting the faith by doing good for the sake of God, the Most Beneficent and Most Merciful, and which includes establishing regular prayer, giving regular charity and having assurance of the hereafter. These fundamental components of the path to success, as outlined above, are repeatedly reinforced for the benefit of the seekers of success, in both the Holy Quran and in this collection of meditations, but summarized brilliantly in the beautiful selected passage of today.

The seeker of success who wishes to reach his goal has unwavering faith in God, the Most Glorious, the Best Doer of good, and the Best Guide, and in His noble messenger, Muhammad. He performs righteous deeds as a manifestation of his faith, including engaging in regular prayer and giving regular charity. He has in his heart, assurance of the hereafter.

# Day 236

We bestowed (in the past) wisdom on Luqman: "Show (your) gratitude to Allah". Any who is (so) grateful does so to the profit of his own soul; but if any is ungrateful, indeed Allah is free of all wants and worthy of all praise.

And (remember) when Luqman said to his son by way of instruction: "O my son! Join not in worship (others) with Allah; for <u>false worship is indeed the highest wrongdoing</u>".

And we have enjoined on man (to be good) to his parents; in difficulty upon difficulty did his mother bear him, and in two years' time was his weaning; (hear the command:) "Show gratitude to Me and to your parents; to Me is (your final) goal".

"But if they strive to make you join in worship with Me – things of which you have no knowledge, obey them not; yet bear company with them in this life with justice (and consideration) and follow the way of those who turn to Me (in love). In the end the return of you all is to Me, and I will tell you the truth (and meaning) of all that you did".

"O my son!" (said Luqman), "if there be (but) the weight of a mustard seed and it were (hidden) in a rock, or (anywhere) in the heavens or on earth, Allah will bring it forth; for Allah understands the finer mysteries, (and) is well-acquainted (with them).

(Cont'd)

# Day 236

The beautiful selected passage of today is part of the same chapter reviewed yesterday, titled "Luqman", the name of one of the honorable messengers of God, the Most Beneficent and Most Merciful – whose distinguishing characteristics are his wisdom and guidance; an example of the depth of his wisdom is given in his firm grasp of faith, and his priceless advice to his son, beginning with the injunction to "show your gratitude to God". Man is reminded that if he is grateful to his Lord, he is only helping himself.

The depth of the wise prophet Luqman's wisdom can be gauged by his caring and detailed advice he gave to his son, and documented in the Holy Quran for the benefit of the seekers of success. A Brief summarization of the comprehensive advice provided by the wise prophet Luqman follows – the seeker of success is referred to the text of the beautiful selected passage itself for further details:

1. Join no one else with God, the One and the Only One, in worship - and the wisdom to understand that one who does so is committing the **highest wrongdoing.**

2. Man is accountable for all his actions in this life, down to the size of a "mustard seed" figuratively.

3. Establish regular prayer - which is the reason for his creation.

4. Enjoin what is right and forbid what is wrong.

5. Practice patience and constancy in all affairs.

6. Avoid arrogant behavior, and be humble.

7. Be moderate in pace – neither being excessively fast nor slow.

8. Speak in a gentle manner and avoid harshness.

The seeker of success who wishes to reach his goal has complete faith in God, the Most Holy, Most Wise and the Most Righteous Teacher, and in His beloved messenger, Muhammad. He joins no others in the worship of his Lord, is kind to his parents, showing gratitude to them and to his Lord; and obeys his parents, except if they instruct him to abandon his faith. He pays close attention to the priceless and timeless advice that the wise prophet Luqman provided to his son, as well as all other men and women, for succeeding, and as is documented in today's beautiful selected passage.

"O my son! Establish regular prayer, enjoin what is just, and forbid what is wrong; and bear with patient constancy whatever comes to you – for this is firmness (of purpose) in (the conduct of) affairs.

"And swell not your cheek (in pride) at men, nor walk in insolence through the earth; for Allah loves not any arrogant boaster.

"And be moderate in your pace, and lower your voice; for the harshest of sounds, without doubt, is the braying of the ass".

(31:12-19)

## Day 237

**Whoever submits his whole self to Allah, and is a doer of good, has indeed grasped** *the most trustworthy hand-hold*; **and indeed with Allah rests the end and decision of (all) affairs.**

(31:22)

# Day 237

The beautiful selected passage of today contains two powerful messages that have been repeated in the Holy Quran and in this collection of meditations with frequency relative to their importance as fundamental components of success. Its distinctive characteristic is the use of an extremely powerful similitude that is, therefore, markedly effective in understanding and retaining its most valuable messages for the seeker of success.

The first powerful message in the beautiful selected passage of today reviews the most important component of success, i.e. faith in God, the Most Beneficent and Most Merciful, arising from contemplation and observation of the innumerable signs in all of existence, including in man himself, of God's Presence and Benevolence, submitting his whole self to Him in awe and thankfulness; additionally, if one believes in the message brought to mankind by the noble prophet Muhammad as that from God, the Most Glorious and the Truth, and recorded in the Holy Quran, such as in the beautiful selected passage of today, this fortunate individual has earned the coveted title of "Muslim", or one who has submitted his whole self to God, the Creator and Sustainer of all – and is on the sure path to the attainment of lasting success.

The second powerful message in the beautiful selected passage of today is a direct extension of faith, as described above, which is its manifestation, including praising, adoring and worshipping God, the Originator and the Sustainer of all that exists, and doing good deeds for the sake of serving Him and for nothing or no one else, including himself. Man craves security at all stages of his life, from childhood to death, and seeks it in various forms, depending on the level of his capability and understanding. Now we can understand the significance of the brilliant similitude used in the beautiful selected passage of today, i.e. the best security possible for man is in acquiring faith, submitting his whole self sincerely to God, and doing good deeds for His sake, as equivalent to having grasped the most trustworthy hand-hold, the one that never breaks, though all other security measures can fail – for indeed, God is Most Powerful, the Best Protector, and with Him rests the end and decision of all affairs.

The seeker of success who wishes to reach his goal has absolute faith in God, the Most Strong and the Best Protector, and in His noble messenger, Muhammad. He submits his whole self to his Lord - in awe and gratitude to Him, performing righteous deeds as manifestation of his faith, and feels secure in knowing that he has grasped the most reliable Handhold that never breaks, in reference to his relationship with his Lord.

# Day 238

O Mankind! Fear your Lord (keeping your duty to Him and avoiding all evil), and fear (the coming of) a day when no father can avail anything for his son, nor a son avail anything for his father. Indeed the promise of Allah is true; let not then this present life deceive you, nor let the chief deceiver (Satan) deceive you about Allah.

Indeed the knowledge of the hour is with Allah (Alone). It is He who sends down rain, and He who knows what is in the wombs. Nor does anyone know what it is that he will earn tomorrow; nor does anyone know in what land he is to die. Indeed with Allah is full knowledge and He is acquainted (with all things).

(31:33-34)

# Day 238

Success is not a matter of coincidence; it requires formulation of a vision, a goal, planning, and striving to turn the vision and goal into reality. In fact, man does exhibit understanding the process of planning and striving for successful outcomes at various stages of his life on the earth. For example, a child is groomed for optimizing his outcome at adolescence/young adult level: of possible acceptance into a prestigious university if he is successful in his earlier education. A young adult prepares for optimal transition from university to work setting. He prepares for the middle age phase of his life, when he himself will be responsible for raising children and also the responsibility for his elderly parents. And he prepares for his retirement and old age. However, man's ability to plan beyond his old age or death, although it should be of many times more significant concern to him than the previous stages discussed above, is usually deficient when compared to his motivation in planning for the various phases in this earthly life, or on a short-term basis. In the beautiful selected passage of today, man is instructed in planning and taking appropriate measures for optimizing a successful outcome in the next stage of his life beyond this world, i.e. after death, which is more important than all his previous stages, as it will be his situation for eternity, whereas the entire duration of the life of this world is like less than one day of the afterlife.

God, the Most Great, the Originator, the Restorer and the Best Appraiser, informs man in the beautiful selected passage of today of the many things that man does not know about – such as what will happen to him tomorrow, or what is in the womb in early pregnancy, or where he will die, etc. But God, the Almighty, the All-aware and the All-comprehending One, knows all; and He instructs man to take appropriate preparatory measures for his life after death – for indeed He is Most Caring and Most Loving, and His word and His promise is true. A summary of the specific steps in adequate preparation of the most important phase of man's life i.e. that after his death, and resurrection is as follows:

1. Have a sense of fear of not fulfilling the duties for which God, the Creator of all and the Best of those who keeps account, created him, as every individual will be called to account for the performance of his duties on the Day of Judgment, when everyone will be accountable for his own actions, and neither a father can avail anything for his son, nor a son avail anything for his father.

2. Let not the life of the present world deceive you – so that all of one's energies and resources are not wasted on the short-term pleasures of this life, with no concern or preparation for the hereafter, which is more important than the present life

3. Let not Satan, the chief deceiver – through himself or his agents – deceive you about God, the Most Great and Most Kind, thus preventing you from fulfilling your duties and attaining success.

The seeker of success who wishes to reach his goal has complete faith in God, the giver of life, the Creator of Death and the Resurrector, and in His noble messenger, Muhammad. He is certain of the hereafter and takes appropriate preparatory measures during his life to prepare for it accordingly.

# Day 239

Only those believe in our Ayat (signs, revelations, etc.) who, when they are reminded of them, fall down prostrate, and glorify the praises of their Lord, and they are not proud.

Their limbs forsake their beds, to invoke their Lord in fear and hope, and they spend (in charity in God's cause) out of what We have bestowed on them.

Now no person knows what delights of the eye are kept hidden (in reserve) for them – as a reward for their (good) deeds.

Is then the man who believes, no better than the man who is rebellious and wicked? They are not equal.

(32:15-18)

# Day 239

The most important components of success are repeated in the beautiful selected passage of today for reinforcement of key points for the benefit of the seeker of success; the characteristics differentiating it from others with similar contents include an effective description of differentiation between success and failure and rich details about faith, the most important component of success, as well as about the magnitude of the reward of attaining success.

An individual who passes a driving examination has more privileges in society than the one who does not. A physician who has failed a licensing examination typically has fewer privileges professionally than the one who has passed. The clear differentiating point between success and failure is identified in today's beautiful selected passage, with the characteristic of faith in God, the Most Holy and the Best Guide, associated with success; and rebelliousness and wickedness, associated with failure. Similar examples can be used between hot and cold, and light and dark: they are completely different characteristics.

Further details about individuals who succeed, or those possessing faith, are provided for the seeker of success. They are described as those who, when they are reminded of the signs of God (evidences, revelations, etc.), feel a special obligation and love for Him, falling down prostrate, glorifying the praises of their Lord, and not being proud. The seeker of success is requested to make prostration to his Lord at this time and glorify Him with praise to strengthen his belief and readiness to serve his Lord, and to continue doing so on a regular basis. Having been enthused with belief and love and awe of their Creator, the seekers of success, further, forsake their beds to invoke their Lord in fear and hope (while the others are still sleeping), and they perform good actions to manifest their faith, along with spending in charity to please their Lord, from what He has bestowed on them.

While serving to inform the believers of the greatness of the reward awaiting them for their efforts in performing good deeds arising from faith, the beautiful selected passage of today also increases their enthusiasm and their motivation for continuing on the righteous path and strengthening their faith, knowing that one is not even able to imagine, based on the comparison to the life of this world, what delights of the eyes are kept hidden in reserve for them. Enthusiasm is also known to the experts on worldly success as an important component of being able to achieve one's goals.

The seeker of success who wishes to reach his goal has absolute faith in God, the Most Righteous Teacher and the Best Guide, and in His beloved messenger, Muhammad. He knows that good and evil are not the same. When reminded of the signs of God, the All-seeing and All-Aware, he falls down prostrate – glorifying His praises and is not proud. In addition, he manifests his faith with regular worship to his Lord, including forsaking the comfort of his bed in part of the night, in order to praise God, the Most Praiseworthy and Most Glorious, and performance of other good deeds, including spending in charity out of what God, the Most Rich and the Most Generous, has provided him.

# Day 240

**O Prophet (Muhammad)! Fear God, and follow not (the advice of) the disbelievers and the hypocrites. Indeed, God is ever All-knower, All-wise.**

**And follow that which is revealed to you from your Lord. Indeed, God is well acquainted with what you do.**

**And put your trust in Allah; and enough is Allah as a Wakil (Disposer of affairs or Trustee).**

(33:1-3)

# Day 240

The beautiful selected passage of today is addressed to the beloved prophet Muhammad; this and similar revelations in the Holy Quran imply the inclusion of the believers as addressees as well, after the message was delivered to the noble prophet Muhammad from God, the Most Great, and the Most Righteous Teacher, and subsequently relayed to mankind. It begins with the reminder to keep one's obligations to God, the Most Beneficent and Most Merciful, and then proceeds to instruct the noble prophet Muhammad and the believers, to follow the Guidance that has been revealed from their Lord, and not to follow the advice of the disbelievers and hypocrites. The guidance from God, the Most Great and the Creator and Sustainer of all, is meant as a Mercy to guide men to all that is good and which will benefit them in this life and the afterlife. The guidance from the disbelievers and the hypocrites is meant to serve their interests, which may benefit men on a short-term basis, in the life of this world, but will be harmful to them in the long-run and in the after-life; it is better termed as misguidance. Indeed, God is ever All-Knower, All-wise and well-acquainted with what every being is doing – and it is His Guidance that supersedes over that of any other source.

Additionally, the honorable prophet Muhammad and the believers are instructed to put their trust in God, the Almighty, the Most Wise, the Light and the Guide – regarding the matter of guidance as well as all other matters. If one puts his trust in any other than God, the Most Great and Most Wise, he will be disappointed, both in this life and, especially, in the hereafter, while the one who puts his trust in God will never be disappointed – neither in this life nor the hereafter. The beautiful selected passage of today ends with the reassurance that the one who puts his trust in God, the Creator and Sustainer of all, will find Him to be the Most Trustworthy, and the Best One to represent and advance his interests.

The seeker of success who wishes to reach his goal has unwavering faith in God, the Best Teacher and the Best Guide, and in His noble messenger, Muhammad. He is cognizant of his obligations to his Lord, prefers the Guidance from Him over that of the enemies of the faith, and puts his trust in God completely, knowing that He is the Most Trustworthy and the Best Disposer of affairs and Trustee.

# Day 241

**Say: "who is it that can protect you from Allah if it be His wish to give you punishment or to give you Mercy? Nor will they find for themselves, besides Allah, any protector or helper.**

(33:17)

# Day 241

The beautiful selected passage of today can help the unfortunate individual who does not possess the most important ingredient of success, i.e. faith or belief in God, the Creator and Sustainer of all, and in His beloved messenger, Muhammad, to acquire it. And for the fortunate individual who has been blessed with faith, it will be strengthened. It was revealed during the time when the enemies of faith were determined to exterminate the believers and, therefore, the believers were called to defend their faith not only with their resources, but with their persons as well. There were some among the believers who professed their belief verbally, but were willing to manifest their faith up to a certain level only, and not to risk physical harm in hostilities – such individuals would be categorized as hypocrites, i.e. saying one thing, while their actions were inconsistent with their sayings .

God, the Most Wise and the Most Righteous Teacher, instructs His beloved messenger, Muhammad, to ask the hypocrites, that if it was His wish to punish them or grant them Mercy – either in this life or in the hereafter, then who is there that can prevent Him from doing so? The answer lies in the brilliance of the question itself, as can be expected from the One Who is Most Wise and is the Best Teacher: of course there is no one that can do such a thing, whether one was to die defending his faith or die during his sleep. This is the crux of faith, and it is not enough to verbally profess faith, but to manifest it with righteous action, up to and including with one's life – if necessary.

The seeker of success who wishes to reach his goal has complete faith in God, the Almighty and Creator of all, and in His beloved messenger, Muhammad. He manifests his faith with righteous actions, up to and including risking and giving his life, if necessary – for he realizes that if it was the wish of his Lord to punish him with death or suffering, or reward him with His Mercy, there is none that can prevent Him from doing so at any time. And he realizes that there is, besides his Lord, no protector or helper.

# Day 242

**You have indeed in the messenger of Allah a <u>beautiful pattern (of conduct)</u> for any whose hope is in Allah and the Final Day, and remembers Allah much.**

(33:21)

# Day 242

    The key components of success are brilliantly summarized in the beautiful selected passage of today, with additional key information for a more thorough understanding for those who are motivated to pursue their aspirations.

    The seeker of success who has reviewed the Holy Quran, either on his own or via the earlier meditations in this collection, will have realized the importance of belief and faith in God, the Creator and Sustainer of all, and in His beloved messenger, Muhammad, as the absolute prerequisite and the most important component of success. For further advancement on the path to success beyond the initial, albeit most important, step, this faith must be manifested by appropriate action, including praising and worshipping God, the Almighty and source of all Power – out of awe and love for Him – and performing righteous deeds for His sake and to earn His pleasure. Therefore, engaging in remembering, praising, and worshipping God, the Owner of all and the One Deserving of all praise, is one aspect (the highest one) of manifestation of one's faith. The other component of the expression of faith besides praise and worship of God, the Almighty and Most Kind, is performance of other righteous deeds done for His sake. The seeker of success can refer to Holy Quran for further Guidance, as well as to this collection of meditations, compiled precisely for that purpose. However, the seeker of success is advised by God, the Most Wise and Best Teacher, that in terms of performance of righteous deeds and conduct, one is recommended to **<u>utilize His noble messenger, Muhammad, as the model to which all seekers of success should aspire.</u>** This has important implications for the seeker of success in the following ways: 1) having a role model or mentor helps to facilitate one's journey in realizing a goal, so that he or she does not have to learn how to invent the wheel again, and can learn from the knowledge gained from others who can guide one to a successful outcome. The beloved prophet Muhammad has been designated a model of success by God, the Best Appraiser and the Wisest Judge, so the seeker of success pays close attention to the life of and practices of the noble prophet Muhammad, and 2) when there is something an individual does not understand in regards to the recommendations given in the Holy Quran, or does not find his specific concern addressed in it, then he should utilize the noble prophet Muhammad's example and what he said and did regarding the issues of concern. The respected reader of this collection should recall that the noble prophet Ibrahim was referred to earlier as the model for the seeker of success, but with the updating, clarification, and purification of the previous messages relayed from God, the All-knowing and Most Wise, the role model for all mankind and especially the seekers of success has been subsequently designated as the noble prophet Muhammad. Another advantage of utilization of the beloved prophet Muhammad as the ultimate role model is that we know a lot more about him on factual basis than any previous historical figure.

    The other key components of success besides faith are reviewed in the beautiful selected passage of today, and include understanding the final day, or Day of Judgment, and being gathered in the presence of God, the Giver of life and Creator of death, the Restorer and the Gatherer, and being held accountable for one's performance in the life of this world with a detailed account, and being rewarded or punished accordingly.

The seeker of success who wishes to reach his goal has absolute faith in God, the Creator and Sustainer of all, and in his noble messenger, Muhammad. He is certain of meeting his Lord on the Day of Judgment, to be held accountable for his life in this world. He manifests his faith with remembering, praising and worshipping his Lord much along with performance of other righteous actions. In addition to the Holy Quran, he utilizes the noble prophet Muhammad as the best model for how he should spend his time on earth and performance of righteous deeds as a manifestation of his faith.

# Day 243

O You who believe! Celebrate the praises of Allah, and do so often;

and glorify Him morning and evening.

He it is who sends Blessings on you and His angels too (ask Allah to bless and forgive you), that He may bring you out from darkness into light. And He is ever Most Merciful to the believers.

Their greeting on the Day they shall meet Him (their Lord) will be "Peace". And He has prepared for them a generous reward (paradise)

(33:41-44)

# Day 243

Several key components of lasting success are reinforced in the beautiful selected passage of today, with particular details about them contributing to a greater appreciation of the subject matter when combined with the understanding of other similar passages in the Holy Quran and this collection of meditations.

We begin with the most important component of success, i.e. belief or faith in God, the Creator and Sustainer of all, and in His beloved messenger, Muhammad, for it is to the faithful that further instructions are addressed and further Guidance is provided on attaining **lasting success.** The seeker of success who has reviewed the earlier meditations will recall that even though faith is of primary importance in the attainment of success, that it will not be of practical benefit unless it is manifested by appropriate action. The seeker of success who has reviewed the earlier meditations in this collection will also recall that the important component of manifesting one's faith is by engaging in praising or worshipping God, the Most Great and the Only One deserving of all praise – and which is the reason for man's creation. And the other form of manifesting one's faith is by performing other righteous acts for God's sake and pleasure, blessed be His Name. Further details are provided in the beautiful selected passage of today about that portion of the faith dealing with praising or worshipping of God, the Most Beneficent and Most Merciful. The seeker of success is instructed to celebrate the praises of his Lord often, and to Glorify Him in the morning and evening (clarified as five obligatory worship times by Muhammad, the beloved messenger of God, and the model for the seekers of success to follow). The seeker of success who has reviewed the earlier meditations will also recall that celebrating the praises of his Lord often, and more than the obligatory requirements, is one way that a believer gains increasing closeness to Him.

As a result of his praise and worship, we are instructed in the beautiful selected passage of today, the seeker of success will attain significant short-term and long-term benefits. The short term benefits include receiving blessings from his Lord and the angels, who are witnessing the beautiful acts of praise and worship, asking God, the Most Glorious and the Responder to Prayer, to bless and forgive the worshipper. Additionally, the seeker of success will be brought from darkness into light. And indeed God is Most Beneficent, Most Merciful to the believers. An example of the long-term benefit of engaging in praise and worship of God, the Most Great and the Most Generous One, is that when the seeker of success meets His Lord on the Day of Judgment, he will be greeted with the greeting of "peace" by angels, heralding the good fortune and what is in store for him, finding from his Lord a most generous reward and being admitted to paradise, attaining **lasting success**. Additionally, since worship of God, the Most Holy and the Most Beneficent, is the best of righteous actions, accumulation of righteous actions to one's credit will help sway the balance of righteous deeds to a favorable position and contribute to being declared a winner on the Day of Judgment

The seeker of success who wishes to reach his goal has unwavering faith in God, the Creator and Sustainer of all, and in His beloved messenger, Muhammad. He engages in the praise and worship of his Lord much – and glorifies Him in the morning and evening, and he does so often.

# Day 244

**O Prophet! Tell your wives and daughters, and the believing women, that they should cast their outer garments over their persons (when outside): that is most convenient, (so) that they should be known (as such, i.e. believing women) and not be molested. And Allah is Most Forgiving, Most Merciful.**

(33:59)

# Day 244

The beautiful selected passage of today is addressed to half of the seekers of success who have been blessed with faith (in God, the Most Magnificent and Most Wise, and in his beloved messenger, Muhammad) – which is the most important component of success, and those who are of female sex, i.e. believing women. Much has been made in recent times about concern for the traditional dressing of Muslim or believing women and women's freedom, with a great degree of sensationalism attached to the topic. For a better understanding of the role of distinctive dressing based on tradition or style, let us examine the dressing preference of physicians, judges and generals. A physician does not need to wear a long white coat, but does so in order that others will recognize him as a physician and considers it an honor; it also helps him perform his duties better, with its convenient pockets, and protects his daily clothes from blood and soiling. A judge does not need to wear a black cloak to perform his duties, but does so out of tradition, as well as considering it a sign of honor. Neither does a general need to wear distinctive clothing, with his stars pinned to his dressing, but does so to be recognized as such and considers it an honor. Let's suppose we suggest to the physicians, judges, or generals to wear shorts on their duty instead of their traditional mode of dressing and to express their individuality; would we expect any physician, judge or general to follow our suggestion?

There is no doubt that a woman's feminine characteristics arouse pleasure in men, and vice versa. Also, once an individual is around another from the opposite sex, it would be an anomaly for the woman to follow her passion with unwelcome physical aggression, but considered a more common response for man, partly due to differences in hormones, body size, strength, and tradition. It is interesting that at present, men can enjoy the pleasure of being aroused by displays of feminine beauty, with all levels of particular societies encouraging nakedness in women. However, men continue to don traditional dressing in those societies championing women's right to dress to express their femininity. In fact, if the women indeed were effective in demanding their rights in societies encouraging dressing to express oneself freely, it would be the women who would be more conservatively dressed, and the men who would be expected to be dressed so that women can more easily enjoy viewing the masculinity of men, including on the most solemn occasions. God, the Most Wise and Most Great, instructs the believing women in the beautiful selected passage of today to cast Jilbab (long outer garment or cloak) for convenience, to be identified as such (faithful), and so they would not be objects of undesired physical aggression. What exactly is instructed to be covered is not specified; however, the aim of modesty, including loose outer garments to minimize the display of femininity to unintended males, is clear.

The seeker of success who wishes to reach his goal has complete faith in God, the Most Wise and the Best Guide, and in His noble messenger, Muhammad. The female seeker of success who wishes to reach her goal is proud of expressing her distinguished status as one who is a believer – with her choice of dressing that includes casting a long outer garment over her person to cover her femininity and features of beauty, when she is outside of her home for convenience, to proudly identify her status (as a believer), and so that she will not be the object of undesired physical aggression. She knows that the entire life is an examination process, which she intends to pass; she is less willing to discard her honorable mode of dressing than a judge who is willing to wear shorts and T-shirt while he is on duty.

# Day 245

O You who believe! Fear Allah, and (always) say a word directed to the Right.

He will direct you to do righteous good deeds and will forgive you your sins. **He who obeys Allah and His messenger, has already attained the highest Success.**

(33:70 -71)

# Day 245

When a teacher repeats particular points to students, the wise student will pay particular attention to those points – in proportion to the number of times they have been repeated. There are five powerful messages in the beautiful selected passage of today for the benefit of the seeker of success, two of which are its distinguishing characteristics from other similar passages, and which will be reviewed in further detail below. The other three powerful messages are also of significant importance and will be listed as summaries, with the seeker of success directed to the earlier meditations for further details – as they have been reviewed in the past, to enable appropriate understanding to the reader, and they are as follows:

The importance of faith in God, the Most Great and Most Kind, and in His beloved messenger, Muhammad. This is the most important component of success.

The importance of fearing God, Who, even though he is the Most Merciful and Most Forgiving, is also the All-Aware, the Best of those who keeps account, the Best Judge and the Avenger. Therefore, one should fear the failure to perform the assigned duties for which man was created.

As a result of the above (2) and also of the two new messages to be discussed for today, that God, the Most Forgiving and the Best Guide, will forgive the sins of the believers and guide them to do righteous and good deeds – the criterion for granting the best rewards in the hereafter, i.e. righteous deeds done as manifestation of faith.

One of the two powerful messages and characteristic features of today's beautiful selected passage instructs the seeker of success to say a word directed to the right. This includes speaking the truth itself; it also includes saying the right things that are honorable and avoiding unnecessary talking, or talking which will lead to harm.

The second of the two powerful messages and characteristic features of today's beautiful selected passage of today is an excellent guide, as well as great news for the believers – the announcement that he who obeys God, the Most Just and Most Forgiving, and obeys His messenger, the beloved Muhammad, is as he **has already attained lasting success.** During the examination and afterwards, until the results are in, the examinees are indeed anxious and uneasy about their performance or the results: and if the results are even suggested to them by the teacher, examiner, or evaluator, they will be greatly reassured!

The seeker of success who wishes to reach his goal has absolute faith in God, the Most Great and the Most Trustworthy, and in His beloved messenger, Muhammad. He fears failing to fulfill the duties required of him from his Lord; he speaks the truth and says righteous words when he speaks; he obeys God, the Best Guide and Most Righteous Teacher, and obeys His noble messenger, Muhammad, and he feels greatly relieved, knowing beforehand that he is one of those will pass the exam of life and attain lasting success.

## Day 246

**Truly, We did offer Al Amanah (the trust or moral responsibility, or honesty and all the duties which God has ordered) to the heavens and the earth and the mountains, but they declined to bear it and were afraid of it (i.e. afraid of failing and incurring God's punishment as a result), but man bore it. Truly, he was unjust (to himself) and ignorant (of its consequences) –**

**(With the result) that God has to punish the hypocrites – men and women, and the Mushrikeen (polytheists, idolaters, pagans, and disbelievers in God and His noble messenger, Muhammad); and God will pardon (accept the repentance of) the true believers – men and women, and God is ever Oft-forgiving, Most Merciful.**

(33:72-73)

# Day 246

The beautiful selected passage of today again reinforces the importance of the two primary components of success for our benefit: Faith and the performance of righteous deeds. Its distinctiveness lies in the understanding of the magnitude of responsibility that is carried by man, the undesirability of hypocrisy, and association of others in the worship of God, the Source of all that exists, and He to Whom belongs all praise and worship, and its consequences, as well as the understanding of imperfection in man.

When something of value is kept with another, two conditions must be met: 1) the one offering the other something of value, trusts in the other's ability to safeguard it and return it, and 2) the one accepting the responsibility to safeguard and return the thing of value to the other believes he has the ability to do so. In the beautiful selected passage of today, we are informed that God, the Most Powerful and the Most Praiseworthy, offered Amanah (the trust or moral responsibility and consequences of selecting the good over the bad) to the heavens, earth, and the mountains, but they declined, due to the fear of failing and incurring the punishment of God, the Resurrector and the Avenger. However, man accepted this responsibility without fully realizing its consequences. This signifies that the level of responsibility borne by man is truly great and if he is not extremely vigilant, he risks failure. This is what distinguishes man from all other created beings. But, along with his special status among the created beings, man carries much greater risk of failure, while failure is not an option for the other created beings at all – as they are constantly in praise, worship and service of God, while man may choose whether or not to do so, although that is God's right upon man.

With our understanding that it is God's right upon man that man should praise, worship and serve God, which man accepted as a trust from Him, and so which must be returned to God, the Creator and Sustainer of all. We are informed in today's beautiful selected passage that God, blessed be His Name, will pardon or accept the repentance of true believers, as he is Most Forgiving and Most Merciful. Who are these true believers who seek God's forgiveness? These are the people who have not been perfect (since it is not possible for a person to be perfect), but who have faith in their Lord, the Creator and Sustainer of all, as relayed to us by His noble messenger, Muhammad, who praise, worship and perform righteous deeds to please and serve God, the Most Appreciative and the Most Generous. These are the people who are returning to God, the Best of those who keep account and the All-Aware, what was entrusted to them. On the other hand, the hypocrites and those who reject the message of the noble prophet Muhammad to submit to God, the Most Holy and the Most Glorious and worship Him Alone, not associating any other in worship with Him; they do not return what has been entrusted to them by God, the Source of all that exists, the Resurrector and the Most Just, and will incur His punishment, as recorded in the beautiful selected passage of today.

The seeker of success who wishes to reach his goal has absolute faith in God, the Most Magnificent and the One to Whom belongs all praise and worship, and in His noble messenger, Muhammad. He realizes the greatness of the responsibility he bears in honoring the trust placed in Him by his Lord and fears the failure of not being able to return it. He realizes his imperfection and seeks his Lord's pardon for that, but makes the most sincere effort to return the trust to his Lord – of praising, worshipping and serving Him with righteous deeds, not associating any other in worship with Him and acting as His vicegerent on earth.

# Day 247

It is not your wealth nor your children that will bring you nearer to Us in degree; but only those who believe and work righteousness – these are the ones for whom there is a multiplied reward for their deeds, while securely they (reside) in the dwellings on high.

Those who strive against our signs, to frustrate them, will be given over into punishment.

Say: "Indeed, My Lord enlarges and restricts the sustenance to such of His servants as He pleases; and nothing do you spend in the least (in His cause) but He replaces it – for He is the Best of those who grant sustenance".

(34:37-39)

# Day 247

    The beautiful selected passage of today contains three powerful messages that will help the seeker of success to reach his goal - the first of which reinforces the most important components of success, i.e. faith in God, the Creator and Sustainer of all, and in His beloved messenger, Muhammad, which is then manifested by appropriate action or working righteousness. Although reviewed in the earlier meditations, the characteristic description of the key components of success, i.e. faith and righteous deeds that is relayed in today's beautiful selected passage, is memorable and quite effective for highlighting their great importance. Those fortunate individuals who have faith and perform righteous work will receive a multiplied reward from God, the Most Generous and the Most Appreciative One, and be secure in high dwellings, i.e. in paradise. A significantly noteworthy point in today's beautiful selected passage is that it is not one's wealth or influence that determines one's nearness to God, the Creator the Most Holy and the Most Loving, which every individual desires, but having faith, piety, and working righteousness.

    The second powerful message of the beautiful selected passage of today is the opposite of the example above, i.e. denial of the signs of God, the Most Great and Merciful - exhibited by lack of faith, and in extreme form, striving against God, the Most Forceful and the Compeller, and against the faithful. And instead of the magnificent reward and closeness to their Lord promised for the group above, i.e. those having faith and working righteousness, this unfortunate group that lacks faith and works against the Lord of all that exists and the faithful, will be taken furthest away from their Lord and into punishment – a truly gruesome and horrendous resting place.

    The third powerful message in the beautiful selected passage of today deals with material possessions. The believer is instructed that his Lord enlarges and restricts the sustenance to whomever He pleases – in this life and the next. One cannot use the evidence of being provided with greater sustenance in this life as a sign that God, the Creator and Sustainer of all, is more pleased with them than the ones who are provided less. On the contrary, righteous individuals may be tested with being provided less material wealth, but an increase in faith, which is more valuable in the long run. Indeed, those who desire the glitter of this temporary world receive what they desire – but for them will be painful punishment in the hereafter for neglecting it. A helpful advice is provided to the seeker of success at the end of the beautiful selected passage of today, i.e. that whatever one spends in the cause of his Lord will be replaced by Him - as we learned from information in the other passages in the Holy Quran, he will be provided with a manifold increase on what he spent, for the reward is being provided by Him Who is Most Rich and Most Generous.

    The seeker of success who wishes to reach his goal has unwavering faith in God, the Most Just, the Constrictor and the Reliever, and in His noble messenger, Muhammad. He performs righteous deeds as a manifestation of his faith, and knows their value in terms of providing outstanding returns in the long run.

# Day 248

Praise be to Allah, Who created (out of nothing) heavens and the earth, Who made the angels messengers with wings – two, or three, or four (pairs); He adds to creation as He pleases – for indeed Allah has power over all things.

What Allah, out of His Mercy, does bestow on mankind, none can withhold it; what He does withhold, none can grant it, apart from Him – and He is the exalted in power, full of wisdom.

O mankind! Call to mind the Grace of Allah towards you! Is there a creator, other than Allah, to give you sustenance from heaven or earth? There is no god but He; how then are you deluded away from the truth?

(35:1-3)

# Day 248

The beautiful selected passage of today provides three powerful messages to help one to acquire faith (in God, the Creator and Sustainer of all, and in his beloved messenger, Muhammad), the central component of lasting success for the unfortunate individual who has not yet acquired it, and to strengthen it - for those who have already been blessed with it.

The first powerful message in the beautiful selected passage of today to help the seekers of success to acquire or strengthen their faith is the announcement from God, the Most Great and Most Glorious, that it is He Who created everything now existing – from nothing. Specific details are provided about one form of His creation, i.e. angels having two, three of four pairs of wings. With our limited senses, we cannot discern or see the angels, but we know that they are in constant praise and service of their Lord, and are without the choice of free will that is characteristic of man. Indeed, God, the Almighty and Most Wise, is able to create what He wills – for He has power to do whatever He wills.

The second powerful message in the beautiful selected passage of today to help the seekers of success to acquire or strengthen their faith is the knowledge and acceptance of the fact that whatever good God, the Most Beneficent and Most Merciful, wishes to bestow on mankind or any of His creation, none can withhold it; and whatever He wishes to withhold, none can grant it apart from Him. This is one of the most central tenets of faith, for without this understanding, man is susceptible to serve or worship other beings than God, to Whom belongs all praise and worship – and indeed, He is the Source of all power and the Most Wise.

The third powerful message in the beautiful selected passage of today to help the seekers of success to acquire or strengthen their faith is to recall the countless presents from God to mankind needed for their sustenance, such as oxygen, light and water, etc. – who else is there that can provide these things to all others than He Who is Most Beneficent and Most Powerful? Indeed, Truth stands clear from error. And to God belongs all power and praise.

The seeker of success who wishes to reach his goal has complete faith in God, the Creator, Sustainer and Nourisher of all, and in His beloved messenger, Muhammad. He manifests his faith with appropriate actions, including regular praise and worship of his Creator and Sustainer, along with the performance of other righteous deeds. He knows that whatever his Lord wills for him, that none can withhold it from him – and that whatever his Lord withholds from him, that none can grant it to him.

# Day 249

**O Mankind! Certainly the promise of Allah is true. Let not then this present life deceive you, nor let the chief deceiver (Satan) deceive you about Allah.**

**Indeed, Satan is an enemy to you – so treat him as an enemy. He only invites his adherents, that they may become companions of the blazing fire.**

**For those who reject Allah is a terrible penalty; but for those who believe and work righteous deeds, is forgiveness and a magnificent reward.**

(35:5-7)

# Day 249

The wise individual who wants to reach a particular goal will not only learn about factors that will help him to achieve his goal, but also about factors that can prevent him from reaching his goal, and take appropriate precautions accordingly. The major portion of today's beautiful selected passage deals with instructions to mankind about factors that can prevent them from attaining success – and we are informed about two such factors by the Grace of God. Both of the identified barriers to success are points that have been reinforced and reviewed elsewhere in the Holy Quran and in this collection of meditations. They are combined in an effective manner, clearly indicative of the serious consequences of neglecting such vital information.

The first factor identified in the beautiful selected passage of today that can prevent the seeker of success from reaching his goal is to be deceived by the glamour and glitter of the life of this world. It is possible for one to be absorbed in the immediate but transient pleasures of this life and, therefore, to neglect the duties that man was created for – which is to worship his Lord, the Creator and Sustainer of all and to see which of mankind will be best in fulfilling their duties. The esteemed reader is referred to the commentary of Day 3 of this collection of meditations on a more detailed discussion of worship. The unfortunate individual who follows this route and neglects his preparation for the hereafter, will have missed his goal of success by rejecting the signs of his Lord, rejecting faith, and neglecting the duties for which he was created, and therefore will incur a terrible penalty associated with such reckless negligence.

The second factor identified in the beautiful selected passage of today that can prevent the seeker of success from reaching his goal is to be deceived by Satan, whose primary goal in existence, is to deceive mankind from remembering God, the Almighty and the Most Magnificent, and to distract man from fulfilling his duties to his Lord; Satan is the chief deceiver in this sustained malicious effort and can use others to assist him, i.e. those who have been already deceived by him and wish to serve him. The seeker of success is warned that Satan only invites his adherents to the terrible penalty awaiting those who have failed the test of the life of this world, in order to become his companions in the blazing fire of hell.

The beautiful selected passage of today ends with a reminder about those who take the appropriate precautions against factors that can prevent them from reaching their goal and who have faith in God, the Creator and Sustainer of all, and in His beloved messenger, Muhammad, and manifesting their faith with righteous deeds: for them is promised forgiveness and a magnificent reward by Him Who is Most Rich, the Most Generous and the Most Forgiving.

The seeker of success who wishes to reach his goal has absolute faith in God, the Creator and Sustainer of all, and in His noble messenger, Muhammad. He engages in regular praise and worship of his Lord, performs righteous deeds as a manifestation of his faith and takes appropriate precautions against the dangers of being deceived by the glamour and glitter of this life at the expense of the hereafter – and especially against Satan, the chief deceiver and the most dangerous enemy of man.

## Day 250

Whosoever desires honor, glory and power – then, (should know that) to God belongs all honor, glory and power. To Him mount up (all) words of purity; it is He Who exalts each deed of righteousness. Those that lay plots of evil – for them is a terrible penalty; and the plotting of such will be void (of result).

(35:10)

# Day 250

    The seeker of success will find in the beautiful selected passage of today three valuable messages that will help him to reach his goal. Man desires all the good things, including honor, glory, and power. The first valuable message in the beautiful selected passage of today brilliantly directs man to the source of all that is good, including glory, honor and power: God, the Lord of all that exists, the Most Glorious, the Source of all power, the Bestower of all honors, and the Humiliator. Certainly, it would be unwise to desire something from someone while being indifferent or hostile to him. Therefore, if man desires honor, glory, power, and indeed all that is good, he must know that all he seeks that is good, is with God, the Creator and Sustainer of all, and the Source of all that is good. It is possible for man to be fooled by the transient honor, glory, and power of life in this world, unless he realizes the foolishness of preferring the transient good in the life of this world in exchange for long-term suffering in the hereafter. The next point clarifies how one can then proceed in accessing the good things that he desires.

    The second valuable message in the beautiful selected passage of today is an extension of the above message. Once man realizes that all good things, including honor, glory and power belong to God, the Almighty and the Most Magnificent, he can take the appropriate route to access the good he desires: God, the Most Beneficent and Most Generous, will exalt each righteous deed and all words of purity, with the most pure of them being His praises, which are done as manifestation of one's faith in Him and His beloved messenger, Muhammad, and to serve God, blessed be His Name. And the goodness that one will attain, including honor, glory, and power - although transient in this world, will, in the hereafter, be eternal.

    The third valuable message in the beautiful selected passage of today serves to warn the enemies of faith to desist in their evil plots – otherwise they will incur a terrible penalty; it also serves to reassure the seekers of success in striving on the Righteous Path, that the plotting of evildoers will be void of result. Of course, an individual with faith need not be reminded that he should not be a party to plotting of evil acts – involvement in which would lead him away from his goal of success, and towards failure, with all the associated consequences previously reviewed in this collection.

    The seeker of success who wishes to reach his goal has unwavering faith in God, the Source of all power, goodness, and honor, and in His beloved messenger, Muhammad. He realizes that all that is good – including honor, glory, and power – belongs to God, the Creator and Sustainer of all and the Most Glorious. He knows the value of faith, worship and righteous deeds to his Lord as fulfillment of his obligations towards Him, and knows God's generosity is unbounded. He continues to strive in serving God, undeterred by the evil plots of the enemies of faith, knowing that his Lord is the Most Powerful and the Best Protector. He stays away from evil.

# Day 251

**O mankind! It is you that have need of Allah – but Allah is Rich (free of all wants), Worthy of all praise.**

(35:15)

# Day 251

    The beautiful selected passage of today contains three very powerful messages that need to be understood by all for obtaining the maximal benefit from the life of this world. All three of the powerful messages are important components of faith (in God, the Creator and Sustainer of all, and in His beloved messenger, Muhammad), which is the most important component of attaining lasting success. It will be of great help for the individual who does not have faith to attain it, and for the fortunate individuals who have been blessed with faith, to strengthen it.

    The first powerful message in the beautiful selected passage of today that will help the seeker of success to reach his goal is attaining the understanding that he is in need of God, the Creator and Sustainer of all, at all times – from the provision of his vital necessities, such as oxygen, water, and the truly amazing functioning of his organs (such as heart and lungs), to the maintenance of the universe in a way that sustains his life. When one understands and appreciates the proper role of God, the Most Glorious and Most Generous, and the impossibility of one's existence without Him, only then, will he be able to praise and worship God with true sincerity and conviction, and attempt to serve Him, as is His right.

    The second powerful message in the beautiful selected passage of today that will help the seeker of success to reach his goal is a proper understanding of the power of God, the Almighty and Source of all power and strength, such that He is free of all needs and is therefore truly the only Rich One in existence, and that everything and everyone else in the entire existence is dependent on Him. A proper understanding of this concept will prevent an individual from the error of worshipping or serving others besides the Only One Who is Deserving of it, which is the greatest error that an individual can make in terms of undermining his chances of success.

    The third powerful message in the beautiful selected passage of today is the logical conclusion to the two vital concepts discussed above, i.e. since everything in existence is dependent on God, the Creator, Nourisher and Sustainer of all that exists, and He is the Only One Who is free of all needs and provides to all of existence their needs, hence, all praise and worship should belong to Him Alone. An individual who is not able to realize the connection between whatever he finds pleasing – whether it is nourishment, safety, or power – with the source which provides it, is susceptible to worshipping others than He to Whom belongs only that right, again committing the most grave error an individual can commit, as we reviewed in the earlier meditations, and undermine his success.

    The seeker of success who wishes to reach his goal has complete faith in God, the Alive, Self-subsisting, and Eternal, and in His noble messenger, Muhammad. He realizes that he, as well as everyone and everything else in existence, is in need of God, the Nourisher and Sustainer of all, at all times – and therefore, all worship and praise, including praise for anything he finds pleasing at any time, belongs only to God.

## Day 252

And no bearer of burdens shall bear another's burden; and if one heavily laden calls to another to (bear) his load, nothing of it will be lifted even though he be near of kin. You (O Muhammad) can warn only those who fear their Lord, unseen, and perform regular prayer. And he who purifies (from all kinds of sins), does so for the benefit of his own self. And to Allah is (final) return (of all).

(35:18)

# Day 252

    The beautiful selected passage of today has four powerful messages that are closely linked and will help one to either acquire faith (in God, the Creator and Sustainer of all, and in His beloved messenger, Muhammad), the most important component of success - if one does not yet possess it, or to strengthen one's faith if one already possesses it.

    The first powerful message in the beautiful selected passage of today is the understanding that every individual is responsible for his own actions, i.e. if he commits an act worthy of punishment in the sight of God, the Most Beneficent and Most Merciful, he cannot expect another to be punished instead of himself on the Day of Judgment, or expect someone else to pardon or bear his sins – for no one has the right to pardon or avert punishment except God Almighty, the Most Just. On the Day of Judgment, no bearer of burdens shall bear another's burden; and if one heavily laden calls on another to (bear) his load, nothing of it will be lifted, even though he be near of kin. The second powerful message in the beautiful selected passage of today to help the seeker of success reach his goal is closely linked to the first: That none shall bear the burden of another's sins, on the Day of Judgment. This is the fundamental flaw and misunderstanding, besides the polytheistic nature of the misunderstanding of the message of the honorable prophet Jesus – that it was misunderstood by some, and relayed as the formal creed, that the honorable prophet Jesus was to be worshipped along with God, the Only One and the Only One Worthy of worship. Additionally, it was misunderstood by some, and relayed as a formal creed, that man's sins will be lightened and void based on them being taken over by the noble prophet Jesus. Thus there was a need for clarification to guide the seekers of success on the right path, and thus the need for our hero, the beloved prophet Muhammad, the seal of prophethood and the one that God Himself, the Most Wise and the Most Righteous Teacher, said should be the model for man and the seeker of success. As the messenger to mankind from God, the Most Kind and Most Wise, if the noble prophet Muhammad wished to lighten the loads of others, he was instructed to only warn the others of terrible punishment for neglecting the duties for which man was created. The third powerful message in the beautiful selected passage of today to help the seeker of success reach his goal is an extension of the second message discussed above, i.e. if one has faith and performs righteous deeds and worships or purifies himself by such actions, he is not benefiting anyone except his own self. Certainly. God, the Eternal and Self-sufficient, is not in need of praise, worship, or any other action from His creation for His benefit – for He is Most Powerful and Able to do all he intends. The fourth powerful message in the beautiful selected passage of today to help the seeker of success reach his goal is one of the fundamental components that is reinforced, reminding him that the return of all beings is to God, the Creator of life, Death, and the Restorer, to be held accountable for their life in this world, and to therefore, prepare accordingly for success in the hereafter.

    The seeker of success who wishes to reach his goal has absolute faith in God, the Most Just and Most Wise, and in His noble messenger, Muhammad. He knows that he is to return to his Lord on the Day of Judgment, to be held accountable for his life in this world, and that on that day no bearer of burdens can bear another's burden. He knows that if he performs righteous deeds and worship for the sake of his Lord and purifies himself, he is helping only himself only and none other.

# Day 253

**Those who recite the Book of Allah, establish regular prayer, and spend (in charity) out of what We have provided for them, secretly and openly, hope for (a sure) investment that will never fail;**

**For He will pay them their wages, and He will give them (even) more out of His Grace – indeed, He is Most Forgiving, most ready to appreciate (good deeds and to recompense).**

(35:29-30)

# Day 253

    Man feels a sense of achievement in getting more in return from his possessions over time than their initial worth, when done in an acceptable manner. In hope of a successful outcome in this matter, he invests his energies and resources in various ways: education, children, marriage, property, precious metals, government bonds, savings, stocks, etc. When looking for optimal results, a wise investor will review the net worth, reliability, and stability for a number of years that a company has been functioning, and the history of rate of return and expected rate of return. Today's beautiful selected passage instructs the seeker of success in the best investment advice from God, the Most Righteous Teacher and the Best Guide, on the three best recommendations in terms of their return.

    The seeker of success is instructed by God, Most Wise and the Best Guide, to invest in recitation of the Holy Quran; with this, he will gain not only immediate spiritual contentment, which is counted among worship and praise of God, the Almighty and Most Kind, but will also receive personal Guidance on all issues of concern. He is also recommended to invest in regular prayer, which counts among worship of God, the Creator and Sustainer of all, to protect him from other evil actions, to purify himself for his own benefit, which indeed the best form of righteous actions - and the reason for his existence. The esteemed reader is referred to the meditation on Day 3 for a more detailed review of worship. The final recommendation deals with investment strategies – the best strategy being spending in charity, out of what is provided to man from his Lord, and for His sake. With the advice on best investment strategies from God, the Most Wise and the Most Great, to the seeker of success for optimal returns – including reciting the Holy Quran, establishing regular prayer, and spending in charity, secretly and openly, for His sake – the seeker of success is assured of having chosen a most sound investment strategy guaranteed to succeed. In addition to the capital invested, he will gain much more profit from the Grace of his Lord – for He is indeed Most Forgiving, and most ready to appreciate and reward all good deeds.

    The seeker of success who wishes to reach his goal has unwavering faith in God, the Most Rich, Most Generous and Most Trustworthy, and in His noble messenger, Muhammad. He knows the value of the potential returns of the most sound investment strategies, which include reciting the Holy Quran, establishing regular prayer and giving regular charity - and engages in them to the greatest extent possible.

# Day 254

Then we have given the Book (Quran) for inheritance to such of Our servants as we have chosen – but there are among them some who wrong their own souls; some who follow a middle course; <u>and some who are, by Allah's leave, foremost in good deeds; that is the highest grace</u> –

Gardens of eternity will they enter; they will therein be adorned with bracelets of gold and pearls, and their garments there will be of silk;

And they will say: "Praise be to Allah, Who has removed from us (all) sorrow – for our Lord is indeed Most Forgiving, ready to appreciate (service);

"Who has, out of His grace, settled us in a lasting abode – no toil nor sense of weariness shall touch us therein".

But those who reject (Allah) – for them will be the fire of hell; no term shall be determined for them, so that they should (neither) die, nor shall its penalty be lightened for them. Thus do we reward the ungrateful one!

(35:32-36)

# Day 254

    The beautiful selected passage of today begins with the announcement that what follows are advanced directives to "servants we have chosen", i.e. those blessed with faith in God, the Creator and Sustainer of all, and in His beloved messenger, Muhammad, and which is the most important component of lasting success. From the point of having attained the "chosen servant" status, we are informed that the individual is able to fall among three possible groups, depending on what he chooses to do with the Guidance that is provided in the Holy Quran: those that fail to follow the guidance from their Lord, who can be considered to be mediocre and who wrong their own souls, by failing to meet their potential; those that follow a middle course, implying a status between the mediocre group discussed above and the successful group discussed below; and those that follow the guidance of their Lord wholeheartedly and are foremost in doing good deeds – having reached **the highest achievement**, with the Grace of God.

    Those fortunate individuals described above, who reach the highest achievement, will be rewarded as a result of their efforts and commendable performance in fulfilling their duties, and are informed of corresponding rewards, consistent with the attainment of their coveted status, by Him Who is the Owner of all and the Most Generous One. The details of the magnificent rewards awaiting these most fortunate individuals is detailed in the text, with a truly magnificent description of being "eternal", and this truly commendable group will continue to praise their Lord, even in the afterlife, for His truly magnificent rewards, as they were in the practice of doing the same in the life of this world.

    The beautiful selected passage of today ends with contrasting the state of the high achievers described above to that of the failures, i.e. those who rejected their Lord, ignoring His signs in existence, while continuing to enjoy the rewards of His Beneficence and refusing to serve Him, and being hostile to those who desired to serve their Lord. The terrible penalty awaiting these truly unfortunate individuals in hell is described in the beautiful selected passage of today, and also is memorable – for their truly despicable state is eternal, and serves as an effective warning.

    The seeker of success who wishes to reach his goal has complete faith in God, the Best Rewarder of thankfulness and the Avenger, and in His beloved messenger, Muhammad. He refers often to the Holy Quran for Guidance from God, the Most Righteous Teacher and the Best Guide, and is foremost in praise and worship of his Lord and doing good deeds as a manifestation of his faith.

# Day 255

**And why should I not worship Him Who created me, and to Whom you shall (all) be brought back?**

(36:22)

# Day 255

Chapter 36 in Holy Quran, titled Ya Sin (two Arabic alphabets), is considered the heart of Holy Quran, from which the beautiful selected passage of today is taken, and in the humble view of the author is the heart of the chapter titled Ya Sin – or the heart of the heart of Holy Quran. Hence, the messages contained in the beautiful selected passage of today are of immense value for all purposes, and especially for the seekers of success. The text of the beautiful selected passage of today is a brilliant question posed by an individual in the sura (chapter) Ya Sin, who had been blessed with the gift of faith in God, the Creator and Sustainer of all, on accepting the invitation to faith by a prophet of God, the Almighty and Most Wise. Therefore, transitioning from an individual to collective experience, the beautiful selected passage of today can serve a useful purpose to instill the seeds of success, or faith, in a large number of people for their benefit – for the aim of the truly successful is not just individual success, but success for as many others as possible.

Let us analyze the brilliance of the question posed – for the answer lies in the question itself: who created me? Just inside of myself, there are countless miracles – those of sight, hearing, reasoning, and emotions, for which I should be, and am immensely grateful. Is it reasonable that I (and also you) should continue to enjoy the treasures I find in my body (and you in yours) -including sight, hearing, love and emotions, as well as numerous other gifts, and not give corresponding praise and express gratitude to Him Who provided these treasures to me and to you and each one of us? The latter part of the question serves to give another reason why one should praise, worship and serve his Lord, i.e. he was created by Him and is to return to Him. Hence, does it make sense that one should serve any other than He to Whom one belongs completely?

The seeker of success who wishes to reach his goal has absolute faith in God, the Creator and Sustainer of all, and the Best Guide and the Most Righteous Teacher, and in His noble messenger, Muhammad. He grasps the irrationality/ungratefulness of worshipping or serving any other being than He Who created him, and to Whom he will return.

# Day 256

Dawood (David)! Indeed, we have placed you as a successor on the earth; so judge between men in truth (and justice) and do not follow your desire - for it will mislead you from the path of Allah. Indeed, for those who wander astray from the path of Allah is a grievous penalty, because they forgot the Day of Account.

Not without purpose did we create the heaven and earth and all between! That was the thought of unbelievers! But woe to the unbelievers because of the fire (of hell)!

Shall We treat those who believe and work deeds of righteousness the same as those who do mischief on earth? Shall We treat those who guard against evil the same as those who turn aside from the right?

(38:26-28)

# Day 256

    The beautiful selected passage of today provides three powerful messages that will help the seeker of success to achieve his goal – with the first one taken from the advice to the honorable prophet Dawood (David), blessed with the gifts of wisdom, justice, and kingly power; the instructions for the path to wisdom and success were directly addressed to him, and also to those who believed in his message and the guidance from their Lord: to judge between men in truth and justice, and avoid following the lusts or emotions of the heart, for they will mislead one from the Right Path and Guidance of God, the Most Wise and the Best Guide. And those who stray from the path of success are warned that they are heading towards the path leading to a grievous penalty, and forgetting that they are accountable for all their actions.

    The second powerful message in the beautiful selected passage of today that will help the seeker of success to reach his goal is possessing awareness that there is a purpose behind the creation of all that exists – lacking this awareness, one is bound to aimlessness, believing there is no purpose to life, and being deluded that one's performance and actions in this life are of no significance, except for immediate consequences, and having no sense of accountability, for it will also place one on the path leading to a grievous penalty – the fire of hell!

    The third powerful message in the beautiful selected passage of today is related to the point above, and explains the foolishness of believing that one's actions have no consequences and thinking there is no difference in outcomes related to one's actions. Man is informed that there is a right way and a wrong way – both are not equal, and they will not be treated equally by Him to Whom is the return of all. Further details are provided about righteousness: Believing in God, the Most Great and Most Kind, and in His messenger, the beloved Muhammad, performing deeds considered righteous – with the highest righteous act being worship of Allah, the Most Holy and the Best of those who do good, and guarding from evil, which will be rewarded accordingly. The wrong way is described as that of those who do mischief on earth and turn away from the right Path, preferring the short-term pleasures – these will be treated differently than those who followed the more difficult Right Path, on the Day of Judgment, and will be punished accordingly.

    The seeker of success who wishes to reach his goal has unwavering faith in God, the Creator of all, the Most Wise and the Gatherer, and in His beloved messenger, Muhammad. He seeks Guidance from His Lord instead of following his lusts or whatever the heart desires. He knows there is a purpose behind all creation. He knows that his actions have long-term consequences beyond the life of this world and chooses the right Path – that of faith, worship and working righteousness, as we noted above.

# Day 257

If you reject (Allah), truly Allah has no need of you; but He likes not ingratitude from His servants; if you are grateful, He is pleased with you. No bearer of burdens can bear the burden of another. In the end, to your Lord is your return, when He will tell you the truth of all that you did (in this life). For He knows well all that is in (men's) hearts.

When some trouble touches man, he cries to his Lord, turning to Him in repentance; but when He bestows a favor upon him as from Himself, (man) does forget what he cried and prayed for before, and he does set up rivals to Allah, thus misleading others from Allah's path. Say: "Enjoy the blasphemy for a little while; surely you are (one) of the companions of the Fire!"

Is one who worships devoutly during the hours of the night prostrating himself or standing (in adoration), who takes heed of the hereafter, and who places his hope in the Mercy of his Lord – (like one who does not)? Say: "Are those equal, those who know and those who do not know? It is those who are endowed with understanding that receive admonition".

(39:7-8)

# Day 257

The beautiful selected passage of today begins with some of the key components that are repeated in the Holy Quran and also in this collection of meditations, to reinforce their importance for the seeker of success, and are summarized as follows:

1. God, the Most Great and Most Kind, has no need for any of His creation, but all creation is dependent on Him for its sustenance.
2. If one rejects God, the Most Magnificent and Most Patient One, he is hurting no one except his own self.
3. God, the Most Beneficent and Most Merciful, is pleased with gratitude expressed by his servants and displeased with ingratitude.
4. Man will be held accountable for all his actions in the life of this world when life as we know it will end, on the Day of Judgment, and the more important afterlife will begin. All of man's actions are known to God, the Hearer and Seer of all, and are recorded accurately, and will be known to man with the end result of lasting success or failure in afterlife, depending on one's performance in the life of this world.
5. No bearer of burdens can bear that of another on the Day of Judgment.

The middle component of the beautiful selected passage of today gives a magnificent example of one of the signs of God, the Most Beneficent and Most Merciful i.e. when some trouble or disaster touches man, he turns automatically to God, the Almighty and Most Kind, seeking help – but after he is given the help and God's Mercy is bestowed on him, he forgets the One to Whom he called for help, going about serving others than He to Whom belongs all praise and worship, therefore incurring a grievous penalty for neglecting to perform the duty he was created for, i.e. praising, worshipping and serving his Lord. The individual who is lacking in faith, the central component of success, is expected to acquire it as a result of the brilliant example of the beautiful selected passage of today – and the one already blessed with it should have his faith strengthened.

The end portion of the beautiful selected passage of today describes how two contrasting parts cannot be equal – such as light and dark, good and evil, right and wrong, etc. Attaining a better understanding of the difference between right and wrong, the seeker of success is directed to choose right instead of wrong, and good instead of evil.

The seeker of success who wishes to reach his goal has complete faith in God, the Most Holy, the Light, and the Judge, and in His noble messenger, Muhammad. He receives admonition from the magnificent examples used in the beautiful selected passage of today, knowing that good and evil, in terms of their outcomes, cannot be the same - and consistently selects good over evil, devoutly praising, worshipping and serving his Lord, and placing his hope for lasting success in the Mercy of his Lord, knowing the importance of all of the above factors in the attainment of success.

# Day 258

Say: "O my servants who believe! Fear your Lord. Good is (the reward) for those who do good in this world. Spacious is Allah's earth! Those who patiently persevere will truly receive a reward without measure!"

Say: "Indeed, I am commanded to serve Allah with sincere devotion;

"And I am commanded to be the first of those who submit to Allah in Islam".

Say: "It is Allah I serve, with my sincere (and exclusive) devotion;

"Serve what you will besides Him". Say: <u>"Truly, those in loss are those who lose themselves and their families on the Day of Judgment; that is indeed the (real and) evident loss!"</u>.

(39:10-15)

# Day 258

The beautiful selected passage of today consists of two portions of interest for the seeker of success – in the first portion are discussed the factors that can help one to achieve his goal; and in the second portion are discussed the factors that can contribute to one's failure. The entire passage consists of instructions to the noble prophet Muhammad from God, the Most Great and the Best Guide, for specific steps one needs to follow to optimize success and minimize failure. The seekers of success, holding the noble prophet as their example to follow, are expected to follow these instructions as well.

In the first half of the beautiful selected passage of today, in regard to factors that will help one to attain success – the foremost is belief, or faith (in God, the Creator and Sustainer of all, and in His beloved messenger, Muhammad). Also, one should fear disappointing his Lord and incurring His penalty on the Day of Judgment, and should perform righteous deeds, for which one will be rewarded with good in this life and in the hereafter as well. The seeker of success is reminded to be patient in his struggle on the righteous path, and that those who patiently persevere in their struggle will receive the highest rewards. If one is unable to practice his faith and serve his Lord in one place, then he is recommended to migrate elsewhere, as the earth is spacious. Man is instructed to serve God, the Source of all that is good and Who is the Most Exalted, and to submit himself to his Lord enthusiastically. In the second half of the beautiful selected passage of today, man is reminded that if he fails to heed the Guidance from his Lord and disobeys, then there will be (a severe) penalty and suffering for him in the hereafter. Those who disobey the call to serve their Creator and neglect the duties that they were created for, and instead serve others besides the One Who created all that exists, are designated as the **biggest losers** – losing themselves and their families on the Day of Judgment.

The seeker of success who wishes to reach his goal has absolute faith in God, the Best Guide, the Most Righteous Teacher, and the Most Patient One, and in His beloved messenger, Muhammad. He submits to his Lord with sincere devotion exclusively, fearing the punishment of his Lord if he fails in his duties, and patiently perseveres in the face of all difficulties in the life of this world.

# Day 259

**Is not Allah enough for his servant? But they try to frighten you with other (gods) besides Him! For such as (those whom) Allah leaves to stray, there can be no guide;**

**And such as (those whom) Allah does guide, there can be none to lead astray. Is not Allah exalted in power (able to enforce His will), Lord of retribution?**

**If indeed you ask them who it is that created the heavens and the earth, they would be sure to say "Allah". Say: "See then? The things that you invoke besides Allah – can they, if Allah wills some penalty for me, remove His penalty? Or if He wills some Grace for me, can they keep back His Grace?" Say: "Sufficient is Allah for me! In Him, those who trust (believers), must put their trust".**

(39:36-38)

# Day 259

There are multiple factors that influence one's actions - including intuition/ awareness, knowledge, evidence, belief, motivation, and resistance. The beautiful selected passage of today sheds light on the contributing factors to action such that the seekers of success will be guided to the righteous actions that will be of most benefit to them and help them to reach their goal.

In a separate passage discussed earlier in this collection of meditations, another reference was made to the inner awareness in man regarding God, the Creator and Sustainer of all; an example is reviewed in which the frightened individual who is faced with a calamity or disaster in a ship (or airplane), will instinctively seek the help of God ("O Lord!"), the Most Trustworthy and the Best Protector,, and after man is safe from the disaster, he is likely to forget on Whom he called for help, and may worship others than He to Whom he called when he was faced with disaster. Similarly, in the example used in the beautiful selected passage of today, if one is asked the question, "Who created the heavens and the earth (and all that exists)?", one's inner awareness will likely answer "God", the Creator of all. Note that it does not answer "gods"; however, in practice, many of these individuals may go about serving and worshipping others than Him Whom the inner heart of the same individual knows that it belongs to no one else.

Utilizing the information gained above, the individual being referred to his inner awareness, additional knowledge from the Holy Quran in other passages, the evidence of the signs of the presence of God, the Most Great and Most Kind, in all of existence (including his own body, and that of the birds flying without falling), and the beauty and perfect order in existence, one can then be led to belief or faith (in God, the Creator and Sustainer of all, and in His beloved messenger, Muhammad), with the Grace of God – which is the most important component of success.

Additional knowledge is provided in the beautiful selected passage of today to both help one to acquire faith and to strengthen it. If God, the Most Wise and the Best Guide, does guide someone, no one can lead him astray, and if He were to leave someone to stray, there will be no one to guide him to the Right Way. And, if God, the Most Beneficent and Most Merciful, were to will someone a penalty or to be provided with His grace, there is none that can hold that back. All of the above information and its understanding is important for development and strengthening of one's faith which would lead him to righteous action. In terms of motivation and resistance to action, the seeker of success will be referred to other meditations in this collection, where more details are provided about the reward/punishment for right/wrong actions, and about resisting the accursed Satan, as well as his agents, and the understanding of trials/tribulations and the necessity for patient perseverance.

The seeker of success who wishes to reach his goal has unwavering faith in God, the Source of all that exists, and the Best Guide, and in His noble messenger, Muhammad. He involves no else in the worship of his Lord, and realizes that the only guidance, help and harm is from God, the Best Guide and the Best Friend and Protector.

# Day 260

Certainly, We have revealed the Book to you in truth, for (instructing) mankind. He, then, that receives Guidance, benefits his own self; but he that strays, injures his own self. Nor are you set over them to dispose of their affairs.

It is Allah Who takes the souls (of men) at death; and those that die not, (He takes) during their sleep – those on whom He has passed the decree of death, He keeps back (from returning to life), but the rest He sends (to their bodies) for a term appointed. Indeed, in this are signs for those who reflect.

(39:41-42)

# Day 260

    The beautiful selected passage of today consists of two extremely important points which will greatly assist the seeker of success on his journey. The first part of the beautiful selected passage of today deals with the Holy Quran as presented in truth from God, the Creator and sustainer of all, through His beloved messenger, Muhammad, as Grace and Mercy, for instructing all with the best Guidance – for their own benefit in this life and forever. He who follows the Guidance from God, the Almighty, Most Wise, and the Best Guide, will benefit only himself and no one else; he who strays and does not follow God's Guidance will harm himself and no other. The noble messenger, Muhammad, as well as the believers, are instructed that the Guidance from Holy Quran is for personal use, as well as for sharing the goodness of the Holy Quran and inviting others to follow the righteous Path to help themselves. However, one is not to force others – as the final option, to either help or harm themselves is their personal choice. Similarly, if an individual is ill, he cannot be forced to take medicine or receive treatment – if he does, he is only helping himself. If one insists on refusing to take the prescribed medication or treatment, however, we can certainly explain the benefits of taking the medication or treatment, or the consequences of not doing so – and hope the individual will choose to help himself.

    In the second part of the beautiful selected passage of today, God, the Most Great, the Giver of Life and the Creator of Death, explains for the benefit of man the matter of death – how his soul is taken from him daily at sleep and returned back to him when he awakes; it will be the same at his death, but the soul is to be returned at his resurrection, on the Day of Judgment, when he will be called to full account for his actions in the life of this world. This is one of the vital components of success – for without this understanding, one cannot fully grasp the importance of how one's actions affect him in long run, beyond their immediate effects, and without an appropriate understanding of this concept, an individual may consider that stealing is fine as long as nobody saw him doing it.

    The seeker of success who wishes to reach his goal has complete faith in God, the Most Great and the Most Wise, and in His beloved messenger, Muhammad. He understands the importance of the Guidance of God, the Best Guide and the Most Wise - and knows how much it helps him, and knows where to seek it. He is certain of the Day of Judgment, when he will be brought back to life from his death, and that he will be called in front of his Creator and Lord, to give a full account for all his actions in the life of this world – to be rewarded or punished accordingly, depending on his performance in the life of this world.

## Day 261

Say: "O my servants who have transgressed against their souls! Despair not of the Mercy of Allah. Indeed, Allah forgives all sins – for He is Most Forgiving, Most Merciful.

"And turn in repentance and in obedience to your Lord and submit to Him (in Islam) before the torment comes upon you, (and) then you will not be helped.

"And follow the best of that which is sent down to you from your Lord (i.e. Quran), before the torment comes on you suddenly while you perceive not!"

(39:53-55)

# Day 261

    The beautiful selected passage of today is addressed primarily to those who are farthest from their goal, and have not yet acquired its absolute prerequisite, i.e. faith (in God, the Creator and Sustainer of all, and in His beloved messenger, Muhammad), the most important component of success. However, the guidance from the beautiful selected passage of today can help the seeker of success at all levels – since maintaining one's faith is also a significant challenge, and one can find himself sometimes in similar situations as prior to having acquired faith.

    The first powerful message in the beautiful selected passage of today is addressed to those who have transgressed against their own souls, i.e. engaged in evil actions, informing them of the tremendous Mercy of God, the Lord of all that exists and the Most Forgiving, such that no one need despair. God, the Most Beneficent and Most Merciful, informs us in the beautiful selected passage of today that He forgives all sins, so that all may benefit from His Mercy and have a chance to succeed, until their death. A later revelation (v 4:116, reviewed in the meditation of Day 70 in this collection) clarified this issue further, without losing the general picture of possible forgiveness of all previous sins, by specifying that all sins can be forgiven except that of worshipping any other than God, the only One to Whom belongs all praise and worship. However, even this would be a non-issue, for one can proceed with the steps reviewed in the remainder of the beautiful selected passage of today, i.e. by seeking forgiveness from God, the Most Great and Most Forgiving, and following His guidance, so he would not be practicing that sin anymore which is not forgivable (including others in the worship of God, to Whom only belongs all praise and worship): This is the foundation of faith and the fundamental component of success.

    The second powerful message in the beautiful selected passage of today instructs the individual who has wronged his own soul by committing sins, on how to obtain forgiveness : First, recognize the errors and sincerely repent; second, if one had not previously done so, then submit to the will of God, the Most Merciful and the Lord of all that exists, without associating any partners with Him, and to accept His message delivered to all, through His beloved messenger Muhammad, and continue on the right path as instructed.

    The third powerful message in the beautiful selected passage of today is to follow to one's best ability the Guidance sent down for the benefit of man from God, the Best Guide and the Most Righteous Teacher, so one can help himself and be able to fulfill the duties for which he was created in this life, after which he would no longer be able to help himself, i.e. after death.

    The seeker of success who wishes to reach his goal has absolute faith in God, the Most Merciful, the Best Guide, the Acceptor of Repentance, and the Most Forgiving, and in His noble messenger, Muhammad. He does not despair of the Mercy of his Lord at any time. For his past errors, he sincerely repents, and he submits to his Lord devotedly, following His Guidance to the best of his ability - and does not repeat his errors from the past.

# Day 262

God is the Creator of all things, and He is the Guardian and Disposer of all affairs.

To Him belong the keys of the heavens and the earth; and those who reject the signs of God – it is they who will be in loss.

(39:62-63)

# Day 262

The beautiful selected passage of today is valuable to the seeker of success because it touches on the most important aspects of life to all individuals – and it provides the best response to one's concerns, guiding him towards lasting success. The first valuable message in the beautiful selected passage of today is that God, the Most Great and Most Wise, is the Creator of all that exists. All intelligent beings will find themselves asking, not infrequently, where all the wonderful things in existence (including life, and their own self) came from; arriving at the correct response to this important question will lead one to the most important ingredient of lasting success, i.e. faith in God, the Most High and the Most Magnificent, and to praise, worship, and serve Him – the reason for which man was created.

The second valuable message in the beautiful selected passage of today is the knowledge that God, the Possessor of all strength, and the Most Just, is the One to Whom belong the keys of the heavens and the earth, and is the Guardian of all that exists and the Disposer of all affairs. Therefore, one need not unnecessarily waste his time on any of the middlemen at any stage of his life – whether it is the employer or the head of the most advanced countries, if one desires connection to the Ultimate Authority and Power, i.e. God.

The third valuable message in the beautiful selected passage of today is the knowledge that if one rejects the signs of God, the Most Great and the Creator of all that exists, then he will not be able to praise, worship or serve Him, i.e. the reason for which he was created, and therefore, will be in loss or, more practically, will be a failure. The wise seeker of success will indeed appreciate knowing not only what he must do – but also what he must avoid, if he is to reach his goal.

The seeker of success who wishes to reach his goal has absolute faith in God, the Creator of all that exists, the Guardian, and the Disposer of all affairs, and in His beloved messenger, Muhammad. He knows that his Lord is the One to Whom belong the keys of the heavens, the earth, and all that exists, and Who is the Best Protector and Guardian of all, and the Final Decider of all matters.

# Day 263

Those who sustain the throne (of God) and those around it, sing glory and praise to their Lord, believe in Him, and implore forgiveness for those who believe, (praying:) "Our Lord! Your reach is over all things, in Mercy and Knowledge. Forgive, then, those who turn in repentance and follow Your path; and preserve them from the penalty of the blazing fire!

"And grant, our Lord! That they enter the gardens of eternity, which You have promised to them and to the righteous among their fathers, their wives, and their posterity! For You are the Exalted in Might, Full of Wisdom.

"And preserve them from (all) ills; and any whom You do preserve from ills that day – on them will You have bestowed Mercy indeed; and <u>that will be truly (for them) the highest Success</u>".

(40:7-9)

# Day 263

    Success of any degree is desirable, as long as one succeeds, according to some individuals – similar to passing instead of failing. Today's beautiful selected passage is of special interest to the seeker of success because it directs him to what God, the Creator and Sustainer of all, has designated to be **the highest form of success**: that of being preserved from ills, or punishment, on the Day of Judgment, in which one will learn if he has passed or failed in the test of life, resulting in either pleasure or pain -  for eternity.

    A careful review of the beautiful selected passage of today leads us to the most important ingredient we have previously identified as the critical ingredient of success, as reviewed in the earlier passages: belief or faith in God, the Most Just and Most Merciful, as relayed to us by the beloved prophet Muhammad, and this faith manifested by turning to God in repentance, praise and worship, seeking and following His guidance, and performing righteous deeds.

    For the wise and fortunate individuals who have faith in God, the Nourisher and Sustainer of all, and who turn to Him in repentance and follow His path, we are informed in the beautiful selected passage of today that they will receive most valuable recommendations from those closest to God, the Most Great and the Most High, i.e. the angels who bear His throne, and those around Him, who glorify His praises. These are indeed recommendations of high value. The recommendation we are referring to is not for something transient, like a job, but for gardens of eternity in which one will reside with bliss. Additionally, the recommendation is not only for the fortunate individual who will succeed – but also the righteous among his family and posterity, directed to Him Who is Exalted in Might, Full of Wisdom, and the Most Generous.

    The seeker of success who wishes to reach his goal has unwavering faith in God, the Most Great and the Most Forgiving, and in His beloved messenger, Muhammad. He turns in repentance to his Lord, and follows the path that leads to Him, with performance of righteous deeds, as a manifestation of his faith.

# Day 264

**... And whomsoever God sends astray, for him there is no guide.**

(40:33)

# Day 264

The most important messages invariably are not those that are written in complex and abstract terms, but those that can be expressed in as simple language as possible. Such is the case with today's beautiful selected passage – although short, it is of profound importance for the seeker of success.

Being blessed with faith in God, the Most Great and the Most High, and in His noble messenger, Muhammad, and manifesting that faith with appropriate righteous actions is the most vital component of success, as reviewed in the earlier passages in this collection of meditations. This beautiful gift of Guidance, leading one to acquire faith, is partly due to the effort of the individual himself, but mostly due to the will of God, the Creator of all and Knower of all. God, Who is most capable of knowing who is most deserving of this priceless gift, leading one to long-term success.

An important concept to gain from the beautiful selected passage of today is that one cannot rely on one's intelligence, strength, or wealth, or any other entities -– unless he also has Guidance and support from God, the Creator and Sustainer of all. Indeed, the unfortunate individual who is lacking the Guidance from his Lord will be hopelessly lost and not be able to be helped by anyone.

The seeker of success who wishes to reach his goal has complete faith in God, the Best Guide and the Best Teacher, and in His noble messenger, Muhammad. He knows that whomsoever God sends astray due to his arrogance and disobedience, for him there is no guidance, and that his situation is hopeless.

# Day 265

**Patiently, then, persevere. Indeed, the promise of God is true. And ask forgiveness for your fault; and celebrate the praises of your Lord in the evening and the morning.**

(40:55)

# Day 265

Today's beautiful selected passage instructs the seeker of success in how to overcome the greatest struggle in one's life, i.e. the inner struggle against one's base desires, or the suggestions and recommendations of the accursed Satan, the avowed enemy of man.

The first recommendation in overcoming the struggle against one's inner self is to patiently persevere. Although one may have opportunity for indulging in all sorts of acts that may lead to immediate gratification, such as stealing, lying, fornication, or the use of illicit substances, one should persevere patiently, denying himself immediate pleasure, in the hopes of attaining long-term gratification. Additionally, when inflicted with a challenge of any magnitude, the seeker of success is instructed to patiently persevere.

Returning to the topic of preference for attaining long-term gratification at the expense of short-term pleasure, the seeker of success, or the individual with faith in God, the Most Great and Most High, and in His noble messenger, Muhammad, is reminded of the benefits of long-term gratification – which is the afterlife – for those who can postpone the immediate gratifications in this life. Indeed, this is the promise of God, the Most Trustworthy and Loving, and the seeker of success would be wise to remember this promise.

Being human and not being perfect, even with the utmost striving, the seeker of success is bound to stray from perfection; therefore, God, the Most Wise and Most Merciful, instructs the seeker of success in this situation to ask forgiveness for his faults. The individuals who stray from perfection, as well as those persevering patiently in all situations, are recommended to celebrate the praises of their Lord in the evening and in the morning (which is incorporated in the obligatory daily Islamic prayers), to help them on their way to success.

The seeker of success who wishes to reach his goal has unwavering faith in God, the Most Glorious and Most Forgiving, and in His beloved messenger, Muhammad. He patiently perseveres in all situations, desiring good in this life as well as in the hereafter, and praises and worships his Lord daily - in the daytime as well as the evening.

# Day 266

And your Lord says: "Call on Me. I will answer your (prayer). But those who are too arrogant to serve Me, will surely find themselves in hell in humiliation!".

(40: 60)

# Day 266

From the time an individual takes the first breath in life, to the last, life is a struggle of varying degrees. Sometimes the struggle is of a minimal degree and at other times it is of relatively massive proportions: when one is too young to meet his own needs, then one's parents will be responsible for his needs, and when one is too old to meet one's own needs, then either his family or the state will be responsible. During the period when one is supposed to be responsible for meeting his own needs, especially, one will undoubtedly encounter situations that will sometimes seem insurmountable on one's own – in that situation, whose help should one seek? Today's beautiful selected passage provides clear guidance in such situations. God, the Most Great and the Most Generous One, invites all to seek His help and He promises: "Call on Me; I will answer your (prayer)".

When faced with a difficult situation, someone who is arrogant may think himself to be self-sufficient, which is inappropriate because the Only One Who is Self-sufficient in actuality is God, the Creator and Sustainer of all that exists. Although realizing the importance of building one's own skills to be of use to himself, as well as the benefit of others, and utilizing the skills of others when necessary, we learn from the beautiful selected passage of today that the most important component of problem-solving is calling on God, the Most Strong and Most Reliable One, for help. This way, one is living the life for which he was created, i.e. praising, worshipping, and serving God, the Most Holy and Only One, and no one else.

The seeker of success who wishes to reach his goal has complete faith in God, the Hearer and Seer of all, and the Responder to prayers, and in His noble messenger, Muhammad. Along with utilizing his own skills and those of others, he knows that the most important component when faced with difficulty, is calling on God, the Source of all power and the Most Trustworthy One. He knows that his Lord hears him and answers his prayer. He realizes that those who are too arrogant to serve God, the Most Great and Most Wise, will find themselves in hell in humiliation.

# Day 267

**So persevere in patience – for the promise of God is true. And whether We show you (in this life) some part of what We promise them – or We take your soul (to Our Mercy before that), in any case it is to Us that they shall (all) return.**

(40:77)

# Day 267

It is indeed a challenge to fulfill the duties for which one was created, which is to worship God, the Creator and Sustainer of all, and which is His right: It requires an understanding of one's role and responsibilities in life as a result of acquiring faith, the most important component of success, as well as loyalty and appreciation towards one's Creator – an individual with this level of understanding will be able to persevere in patience and fulfill the duties for which he was created, with enthusiasm.

On the other hand, for those who prefer instant gratification and are not concerned about the duties for which they were created, this life is quite comfortable. They often like to say: "How do we know there is any other life except that on earth? We might as well enjoy it", and "How do we know that God Created us, and we did not appear by chance only?"

In the beautiful selected passage of today, the seeker of success is encouraged to persevere in patience in his daily life, fulfilling the duties for which he was created; contrasting this group is its counterpart, which is addressed in today's beautiful selected passage as "them" and explained in further detail in the earlier verses as those who include others in the praise and worship of God, the Most Great and the Only One, exulting without any right, committing crimes and rejoicing in their errors.

For those who persevere in patience, as well those who prefer instant gratifications and the enjoyment of this world, we are reminded that the promise of God, the Originator and Restorer, is true – each shall have his appropriate reward or punishment, and it is to Him that is the return of all. The understanding that one is to return (after death) to God, the Giver and Taker of life and the Restorer, is important because it highlights the importance of accountability, i.e. that one is responsible for all his actions, which may result in reward or punishment, on the Day of Judgment.

The seeker of success who wishes to reach his goal has absolute faith in God, the Most Wise, Most Beneficent and Most Merciful, and in His noble messenger, Muhammad. He perseveres patiently in all situations throughout his life. He knows that the promise of his Lord is true, and it is to Him that all shall return.

# Day 268

.... "Your God is One God; so take the straight Path to Him and obedience to Him. And ask for His forgiveness". And woe to those who join gods with God;

Those who practice not regular charity, and who even deny the hereafter.

For those who believe and work deeds of righteousness, is a reward that will never fail.

(41: 6-8)

# Day 268

    The beautiful selected passage of today has three powerful messages for the benefit of the seeker of success to help him reach his goal - the first of which is the explanation that there is only One God and none other than Him. A proper understanding of this most important concept is necessary so that one takes the straight path to God and practices obedience to Him, Who created all and sustains all out of His Love and Mercy. Also, since man is not perfect, when he makes a mistake, he is advised to seek forgiveness from his Lord, the Most Great and the Most Forgiving One.

    The second powerful message in the beautiful selected passage of today provides us with a list of things that the seeker of success is advised to avoid: 1) joining other gods with God, the Most Great and the Only One, which is the greatest sin, because it is not only a sign of ingratitude, and prevents one from fulfilling the duties for which one was created, but it is the only unpardonable sin; 2) not practicing regular charity. Giving regular charity falls under worshipping God, the Most Kind and Most Rich One. It is also an opportunity that man has to emulate the Beneficence of God. Certainly the best compliment one can give another is to emulate him, and 3) denying the hereafter – for it leads to choosing pleasure and success in the short term, at the expense of pain and suffering in the long term.

    The third powerful message in the beautiful selected passage of today is a reinforcement of the key component of success, i.e. faith in God, the Most Great and the Righteous Teacher, and in His beloved messenger, Muhammad, and performing deeds of righteousness as a manifestation of that faith – for such who follow this most righteous advice and heed the above injunctions is a reward that will never fail, and they will be the ones to attain lasting success.

    The seeker of success who wishes to reach his goal has absolute faith in God, the Creator and Sustainer of all, and the Reckoner, and in His beloved messenger, Muhammad. He joins none other in the worship of his Lord, performs righteous deeds as a manifestation of his faith, gives in regular charity from what his Lord has provided him, and is certain of the hereafter.

# Day 269

In the case of those who say: "Our Lord is God," and further, stand firm and steadfast, the angels descend on them at the time of death; "Fear not!" (they say), "nor grieve! But receive the glad tidings of the garden (of bliss) that which you were promised!

"We were your protectors in this life and will be so in the hereafter; <u>therein shall you have all that your souls shall desire</u>; therein shall you have all that you ask for!

"A hospitable gift from One Most Forgiving, Most Merciful".

(41:30-32)

# Day 269

The beautiful selected passage of today reinforces to the seeker of success the key component needed to reach his goal, i.e. faith (in God, the Creator and Nourisher of all, and in His noble messenger, Muhammad). As previously mentioned, when a teacher repeats a particular concept, it is for the benefit of the student so that he will realize its importance.

Having faith is manifested by the believer and the seeker of success as he says: "My Lord is God", and afterwards stands firm and steadfast. The believer rejects the authority of anything that prevents him from fulfilling his duties towards his Creator and Sustainer, to Whom only belongs all praise and worship. After this important declaration of faith that includes recognizing the prophethood of the honorable prophet Muhammad, the seeker of success will have to stand firm and steadfast by avoiding all sins – this will indeed require patient perseverance.

We are provided in the beautiful selected passage of today a description of the success awaiting one who has faith in God, the Most Great and the Most Righteous Teacher, and in His beloved messenger, Muhammad, who performs righteous deeds as a manifestation of his faith, and stands firmly, avoiding all sins: Angels will descend on such fortunate souls at the time of their death, supporting them, and reminding them that they were in their protection in life and will also be under their protection in death – and they will be given glad tidings of the eternal paradise and garden of bliss that was promised to the believers by God, Most High and the Most Trustworthy. **Therein shall a soul have all that it desires, and all that one can ask for will be provided: Truly, this is the success worth pursuing.**

The seeker of success who wishes to reach his goal has complete faith in God, the Most Wise, the Most Trustworthy, and the Most Generous, and in His noble messenger, Muhammad. He praises and worships his Lord with enthusiasm and performs righteous deeds as a manifestation of his faith and avoids all sins, standing firm in his faith.

# Day 270

**Who is better in speech than one who calls (men) to God, works righteousness, and says: "I am one of the Muslims"?**

(41:33)

# Day 270

    The propensity for a great majority of people is to expend enough effort to be able to succeed at any task, but without having to utilize a tremendous amount of one's resources or energy. Therefore, statistically, most of the measurable outcomes will follow the bell-curve pattern, i.e. those falling below the 2.5 percentile can be labeled the least successful and those above the 97.5 percentile can be labeled as the most successful.

    If the respected reader attains from this humble collection of meditations the most important and primary ingredient of success, i.e. faith in God, the Most Great and the Only One, and in His beloved messenger, Muhammad – and does righteous deeds as a result of his faith, then the author will have realized the greater portion of his intent. The esteemed reader will then most likely be in the group to have attained success. However, there is bound to be a group of people, who, for their own benefit, are avowed over-achievers, i.e. in the highest 2.5 percentile, and it is to this group of individuals to whom today's beautiful selected passage is addressed.

    The super-achiever is not content with the security of success with which a majority of people would be delighted and which awaits those who have faith in God, the Most Great and Most Generous, and in His noble messenger, Muhammad, and who perform righteous deeds as a manifestation of their faith; he wishes these good things for others as well, and therefore identifies himself as one who has submitted himself to God, the Originator of all that exists and the most Righteous Teacher, i.e. identifies himself as Muslim and also invites others to the way of God, the Most Gracious and Most Generous One. Notice that the term "call", equivalent to "invitation" is used. It would be unreasonable to think that one can forcefully encourage others to partake of something good, such as a bounteous feast. Similarly, one can graciously invite a less fortunate individual to the Way of God, the Most Magnificent and the Best Guide, or towards lasting success – but cannot force him on that path.

    The seeker of success who wishes to reach the highest level of success has absolute faith in God, the Most Glorious, and the Creator and Sustainer of all, and in His beloved messenger, Muhammad. He knows that in the eyes of his Lord, there is no person better than he who possesses faith, praises and worships his Lord regularly with enthusiasm, works righteous deeds as a result of faith, identifies himself as one who has submitted himself to God, the Creator and Sustainer of all, i.e. Muslim, and invites others to His path, so that they too may succeed.

# Day 271

**And no one will be granted such goodness except those who exercise _patience and self-restraint;_ none but persons of the greatest good fortune.**

**And if at any time an incitement to discord is made to you by the evil one (Satan), seek refuge in God; He is the One who hears and knows all things.**

(41:35-36)

# Day 271

The beautiful selected passage of today identifies two characteristics that someone who hopes to reach the **highest degree of success** is expected to attain; in addition, we are provided with clear instructions on how we can attain these two very valuable characteristics.

Patience and self-restraint are identified as the two very valuable characteristics in the beautiful selected passage of today that persons of the greatest good fortune will be so fortunate to have attained, and who will accordingly be rewarded with the corresponding measure of goodness by God, the Most Great and the Most Generous One. Being unable to control oneself and not exhibiting patience are both related and sometimes indistinguishable except when referring to short-term or long-term situations. When looking at negative situations retrospectively, people frequently cite above two factors as something they wish they had practiced in order to avoid the negative situation. Unfortunately, neither in this world nor on the Day of Judgment, are we able to turn the clock back and undo our failure.

It is not surprising, then, that the greatest impediment to man in attaining these two very valuable characteristics that will help him to succeed, i.e. patience and self-restraint, is his avowed enemy, Satan, referred to as "the evil one" in the last verse of the beautiful selected passage of today. And when the evil one incites discord, with the intention of neutralizing the virtues of patience and self-restraint, we are so generously instructed by God, the Most Kind and the Most Righteous Teacher, on how we can out-maneuver the evil one: By seeking refuge in God, the All-hearing, All-knowing, and the Best Protector.

The seeker of success who wishes to reach his goal has unwavering faith in God, the Most Patient, the Most Righteous Teacher, and the Best Friend and Protector, and in His noble messenger, Muhammad. He knows that patience and self-restraint throughout his life are crucial to his success; and whenever the evil one (Satan) attempts to make an incitement to discord, he seeks refuge in God, the Most Powerful and the Best Protector.

# Day 272

Among His signs are the night and the day, and the sun and the moon. Adore not the sun and the moon, but adore God, Who created them, if it is Him you wish to serve.

But if the (unbelievers) are arrogant, (no matter); for in the presence of your Lord are those who celebrate His praises by night and by day. And they never tire (nor feel themselves above it).

(41:37-38)

# Day 272

The vision of the sun rising in the day and setting in the evening inspires awe in most people; so does the vision of a full moon in the night, and that of the starry sky, as well as the vision of the first signs of spring after a long winter. The alternation of night and day with perfection, year after year, inspires awe as we realize what would happen if we could no longer rely on their predictable transformation. There are many other things in existence that command awe: earth, mountains, sea, sky, and stars, among innumerable other things.

When man sees something beautiful, he has a tendency to adore it. Hence we find that, throughout the world, people at various times and various places showed their wonderment to some of the things noted above by actually worshipping them. We see that people in the past, and sometimes even today, have taken things such as the sun, the moon, the stars, fire, water, trees, or mountains, among other things, for worship.

In the beautiful selected passage of today, man is instructed to be careful that in marveling at the truly amazing things in existence, such as the sun and the moon, among countless others, he does not forget Who has created them – because only then will he be able to fulfill the requirements for which he was created, i.e. to praise, worship and serve God, the Creator and Sustainer of all. Our praise and worship of God, the Most Holy, to Whom belongs all praise and worship, neither requires our worship, nor is His stature increased by it – although we know from other verses in Holy Quran, that God, the Most Holy and Most Wise, created everything in existence to worship Him. The entire existence continues to worship and celebrate the praises of God by night and by day, without tiring, unlike man. The esteemed reader is referred to the commentary of Day 3 of this collection of meditations on a more detailed discussion of worship. And, if an unfortunate individual is arrogant and fails to recognize and worship and serve the Creator, Who is the Originator of all – we are informed, regardless, in God's presence are those who celebrate His praises by night and by day, and they never tire, nor feel themselves above worshipping Him.

The seeker of success who wishes to reach his goal has complete faith in God, the Originator of all and the Most Glorious, and in His beloved messenger, Muhammad. When he encounters things commanding awe, such as the sun or the moon or anything else, he does not adore or worship them, but praises and worships God, Who created these things and everything else in existence.

# Day 273

**And among His signs is this: you see the earth barren and desolate; but when We send down rain to it, it is stirred to life and yields increase. Truly, He Who gives life to the (dead) earth, can surely give life to (men) who are dead – for He has power over all things.**

(41:39)

# Day 273

    The beautiful selected passage of today has two powerful messages for the seeker of success to help him realize his goal - the first of which is a continuation on the reflection of the message in the meditation from that of yesterday, i.e. another sign of God, the Most Great, the Creator of good as well as the Creator of harm, being the barren earth, which is stirred to life after He sends down rain to it in the spring. The wise seeker of success does not adore or worship the rain or the spring or trees, but gives praise where it most appropriately belongs, i.e. to Him Who created these things, as well as all other things in existence. This fortunate individual can be said to have freed himself from the shackles of idolatry and polytheism, like his prototype on the path to success, the beloved prophet Ibrahim, who submitted himself to the service of God, the Most Wise and the Truth, by dissociating himself from worshipping anything other than He to Whom all worship rightly belongs.
    The second powerful message in the beautiful selected passage of today uses the same example as in the first message, i.e. the barren earth being revived to life, and reminds any skeptic that he too can so be revived after his death, by Him Who is Most Great and the Giver and Taker of life. This example will help the fortunate individual to understand that he will be held accountable for his actions in this life and will result in increased likelihood that he will choose the path of success rather than that of failure.
    The seeker of success who wishes to reach his goal has absolute faith in God, the Most Pure, the Originator and the Restorer, and in His noble messenger, Muhammad; every year when he sees the barren earth revived to life in the springtime, he contemplates his own resurrection. He knows that he is responsible for all his actions in this life, as well as the consequences of neglecting his responsibilities.

# Day 274

Whoever works righteousness, benefits his own soul. Whoever works evil, it is against his own soul – nor is your Lord ever unjust (in the least) to His servants.

(41:46)

# Day 274

One has to constantly make decisions at every moment of his life. In the extreme ranges of one's life, i.e. very young or very old, typically, or in the case of one with impaired mental faculties, others will have to make decisions for that individual. Sometimes the difference will be more apparent than other times, but one makes conscious decisions between good and evil on a constant basis.

Among the different religions and social systems we have seen throughout history, the vast majority purport to promote right over wrong, and to promote good over evil. But why should one choose right over wrong? And why should one choose good over evil? Some people believe they are helping society by choosing right and good over wrong and evil. Others naively believe they are doing God, the Most Glorious and the Only One free of all needs, a favor by choosing right and good over wrong and evil. The beautiful selected passage of today makes it clear that if an individual chooses and works righteousness, he is not benefiting anyone but his own self. Conversely, if he chooses and works evil, then he is not harming anyone other than his own self. Therefore, it's clear that if a man wants to help himself, then he should work righteousness, and if he wants to avoid harming himself, then he should avoid evil.

Today's beautiful selected passage closes by reminding man that his entire life, and every moment in it, is an opportunity for him to either increase his chances of success by working righteousness, or an opportunity to lessen his chances of success by choosing evil - for God, the Most Supreme and the All-aware is also the Best of those who keep accounts, and no deed of man will be left unaccounted for. The seeker of success should be reminded that in order to receive an appropriate reward for a righteous deed, it should be combined with faith in God, the Most Wise and the Most Generous One, and in His noble prophet, Muhammad. Otherwise, the individual who performs a good deed for anything or for anyone else other than God, the All-hearing and All-seeing, then would already have been recompensed for that good deed prior to the Day of Judgment by whom he attempted to please, and is not expected to be recompensed by God the Most Rich and the Most Generous, since it was not done for His sake. Similarly, if an individual performs an evil deed, he will be the one most negatively affected by the evil act. The other individual to whom the evil act is directed may suffer transiently in the life of this world, with the permission of God, the One Who controls every matter and incident, but the one performing the evil act will suffer long-term consequences - both in this life as well as on the Day of Judgment, the effects of which may be eternal suffering.

The seeker of success who wishes to reach his goal has unwavering faith in God, the Most Great, the Bestower of honors, as well as the Humiliator, and in His beloved messenger, Muhammad. He knows that if he works righteousness, he is the greatest beneficiary of the act; and if he works evil, he is the greatest loser as a result of the act.

# Day 275

Man does not weary of asking for good (things from God), but if ill touches him, he gives up all hope (and) is lost in despair;

When we give him a taste of some Mercy from Ourselves after some adversity has touched him, he is sure to say: "This is due to my (merit). I think not that the hour (of Judgment) will (ever) be established – but if I am brought back to my Lord, I have (much) good (stored) in His sight!". But We will show the unbelievers the truth of all that they did, and We shall give them the taste of a severe penalty.

When We bestow favors on man, he turns away and gets himself remote on his side (instead of coming to us); and when evil seizes him, (he comes) full of prolonged prayer!

(41:49-51)

# Day 275

A proper understanding of the beautiful selected passage of today will help the seeker of success to develop a strong foundation for success and be able to weather the storms in life, as well as to avoid being lost and carried away during the times of ease and calm. The wise seeker of success realizes that both of these periods, i.e. adversity and ease, are a natural component of life and that both periods are an opportunity to prove himself and to come closer to his goal.

All beings desire what is good and brings them happiness. When man asks for something from God, the Most Great and the Most Generous invariably, it is something that will bring him happiness. The desire to seek goodness and happiness is necessary for the seeker of success. However, it is a sign of foolishness for one to desire good in the short term at the expense of suffering in the long term.

During the course of life, all individuals will be affected by harm or illness to a varying degree. During such periods, there is a tendency for man to be lost in despair, promptly seeking the assistance of God, the Hearer and Seer of all. As noted above, in his life, man will experience not only periods of turbulence, but also periods of comfort and ease; in such periods of comfort and ease, man has a tendency towards arrogance, thinking that he is entitled to such rewards as a result of his efforts primarily, and that it will last forever, and frequently forgetting to acknowledge the role of God, the Most Merciful, the Creator of harm and the Creator of good, in allowing him to have this period of comfort and ease. However, having knowledge of the factors described in the beautiful selected passage of today, the wise seeker of success will not look at the times of ease as an opportunity to relax and congratulate himself, but continue to work to improve himself, realizing that like all things, this is a gift from God, the Source of all that is good and the Source of peace.

The seeker of success who wishes to reach his goal has complete faith in God, the Almighty, the Constrictor and the Reliever, and in His noble messenger, Muhammad. He knows that his life will include periods of turbulence as well as ease. He attempts to remember his Lord in the periods of tranquility as much as he remembers and calls on Him in the periods of adversity.

# Day 276

Whatever you are given (here) is (but) a convenience of this life; but that which is with God is better and more lasting – (it is) for those who believe and put their trust in their Lord:

Those who avoid the greater crimes and shameful deeds, and when they are angry - even then forgive;

Those who hearken to their Lord and establish regular prayer; who (conduct) their affairs by mutual consultation; who spend out of what we bestow on them for sustenance;

And those who, when an oppressive wrong is inflicted on them, (are not cowed but) help and defend themselves.

(42:36-39)

# Day 276

    The beautiful selected passage of today is directed specifically to the seeker of success and a proper understanding of it would provide him with a definite advantage that can help him to realize his goal. Let us take as an example the different stages in a person's life for a proper understanding of today's beautiful selected passage, so that it can optimally benefit the seeker of success.

    In the stage of childhood, a person considers himself very happy if he is in possession of large amounts of candy and toys. In the stage of adolescence, a person considers himself very happy if he acquires greater mobility in his community, such as with the use of an automobile, and acquires the ability to enjoy some other aspects of adulthood at an earlier stage in life, i.e. in adolescence, without the associated responsibilities of an adult. In the stage of adulthood, a person considers himself very happy if he is in possession of a large amount of wealth and property, along with having good health, love and affection from his relatives, as well as friends and power. Because a person spends a greater period of time in his adulthood compared to other phases in life, the topic of success and its study is a popular subject that focuses on success as envisioned by a person in the adult phase of his life.

    However, beyond the various stages of one's life on earth, a man who would truly be successful will contemplate what will happen to him after his death, in the period of time not measured in years or decades, but for eternity. The wise man who contemplates on this matter will then realize that whatever he has been given in this life – indeed, whatever can possibly be acquired in this life – is but a trifle for the convenience of this life; and he will realize that what is with God, the Most Rich and the Most Generous, is better and more lasting. The wise reader is referred to the text of the beautiful selected passage of today to acquire the characteristics which will lead him towards success that is not counted in years or decades, but that which will be for more than millions or billions of years – and indeed, forever.

    The seeker of success of success who wishes to reach his goal has unwavering faith in God, the Most Great, the Creator and Sustainer of all, and in His noble messenger, Muhammad. He realizes that what is with his Lord is better and more lasting than all the riches in this world. He believes in his Lord and puts his trust in Him. He avoids the greater crimes and shameful deeds and forgives others even when he is angry. He rushes to his Lord and yearns for closeness to Him and establishes regular prayer. He conducts his dealings in consultation with others who also have faith in God, the Most Beneficent, Most Merciful, and in his honorable messenger, Muhammad, and spends out of that which has been provided to him by his Lord. And when an oppressive wrong is done to him, he is not cowed, but exhibits courage and defends himself.

# Day 277

The recompense for an injury is an injury equal to it (in degree); but if a person forgives and makes reconciliation, his reward is due from God – for (God) loves not those who do wrong.

But indeed if any do help and defend themselves after a wrong ( is done) to them, against such there is no cause of blame;

The blame is only against those who oppress men with wrongdoing and insolently transgress beyond bounds through the land, defying right and justice; for such, there will be a penalty grievous.

But indeed if any show patience and forgive, that would truly be an exercise of courageous will and resolution in the conduct of affairs.

(42:40-43)

# Day 277

    The beautiful selected passage of today is a continuation from yesterday's passage on instructions for the seeker of success to help him reach his goal – but was separated from the yesterday's meditation due to a distinct characteristic the seeker of success is recommended to acquire that will help him to realize his goal. We learned in yesterday's beautiful meditation that one of the characteristics that the seeker of success should instill in himself is courage – so that when an oppressive wrong is inflicted on him, then he is not cowed, but helps and defends himself. However, in the process of defending himself against oppression, the seeker of success is instructed by God, the Most Wise and the Best Protector and Helper, that even though the oppressor and wrongdoer is the one who is blameworthy and responsible for the suffering, even still, the one who is helping and defending himself must not exceed certain boundaries. The one who helps and defends himself against an oppressive wrong is instructed not to inflict an injury greater than what he suffered in the process of helping and defending himself.

    We are instructed in today's beautiful selected passage, by God, the Most Great and the Most Righteous Teacher, that if we wish to attain a position of high standing in the sight of God, the Best Appraiser and the Best One Who keeps account, then we should acquire the characteristics of patience and forgiveness. Therefore, while in the process of defending and helping ourselves against oppression, even though we have the right to inflict injury towards the oppressor – at least to the same level that we suffered, we are encouraged to exhibit patience and forgiveness. This truly is an exercise in courage, and may lead the oppressor away from evil and towards God, the Most Beneficent and Most Merciful, by the way of example.

    The seeker of success who wishes to reach his goal has complete faith in God, the Most Great and the Most Forgiving One, and in His beloved messenger, Muhammad. He realizes that even though he has the right and duty to help and defend himself when an oppressive wrong is inflicted on him, he cannot inflict a greater injury than what he suffered in the process of helping and defending himself. He knows that exhibiting patience and forgiveness is a sign of courage and more pleasing to God, the Most Wise, Most Patient, and the Most Forgiving, than exacting retribution.

# Day 278

**And no protectors have they to help them other than God. And for any whom God leaves to stray, there is no way (to the goal).**

(42:46)

# Day 278

Today's beautiful selected passage helps the seeker of success immensely by identifying how two of his essential needs can be met so he can be successful in reaching his goal. One of the essential needs of man, as well as of all living beings, is protection. From his birth and up to his death, man is in need of protection. He is in need, whether he realizes it or not, of protection from the elements; from other living beings, such as wild animals, who will have met their needs by destroying him; from other living beings, such as man himself, who stands to gain by destroying him; and from anarchy and disorder. And although he may not realize it, his greatest need for protection is from the evil within himself, so that the goodness within himself prevails over the evil within himself. Man seeks help throughout his life from various sources – whether from parents, relatives, society, the government, his employer, or spiritual leader, etc. – in various situations. However, the wise individual will realize, as mentioned in the beautiful selected passage of today, that there exists for man no one or anything that can protect or help him, except God, the Most Great and the Best Protector and Helper, as every action in the universe is under His control – even an action as mundane as the falling of a specific leaf from a tree.

Another essential need for man if he is to have any measure of success is guidance – in childhood, man looks to his parents for guidance in all matters, and later he seeks it from teachers, peers, employers, or other experts. Guidance from each of the sources mentioned above will result in success in a limited phase of one's life. However, an individual who desires success in all phases of his life on earth, as well as eternity, will realize that the best source of Guidance for all matters and for eternity is none other than God, the Creator of all, the Source of all power, and the Best Guide. The unfortunate individual who does not seek the guidance of God, the Most Great and the Most Wise, will thus be left to stray, for whom there is no way to the goal of success, either in this life or the hereafter.

The seeker of success who wishes to reach his goal has absolute faith in God, the Creator and Sustainer of all, the Best Protector and the Best Guide, and in His noble messenger, Muhammad. He realizes that he has no protector or helpers other than God, the Most Beneficent and Most Merciful One, and if He were to leave him to stray, there is none other who could guide him towards his goal.

# Day 279

...And truly, when we give man a taste of a Mercy from Ourselves, he exults – but when some ill happens to him on account of the deeds which his hands have set forth, truly then, is man ungrateful!

(42:48)

# Day 279

    The beautiful selected passage of today provides the seeker of success with proper guidance on etiquette in life that is pleasing to God, the Most Forgiving and the Most Refined One – in all phases of one's life, including when one is in a state of comfort, and also when one is faced with difficulty. From the time that one wakes up until the time that he goes to sleep, and again throughout the night until one wakes up in the morning, an individual is the recipient of numerous invaluable gifts from God, the Most Beneficent and the Most Merciful One. Certainly, the rising and setting of the sun at the proper times, the invaluable faculties of hearing, seeing, and reasoning, the restful sleep in the night and return to wakefulness in the daytime, are all gifts we enjoy on a daily basis and that cannot be provided by anyone except from the Mercy of God, the Creator and Sustainer of all. However, how many of us appreciate these truly invaluable gifts that we enjoy on a daily basis from the One Who provides them to us out of His infinite Mercy? Indeed, we may even get in the habit of expecting these invaluable gifts as our right.

    Occasionally, but certainly on a less frequent basis than with the ease and comfort we enjoy as described above, man may experience some ill or discomfort. Man experiences this ill or discomfort as a result of his own actions, as per the Word of God, the Most Forbearing and Most Just - which we reviewed in an earlier meditation. In this situation, the typical response of man is that he loses hope and is filled with despair, having forgotten the countless mercies and gifts from God, the Most Beneficent and Most Merciful, i.e. he shows ungratefulness. A more proper response for man in this situation would be to seek forgiveness from God, the Most Merciful and the Most Forgiving, and to show patience during such times, as a result of which, the individual will emerge wiser and stronger.

    The seeker of success who wishes to reach his goal has unwavering faith in God, the Lord of all majesty and reward and the Most Patient One, and in His beloved messenger, Muhammad. He is thankful to His Lord every day when he is in comfort and ease. During the times when he is ill, or not in comfort, he realizes that it is as a result of some punishment for his own actions, and shows patience and is hopeful of his Lord's Mercy and Forgiveness.

# Day 280

**We have made the (Quran) a Light, wherewith we guide such of Our servants as We will; and certainly you do guide (men) to the straight Way:**

**The Way of God, to Whom belongs whatever is in the heavens and whatever is on earth. Behold (how) all affairs tend towards God.**

(42:52-53)

# Day 280

Man is the only created being having the free will to choose between right and wrong that we know of. All other created beings are pre-occupied with survival: obtaining shelter, obtaining the food for the survival of their self and family, and procreation, so that their genes are passed along into the next generation. In addition to the challenges of survival, and because of his unique gifts, man is the only being in creation we know of, who asks himself: "Why am I here?".

Unfortunately, some human beings never go past the stage of addressing the challenges of survival – but the wise ones, who do begin to utilize their unique gifts and start to contemplate the reason for their existence, will need to utilize their gifts of sight, hearing and contemplation to help them to answer the question "Why am I here?". When the wise individual sees the bird sustaining itself in mid air, he will ask himself how that is possible; when he talks to other individuals like himself, he will realize that the quest to answer the question "Why am I here?" in man is as strong as the quest for survival, if not stronger than that – and that different people have answered that question in different ways. When he contemplates the beauty and perfection wherever he turns, he will arrive at only one reasonable answer that will answer all his questions: the unity, design and harmony of everything in existence can only be possible if all that is in existence is under the control of One Source and Who is God, the Only One and the Only One deserving of all praise and worship. The next question a wise individual will then ask himself is: "How do you find out what the One Source, Who Created all and Sustains all that is in existence expects from me?". Using his intellect and reasoning, he will realize that God, the Most Great, Most Wise, and the Best Teacher, has, for this very purpose, in His Mercy, sent messengers to mankind, including the honorable prophets Noah, Abraham, Moses, Jesus. Further, he will learn that when the message through the earlier prophets was corrupted by mankind - by negligence or intention, God, the Most Wise and the Most Kind, chose as a Mercy to mankind and the worlds, to send the last prophet, the beloved Muhammad with His message, the Holy Quran, as a Light with which to guide all to the straight path for which they were created and to attain eternal success of the highest kind, and which He promised to safeguard Himself for eternity.

The seeker of success who wishes to reach his goal has complete faith in God, the Creator and Sustainer of all and the Best Guide, and in His noble messenger, Muhammad. He knows that he was created for a purpose – and refers often and regularly to the Holy Quran to guide him to the straight Path, leading to attainment of **success of the highest degree**, which will last for eternity.

# Day 281

**We created not the heavens and the earth and all between them merely in idle sport;**

**We created them not except for just ends – but most of them do not understand.**

(44:38-39)

# Day 281

In addition to the gifts of sight and hearing that man has in common with other created beings, he has the unique gift of intellect and reasoning, which, as we learned in yesterday's meditation, he can use to ask vital questions, such as the reason for his existence. The correct answer, which can be deduced from the invaluable faculties provided to us by God, the Most Rich and the Most Wise, will lead one to the path of success. Unfortunately, some individuals fail to utilize their faculties properly and fail to realize the seriousness of creation and existence. For them, the reason for existence and life appears to be a random act, of no significance, or possibly an idle sport. The beautiful selected passage of today informs man clearly that the creation of existence and all that is within it, was not for idle sport. This is a crucial point to grasp if one is to proceed to the next level on the path to success.

After the fortunate individual realizes that creation was not an act of randomness or for idle sport, he is informed of the role that he himself plays in the creation, i.e. that he is created for just ends, i.e. for praising, worshipping and serving his creator, and to test mankind to see which of them will carry out the responsibilities for which they were created, and which of them would fail. Man will then be judged on the Day of Judgment and be either rewarded or punished accordingly; unfortunately for mankind, many of them do not realize this and will therefore be prevented from attaining success. The esteemed reader is directed to the meditation of Day 3 of this collection for a more detailed review of what constitutes worship.

The seeker of success who wishes to reach his goal has absolute faith in God, the Most Wise and the Most Just, and in His beloved messenger, Muhammad. He knows that all that is in existence was not created merely in idle sport or as a result of random events. He knows further that the reason for his own creation is to praise, worship, and serve his Creator; he knows that he will be tested in life to see whether he will be obedient and fulfill his responsibilities to God, the Lord of all Majesty and Reward, or be disobedient and neglect his responsibilities. He knows that he will be judged on the Day of Judgment, based on his performance in life and duties, and will be rewarded or punished accordingly.

# Day 282

**If anyone does a righteous deed, it is to the benefit of his own soul; if he does evil, it works against (his own soul). In the end will you (all) be brought back to your Lord.**

(45:15)

# Day 282

From the time that one gets up to the time that he goes to sleep – and from the time he first acquires awareness between right and wrong, up to his death – man must make decisions continually whether to select the good or bad, whether to do the right thing - usually the harder of the two options, or to select what he knows is not right, which is usually easier and temporarily more enjoyable than the right option.

Because man is encouraged to choose good over bad by God, the Most Glorious and the Best Doer of good, in the Holy Quran, and by His noble messenger, Muhammad, and those who wish for others to succeed, by inviting them to the way of God, the Creator of good and the Lord of majesty and reward, man may erroneously conclude that he is benefiting others by doing righteous deeds. He may feel that his righteous deeds benefit God, the Provider of all and the Only Self-existing One, or those who invite him to the way of God, blessed be His Name – but the beautiful selected passage of today informs us, that is not the case. In fact, if man does a righteous deed with the intention of helping another man, woman or being in this world, still the greatest beneficiary is the one doing the righteous deed himself, as he will have obtained the reward from the other in the form of gratification, appreciation, and increase in one's reputation or esteem. And if the righteous deed was done for the sake of God, the Most Great and the Best One Who keeps account, then his reward is due to him from God, the Most Appreciative One and the Best Rewarder. Indeed, God is the Creator and Sustainer of all that exists and He can meet every need of all His creation, without any assistance from anyone in any form. In the same fashion, if a man does an evil deed, then he is harming no one but himself.

Therefore, man has the option to either help himself every day by choosing right over wrong and good over evil – or he has the option to harm himself by choosing the opposite, until the Day of Judgment, when all men and women will be brought back to God, the Gatherer and the Most Just; it is then that man will know for sure who has been successful. Whoever is saved from the hell-fire on that day will have attained the **highest form of success.**

The seeker of success who wishes to reach his goal has unwavering faith in God, the Most Wise and the Creator of good and harm, and in His noble messenger, Muhammad. He knows that if he does a righteous deed, the greatest beneficiary of that is himself; and that if he does an evil deed, the one who is most harmed by that is himself.

# Day 283

**God created the heavens and the earth for just ends, and in order that each soul may find the recompense of what it has earned, and none of them be wronged.**

(45:22)

# Day 283

Today's beautiful selected passage contains the concepts reviewed in the recent meditations. God, the Most Wise and the Best Teacher, repeats certain concepts in the Holy Quran for emphasis, so that the important concepts are reinforced for the benefit of mankind - the first of which is that man should realize that the earth, life, and all that is in existence, is not a matter of chance, but created for a purpose. The unfortunate individual who does not have a grasp of this concept will be unable to proceed to the next level, which is a requirement for attaining any degree of success.

Once man realizes that he is created for a purpose, he will be able to act in a way that helps him fulfill that purpose. As reviewed in the recent meditations and repeated in the beautiful selected passage of today for reinforcement regarding the purpose for man's existence: it is so that mankind could be tested to see which of them will fulfill the duties for which they were created, i.e. praising and worshipping God, the Only One deserving of all praise and worship and the Most Glorious One, and serving Him by performing good deeds - the best of which is the worship of God, the Most Holy and the Greatest, and consistently choosing good over evil, and therefore passing the test of their life on earth.

Each soul shall have a recompense of what it has earned during its life on earth, to be gathered before God, the most Equitable One and the Gatherer, on the Day of Judgment. No soul shall be wronged in the least on that day by God, Who is the Most Just and Best of those who keep accounts. Every soul that has done the smallest amount of good shall see its result that day; and every soul that has done the smallest amount of evil shall also see its result that day. The truly successful will be those who had faith and whose good deeds outweigh their evil deeds – and so they are saved from the hell-fire; and the true failures will be those who lacked faith and whose evil deeds outweigh their good deeds.

The seeker of success who wishes to reach his goal has complete faith in God, the Creator, Resurrector and the Gatherer, and in His beloved messenger, Muhammad. He knows that he was created for a purpose and does his best to maximize his good deeds and minimize his evil deeds. He knows that he is accountable for all his actions on the Day of Judgment, and prepares himself accordingly, to maximize his prospects for the highest degree of success.

# Day 284

**Indeed, those who say: "Our Lord is (only) God" and remain firm (on that path) – on them shall be no fear, nor shall they grieve;**

**Such shall be companions of paradise, dwelling therein (forever) – a recompense for their (good) deeds.**

(46:13-14)

# Day 284

Although we have reviewed in some of the earlier meditations the dynamic nature of man's journey of his life on earth, the beautiful selected passage of today relays this information to the seeker of success in a manner which covers the most important aspects of this concept and also reinforces it as well for our benefit.

Man is in awe of those exercising power over him at different stages of his life. For example, in his childhood the parents are the ultimate authority; in school, it is the teacher and the principal; in adolescence, it is usually the celebrity figures and peers; in his workplace, it is the employer; and in adulthood, as a citizen, it is the leader of his country or a similar figure. Also, the fact that all that one had worked so hard to attain in one phase of his life could so easily be lost, is difficult for man to comprehend and it can be a cause of major grief – such as loss of one's parent in childhood, loss of one's limbs at a young age, loss of one's career that one had worked hard to develop, or loss of confidence in one's leaders or government to provide an environment of a basic necessity such as safety, security, justice, and a right to pursuit of happiness and care for oneself and his family.

From the beautiful selected passage of today, we are taught an extremely valuable lesson in our pursuit of success: That the only people who will not err in any phase of life in relying on an authority figure to meet their needs at all times are those who realize and proclaim: "Our Lord is only God", and remain firm on that path. On those people who rely on God, the Most Great and the Best Protector, will be no fear, because there is nothing and no one greater than the One Who created all that exists and on Whom everything in existence is dependent. They shall also not have any cause to grieve because God, the Owner of all and the Inheritor of all, provides for them most amply at every stage of their life – both on this earth and in the hereafter, for eternity. Therefore, those who have faith in their God, the Creator and Sustainer of all, and perform good deeds as a result shall be companions of paradise, dwelling therein forever.

The seeker of success who wishes to reach his goal has absolute faith in God, the Source of all power and the Most Generous One, and in His noble messenger, Muhammad. He knows that at every stage in his life, and for eternity, that there is no power greater than God, the Most Beneficent and Most Merciful. Therefore, he believes and says: "My Lord is only God (and none other)", and remains firm on that path. He engages in regular praise and worship of his Lord and performs other good deeds as a manifestation of his faith.

# Day 285

We have enjoined on man kindness to his parents; in pain did his mother bear him, and in pain did she give him birth. The carrying of the (child) to his weaning is (a period of) thirty months. At length, when he reaches the age of full strength and attains forty years, he says: "O my Lord! Grant me that I may be grateful for your favor which you have bestowed upon me and upon both my parents, and that I may work righteousness such as you may approve – and make my offspring good. Truly have I turned to you and truly do I bow (to you) in Islam".

Such are they from whom We shall accept the best of their deeds and pass by their ill deeds; (they shall be) among the companions of the Garden – a promise of Truth, which was made to them (in this life).

(46:15-16)

# Day 285

The beautiful selected passage of today provides the seeker of success with two powerful messages to help him reach his goal - the first of which is that man is instructed by God, the Most Kind and the Most Wise, to be kind to his parents. The examples provided to help us understand the reason for this injunction include the discomfort suffered by the mother during pregnancy, the truly discomforting pain of labor, and the period of breastfeeding (approximately two years). Providing support and comfort to the mother during the critical period of a new life in the early period, the father will share in the honor accorded to the mother.

The second powerful message in the beautiful selected passage of today to help the seeker of success to reach his goal regards the characteristics he needs to acquire in his adulthood – these he should start initiating at an early age in his life and they should be refined by the age of forty, when he has typically acquired the optimal level of intellect, patience, understanding and maturity, and which afterwards, typically begins to gradually diminish. These characteristics, which the seeker of success should make an effort to acquire and then refine, begin with gratefulness to God, the Creator and Sustainer of all, Who made each and every individual, and everything in existence from nothing, and Who sustains each one of his creations in the most excellent manner in perfection – from the oxygen that is inhaled by the living organism, to the energy that is then derived from the oxygen to carry out the wishes of the organism. Another characteristic that the seeker of success needs to acquire, starting at an early age and then refined in adulthood, is concern for doing righteous work for the sake of God, the Most Supreme and the Rewarder of thankfulness. In adulthood, in addition to one's self, man usually has concern for his offspring – and he should be concerned that they acquire characteristics of success as well, because they are his responsibility, and one will be held accountable for all his responsibilities. The beautiful selected passage of today ends with the reminder of the most valuable characteristic required for achieving success: Faith in God, the Most Supreme, the First and the Last, as relayed to us through His noble messenger, Muhammad, and manifested by submitting oneself and his life to Him wholeheartedly. One who acquires these characteristics is promised not just love and happiness for the few years that one typically works so hard for on earth, but that which lasts for eternity – this is a promise from God, the Truth and the Most Trustworthy.

The seeker of success who wishes to reach his goal has unwavering faith in God, the All-comprehending and the Most Wise One, and in His beloved messenger, Muhammad. He shows kindness to his parents. He acquires the characteristics of gratefulness to his Lord, and yearns to work righteousness. He hopes to guide his offspring to the path of goodness and success, and turns to his Lord in submission, and bowing to Him in praise.

# Day 286

And to all are (assigned) degrees according to the deeds which they (have done) and in order that (God) may recompense their deeds and no injustice be done to them.

And on the day that the unbelievers will be placed before the fire, (it will be said to them): "You received your good things in the life of the world and you took your pleasure out of them; but today, you shall be recompensed with a penalty of humiliation – for you were arrogant on earth without just cause and that you (ever) transgressed".

(46:19-20)

# Day 286

The beautiful selected passage of today provides in an excellent manner a glimpse of the outcome from not attaining success, so that one would be motivated to succeed. Additionally, one who is interested in following the path to success is instructed in how to attain the highest degree of success.

As noted earlier in this collection of meditations, one must constantly make decisions from the time he wakes up to the time he goes to sleep, and from the time one is capable of making decisions up until his death. One can make a decision to do good – which is invariably the more difficult of the two options, or he can choose the alternative. One can choose to either help himself or harm himself with every single decision that he makes. Therefore, one acquires a net reward due to him depending on his actions, and according to his deeds. The key aspects of success are again reinforced for our benefit: Faith in God, the Most Great and the Most Generous One, as relayed to us through His noble messenger, Muhammad, and performance of righteous deeds as a result of this faith. If one does any good deed or righteous action other than as a result of faith in God, the Truth and the Light, then one will have received his reward in this world, i.e. to earn the good pleasure of others or even to feel good about oneself. However, if one does good deeds as a result of faith in God, the Most Rich and the Most Generous One, then its reward is promised to him both in this life, and, more importantly, in the hereafter.

We are also shown a picture of what awaits us as an alternative to the achievement of success in the important selected passage of today: Punishment – with fire and humiliation for neglecting one's duties and being arrogant. Someone may make a comparison between a loving parent and his child as to why the parent would want to punish his child with what seems to us to be a severely painful form of punishment with the example that is given, i.e. with fire. Consider for a moment a parent who has showered his child with the greatest blessings and affections and has instructed him to carry out the parent's wishes. Instead, the child is neglectful of his duties and, for the sake of short-term pleasures, has failed to carry out his duties. Certainly, the child who has diligently carried out his duties cannot be equal in receiving the love of the parent than the child who has been neglectful. In fact, the physical pain and punishments described in the Holy Quran may be the lesser of the painful sequel for the evil folks and those who neglected the duties of their Lord, when compared to the fact that they will feel the loss of the Love and Closeness to God, the Most Loving Creator and Sustainer of all that exists, on the Day of Judgment.

The seeker of success who wishes to reach his goal has complete faith in God, the Most Great and the Lord of all majesty and reward, and in His noble messenger, Muhammad. He is able to patiently endure short-term sufferings for long-term pleasures and for the pleasure of closeness to his Lord. He knows that the degree of his long-term success is proportional to the righteous deeds he performs as a result of his faith.

# Day 287

**O you who believe! If you will aid (the cause of) God, He will aid you, and plant your feet firmly.**

(47:7)

# Day 287

The beautiful selected passage of today reinforces the key components of success for our benefit: Faith and righteous action as a result of the faith. A specific example of righteous action is also provided for our benefit. As we learned in the earlier meditations in this collection, faith in God, the Creator and Sustainer of all that exists, as relayed to us by His noble prophet Muhammad, is the essential foundation on which all success rests; for this reason, even though the main message of the beautiful selected passage of today could be relayed on its own, it is preceded by a reminder of this essential characteristic, i.e. faith, without which even good deeds are of no benefit when it really matters. On the other hand, a person who performs actions for the sake of God, the Abaser and the Exalter, i.e. the person who has faith and believes, is recommended in the beautiful selected passage of today, to aid the cause of God, the Only One, the Eternal, and the Self-existing One. What forms of aid could one give to the cause of God, Who is Most Strong, Most Rich and Free of all needs? The simplest could be provision of emotional support to others who are serving in the cause of God, the Most Beneficent and Most Merciful, followed by provision of financial resources or meeting their other needs, followed by the highest form of assistance, which is by assisting with their persons or selves. The individual who believes and aids the cause of God, the Creator and Sustainer of all, is promised support from Him. He who has the support of God, the Source of all power and the Best Friend and Helper, is indeed the most fortunate one - and is certain to succeed.

The seeker of success who wishes to reach his goal has absolute faith in God, the Most Powerful and the Most Trustworthy, and in His beloved messenger, Muhammad. He enthusiastically aids the cause of God, the Most Great, the Most Appreciative, and the Most Generous One, as a manifestation of his faith.

# Day 288

**Indeed, God will admit those who believe, and do righteous deeds, to gardens beneath which rivers flow – while those who reject (God) will enjoy (this world) and eat as cattle eat, and the fire will be their abode.**

(47:12)

# Day 288

The beautiful selected passage of today reinforces the key points for the seeker of success, by contrasting the outcomes of those who succeed, with the outcomes of those who never tried to succeed at all. Although these concepts are mentioned in other meditations in this collection also, they are worth repeating as the important concepts themselves are repeated often for the benefit for the seeker of success in the Holy Quran. The first important concept for the benefit of the seeker of success in the beautiful selected passage of today, and the key ingredient of success, is that those who believe in God, the Most Great, the Creator and the Resurrector, as relayed to us through His noble messenger, Muhammad, and who do righteous deeds as a result of their faith, will be rewarded with being admitted to gardens beneath which rivers flow – where they will abide for eternity. This is indeed the **highest accomplishment** and will be the desire of all mankind on the Day of Judgment.

The second important concept for the benefit of the seeker of success in the beautiful selected passage of today is related to the above concept in that it is the opposite extreme of the recommended factors for success, i.e. if an individual rejects God, the Most Great, the First, and the Last, even though the signs of His presence are everywhere, and continues to enjoy His myriad blessings, while refusing to carry out the responsibilities for which he was created, specifically to praise, worship and serve Him, then he is no better than the cattle who enjoy whatever is given to them but are unable to reason logically. The cattle, however, will not be called to account. The ungrateful man, who preferred the short-term pleasure of this world at the expense of the long-term outcome by neglecting his responsibilities, however, will be called to account – with appropriate consequences, and instead of the garden in paradise for the successful individuals, the failures will have as their abode, eternal fire – a fitting punishment from God, the All-comprehending and the Most Wise One.

The seeker of success who wishes to reach his goal has unwavering faith in God, the Most Great, the Giver and Taker of life, and in His noble messenger, Muhammad. He praises and worships his Lord enthusiastically, and performs righteous deeds as a manifestation of his faith. He knows that those who reject God, the Creator and Sustainer of all, and who choose short-term benefits at the expense of long-term benefits, while neglecting their responsibilities, are doomed for failure of the worst kind.

# Day 289

**And as for those who accept guidance (from God), He increases them in Guidance, and bestows on them their piety and restraint (from evil).**

(47:17)

# Day 289

The beautiful selected passage of today can help the seeker of success to reach his goal by strengthening him in certain characteristics that will be of great help to him on his journey. The example of today's beautiful selected passage is contrasted with the verse earlier in the same chapter, in which is mentioned about the people who have heard the noble prophet Muhammad's message from God, the Creator and Sustainer of all, but have not accepted it wholeheartedly. These people are certainly unfortunate who are following their lusts and whose hearts have been sealed by God, the Most Great and the Best Guide; this situation is certainly to be avoided by the seeker of success. Contrast the above unfortunate situation with that of the individual who has faith in God, the Maker of order and Shaper of beauty, and in His noble messenger, Muhammad. This is the fortunate individual, who is promised by God, the Most Glorious and the Most Trustworthy One, that he will be increased further in Guidance, and also bestowed with piety and restraint from evil.

The characteristics of piety or God-consciousness and restraint from evil are, then, special rewards reserved for special people pleasing to God, the Creator and Sustainer of all that exists. These are clearly the positive indicators of success, both in this life and in the hereafter, and the seekers of success are recommended to ensure that they acquire and increase these characteristics as much as possible to ensure a favorable outcome. The esteemed reader is reminded of the two most vital components of success: Faith in God, the Most Righteous teacher and the Most Generous One, and performance of righteous action, which is related to the above gifts, i.e. being provided with Guidance, piety, and restraint (from evil).

The seeker of success who wishes to reach his goal has complete faith in God, the Most Praiseworthy and the Possessor of all strength, and in His beloved messenger, Muhammad. He searches for Guidance from his Lord in the Holy Quran, and from the recommendations of the beloved messenger, Muhammad (from sunnah or tradition). As a result, he hopes to be increased further in his consciousness of God, or piety, and restraint (from evil).

## Day 290

And We shall try you until We test those among you who strive their utmost and persevere in patience; and We shall try your reported (determination).

Those who reject God, hinder (men) from the path of God, and resist the messenger after Guidance has been clearly shown to them, will not harm God in the least, but He will make their deeds fruitless.

(47:31-32)

# Day 290

    The beautiful selected passage of today helps the seeker of success in regards to his faith, which is the most valuable ingredient of success. With regard to the believer's faith in God, the Provider and Sustainer of all, and in His beloved messenger, Muhammad, we can categorize that into three phases: acquisition of, maintenance of, and increase in faith.

    Acquisition of faith, whether by birth of by choice, is a special blessing bestowed on an individual, directing him towards success. This is dealt with in detail in multiple chapters elsewhere in this collection of meditations, and so we will discuss the phases of maintenance and increase in the believer's faith, which is dealt with in the beautiful selected passage of today.

    From the time of the noble prophet Muhammad up until now, just as surely as there has been Satan trying to direct men away from the remembrance of God, the Originator and the Resurrector, there have also been individuals and groups whose goal is to hinder men from the Path of God, the Guardian of faith and the Protector, and to resist the efforts of the noble messenger Muhammad after Guidance has clearly been shown to mankind. The believers in this situation should guard their most valuable asset, i.e. faith, and remember that these unfortunate individuals are harming no one but themselves; certainly, they are not able to harm God, the Source of all power and the Compeller, in the least, and their efforts will be fruitless. This is the promise of God, the Truth and the Most Trustworthy One.

    If man does profess faith, he should be prepared that this will be tested at times in his life by God, the Most Wise and the Best Appraiser, to see if he exhibits sufficient determination, patience, perseverance and effort, and strives to exhibit the sincerity of his faith. This is the susceptible period when the maintenance of faith is of prime importance. Professing faith is not sufficient unless it is accompanied by appropriate action. When actions are regularly performed that are good, and which are a manifestation of one's faith, including actions deserving of high merit and pleasing to God, the Creator and Sustainer of the world, this results in increase in one's faith, in a mutually responsive cycle, i.e. faith leads to action, which leads to increase in faith, which leads to further increase in good actions, and so on, with the end result being that this individual reaches ever closer to his goal of **lasting success**.

    The seeker of success who wishes to reach his goal has absolute faith in God, the Most Wise and the Most Just, and in His noble messenger, Muhammad. He knows that those who reject God, hinder men from the Right Path, and resist the noble messenger, Muhammad (and his teachings), after Guidance has been clearly shown to them, will neither harm God in the least, Who is the Most Strong and the Best Protector, and nor do their actions have any effect on the level of his faith. He also knows that just as a diamond cannot be perfected unless it is stressed, he himself will have to pass through rigorous tests in his life to test his faith. He seeks God's help, Who is the Best Guide, the Most Righteous Teacher and the Most Patient One, during these trials, with patient perseverance.

# Day 291

**That He may admit the men and women who believe, to gardens underneath which rivers flow, to dwell therein forever, and remove their ills from them – <u>and that is in the sight of God, the highest success (for man)</u>.**

(48:5)

# Day 291

The beautiful selected passage of today has special significance for the seeker of success, as it is addressed specifically to him or her, and moreover, it classifies practically for the seeker of success, his concern in a most excellent manner: If I were to attain the highest degree of success, how will that be manifested?

The question that has been posed above is an extremely important one. To put this question in its proper perspective, let us take the example of the time period itself. From what is known to us about the universe and its existence, human life as we know it has been around for an extremely short duration compared with formation of the earth– and an individual's lifetime is figuratively like a moment in this timeframe and the overall picture. However, during one's lifetime, the individual does experience many emotions, and at this time lives on average for 70 years. With regard to the completion of one's life on earth, then, one needs to contemplate where he will be afterwards. The intelligent reader and the seeker of success is reminded to consider the relatively miniscule period of life that he spends on earth and to contemplate where he will be in the cosmos after his life on earth, and which is a much longer duration - literally, for eternity.

Certainly, being successful during one's life on earth is a worthwhile pursuit, and no one should neglect it – but being concerned about one's success in life for a period of about 70 years, while neglecting the remainder of one's life, which is eternity, would indeed be foolish. God, the Most Great and the Eternal, wants all men and women to succeed, both in this life and for eternity. He has identified the men and women who will succeed: Those who believe in God, the Most Glorious and the Most Generous, and in His beloved messenger, Muhammad (which will subsequently lead to good actions, as we learn elsewhere in the Holy Quran) – they shall be admitted to gardens underneath which rivers flow, to dwell therein for eternity, and their ills will be removed from them. In the sight of God, the Creator and Sustainer of all, **this is the highest form of success** for man. All the seekers of success shall be eternally grateful to God, the Best Guide and the Best Teacher, for the Guidance they receive from the beautiful selected passage of today.

The seeker of success who wishes to reach his goal has unwavering faith in God, the Best Guide and the Bestower of honors, and in His beloved messenger, Muhammad. He knows that success in this life is of a transient nature. He realizes that the highest form of success is reserved for men and women who have faith, who manifest that faith by the regular praise and worship of God, the Most Rich and the Everlasting One, along with performance of other good deeds – and who will be admitted by Him, to gardens underneath which rivers flow, to dwell therein for eternity.

# Day 292

O you who believe! Avoid suspicion as much (as possible) – for suspicion in some cases is a sin. And spy not on each other, nor speak ill of each other behind their backs. Would any of you like to eat the flesh of his dead brother? No, you would abhor it! And fear God, for God is the One Who forgives and accepts repentance, and is Most Merciful.

(49:12)

# Day 292

The beautiful selected passage of today reinforces two key points that are repeated a number times in this collection of meditations, to emphasize their importance to the seeker of success. In addition, we are provided with other new information that the seeker of success should add to his armamentarium of skills that will be useful to him in helping him to reach his goal.

The two key points that are reinforced for one's benefit are 1) faith in God, the Creator and Sustainer of all, and in his noble messenger, Muhammad, and 2) fear of God, the Most Beneficent and Most Merciful – not because of His harshness, but because of the great responsibilities that man has on earth as the deputy for God, the Most Great and Most Magnificent. No reasonable man who understands the riches with which he has been endowed (such as sight, hearing, and reasoning), should feel content abusing these riches. On the contrary, he should be fearful of using them for any purpose except for praising, and serving the cause of, the One Who provided these riches to him; if in the past, he has misused these priceless treasures from God, he should seek His forgiveness and he will find Him to be the One Who is most willing to forgive, Who accepts repentance, and is the Most Merciful.

The new information from the beautiful selected passage of today that the seeker of success should add to his armamentarium, in order to reach his goal, is to avoid suspicion as much as possible, and also avoid spying on each other as individuals. A country may need for its safety and protection a department of intelligence for maintaining its interests, which practices within ethical boundaries - but the beautiful selected passage of today is addressed to individuals, to foster brotherhood and overcome the barriers to fostering an increased level of brotherhood among individuals. Suspicion in some cases is categorized under sinful acts, and the seeker of success turns away from all sinful acts which will prevent him from reaching his goal. Going one step beyond suspicion in undesirable acts is spying on each other and gossiping or speaking ill of each other behind each other's backs. Spying on each other and gossiping behind people's backs is much more harmful, and prevents the feeling of brotherhood and camaraderie to a much greater degree, than suspicion. Therefore, the harmful effect of gossiping and spying on others is characterized as equivalent to eating the flesh of one's dead brother. Even though he may have engaged in it previously, thinking it was of no significant harm, the seeker of success from now onwards will not engage in gossiping, knowing that it is as if he were eating the flesh of his dead brother – and he seeks forgiveness from God, the Most Great, Most Wise, and the Most Forgiving One.

The seeker of success who wishes to reach his goal has complete faith in God, the All-Hearing, All-Seeing, the Best Guide, and the Most Forgiving One, and in His noble messenger, Muhammad. He fears that the invaluable treasures that His Creator and Sustainer has endowed him with would be misused by his negligence. He is neither suspicious of others, nor spies on them. He realizes that gossiping about others is not a trifling matter - but a serious issue, and which is repulsive in the sight of his Lord, similar to eating the flesh of his dead brother.

# Day 293

**O mankind! We created you from a single (pair) of a male and a female, and made you into nations and tribes, that you may know each other (not that you may despise each other). Indeed, the most honored of you in the sight of God is (he who is) the most righteous of you. Indeed, God has full knowledge, and is well-acquainted (with all things).**

(49:13)

# Day 293

    The beautiful selected passage of today provides advice for mankind to interact and live with each other harmoniously, and to succeed both at an individual level and collectively, on societal level. Mankind has practiced various kinds of racism from ancient times, and continues to do so up to now. We have seen one group of people discriminate against another for all sorts of reasons: gender, color of skin, religion, country of birth, language, level of education, nationality, amount of wealth, and political affiliation, among other factors. With one powerful verse, God, the Most Kind and Most Just, leveled the playing field for all mankind over fourteen hundred years ago – something which the most enlightened societies at this time are proud to have put into their laws over the past few decades after long and bitter struggles, but not yet followed in spirit.

    God, the Most Righteous Teacher and the Most Equitable One, informs us in the beautiful selected passage of today that all individuals are derived from a single male and female. There is no simpler way to explain how much all individuals have in common and, in a literal sense, are brothers and sisters of each other, if we go back enough generations, including the first pair of humans, Adam and Eve. Besides fostering increased sense of brotherhood in society, the beautiful selected passage of today effectively dispels all notions of superiority based on race, sex, language, nationality etc. Our present society as well, will benefit a great deal by following the recommendations from the beautiful selected passage of today, where we are instructed to celebrate the differences among each other, knowing that eventually we all form one family. Unfortunately, at present, our society has degenerated and suffers because in practice, if not in theory, the base members of society are intent on exploiting the differences among mankind, making them forget that they have so much in common.

    If all members of mankind are equal, as we discussed above, then what makes one superior to another? This is a valid question that is applicable in pre-school, kindergarten, college, the workplace and the soccer field as well; and of course the seeker of success would be especially interested in knowing the answer to this question. We are instructed by God, the Most Magnificent and Most Generous One, that the only distinction in His sight among mankind for honor is **righteousness**, which everyone who wants to succeed aims to practice – and God has full knowledge of, and is well-acquainted with, all that we do.

    The seeker of success who wishes to reach his goal has absolute faith in God, the Creator and Sustainer of all, and in His beloved messenger, Muhammad. He knows that all of mankind forms one brotherhood – and that the most honored in the sight of his Lord is he who is the most righteous, and that God has full knowledge of all matters and is well-acquainted with everything that every individual does at all times.

## Day 294

**Only those are believers who have believed in God and His messenger and have never since doubted, but have striven with their belongings and their persons in the cause of God; such are the sincere ones.**

(49:15)

# Day 294

Today's beautiful selected passage helps the seeker of success to strengthen his faith – the one key characteristic that will most determine whether he will be able to reach his goal or not. Because of their relative importance, the key characteristics of success have been reinforced a number of times by a number of methods in the Holy Quran, and also in this collection of meditations, for the benefit of the seeker of success. The serious seeker of success, knowing its importance, would desire to be sincere in acquiring and maintaining that characteristic which is the critical determinant for him as to whether he reaches his goal and becomes a raging success or fails to reach his goal (and the alternative result is utter failure).

A sincere believer having faith is one who is characterized as having believed in God and His noble messenger, Muhammad, and afterwards, never doubting. There are plenty of opportunities for distractions for man daily in his life, and the accursed Satan's mission is to distract the believers from the straight Path, utilizing his accomplices. Imagine what would happen if a player on the football field forgot his mission or even did not feel strongly about it? Of course he would not succeed. In addition to not wavering from his faith, the sincere believer strives with his assets in the cause of God, the Source of all that exists and the Source of all power, including, if necessary, his most valuable asset, and that is his person.

The seeker of success who wishes to reach his goal has unwavering faith in God, the Originator and the Restorer, and in His noble messenger, Muhammad. He knows that, just as the player who lacks confidence in his mission on the playing field has a distinct disadvantage compared to the opponent who does have confidence, the seeker of success who has doubts about his faith has a similar disadvantage in life compared to someone else who does not have doubts. He strives with his assets in the cause of God, the Truth, and the Most Glorious - including his greatest asset, i.e. his person, if necessary.

# Day 295

**They impress on you as a favor that they have embraced Islam. Say: "Count not your (acceptance of) Islam as a favor upon me. On the contrary, God has conferred a favor upon you that He has guided you to the faith – if you are true and sincere".**

(49:17)

# Day 295

I have avoided using examples from my own personal life or that of others', except from that of the beloved prophet Muhammad, when needed, or that of other prophets from the selected passages of the Holy Quran for the benefit of the seekers of success – I feel that these passages have been meant for use for the benefit of all mankind in all ages and utilizing an example from my own life, and current or other historical figures, except those specifically addressed in the passages would be detracting from the universal applicability of the Holy Quran, which is addressed to all the seekers of success. However, I will present to the esteemed reader an example from my own personal life which has helped me best to understand the beautiful selected passage of today and which I hope will do the same for the honorable reader and the seeker of success.

My six year old son, who is in first grade, called me on my mobile phone at work, a call which I was not able to receive due to being busy. He continued calling until I was free and excitedly told me that he had done well in his spelling test. It was not enough that I congratulated him on his hard work. He told me in no uncertain terms that he had done me a favor by doing well in his exam and that he expected to be rewarded for that. How I wished I could explain to him that by working hard and doing well in his exams, he was not helping me but helping himself to make a better future for himself? But this would have to wait for some other day, as I felt he deserved to feel good about his accomplishment. The above example conveys the spirit of the beautiful selected passage of today well and is therefore presented for the benefit of the seeker of success. From the other meditations in this collection, the esteemed reader is expected to have acquired the information that the acquisition of faith and believing in God, the Most Great and Most Kind, and His beloved messenger, Muhammad, and accepting a life of submission to God, i.e. Islam, is the most important characteristic of success. However, it would be inappropriate to feel that by embracing Islam, one is conferring a favor on anyone or benefiting anyone. On the contrary, the fortunate individual who has been guided to Islam by God, the Light and the Guide, has had a favor conferred upon him that is of immeasurable value, i.e. by being guided towards acquisition of faith, the most valuable component of success and which will be of immense benefit to him both in this life and for eternity.

The seeker of success who wishes to reach his goal has complete faith in God, the Most Praiseworthy, the Best Guide and the Most Magnificent, and in His beloved messenger, Muhammad. He knows that the life he lives in submission to his Lord as a result of his faith is an immense favor that God, the Most Beneficent and Most Merciful, has conferred upon him and that the one who benefits most as a result of his faith is himself.

# Day 296

And paradise will be brought near to the pious – no more a thing distant.

(It will be said:) "This is what was promised for you – for everyone who turned (to God) in sincere repentance, who kept (His law) – i.e. did what was commanded by God.

"Who feared (God) Most Gracious, unseen, and brought a heart turned in devotion (to Him);

"Enter therein in peace and security – this is a Day of eternal life!"

There will be for them therein all that they wish – and more besides, in Our Presence.

(50:31-35)

# Day 296

    The beautiful selected passage of today is addressed specifically to the seeker of success in very clear terms. The details provided about those factors that will contribute to one's success are clearly outlined and will be much appreciated by all the seekers of success. Additionally, the details provided about the benefits of succeeding will not only convince those who have already made success a plan for their life to be diligent in their efforts, but will be valuable for also convincing those who are lazy and satisfied with the short-term pleasures, although shortchanging themselves greatly in the long-run.

    The fortunate individuals who will succeed are categorized generally by God, the All-knowing and Most Wise, as being pious. What characterizes the pious individuals is further detailed for our benefit: They are those who turn to God, the Most Holy and the Source of all that exists, in sincere repentance; thus they recognize His superiority over all that exists – and they believe in the messengers He sent to guide mankind, including the last messenger, the beloved Muhammad. Therefore, they do what is commanded by God, the King and the Most Glorious, in Holy Quran, and refrain from what He instructed mankind to refrain from. They recognize the immensity of the treasures that have been bestowed upon them by God, such as sight, hearing, and reasoning, and fear the consequences of neglecting the duties for which they were created. And out of love, awe, and fear, they turn to God, the Most Great and Most Loving One, in sincere devotion.

    When the most fateful day will come to pass, as reported by the prophets, when the sky shall be glowing red and mountains will become like carded wool, and there will be utter confusion and anxiety, the Judgment will come from God the Giver and Taker of life and the Restorer - and those who fail the test of life will be utterly humiliated and condemned for eternal suffering, while the fortunate individuals will be the pious ones, as described above, to whom paradise will be brought near as promised – no more a thing distant. They will enter therein in peace and security – to abide therein forever. Here they shall have all that they wish for, unlike on earth, where no amount of money or riches can fulfill anyone's desires. And they shall receive something much more valuable: the nearness to their Lord, the Creator and Sustainer of all. **This is indeed success of the highest degree.**

    The seeker of success who wishes to reach his goal has absolute faith in God, the Most Rich, the Most Righteous Teacher and the Satisfier of all needs, and in His noble messenger, Muhammad. He turns to God, the Most Forgiving and Most Loving, for guidance, and does what is commanded and refrains from what is forbidden by Him. He fears his Lord, Most Gracious, unseen, and turns his heart to Him in devotion.

# Day 297

**Indeed, it is We Who give life and death; and to Us is the final goal.**

(50:43)

# Day 297

Although the beautiful selected passage of today is short, it contains information of profound significance, and all individuals who hope to succeed need to ponder deeply on its contents. This is also an example of how the most important messages are best expressed in the simplest form. One who appropriately understands the message of the beautiful selected passage of today will acquire faith and desire to do good actions – both being key characteristics of success, and reinforced in various forms in the Holy Quran and other passages in this collection, for the benefit of the seeker of success.

First, contemplation on life and death will eventually lead one to God, the Most Beneficent and Most Merciful One. A human being is a collection of billions of cells, each cell being a miracle in itself, and every one of them working together in perfect harmony for the benefit of one organism is truly a work of profound awe and wonder. Who created this perfect harmony that allows the organism to see, and hear and reason? Is it chance? When the individual correctly realizes that it is absurd to attribute such precious and intelligent work to chance, he is on the right path to acquiring the most important characteristic of success: Faith in God, the Creator and Sustainer of all, as relayed to us through His noble messenger, Muhammad.

Second, what does man do with the precious resources he has been granted, i.e. the ability to see, hear, reason, work and accomplish truly amazing feats? Does he utilize these to please himself – or please someone else, whether it is the strongest man in the village, his employer, or the king or president? When man realizes that the best use of all his resources is for the One Who provided them to him, i.e. by praising, worshipping, and serving God, and that it is to Him that he and all else shall return, then he will have developed the second key characteristic of success: the desire to do good actions as a result of faith. The esteemed reader is referred to the meditation of Day 3 in this collection for a more detailed review on worship. The intelligent man who realizes that life and death are not under anyone's control except God, the Giver and Taker of life, and that to Him is his final Goal, is well on his way to lasting success and being free from the potential abuse from many who can abuse him and rob him of the rewards of his labor that are due to him.

The seeker of success who wishes to reach his goal has unwavering faith in God, the Originator, the Restorer and the Best Judge, and in His beloved messenger, Muhammad. He knows that it is only God Who gives life and death, and to Him is the final goal of all. He prepares himself accordingly for success in this life and the hereafter.

# Day 298

As for the righteous (or pious), they will be in the midst of gardens and springs (in paradise) –

Taking joy in the things which their Lord gives them because, before then, they lived a good life:

They were in the habit of sleeping but little by night;

And in the hours of early dawn, they (were found) praying for forgiveness;

And in their wealth and possessions (was remembered) the right of the (needy) – him who asked, and him who (for some reason) was prevented (from asking).

On the earth are signs for those who have faith with certainty;

As also in your own selves – will you not then see?

And in heaven is your sustenance, as (also) that which you are promised;

Then, by the Lord of heaven and earth, this is the very Truth, as much as the fact that you can speak intelligently to each other.

(51:15-23)

# Day 298

    Today's beautiful selected passage brilliantly links the goal of the seeker of success to those factors that can help him to reach his goal. Unfortunately, many people - including this humble author at one time, are misled into the concept as to what constitutes success: they are led to believe that one's assets, social standing, and happiness on earth are the markers of success. Then the gullible folks are instructed in ways to achieve the highest levels of these factors. As we have learned elsewhere in this collection of meditations, our entire life here on earth is like less than a day of time in the life after death. Therefore, an intelligent person will not only be concerned about his life on earth, but also will be concerned about – indeed, much more concerned about – his life after death. We learn in the beautiful selected passage of today that the successful individuals will be living in the midst of gardens and springs in paradise, living in joy for eternity – for having lived a good life on earth. Who are these fortunate people? They are identified by God, the Most Great and the Best Appraiser, as the righteous or pious people.

    The seeker of success should now be interested in what he needs to do to be placed in the category of the righteous or pious individuals. First, one who wishes to attain success should have faith in God, the Creator and Sustainer of all, and in His noble messenger, Muhammad. As instructed in the beautiful selected passage of today - indeed, in the earth as well as the heavens, there are many signs pointing to God, the Most Beneficent and Most Merciful: how the earth is revived every year predictably; and how a new being is formed from a man and a woman, attains full strength and then regresses (also predictably), among countless other wonders. It seems that the only individual who cannot experience the presence of God from what he sees would have to be living in a vacuum. Even the fact that one being could formulate utterances that another could understand, is a wonderful sign of the presence of God, the Most Great and Most Magnificent, and points to His presence as Magnificent and Glorious. Having formulated his faith in God, the Truth and the Eternal One, which was most faithfully relayed to mankind by His beloved messenger, Muhammad - and without His message being corrupted, the seeker of success would be interested in fulfilling the duties for which he was created; when he does this diligently and lovingly, he can be placed in the category of the righteous (or pious). We are provided with further details about the actions that the righteous individual would perform, i.e. sleeping little and instead, worshipping and praising his Lord in the night; in the hours of early dawn, praying for forgiveness; and remembering to share his wealth and possessions with the needy – those who ask, as well as those who don't ask.

    The seeker of success who wishes to reach his goal has complete faith in God, the Eternal and the only Self-sustaining One in existence, and in His noble messenger, Muhammad. He is in the habit of sleeping little in the night, preferring to praise and worship his Lord and seek His forgiveness, which he also continues in the early hours of dawn. He shares his wealth and possessions with the needy – those who ask, and also those who don't ask.

# Day 299

**I have only created jinn and men that they should worship Me (Alone).**

(51:56)

# Day 299

    Although it is quite short, the beautiful selected passage of today is one of the most important ones, and contains the most important concept that the seeker of success needs to understand. The mark of a great teacher is the ability to relay complex ideas and concepts in simple terms. And God is indeed the Best Teacher and the Best Guide. The beautiful selected passage of today also confirms to us that the most valuable concepts are best understood when expressed in simple terms.

    Along with all living things, man finds sustenance in this world, so lovingly provided for the benefit for all by God, the Creator and Sustainer of all that exists. However, man differs from all other animals and living things that we are aware of, in having control over his actions and having the ability to forego instant gratification for delayed reward based on his long-term goals.

    If man is to have any degree of success, he must ask himself the question: "Why was I created?" If the answer that he arrives at is " To enjoy yourself", he may be inclined to seek pleasure from those things that would provide him with the greatest amount of pleasure in the shortest amount of time possible, without regard to long term consequences, such as abuse of illicit substances, stealing, rape, etc. If the answer that he arrives at, and which many people seem to conclude, is to have his life on earth to be considered "successful", often implying financial abundance and a sense of happiness during most of one's remaining life on earth until death, he may try to reach those goals by all methods available to him – both ethical and unethical.

    However, the individual who has attained the most important ingredient of success, i.e. faith in God, the Creator and Sustainer of all, and in His noble messenger, Muhammad, will be guided by his Lord to the true reason for which he was created, i.e. to worship God, the Originator, Guide, and the Restorer. The esteemed reader is referred to the meditation on Day of this collection for a more detailed review of worship. Worship of God, in its various forms we have reviewed earlier, often means we have to curtail another activity which might have provided us with instant gratification. Therefore, the truly successful individual is the one who is able to delay gratification, not only on an immediate basis, but even while living on earth, in exchange for the afterlife, which is of much greater significance due to it being eternal. One other concept needs to be understood in order to grasp the benefit from the beautiful selected passage of today – and that is one of jinns. God, the Most Beneficent and Most Merciful, informs us that He has created mankind and jinns for worshipping Him. How should we understand the concept of jinns? It is best to consider that at present our senses are not sufficient for us to be able to appreciate the presence of jinns – as a shark in the ocean is not aware of the presence of man on land.

    The seeker of success who wishes to reach his goal has absolute faith in God, the Creator of all power, the Light and the Guide, and in His beloved messenger, Muhammad. He knows that the reason he was created was to worship God, the Creator and Sustainer of all that exists - which includes praise, and performance of other righteous actions, for the sake of God, the Most Holy and to Whom belongs all praise, and to Whom is the return of all.

# Day 300

Therefore, shun those who turn away from Our message (this Quran) and desire nothing but the life of this world;

That is as far as knowledge will reach them. Indeed, your Lord knows best those who stray from His path, and He knows best those who receive guidance.

And to God belongs all that is in the heavens and on earth – so that He rewards those who do evil according to their deeds, and He rewards those who do good, with what is best.

(53:29-31)

# Day 300

An individual who has not been blessed with faith in God, the Creator and Sustainer of all - as relayed to us through His beloved messenger Muhammad, will depend on his limited intelligence to guide him; this will result in significant limitations for the individual, for his goals are now limited by his knowledge. Therefore, the best he can hope to achieve is maximal pleasure and accumulation of wealth and power in this world.

On the other hand, the fortunate individual who sees the countless signs of God, the Greatest, the Creator of all and the Maker of order, in everything - from the light, to the planets, to his own organs and how perfectly they work, will be blessed with the most valuable characteristic of success: Faith. He realizes that to God belongs all that is in heavens and earth and in existence. He realizes the importance of the Holy Quran in his life – sent as a Mercy to all, through the beloved prophet Muhammad, containing extremely valuable messages for mankind to help men and women to attain lasting success. Like the child attaining wisdom, who realizes that there is more to life than candy and play, which gave him so much pleasure earlier, the fortunate individual who acquires faith realizes that there is more to life than enjoyment on earth. He knows that good deeds will be rewarded by his Lord and that evil deeds will be punished accordingly.

If an individual is to be successful in his mission, whatever it is, it would help if he has assistance from others – and indeed interdependence on others is frequently of great importance. Certainly, he would be prevented from accomplishing his mission if he is influenced by those who are hostile to his mission. In the beautiful selected passage of today, the seeker of success is instructed to avoid those who turn away from God's message (the Holy Quran) and desire nothing but the life of this world, and are therefore, hostile to his mission in life, i.e. to worship and serve God, the Creator and Sustainer of all.

The seeker of success who wishes to reach his goal has unwavering faith in God, the Most Wise and the Most Righteous Teacher, and in His noble messenger, Muhammad. He shuns those who are hostile to his mission in life, i.e. to worship and serve God, and shuns those who desire nothing but the life of this world - due to their negative influence on the ability to realize his mission and reach his goal. He is kind and courteous to everyone.

# Day 301

Do you (O Muhammad!) see the one who turns back (from Islam)?

Gives a little, then hardens (his heart)?

What! Has he knowledge of the unseen so that he can see?

Or is he not acquainted with what is in the books of Moses –

And of Abraham, who fulfilled his engagements (ordered by God)?

Namely, that no bearer of burdens can bear the burden of another;

That man can have nothing but what he strives for;

That (the fruit of) his striving will soon come in sight;

Then will he be rewarded with a reward complete;

That to your Lord is the final goal;

That it is He who grants laughter and tears;

That it is He who grants death and life;

That He did create in pairs – male and female;

From a seed when lodged (in its place);

That He has promised a Second Creation (raising of the dead)!

That it is He Who gives wealth and satisfaction.

(53:33-48)

# Day 301

    The beautiful selected passage of today serves an invaluable purpose for the seeker of success: if he does not possess the most valuable characteristic of success, i.e. faith, it enriches him with it; and if he does possess it already, it is further strengthened, in order that his chances of reaching his goal will be optimized. An example is provided in today's beautiful passage from the time of the beloved prophet Muhammad, of the unfortunate individual who turns his back on the message from God, the Most Great and Most High, to have mankind submit to Him and serve Him willingly, and instead turns away in arrogance and refrains from sharing his wealth with the needy. Indeed, this scenario can also be witnessed in our time. The unfortunate individuals described above refuse to believe in anything they cannot see – because they are blinded by their arrogance in refusing to accept that their intelligence has limitations. Imagine if a child would refuse to follow his parents because of his limited intelligence!

    The beautiful selected passage of today cites faith from the older scriptures – from that of the honorable prophets Abraham and Moses, with the same message relayed to mankind from God, the Hearer and Seer of all, through His final prophet to mankind, the noble and beloved prophet Muhammad: To serve and submit to Him Who created man and everything else in existence and has sole power over all; it can be divided into two components – the first component deals with the characteristics of God, the Creator and Sustainer of all, that lead one to have faith in Him, to adore, worship and yearn to serve Him. The second component deals with specific actions that will increase the likelihood of attainment of success after acquisition of faith.

    The describing characteristics of God, the Most Great, the Hidden and Manifest in the beautiful selected passage of today, are directed towards the unfortunate individual who lacks God's awareness and the realization that it is He Who creates a new individual from two; that it is He who gives wealth and satisfaction; that it is He Who grants laughter and tears; that it is He Who grants life and death; and that it is He Who will raise man again after his death, as easily as He awakens man in the morning after his sleep daily. The specific actions that are identified in the beautiful selected passage of today to increase our likelihood of success after attainment of faith are:

1. To share our wealth with the needy.

2. All individuals are responsible for their own actions, and that no one can bear the burden of another in terms of fulfilling the responsibilities for which one was created.

3. Goals are extremely important – and man will attain only that for which he has strived. He will not stumble on to success.

4. Realization that to God, the Truth and the Best Judge, is the final return of all, and that man will be either rewarded or punished according to his actions in the life on this earth.

The seeker of success who wishes to reach his goal has complete faith in God, the Most Praiseworthy and the Greatest, and in His beloved messenger, Muhammad. He shares his wealth with the needy, realizes that no soul can bear the burden of another, that he shall attain only that for which he has strived, and knows that his final return is to God, the Originator, the Restorer, and the Best of those who keep account, and has prepared himself accordingly.

# Day 302

**All that is on earth will perish;
But will abide (forever) the Face of your Lord – full of Majesty, and Reward and Honor.**

**(55:26-27)**

# Day 302

The beautiful selected passage of today contains two very powerful messages for the seeker of success – and if he is able to grasp these two concepts, it will be of great help to him in reaching his goal. We all understand that children love candy and playing games. Children get pleasure from these things, and those who love them are happy to provide them with things and situations which give them enjoyment. A child who continues to derive pleasure from candies and games in his adolescent or adult phase of life and continues to place these at the same level of priority as in the other stages of his life will be at a handicap and suffer long-term failure for not having prepared adequately for the later, more important phases of his life.

The first powerful message in the beautiful selected passage of today for the benefit of the seeker of success is that everything on earth will perish. Like the child who yearns for as much candy or as much pleasure from games, it is not uncommon to see individuals interested in accumulating as many material possessions as possible during this life, or in attaining the greatest pleasure as possible during their life on earth. With the knowledge that everything on earth will perish, then, man can prepare himself to acquire that which will not perish but which he can attain and which is more valuable for him in the next and more important stage after his life on earth.

The second powerful message in the beautiful selected passage of today for the seeker of success is a continuation of the above point, i.e. if everything on earth will perish, then what is it that man should concentrate on attaining if he can help himself? We are informed for our benefit about that which will not perish and we should concentrate on enriching ourselves – if we are to be counted among the successful. Only God – full of Majesty, Reward and Honor will abide forever. Therefore, if one wishes for wealth, honor and glory for this life, as well as for the more important phase of his life, i.e. the afterlife, he will sincerely make an effort to do those things which are pleasing in the sight of God, the Creator, Sustainer, Restorer and the Most Rich One.

The seeker of success who wishes to reach his goal has absolute faith in God, the Eternal and the Self-existing One, and in His noble messenger, Muhammad. He knows that all that is on earth will perish except God – Owner of all Majesty, Reward and Honor. He knows that his most valuable treasure is the accumulation of good deeds for the pleasure of his Lord, the Most Glorious, Most Kind and the Bestower of all honors.

# Day 303

**Is there any reward for good – other than good?**

(55:60)

# Day 303

The beautiful selected passage of today, although short, contains one of the key concepts pertaining to success, and, if understood correctly, will help the seeker of success to reach his goal; and, if not understood correctly, can be a barrier to the attainment of success.

All individuals have an inherent desire to do "good" i.e., to choose favorable things over unfavorable things. The difference arises only depending on who is judging a particular action. Therefore, every action that a person performs is chosen by him as a favorable option with which he is rewarded accordingly, and all actions fall into a range, from one extreme to another, in regard to the benefits attained from them.

On the one extreme we have actions that are chosen by individuals that are of benefit to them only, at the expense of the suffering of the other; in this category, we can place such actions as stealing, rape, torture and murder. The individual committing these acts does so for the material or other benefits that he attains from committing them. He fails to realize at the time of committing such acts that he will be held accountable for committing these acts by the worldly authorities if he is caught; and, more importantly, that he will be held accountable and punished by God, the Most Great, the All-seeing and All-hearing One on the Day of Judgment.

In the middle of the range we described above, are those actions that are chosen by individuals so that those actions are of benefit not only to oneself but also to those that are from his family tribe, race, or religion. This individual will receive his reward from a feeling of well-being, as well as receiving his reward from appreciation from those that are from his family, tribe, race or religion.

And on the other end of the range we have discussed above, are those actions performed by individuals which are desirable in the sight of God, the Most Just and the Most Wise, even if they are unfavorable to the individual himself temporarily, such as charity and justice, and even if the judgment is against oneself or one's family and the reward for these actions will not only be in this world from a sense of well being from oneself, or from appreciation from others, but most importantly, the reward will be due to the individual from God Himself, the Most Rich and the Most Generous, both in this life, and more importantly, on the Day of Judgment.

The seeker of success who wishes to reach his goal has uncompromising faith in God, the Truth and the Witness, and in His beloved messenger, Muhammad. For every action that he performs, he considers whether it is pleasing or displeasing to God, the Best Doer of good, the Most Rich, and the Most Generous

# Day 304

When the Event (i.e. the Day of Resurrection) befalls;

And there can be no denial of its befalling -

Bringing low (those who enter hell) and exalting (those who enter paradise);

When the earth will be shaken with a terrible shake;

And the mountains will be powdered to dust,

So that they will become floating particles;

And you all will be in three groups:

Then there will be those on the right hand: how (fortunate) will be those on the right hand!

And those on the left hand: how (unfortunate) will be those on the left hand!

<u>And those foremost (in faith) will be foremost (in the hereafter);</u>

<u>These will be nearest to God.</u>

(56:1-11)

# Day 304

The beautiful selected passage of today has three powerful messages that are useful for the seeker of success to help him reach his goal - the first of which is the realization that life as we know it is expected to end on the Day of Judgment. On that Day, even the most majestic mountains will be powdered to dust as a result of the terrible shaking of the earth and become like floating particles. On that Day, all of mankind, from the earliest to latest times, will be resurrected by God, the Most Great, the Creator and the Resurrector.

The second powerful message in the beautiful selected passage of today for the seeker of success to help him reach his goal is that, on the Day of Judgment, every single individual will be held accountable for all his actions, in the presence of God, the Most Magnificent, the Gatherer and the Best of those who keep accounts – and on that day will the results be known of every individual's performance during his life on earth, with **three possible outcomes: those on the right hand, or** *those who are successful*; **those on the left hand, or the** *failures*; **and those who are foremost, or** *the super-achievers.*

The third powerful message in the beautiful selected passage of today for the seeker of success to help him reach his goal is the one of most interest to him, since it identifies the requirements for the attainment of the highest degree of success – which tells us that attainment of the highest degree of faith (in God, the Most Holy and the Only One Worthy of worship, and in His beloved messenger, Muhammad) in the life of this life of this world corresponds to the one being placed in the **highest category of achievers.** This is the enviable group that will be closest to God, the Most Great and Most Glorious. People in this life feel pride being in the company of presidents and kings. Could anyone feel any more satisfaction than being close to Him Who created all that exists and is eternal? This is indeed **the objective of those who desire true success.**

The seeker of success who wishes to reach his goal has complete faith in God, the Most Great, the Creator and the Resurrector, and in His noble messenger, Muhammad. He knows that he is accountable for all his actions personally to God, the Best of those who keep account and the Most Just, on the Day of Judgment, and has prepared himself accordingly. He also knows that the **highest degree of success** is reserved for those having the highest degree of faith.

# Day 305

We created you. Then why do you not believe?

Then tell me (about) the (human) semen that you emit.

Is it you who create it (i.e. make it into a perfect human being) or are We the Creator?

Then tell me (about) the seed that you sow in the ground.

Is it you that cause it to grow, or are We the cause?

Then tell me (about) the water which you drink.

Do you bring it down (in rain) from the cloud or do We?

Then tell me (about) the fire which you kindle.

Is it you who grow the tree which feeds the fire or do We grow it?

(56:57-72)

# Day 305

Today's beautiful selected passage is not only rich because of its superb use of language and imagery, but, more importantly, because of the conclusions to which any reasonably intelligent individual will reach as a result of contemplating on its contents. This will result in empowering the individual who does not already possess the most valuable characteristic of success, i.e. faith, to be endowed with it – and for the individual who is fortunate to be in possession of it already, to have it strengthened.

Attaining success, as well as practicing those habits which lead to success, is hard work. Many times we see that even if an individual has attained some level of success in this life, it is not a guarantee that those who follow that individual's actions – including, often, his own children – will be able to attain the level of success that individual was able to attain in the past. The key here is appreciating the real reason behind particular actions, and the lack of synergy with other associated actions which results if one does not appreciate the real reasons behind particular actions leading to success.

We find that many individuals engage in prayer and worship because they have been instructed that it is good for them. The act of worship from an individual who lacks faith can be compared to the donning of a doctor's white coat by an individual in the belief that he will attain the ability to heal if he puts on the coat. In order to truly worship, in the literal as well as philosophical sense, we need to understand the factors which lead us to turn to the object of worship, devotion and adoration. The ability to create the masterpiece we know as a human from a few drops of semen from the male, combined with the similar equivalent from the female, the ability to cause a seed to grow into a tree that nourishes us, the ability to provide us with water (without which we cannot survive for long), and the ability to provide fire for our comfort, are the examples mentioned in the beautiful selected passage of today, that if one contemplates on sincerely, will guide us to faith – the most important ingredient of success, and which leads to the best form of worship, i.e. emanating from adoration, awe, love and gratefulness. The esteemed reader is referred to the meditation of Day 3 in this collection for a more detailed discussion of worship.

The seeker of success who wishes to reach his goal has absolute faith in God, the Creator, Provider and Sustainer of all that exists, and in His beloved messenger, Muhammad. His praise and devotion to his Lord results from sincere contemplation and awe, and counts as worship. His actions are all for the sake of God (glorified be His Name), for which he will be rewarded immensely, both in this life and the hereafter.

# Day 306

This is a revelation from the Lord of the worlds;

Is it such a message that you would hold in light esteem?

And instead (of thanking God) for the provision He gives you, you deny (Him in disbelief)!

Then why do you not (intervene) when (the soul of the dying man) reaches the throat –

While you (sit) looking on?

But We are nearer to him than you, and yet you see not.

Then why do you not – if you are exempt from (future) account,

Send back the soul if you are true (in claim of independence)?

(56:80-87)

# Day 306

    The beautiful selected passage of today reinforces for the benefit of the seeker of success the two key ingredients of success: faith and righteous actions as a result of the faith. Repetition of these key points in the Holy Quran signifies the concern by God, the Most Beneficent, the Most Merciful and the Most Righteous Teacher, for man to grasp these key concepts. An extremely effective and memorable example is provided, so that as many individuals as possible can grasp the important concept of faith for their own benefit.

    The man who is arrogant and refuses to submit to the authority of God, the Most Pure and the First and the Last, and instead relies completely on his own intelligence, is challenged to the effect that, if he considers himself independent and not under the authority of God, the Creator and Sustainer of all, then he should consider the time when someone, or he himself, is about to die, and should return the dying man's soul back into his body; and if one is not able to fulfill the stated challenge, than he should logically submit to the authority of God, the Most Great and the Source of all power. That man is now fortunate that he has attained faith, which is the foundation of all success.

    In addition to the attainment of faith, man needs to perform good deeds as a manifestation of his faith. For this, he needs to turn to the Holy Quran for Guidance, and accept it as a revelation from the Lord of the worlds, and give it the respect that it deserves accordingly. The foremost among good deeds is worship of God, the Most Beneficent and Most Merciful, and which is the purpose of man's creation. The esteemed reader is referred to the commentary of Day 3 of this collection of meditations on a more detailed discussion of worship.

    The seeker of success who wishes to reach his goal has uncompromising faith in God, the Most Great and the Creator and Sustainer of all, and in His noble messenger, Muhammad. He performs good deeds as a manifestation of his faith and turns to the Holy Quran for guidance on all matters – giving it the proper respect that it deserves as a revelation to mankind from the Lord of the worlds.

# Day 307

Whatever is in the heavens and on earth, let it declare the praises and glory of God, for He is the Exalted in might, the Wise;

To Him belongs the dominion of the heavens and the earth; it is He who gives life and death – and He has power over all things;

He is the First and the Last, the Evident and the Hidden – and He has full knowledge of all things.

(57: 1-3)

# Day 307

The beautiful selected passage of today guides us toward the performance of the duties for which man was created, so that he may succeed.

We have been informed in the Holy Quran, and it has also been referred in the other meditations in this collection, that man was created in order to worship God, the Most Great, his Creator and the Creator of all that exists. We are informed in the beautiful selected passage of today that whatever is in the heavens and earth should declare the praises and glory of God, the Exalted in might and the Most Wise. We are informed elsewhere in the Holy Quran that whatever is in existence does declare the praises of God, the Most Beneficent and Most Merciful; however, of the beings we are aware of, only mankind is given the ability to voluntarily praise, worship and serve God, the Source of all power and the One Who gives life and death. The esteemed reader is referred to the commentary of Day 3 of this collection of meditations on a more detailed discussion of worship.

The individual who utilizes his faculties and appreciates the greatness of God, Who has complete control of all matters at all times, on earth and in the universe, Who alone gives life and death, Who is the First and the Last, the Evident and the Hidden, will sincerely declare the praises of God (the Most Praiseworthy), worship and wish to serve Him. This is the individual who is fulfilling the duties for which he was created, i.e. by praising, worshipping and serving Him Who created man and all that exists and by performing good deeds; this is the man who will have attained the objective of his life and will be rewarded with lasting success.

The seeker of success who wishes to reach his goal has complete faith in God, the Most Great, the All-knowing and All-seeing, and in his beloved messenger, Muhammad. He knows that he was created to praise, worship, and serve God - Who is the Only One, the Exalted in might and the Most Wise, and that it is to Him that he will return and be held accountable for his life on earth. He praises and worships God (glorified be His Name) with enthusiasm and performs other righteous deeds as a manifestation of his faith.

# Day 308

To Him (God) belongs the dominion of the heavens and the earth, and all affairs are referred back to God.

He merges night into day and He merges day into night; and He has full knowledge of the secrets of (all) hearts.

Believe in God and His messenger, and spend (in charity) out of the (substance) whereof He has made you heirs. For those of you who believe and spend (in charity) - for them is a great reward.

(57:5-7)

# Day 308

The beautiful selected passage of today again reinforces the two fundamental requirements for success – faith and good actions as a result of faith – for the benefit of mankind, so that as many people can grasp the valuable message and be guided toward success as possible.

The characteristics of God, the Most Kind and the Absolute Ruler, to Whom belongs the rule of the heavens and the earth, and to Whom all affairs are referred (so that nothing ever happens in the entire existence without His permission), are described, so that man may reflect on, understand, accept and serve his Lord. Additional characteristics of God and His Greatness, with His ability to merge night into day, and merge day into night, as well as His ability to have full knowledge of every individual's actions and intentions, serve to further increase the faith of the individual, and the desire to praise, worship and serve his Lord.

Having acquired faith, it remains for man to perform good actions that reflect the faith in order to attain success. Belief in the beloved prophet Muhammad as the messenger of God, the Creator and Sustainer of all, is identified as part of faith; therefore, one will have a guide for performing good actions as instructed in the Holy Quran, along with the example of the noble prophet Muhammad (in the sunnah or traditions of the prophet), to properly guide one towards success. The foremost among good actions, as we discussed in the previous meditations, is praising and worshipping of God, the Most Praiseworthy and the Only One deserving of worship. A specific and important good action is mentioned in the beautiful selected passage of today that is pleasing to God, the Most Beneficent and Most Merciful: spending in charity, along with faith. The individual who spends in charity without having faith will have earned his reward on earth by being appreciated for giving charity and by gaining a sense of well-being from sharing his wealth; but he who gives in charity from his wealth and possessions, as a result of his faith, will have a great reward from God, the Most Rich and the Most Generous.

The seeker of success who wishes to reach his goal has absolute faith in God, the Almighty and the All-Hearing, All-Seeing and All-Knowing, and in his noble messenger, Muhammad. He praises and worships God (glorified be His Name) with enthusiasm and spends in charity from his wealth and possessions, as a manifestation of his faith.

# Day 309

He (God) is the One Who sends to His servant manifest signs (verses) – that He may lead you from the depths of darkness into the Light. And indeed God is to you Most Kind and Merciful.

(57: 9)

# Day 309

    In order to appreciate the importance of today's beautiful selected passage, the esteemed reader will be provided with an example of an employee in a corporation, so that he may better understand its implication and its relevance in his pursuit of success. Let us suppose that an employee in a large corporation has been assigned a particular duty by his employer, to be performed in a distant city, and that the employee continues to be supported during his mission by the employer, but that during this time the employee is neglectful of his mission, doing instead, whatever pleases him and what he thinks ought to be done. When the employee returns to his employer at the end of the contract, he will be held accountable for his actions – and either rewarded appropriately for fulfilling his duties, or punished accordingly for being neglectful of his duties. Not being rewarded in itself, can be considered a punishment. The employee may actually feel more pain in knowing that the CEO corporation is displeased with him and his office is changed to far away from the CEO; and he may feel extreme pleasure if his performance is acknowledged and knows that the CEO is pleased with him for fulfilling his duties, and his office has been moved next to that of the CEO

    We have learned elsewhere in the Holy Quran, and expounded further in this collection of meditations as well, that God, the All-powerful and the Owner of all that exists, has created man to worship Him. The esteemed reader is referred to the meditation of Day 3 in this collection for a more detailed discussion of worship. Throughout his life, man continues to draw sustenance from God and is dependent on Him for every breath that he takes. In this state, if he is neglectful of the purpose for which he was created, and instead does as he pleases, he is indeed setting himself up for a very painful failure. Instead, if he recognizes the Greatness of the One Who created and sustains him, and so realizes and fulfills the obligations that he has towards his Lord, he is beginning to take the path of success. Additionally, man has not been abandoned to his own fate, but clear guidance from God, the Best Guide and the Most Righteous Teacher, has been provided to him through His honorable messengers, including His last messenger to mankind, the beloved Muhammad, who completed God's revelation or instructions on Guidance, to us, so that everyone may succeed. Therefore, if man realizes that God, the Most kind and Most Merciful, is He who sent His servant, the beloved prophet Muhammad, with a message for mankind, so as to guide them to the right path, then we can say that this individual has been led from the depths of darkness and the goal of pleasing himself, into the most brilliant light, and towards the goal of pleasing the One Who created and sustains all that exists. Upon acting righteously as a result of attaining Guidance, he will be rewarded accordingly by God Himself, Who is Most Rich and Most Generous.

    The seeker of success who wishes to reach his goal has unwavering faith in God, the Most Kind and Most Merciful and the Most Righteous Teacher, and in His beloved messenger, Muhammad. He knows that he is on a mission from his Lord during his life on earth and recognizes God's signs everywhere in existence and especially in the verses of the Holy Quran; he refers to the Holy Quran often, to help him on his mission and to reach his goal.

# Day 310

Who is he that will loan to God a beautiful loan? For (God) will increase it manifold to his credit and he will have (besides) a liberal reward.

One day you shall see the believing men and women – how their light runs forward before them and by their right hands. (Their greeting will be:) "Good news for you this day! Gardens beneath which rivers flow! To dwell therein forever! <u>This is indeed the Highest Success</u>".

(57:11-12)

# Day 310

The beautiful selected passage of today reinforces again the two fundamental components of success: faith and good actions as a result of faith. We are thankful to God, the Most Kind and the Most Righteous Teacher, Who has instructed and guided us towards faith from so many different aspects by a preponderance of evidence, so that we should not be left in darkness. The major component of today's beautiful selected passage deals with the explanation and encouragement of a specific form of righteous action that will be of great benefit to those who are interested in attaining success.

The giving of charity is an act that is encouraged in many societies, beliefs and cultures - even those who do not acknowledge the authority of God, the Lord of Majesty and Reward. These individuals will have their reward in the life of this world with a sense of well-being from sharing, and with the appreciation of those whom they have benefited, as well as with the appreciation of society. However, for those individuals who have attained faith, they are instructed to share their wealth for the sake of God, the Most Beneficent and Most Merciful, and their reward will be due from God Himself, the Most Great and the Most Generous.

The fortunate individual possessing faith is encouraged in the beautiful selected passage of today to give a "loan" to God, the Self-existing and the Most Rich One, in a figurative sense, as God is free of all needs, and is the Nourisher of all. However, an individual who spends his wealth in the cause of God, the Most Supreme and the Doer of Good, including the giving of charity, will be treated as if he has given a loan to his Lord and the Lord of all that exists. He shall have in return a manifold increase in credit – both in this life and in the hereafter. Indeed, God is not in need of anything from anyone, but the act of sharing from one's wealth for the love of God, the Most Appreciative and the Most Generous, will be acknowledged and rewarded accordingly. These fortunate individuals shall be granted Light, while others will be suffering in darkness, on the Day of Judgment, and they will be informed of their reward of being granted gardens beneath which rivers flow, to dwell therein forever**. This will indeed be the Highest Achievement possible, and should be the object of every individual's desire; this is true success**.

The seeker of success who wishes to reach his goal has complete faith in God, the Most Great, Most Rich and the Most Generous, and in His noble messenger, Muhammad. He spends his wealth in the cause of God (glorified be His Name), as a manifestation of his faith.

# Day 311

Know you (all) that the life of this world is but play and amusement, pomp and mutual boasting and multiplying (in rivalry) among yourselves, riches and children. Here is a similitude: How rain and the growth which it brings forth, delight (the hearts of) the tillers; soon it withers – you will see it grow yellow, then it becomes dry and crumbles away. But in the hereafter is a penalty severe (for the devotees of wrong). And forgiveness from God and (His) good pleasure (for the devotees of God). And what is the life of this world but goods and chattels of deception?

Be foremost (in seeking) forgiveness from your Lord, and a garden (of Bliss), the width of which is as the width of heaven and earth, (will be) prepared for those who believe in God and his messengers: that is the Grace of God, which He bestows on whom He pleases. And God is the Lord of Grace abounding.

(57:20-21)

# Day 311

    The beautiful selected passage of today contains two powerful messages to help the seeker of success to achieve his goals - the first of which is the realization that the life of this world is less in importance compared to the life of the hereafter, and that it is a preparation for life in the hereafter, for eternity. A wonderful example is provided in the beautiful selected passage of today of the rain and the growth in spring that we see in the land, and how it withers away in the fall. Similarly, the life of this world shall also end, bringing the individual into the next phase of his life. Many people are deceived by the life of this world, thinking that the riches we see in life should be the object of desire of one's life, and that an individual should accumulate as much wealth as possible in this life. Indeed, a significant number of persons wrongly equate success only with the accumulation of wealth in life; such individuals will be sorely disappointed on the Day of Judgment, when they will incur a severe penalty for neglecting the duties for which they were created, and for not having prepared themselves adequately for the hereafter.

    The second powerful message in the beautiful selected passage of today to help the seeker of success to reach his goal is to seek forgiveness from God, the Most Forbearing and the Most Forgiving One, and to be foremost in seeking His forgiveness. Having been endowed with free will, man is not expected to be perfect. However, he is expected to strive towards goodness and towards the path leading to his Lord, despite his imperfections. Such an individual will earn the forgiveness of God, the Almighty, the Most Kind and the Most Forgiving. For such individuals, who believe in God and His messengers - including the noble prophet Muhammad, is prepared a garden of bliss, as wide as the heaven and earth. ***This is true success.***

    The seeker of success who wishes to reach his goal has absolute faith in God, the Most Great, the Most Forgiving, and the Most Righteous Teacher, and in His beloved messenger, Muhammad. He knows that all the possessions one can accumulate in this life are insignificant compared to what is possible to have and experience in the hereafter, and he prepares himself accordingly. He is foremost in seeking the forgiveness from God, the Most Forgiving and the Most Merciful.

## Day 312

**No misfortune can happen on earth, or in your souls -but is recorded in a decree before We bring it into existence; that is truly easy for God;
In order that you may not despair over matters that pass you by, nor exult over favors bestowed upon you, for God loves not boasters.**

(57:22-23)

# Day 312

The esteemed reader will be provided with an example, in an attempt at understanding the beautiful selected passage of today, which addresses complex issues that are explained in condensed format for our benefit. A lack of knowledge or understanding of the issues addressed in the beautiful selected passage of today can be a source of great anguish in life, and its awareness and understanding can be a significant advantage in one's quest for success.

Let us take the example of the relationship between a child and his parent – for this is an appropriate example of man's relationship to God, the Most Kind and the Most Compassionate, although none of us are His children in the literal sense. A child typically desires as much candy as possible, but the parent sometimes declines this request, for the child's benefit. A child who is engaging in harmful behavior is disciplined, to help him realize his error and to prevent him from continuing to harm himself, for his own benefit. We are instructed in the beautiful selected passage of today that all events at all times are under the complete control of God, the All-powerful and the Most Wise. Attributing the cause of misfortune to one's enemy, or anyone else except God, indicates a deficiency in faith and a lack of proper understanding of the attributes and abilities of God, i.e. faith, which as we have repeatedly seen, in the Holy Quran and in this collection of meditations, is the most important component of success. In the same sense, attributing any fortunes or blessings to any source other than God also indicates a deficiency of faith. All good, as well as all misfortune, is not able to occur except with the permission of God, the Creator of all, and the Most Just. This does not mean that man has no control over his destiny, for God, the Most Wise and Most Great, informs us elsewhere in the Holy Quran that He does not change the situation of a people until they change what is in their hearts, and first make an effort towards the change.

With the knowledge that we gain from the beautiful selected passage of today, then, if a man were to be afflicted with misfortune, or be blessed with God's favors, he should neither despair in misfortune, nor exult over the favors that he has been blessed with. Instead, he should trust in the wisdom of God and show patience during misfortune, and should remember and thank Him when blessed with his favors, rather than exulting, boasting and being prideful.

The seeker of success who wishes to reach his goal has uncompromising faith in God, the Most Great, the Best Doer of good, and the Creator of Good and Harm, and in His noble messenger, Muhammad. He knows that neither any misfortune can happen, nor can any favor be bestowed on him, except with the permission of God, the Source of all strength and the All-Aware.

# Day 313

O you who believe! Fear God and believe in His messenger (Muhammad); He will bestow on you a double portion of His Mercy. He will provide for you a Light by which you shall walk (straight in your path) and He will forgive you (your past) – for God is Most Forgiving, Most Merciful.

(57:28)

# Day 313

    One of the most favored combinations of characteristics of God that He prefers to describe Himself with is that of Beneficence and Mercy. Consistent with those attributes, God, the Most Beneficent and Most Merciful, has provided mankind with the beautiful selected passage of today, in order that as many people as possible can be guided towards lasting success. Although originally addressed to certain people in the time of the beloved prophet Muhammad, the beautiful selected passage of today has as much relevance today as at anytime, as is expected of the Holy Quran - which is the ultimate source of guidance and success for all times.

    In a benevolent society, rules are made for the benefit of every member of the society. There are rules that have to be followed in government, in school, at the workplace, on the road, and in the home. One does not have the luxury of selecting which rules to follow, or of following a part of the rule and disregarding another portion, if one is to enjoy the benefits of a family, employment, educational facility, or citizenship.

    The esteemed reader who has followed these meditations to now, is reminded that the two fundamental requirements for success are faith in God, the Most Beneficent and Most Merciful, and in His noble messenger, Muhammad, along with the performance of good actions as a result of faith. The original reference to those "who believe" was to the Jews and Christians, who already possessed faith in God, but did not yet accept the message of the noble prophet Muhammad. Therefore, in order for them to meet the correct requirements of faith, they were reminded to not only believe in God, blessed be His Name, but also to fear Him (as he should be feared), and also to believe in His noble messenger Muhammad. With the proper grasp of faith, one can then be able to perform the righteous actions, both of which together are the most important ingredients of success. We learn, further, that once an individual has the proper grasp of faith, i.e. belief in God, the Most Great and Most Kind, and in His beloved messenger, Muhammad, he will be provided with a Light from God (Guidance from the Holy Quran), to follow the straight path and perform righteous actions, which will lead him towards lasting success, and away from punishment and the wrath of God for neglecting his duties. And consistent with His Beneficence and Generosity, God promises such persons, as described above, a double portion of reward and forgiveness for their past sins. The same is applicable to all those who have not yet been bestowed with faith, or who possess only a portion of it.

    The seeker of success who wishes to reach his goal has complete faith in God, the Most Beneficent, Most Merciful and Most Forgiving, and in His beloved messenger, Muhammad. He praises, worships and serves God, the Light and the Best Guide, with enthusiasm and performs other righteous actions as a result of his faith, fears neglecting the duties for which he was created, and often refers to the Holy Quran to guide him towards righteous actions and success.

# Day 314

**<u>Those who oppose God and His messenger (Muhammad) will be among those most humiliated.</u>**

**God has decreed: "It is I and My messengers Who must prevail"; for God is One full of strength, and the One able to enforce His will.**

**(58:20-21)**

# Day 314

    The beautiful selected passage of today is addressed to those who are endowed with faith (in God, the All-powerful and the Creator of all power, and in His noble messenger, Muhammad), as well as those who are lacking this vital component of success, and also those who actively prevent others from accepting faith. As for those who are already in possession of faith, they will bear with patience the taunts and persecution from those who oppose God, the Compeller and the Trustee, and in His beloved messenger, Muhammad, knowing that they will be victorious in the end. Those who are lacking in faith will benefit from being blessed with it, knowing that with the acquisition of faith they will be prevented from ignominy and failure. As for those who are not only lacking in faith, but who also oppose God, the Most Great and Most Glorious One, and His noble messenger, Muhammad, by persecuting the faithful and preventing the spread of faith, they should take note that if they persist, they will be among the most humiliated, for it is God and His messengers that must prevail, and God is the One full of strength, Able to enforce His will – while they depend on His Grace for every breath that they take, yet show their ungratefulness by opposing Him. And if they desist, and accept faith, then they will benefit from being saved from sure humiliation and ignominy to last forever – both in this life and in the hereafter.
    In the time of the noble prophet Muhammad, there were those who opposed God, the Most Beneficent and Merciful, and also the noble prophet, attempting to kill him and prevent the spread of faith. At present, we see as much, if not more, zeal from those who oppose God, the Most Great and the Victor, and His beloved messenger, Muhammad, uniting in their hatred and persecution of the faithful along with preventing the spread of faith. As promised by God, the Possessor of all strength and the Most Forceful One, in today's beautiful selected passage, the enemies of faith in the time of the holy prophet were overcome – and such will be the case with the enemies of faith at present. More importantly, the enemies of faith can save themselves from perpetual ignominy in the hereafter by desisting from treason and working against God, Who created and sustains them, as well as all that exists.
    The seeker of success who wishes to reach his goal has absolute faith in God, the Inspirer and Guardian of faith, and in His noble messenger Muhammad. If he encounters persecution from those who oppose God (the Most Praiseworthy) and His beloved messenger, Muhammad, he is reassured by knowing that the persecutor is the one at loss and that it is God (glorified is His Name) and His messengers who must prevail – for God is the Source of all strength, and Able to enforce His will at all times.

# Day 315

**Whatever is in the heavens and on earth, let it declare the praises and Glory of God - for He is the (One) Exalted in Might, the Wise.**

(59:1)

# Day 315

    The beautiful selected passage of today, although short, is rich in content and a proper understanding and application of it in one's life will be of tremendous benefit to him who hopes to attain success.

    Man is unique among the entire creation that we are aware of, in having the ability to reason; however, with this awesome gift also comes tremendous responsibility. Everything in creation, except man, praises and glorifies God, the One Exalted in might and the Most Wise, as an inherent characteristic of nature and creation. As for man, he must use his tremendous gifts of sight, hearing and reasoning with one logical conclusion only, declaring: Praised be He Who provided these gifts to me – such beautiful sights and colors to be appreciated by the eyes; such a vital means of communication as hearing and speaking, which enables one to interact effectively with others; and such impeccable order in the universe, from the tiniest subatomic particles to the huge stars and galaxies, that man is awed by Him Who created all that exists and sustains the creation - and that is God, the recognition of Whom is the foundation of all success. The next step then is praise, glorification and worship of God, the Supreme One and the Most Praiseworthy, Who governs and sustains all of His creation, which is followed by other righteous actions performed for the love of God, the Creator and Sustainer of all that exists.

    In fact, we are informed elsewhere in the Holy Quran that the purpose of man's creation is to praise and worship God, the Most Great and Most Glorious One. The man who engages in praise and worship of God, the Maker of order and the Shaper of beauty, is fulfilling what he was created for. Therefore, we can say that a man's success is in proportion to how much he engages in the praise, worship and serving God, the Most Great, the One Exalted in might, and the Most Wise, and performs other righteous deeds as a result of his faith. The esteemed reader is referred to the meditation on Day 3 in this collection for a more detailed discussion on worship.

    The seeker of success who wishes to reach his goal has uncompromising faith in God, the Most Praiseworthy and the Best Appraiser, and in His beloved messenger, Muhammad. He is awed by and thankful for his innumerable gifts, including the faculties of hearing, seeing and reasoning, and engages profusely in the praise, worship and glorification of God, Who granted them to him, and performs other righteous deeds as a manifestation of his faith.

# Day 316

**O you who believe! Fear God, and let every person look to what (provision) he has sent forth for tomorrow. And fear God - for God is well-acquainted with (all) that you do.**

(59:18)

# Day 316

The beautiful selected passage of today reinforces the importance of the two primary ingredients of success: faith in God, the Provider of all and the Most Forgiving, as relayed to us through His honorable messenger, Muhammad, and performance of good actions as a result of the faith. It can be placed in the category of higher level instructions or training on the path to success, because it addresses those who have already achieved the status of believers, having acquired faith. It concentrates on good actions that need to be performed in order to attain success.

There are three specific actions recommended in the beautiful selected passage of today for those who wish to attain success, and they are inter-related. First, the believer is instructed to fear God, the Almighty and the Giver and Taker of life, and this is mentioned twice in the same verse. The fear one should have of God, the Most Beneficent and Merciful One, is different from the fear one would have of a vicious animal – it is the fear one may encounter if he were to take responsibility of extremely precious assets and the fear he would experience of not being able to return them, were he not careful with safeguarding them.

Man has been blessed with the most precious of resources – with eyes to see, ears to hear, the heart and brain to reason, and limbs to carry out his intentions. He should indeed fear being negligent of those precious resources – for he is accountable for them on the Day of Judgment to God, Who provided these precious resources to him. Therefore, man is reminded to look into what provision he has made for himself by utilizing his precious resources he has been provided with, in preparation for the Day of Judgment; this is the second of the three recommendations in the beautiful selected passage of today. Third, man is instructed that all his actions are known to God, the All-Hearing, All-Seeing and All-Knowing One, and He Who keeps the most accurate account of them, to recompense man accordingly on the Day Judgment - so man will engage in those actions that will be rewarded by God, the All-Aware and the Most Generous, and refrain from those actions that will be punished by Him.

The seeker of success who wishes to reach his goal has absolute faith in God, the Most Great, the Originator, Restorer and the Most Trustworthy, and in His noble messenger, Muhammad. He fears disappointing his Lord, Who has entrusted him with the precious gifts that include his ability to see, hear and reason. He utilizes them to create a provision for himself on the Day of Judgment, by praising, worshipping and serving his Lord enthusiastically, and he knows that his Lord is acquainted with all that he does.

# Day 317

**And be not like those who forgot God (i.e. became disobedient to God), and He caused them to forget their own selves (i.e. He let them to forget to do righteous deeds). Such are the rebellious transgressors!**

(59:19)

# Day 317

    Man finds it easy to remember God, the Most Great, the Constrictor and the Reliever, during times of distress. However, he finds it more difficult to remember God, the Nourisher and Sustainer of all, during times of ease. And it is during the times of ease that man is more susceptible to harm himself. The beautiful selected passage of today will help the seeker of success to be wary of the factors of complacency and lack of focus that can interfere with, and sabotage, his path to success. Man is instructed for his own benefit to not forget God, the Most Beneficent, Most Merciful, at all times – for doing so causes him to forget the reason for his existence. Also, when he forgets God, man is likely to forget what is required of him – and instead of being one who obeys God, he becomes one who is disobedient to Him. In other words, if one is not working for the sake of God, the Owner and King of all that exists, then he is, in effect, working against Him indirectly.

    If one forgets God, blessed be His Name, and the reason for his existence, then the one who stands to lose most as a result is man himself, because then he will fail to perform righteous deeds for the sake of God, including worship ( which is the reason for man's creation), since he has forgotten God (glorified be His name) in the first place. Therefore, this unfortunate individual has actually forgotten himself, for he is not accumulating any spiritual capital that would be of benefit to him on the Day of Judgment. Such an individual who continues to enjoy the numerous blessings and sustenance from God daily, yet forgets Him and is disobedient to Him, is categorized in the beautiful selected passage of today as a rebellious transgressor, rebelling against God, the Owner and Sustainer of all, and is deserving of His wrath and displeasure.

    The seeker of success who wishes to reach his goal has uncompromising faith in God, the Most Great, Most Wise and the Most Righteous Teacher, and in His beloved messenger, Muhammad. He remembers his Lord at all times and knows that he will be at a significant loss if he forgets Him. He knows that he is at greatest risk of forgetting God, the Creator and Sustainer of all, during the times of ease, and makes a special effort to remember Him especially during those times.

# Day 318

**Not equal are the dwellers of the Fire and the dwellers of paradise; it is the dwellers of paradise that will achieve Success.**

(59:20)

# Day 318

Passing examinations requires effort. Generally, the more important the examination, the more complex and difficult it is, and the more effort that is required to succeed in the examination. Suppose that we have two candidates who are taking an examination – one of them prepares himself accordingly and is diligent in his studies and completes the requirements for succeeding in the exam, despite suffering hardships during his preparation; the other is lax in his preparation, fails to recognize what is required of him to succeed in the exam, and enjoys himself during the preparation phase. When the results are announced, one of them will be pleased with the result and the effort he has expended, while the other will be sorry that he did not prepare accordingly, and instead, elected to have immediate gratification in the preparation phase, for which he has to suffer the long-term consequences of failure.

The beautiful selected passage of today reminds us, while we are in the examination of life, to be patient and diligent, to delay the immediate gratification for long-term gains, to give the examination of life the attention and effort that it deserves, for it is the most important examination of each individual - the consequences of which will be of utmost importance. On the Day of Judgment, when the results will be known, those who pass the test of life will have attained **<u>lasting success</u>** and will be granted paradise – with gardens of bliss, under which rivers flow, to dwell therein forever; while those who took life for a joke and failed to prepare accordingly, preferring short-term pleasures in the life of this world instead, will be sorely disappointed – with immense punishment, to dwell in the fire and its punishment therein, forever. This is the Judgment of God – and He is Most Just, Most Wise. Indeed, not equal will be the dwellers of fire and the dwellers of paradise.

The seeker of success who wishes to reach his goal has complete faith in God, the Most Beneficent, Most Merciful and the Most Equitable One, and in His noble messenger, Muhammad. He knows that this life is a preparation for the hereafter and prepares accordingly – by being willing to forego short-term pleasures for more lasting gains. He is willing to work hard in order to achieve lasting success.

# Day 319

**Had We sent down this Quran on a mountain, you would have surely seen it humble itself and cleave asunder for fear of God; such are the similitudes which We propound to men that they may reflect.**

(59:21)

# Day 319

We are provided with a marvelous example in way of similitude in the beautiful selected passage of today that conveys its important message in a most effective way and that is also memorable – for the benefit of the seeker of success, so that he may reflect upon it and grasp its importance. The concept of the fear of God, the Most Beneficent and Most Merciful, is again reinforced for its importance, which we reflected upon in verse 19 of the same chapter, reviewed in the meditation of three days earlier. Again we reiterate the different types of fear and that the type of fear one should feel from God, the Most Forbearing and the Most Forgiving, is different from the fear one would feel from a vicious animal: This is the fear of taking responsibility of precious assets and fear of not utilizing them wisely and fear of not being able to safeguard them.

The precious assets that man has been given responsibility for, include the eyes that he sees with, the ears that he hears with, the mind and heart with which he reasons and understands, and the limbs with which he carries out his intentions. Although a mountain can be said to be of great physical strength compared to man, it is lacking in the precious assets that we have just described above. Therefore, we understand from the beautiful selected passage that the responsibility placed on man in safeguarding and using wisely his assets is greater than that of a mountain. Thus, man is given the responsibility of understanding and acting on the instructions directed to him from God, the Most Great and Most Wise. If such responsibility were to be given to a mountain, we are told in the beautiful selected passage of today, that it would humble itself and cleave asunder for fear of God and the immense responsibility placed upon it - despite its immense strength. Hence, man is reminded that he should fear God and of misusing the precious assets that he has assumed the responsibility of - which is immense, as we noted.

The seeker of success who wishes to reach his goal has absolute faith in God, the All-Encompassing, the Most Wise, and the Best Guide, and in His beloved messenger, Muhammad. He knows that the responsibility that he carries in safeguarding and using wisely his precious assets given to him by God, the All-Seeing, All-Hearing and the All-Aware, such as seeing, hearing, and reasoning, the value of which is proportionate to their worth. He refers to the Holy Quran often, as to the best use of his precious assets.

# Day 320

God is He, beside Whom there is no other god – Who knows (all things), both secret and open; He is the Most Gracious, Most Merciful.

God is He, other than Whom there is no other god – the King, the Holy One, the Source of peace (and perfection), the Guardian of faith, the Giver of safety, the Exalted in Might, the Irresistible, the Supreme. Glory to God! (High is He) above the partners they attribute to Him.

He is God, the Creator, the Evolver, the Fashioner; to Him belong the most beautiful names; whatever is in the heavens and on earth, does declare His praises and Glory – and He is the Exalted in Might, the Wise.

(59:22-24)

# Day 320

    Today's beautiful selected passage is truly a masterpiece – considering its beauty, rhythm and imagery, and its relevance to those in pursuit of success. Its focus is mainly on faith, the most vital component of success. Anyone lacking faith in God, the Creator and Sustainer of all, should have a firm grasp of it as a result of its understanding and appreciation; his acquisition of faith should be completed, by recognizing the noble prophet Muhammad as a servant of God, relaying the message from God to all. One who is already blessed with faith should have it invigorated as a result of the understanding and appreciation of the beautiful selected passage of today.

    The most important characteristics of God are magnificently described in the beautiful selected passage of today, including His Power, Beneficence, Mercy, and Beauty, culminating in the logical conclusion and the key to faith, i.e. that there is no god other than God, and that there is no other being that shares in His divinity, and that none other than Him has the right to be worshipped. Why does God, the Most Beneficent and Merciful One, emphasize that none other than He should be worshipped? Because of His compassion and love for mankind, so that they should not be neglectful of the duties for which they were created, i.e. to worship their Creator and Sustainer. Seventeen out of the ninety-nine beautiful names of God that are known to us (blessed be His Name), are listed in the beautiful selected passage of today. It is hoped by this humble author that, after the reading and review of the beautiful selected passage of today, the esteemed reader declares the praises and glory of God, the Most Great, the Exalted in might, and the Most Wise One, like everything else in the heavens and earth does – thus helping himself and proceeding on the path towards lasting success.

    The seeker of success who wishes to reach his goal has uncompromising faith in God, the Most Beneficent, Most Merciful and Most Praiseworthy, and in His noble messenger, Muhammad. He knows that there is no one worthy of worship except for God – to Whom belong the most beautiful names. And He declares the praises and glory of His Lord, with the greatest sincerity.

# Day 321

**"Our Lord! In You (Alone) do we trust, and to You (Alone) do we turn in repentance; and to You (Alone) is (our) final return".**

(60:4)

# Day 321

The beautiful selected passage of today is a part of supplication of the beloved prophet Ibrahim, whom God, the Most Great and Most Wise, has recommended in the Holy Quran as an excellent example for believers to emulate, along with the noble prophet Muhammad. It contains three powerful messages that will be helpful for the seeker of success in achieving his goal - the first of which is that the Best One and the Only One to trust is God. This is not to discount trust in other humans, whether they are relations, friends or acquaintances. But all humans have the primary goal of seeking their benefit first; only God, the Most Beneficent and the Most Merciful, has the primary goal of seeking the benefit of every individual, as He Himself is Self-sufficient and the Provider of all.

The second powerful message in the beautiful selected passage of today that can help the seeker of success to achieve his goal is to turn in repentance to God, the Most Merciful and the Most Forgiving. As human beings we are not expected to be perfect and without sin. However, the believer strives toward goodness and turns to his Lord in repentance, knowing that He alone can forgive and guide him on to the straight Path. And God is indeed Most Forgiving and Most Merciful.

The third powerful message in the beautiful selected passage of today that can help the seeker of success to achieve his goal is the awareness that to God Alone, the Creator and Sustainer of all, is the final return of himself, and everyone else. Without this awareness, man is susceptible to live a life of aimlessness, and neglecting the duties for which God, the Creator and Sustainer of all, created him. With this awareness, man can better prepare himself daily for a more successful outcome on the Day of Judgment.

The seeker of success who wishes to reach his goal has complete faith in God, the Eternal and the Self-existing One, and in His beloved messenger, Muhammad. He puts his trust in God Alone, turns to Him in repentance, knowing that he is not perfect, and is always aware that to God is his final return, and prepares himself accordingly for the Day of Judgment.

# Day 322

Who does greater wrong than one who invents falsehood against God, while he is being invited to Islam? And God guides not those who do wrong.

They intend to put out the light of God (i.e. the religion of Islam, the Holy Quran, and the prophet Muhammad) with their mouths. But God will bring His Light to perfection, even though the disbelievers hate (it).

(61:7-8)

# Day 322

Man can make an effort towards attaining success; however, he will be in need of help from God, the Most Great, the Best Guide and the Most Righteous Teacher, in guiding him towards success. We are informed in the beautiful selected passage of today that those who do wrong will not be guided by God, the Most Beneficent and Most Merciful One, and therefore cannot hope to achieve success. The truly successful individuals like to see others succeed as well. Those who have been most blessed with Guidance from God, the Most Beneficent and Merciful One, often invite others to His path for the sake of His love and for the love of mankind, so that they too, could succeed, and invite others to submit their life to God in the religion of Islam. We are informed in the beautiful selected passage of today that one who not only rejects the invitation on path to success, but invents a falsehood against God, the Most Pure and Most Holy One, to justify his rejection, is engaging in a great, or the greatest, wrong. This would be similar to someone with an advanced infection not only refusing the medication ordered by the doctor, but intent on also passing his deadly infection to others

In the time of the beloved prophet Muhammad, there were people who were interested in discrediting him, the Holy Quran as the message of God, blessed be His Name, and the religion of Islam, wishing to put out the Light of God, the Source of all that is Good and the Best Guide, with their mouths, i.e. by slander. We still have such people in our time – and probably with more zeal and hatred. However, God, the Truth and the Most Trustworthy, promises us that He will bring His Light to perfection, even though the disbelievers hate it. Those who meet resistance in their effort to advance the word of God, the Owner of all majesty and Honor, and invitation to success for their fellow men, should therefore take heart and continue in their noble quest, knowing that God's help is with them – for indeed God is All-powerful, Most Wise, and entirely able to enforce His will.

The seeker of success who wishes to reach his goal has absolute faith in God, the Truth, the Most Forceful One, and the Best Friend and Protector, and in His noble messenger, Muhammad. He refrains from wrong, and hopes for Guidance from his Lord. He is not disheartened by the zeal and hatred of the enemies of God, knowing that God is the Sovereign King of all existence, and is fully able to enforce His will at all times and under all circumstances.

# Day 323

O you who believe! Shall I lead you to a bargain that will save you from a grievous penalty?

That you believe in God and His messenger, and that you strive (your utmost) in the cause of God with your property and your persons. That will be best for you, if you only knew!

He will forgive you your sins and admit you to gardens beneath which rivers flow, and to beautiful mansions in gardens of Eternity; <u>that is indeed the Great Success.</u>

And another (favor He will bestow), which you love: help from God and a speedy victory. So give the glad tidings to the believers.

(61:10-13)

# Day 323

The beautiful selected passage of today has great relevance to the seeker of success – for, in it is outlined the path to success of the highest degree, clearly and concisely. The first requirement for the attainment of success is faith or belief in God, the Beneficent and Merciful, and in, His beloved messenger, Muhammad. This has been reinforced in various forms both in the Holy Quran and in this collection of meditations, for the benefit of the seeker of success, and to signify its importance.

We have also reviewed in the earlier meditations that the second primary ingredient of success, in addition to faith is performance of good actions that reflect one's faith. The best example of good actions is praise and worship of God, the First and the Last. Additional good actions listed in the beautiful selected passage of today, summarized for the benefit of the seeker of success, include striving with one's capability in the cause of God, with one's property as well as with one's person or self. Striving with one's person in the cause of God, the Most Great and Most Glorious, will range from performing service in His cause – such as providing education, safety, and support to the believers and mankind – and can include defending the faith and believers with one's person, including its highest form, which is martyrdom.

To those who follow the above instructions, God, the Most Supreme and the Owner of all, promises forgiveness for their sins and the granting of paradise, in gardens beneath which rivers flow and in which there are beautiful mansions, for eternity. And in this life, those who believe and follow the above instructions are promised help from God, the Most Trustworthy and the Best Protector, along with a speedy victory against the enemies of faith. The path to being saved from grievous penalty and being admitted to live in beautiful mansions in gardens of eternity is superbly outlined in the beautiful selected passage of today – a truly magnificent bargain!

The seeker of success who wishes to reach his goal has uncompromising faith in God, the Most Great, the Best Guide and the Most Righteous Teacher, and in His beloved messenger, Muhammad. He praises and worships his Lord enthusiastically, and strives his utmost in the cause of God, with his property as well as his person, if necessary.

# Day 324

O you who believe! When the call is proclaimed to prayer on Friday (the day of community assembly), hasten earnestly to the remembrance of God and leave off business (and traffic); that is best for you if you only knew!

Then, when the (Friday) salat (prayer) is ended, you may disperse through the land, and seek the bounty of God (by working, etc.) <u>and remember God much – that you may be successful.</u>

And when they see some merchandise or some amusement (beating of drum, etc.) they disperse headlong to it and leave you (while delivering the Friday sermon). Say (to them): "That which God has is better than any amusement or merchandise! And God is the Best of providers".

(62:9-11)

# Day 324

    The beautiful selected passage of today instructs the believers in the importance of the Friday prayer and sermon (Friday being the day of community assembly), its relationship with business obligations, and the prioritization in case of conflict of business or recreation with worship.

    The importance of the Friday prayer and sermon on the believer's weekly agenda is clarified: when the call is proclaimed for the weekly Friday afternoon prayer, the believer is instructed to hurry earnestly to assemble with the community, for the sake of remembrance of God, the Creator and Provider of all, leaving behind work and business – for the collective benefit of the community, as well as for the benefit of the individual. After the completion of the important Friday afternoon assembly for the remembrance of God, the Most Great and the Most Holy, the believer is free to disperse, and recommended to resume seeking the rewards on earth of God, the Nourisher and Sustainer of all, such as by work, trade and business. In addition to attending to his work or occupation, the believer is recommended to remember God much – so that he will truly be successful, both in this life and in the hereafter.

    Finally, an example is provided from the time of the beloved prophet Muhammad, of when some people left the honorable prophet Muhammad's sermon to examine the merchandise that was being hawked outside the mosque. Those who were negligent at that time are admonished in the beautiful selected passage of today – as a lesson for all believers to realize that, when there is a conflict between worship and business or recreation, to realize that what God is able to provide is better than any amusement or merchandise. And God is the Best of providers indeed.

    The seeker of success who wishes to reach his goal has complete faith in God, the Most Great and the Creator, Nourisher, and Sustainer of all, and in His noble messenger, Muhammad. He sets aside the Friday afternoon sermon and prayer time on his schedule, for the remembrance of God the Most High and Most Glorious with the community of believers, and resumes his business after the completion of the Friday prayer, if necessary. He is not distracted during the Friday sermon and prayer by amusement or business. He knows that what God, the Most Rich and the Most Generous, is able to provide him is better than any amusement or merchandise, and prefers worship when there is conflict between worship (especially that of Friday afternoon) and business or recreation.

# Day 325

O you who believe! Let not your riches or your children divert you from the remembrance of God; and whoever does that, the loss is their own.

And spend something (in charity) out of the substance which we have bestowed on you, before death should come to any of you and he should say: "O my Lord! Why did you not give me respite for a little while? I should then have given (largely) in charity, and I should have been one of the doers of good".

But to no soul will God grant respite when the time appointed (for it) has come; and God is well-acquainted with (all) that you do.

(63:9-11)

# Day 325

The beautiful selected passage of today again reinforces the two fundamental components of success for our benefit: Faith (in God, the Most Beneficent and Most Merciful, and in His noble messenger, Muhammad) and good actions as a result of faith. It is addressed to those already possessing faith and concentrates on details regarding good actions that the seeker of success can benefit from.

First, the believer is instructed to engage in the remembrance of God, the Best Guide and the Most Righteous Teacher – as a matter of fact, this is the primary reason for the creation of man, i.e. to praise and worship God. If one has been blessed, in the life of this world, with riches of any kind, the proper response should be to express one's appreciation and thankfulness to God, the Creator and Sustainer of all. If one becomes preoccupied with his wealth and possessions, and lets his riches or his children divert him from the remembrance of God, then he is not able to perform what he was created for, i.e. praise and worship his Lord – and whoever is neglectful in that way, should know that the loss is his own. The esteemed reader is referred to the meditation of Day 3 in this collection for a more detailed discussion of worship.

Another righteous action in which the believer is instructed in today's beautiful selected passage is spending from one's wealth in charity. Unfortunately, some individuals will find out too late about the benefits of giving charity, i.e. after their death. Then they will request God for respite for a while – to be able to engage in charity, but that will be too late, for the test of life is over by that time, and exceptions will not be made to retake the test.

The seeker of success who wishes to reach his goal has absolute faith in God, the Most Great, the Best of those who keep accounts, and the All-aware, and in His beloved messenger, Muhammad. He does not let his riches or his children divert him from the remembrance of God. He realizes the importance of giving charity during his lifetime and practices regular charitable giving from his wealth. He knows that he will not have an opportunity to re-take the examination of life.

# Day 326

Whatever is in the heavens and on the earth declares the praises and glory of God; to Him belongs the dominion and to Him belongs (all) praise. And He has power over all things;

It is He Who has created you; and among you are some that are unbelievers and some that are believers. And God sees well all that you do.

He has created the heavens and the earth in just proportions and has given you shape and made your shapes beautiful. And to Him is the final return.

He knows what is in the heavens and on earth; and He knows what you conceal and what you reveal, indeed God knows well the (secrets) of (all) hearts.

(64:1-4)

# Day 326

The beautiful selected passage of today again reinforces the two fundamental components of success for our benefit: faith and good actions. The repetition of the important concepts in different formats is appreciated by the seekers of success and indicates great concern by God, the Most Great, Most Loving and the Most Righteous Teacher, for the success of man. The beautiful selected passage of today informs us that God, the Most Glorious and the Most Praiseworthy, has power over all things at all times, and it is to Him that whatever is in the heavens and earth (besides man) declares praises and glory. Man should also be inspired to do the same. Those who recognize God and His greatness in the universe and on earth are known as believers, having faith in Him, and also declare His praises and glory. The acceptance of faith is completed when the believer recognizes the words of God through His beloved messenger, Muhammad, as recorded in the Holy Quran. This is the fundamental component of success.

The second of the two fundamental components of success is the performance of righteous actions as a result of faith, knowing that God's awareness encompasses all that is in heavens and on earth at all times, and that He has knowledge of the intentions and actions of every individual, and to Whom is the final return of all, when he will be judged regarding his performance in the test of life on earth, and punished or rewarded accordingly. Those who have an appropriate understanding and appreciation of the above two factors or components of success are truly fortunate and can be said to have passed through the most difficult obstacle to success – hence the need for the repetition of these two extremely valuable components of success.

The seeker of success who wishes to reach his goal has uncompromising faith in God, the Maker of order, the Shaper of beauty, and the Creator and Sustainer of all that exists, and in His noble messenger, Muhammad. He performs righteous actions as a result of his faith, and knows that his final return is to God, Who will hold him accountable for all his actions in the life of this world, and either punish or reward him accordingly.

## Day 327

The day that He assembles you (all) for a day of assembly – that will be a day of mutual loss and gain (among you). And those who believe in God and work righteousness – He will remove from them their ill, and He will admit them to gardens beneath which rivers flow, to dwell therein forever; <u>that will be the Great Success.</u>

But those who reject faith and treat our signs as falsehoods – they will be dwellers of the fire, to dwell therein forever, and evil is that goal.

(64:9-10)

# Day 327

The beautiful selected passage of today compares those who will have passed the test of life with those who have failed. The contrast between the two is remarkable, and it is an effective passage directing those who are able to reason, towards a positive outcome for themselves. The two fundamental components of success – faith and good actions – are again reinforced for our benefit, and the mention of "great success" should be of particular interest to the seekers of success.

The test of life for man will end on the Day of Judgment– and all men and women who ever lived will be assembled in front of God, the Creator and the Resurrector. That will be a day of gain and blessing for those who passed the test of life, and a day of loss and shame for those who failed. Those who believed in God, based on His countless signs in heavens and on earth and in themselves, and who worked righteousness as a result of their faith, will have their ills removed from them, and be admitted to gardens beneath which rivers flow, to dwell therein forever; **that will indeed be the great success**, and far more valuable than the accumulation of any wealth possible in one's life.

As for those who rejected faith and treated the signs of God as falsehoods, it will indeed be a day of loss and shame for them. These are individuals who preferred the pleasures of immediate gratification during their life on earth, behaving arrogantly even as they were being provided with provision and sustenance from God, during their life - disobeying Him, and failing to perform the duties for which they were created, i.e. to praise and worship the Creator and Sustainer of all. God, blessed be His Name, has decreed that those who persist in evil and fail the test of life will be placed in the punishment of fire, to dwell therein forever. And while God is the Most Beneficent and Most Merciful, He is also the Most Just, the Most Equitable and the Avenger.

The seeker of success who wishes to reach his goal has complete faith in God, the Most Great, the Giver, Taker and the Restorer of life, and in His beloved messenger, Muhammad. He works righteousness as a result of his faith. He knows the significant contrast between those who pass the test of life and those who fail. He makes diligent effort towards and hopes to be of those who are informed on the Day of Judgment that they have passed the test of life, which is indeed **the greatest success for man**, and to which all should aspire.

## Day 328

No kind of calamity can occur, except by the leave of God. And if anyone believes in God, (God) guides his heart (aright); for God knows all things.

So obey God and obey His messenger; but if you turn back, the duty of Our messenger is only to proclaim (the message) clearly and openly.

God! There is no god but He. And in God, therefore, let the believers put their trust.

(64:11-13)

# Day 328

    The beautiful selected passage of today has three powerful messages to help the seeker of success to reach his goal - the first of which is the knowledge that no harm can come to him or anyone in existence, except with the permission of God, the Most Great, the Creator of harm and good. Therefore, an individual who has an appropriate understanding of faith (the essential ingredient of success) believes in God as the One Who knows all things and has power over all situations as relayed to us through his beloved messenger, Muhammad; he will not be overly sad or angry at any of the events he observes, for he believes in the wisdom and goodness of God. Such an individual will be guided aright by God, the Best Guide and Knower of all.

    The second powerful message in the beautiful selected passage of today to help the seeker of success to reach his goal is the instruction from God, the Most Great and Most Powerful One, that man should obey God and His messenger – for God and His messenger know what is better for man than what man has knowledge of. The duty of God's beloved messenger, Muhammad, was only to proclaim the message of God, the Most Beneficent and Merciful One, which he performed beautifully. The duty of man is to follow the message of God, the Most Great and the Creator and Sustainer of all, for which he will be rewarded or punished accordingly for following or neglecting his duties.

    The third powerful message in the beautiful selected passage of today is the reminder that there is no one greater than God, the All-powerful and the Source of all power, and there is no god but He. Therefore, if one is to put his trust in anyone or anything, he should put his trust completely in God, the Almighty and the Most Magnificent One.

    The seeker of success who wishes to reach his goal has absolute faith in God, the Most Great, Most Powerful, and the Best Guide, and in His noble messenger, Muhammad. He knows that no calamity can occur to him or anyone else, except with the permission of God. He obeys God, the Creator and Sustainer of all and His beloved messenger, Muhammad. He knows there is no one worthy of worship except for God, the Most Holy and the Most Trustworthy, and puts his trust in Him completely.

# Day 329

Your riches and your children are only but a trial; <u>but in the presence of God is the highest reward.</u>

So keep your duty to God and fear Him as much as you can. Listen and obey; and spend in charity for the benefit of your own souls. <u>And those saved from the covetousness of their own souls – they are the successful ones.</u>

If you loan to God a beautiful loan (i.e. spend in His cause), He will double it to your (credit), and He will grant you forgiveness; for God is Most ready to appreciate (service), Most Forbearing,

Knower of what is hidden and what is open, Exalted in might, Full of wisdom.

(64:15-18)

# Day 329

    The beautiful selected passage of today contains three powerful messages that can help the seeker of success to reach his goal - the first of which is the knowledge that all riches in the life of this world – including wealth and the closest relationships of love, are insignificant compared to the riches of God, the Most Rich and the Most Generous, and the satisfaction in attaining closeness to Him, providing one with the highest reward, which is not of fleeting nature like that of this world, but which he will enjoy for eternity.

    The second powerful message in the beautiful selected passage of today that can help the seeker of success to reach his goal is the instruction from God, the Most Great, the Best Guide and the Most Righteous Teacher, to keep one's duty to Him, and to fear the consequences of neglecting the responsibilities for which he was created. The honorable reader is reminded, as reviewed in the earlier meditations, that the primary duty of man and all beings is to praise and worship God, Who is the Most Glorious and the Most Praiseworthy. Another righteous action mentioned in the beautiful selected passage that one is strongly encouraged to engage in, is the giving of charity, with the greatest benefit being accorded as a result – not to the recipient of charity, but the one giving it. And God is the Best to keep account, the Most Generous and Most Appreciative One. Specifically, being free of covetousness, which allows for being more generous in charitable giving, is clearly correlated in the beautiful selected passage of today with achieving success.

    The third powerful message in the beautiful selected passage of today that can help the seeker of success to reach his goal is knowledge that, when spending in the cause of God, the Most Rich and the Most Magnificent one, which is labeled as a "beautiful loan". God is not actually in need of a loan from His creation – He is the Creator and Owner of all. But the spending from one's wealth in God's cause indicates one's love and commitment to Him, and which will be repaid to man, listed as double remuneration, along with the granting of forgiveness and other forms of acknowledgment and appreciation from God, the Most Great, Most Forbearing and Most Ready to appreciate service.

    The seeker of success who wishes to reach his goal has uncompromising faith in God, the One Exalted in might, Full of wisdom, and Knower of what is hidden and open, and in His beloved messenger, Muhammad. He knows that what one finds in the presence of God is far greater than any of the riches of the life of this world. He keeps his duty to his Lord, fears Him much, and spends in regular charity in the way of his Lord as a reflection of his love and commitment to Him.

# Day 330

...And whosoever fears God and keeps his duty to Him, He will make a way for him to get out (from every difficulty).

And He will provide for him from (sources) he never could imagine. And if anyone puts his trust in God, sufficient is (God) for him – for God will surely accomplish His purpose. Indeed, for all things has God appointed a due proportion.

(65:2-3)

# Day 330

Difficulties are part and parcel of life, and vary from trivial to seemingly unbearable ones. When faced with a difficulty, what should be the response of one who is in pursuit of success? First of all, one needs to have faith, the primary ingredient of success, i.e. faith in God, the Most Great, the Opener and the Responder to prayer, as relayed to us through His noble messenger, Muhammad. Faith in God, the Source of Peace and the Creator of all that exists, leads an individual to fear God and to keep his duty to Him at all times – and whoever does so will find out that God Almighty will make a way for him to get out of every difficulty. He will find that God, the Most Great and the Best Provider, will provide for him from sources he never could imagine.

Secondly, at all times, and including when one is faced with a difficulty, he should put his trust in God, the Most Trustworthy and the Best Friend and Protector. He will find that sufficient is God for him and that God is able to accomplish His purpose at all times and under all situations. Putting one's trust in anyone else other than God, the Most Trustworthy and the Best Protector, is indicative of a lack of faith - which is unfortunate because faith is the primary ingredient of success.

Thirdly, one needs to understand that for all things, God, the Best Fashioner and the Originator, has appointed a due proportion, so if the outcome is different in any situation from what one had hoped for, he relies on the wish of God to do as He pleases, for He is all All-Aware, the Supreme One, the Best Doer of good, Most Just, and knows what is better for us than we know ourselves. This is also an important component of faith, the primary ingredient of success.

The seeker of success who wishes to reach his goal has complete faith in God, the Most Great, the Truth and the Trustee, and in His noble messenger, Muhammad. When faced with a difficulty, he does not waver in his faith, and continues to fear God, keeping his duty to Him. He puts his trust only in God, and knows that is sufficient. In any situation, if the outcome is different from what he hoped for, he trusts in the Wisdom of God and knows that his Lord knows better than himself what is good for him.

# Day 331

**Blessed be He in Whose hands is the dominion, and He has power over all things;**

**He Who created death and life, that He may try which of you is best in deed. And He is the Exalted in Might, Most Forgiving.**

(67: 1-2)

# Day 331

The beautiful selected passage of today again reinforces the two primary ingredients of success: faith and good actions, and it does so in the most beautiful manner throughout the entire chapter. Hence passages from this particular chapter are selected for reflection for the next four meditations also. Repetition and reinforcement of the vital concepts indicate concern for retention by the teacher, and God is indeed the Most Righteous Teacher, the Best Guide, the Most Beneficent and the Most Loving One. In regard to faith in God, the Most Great, the Giver and Taker of life, His vital characteristics are presented – including having power and sovereignty over all things, as He is the Creator and Sustainer of all that exists. Therefore, everything in existence praises and glorifies God, as do the believers, i.e. those who believe in, and have faith in, God and in His noble messenger, Muhammad. Anyone who is not able to appreciate this fact is at a great disadvantage, and lacking in the most important component of success. We are further informed that God, blessed be His Name, created life and death so that He might try which of us is best in deed. The best deed that an individual can perform is praise and worship of God, the Creator and Sustainer of all that exists - which, we are informed elsewhere in the Holy Quran, was the reason for creation of all that exists, with man having this ability under voluntary control. Therefore, in life we are in a test to see who is able to perform the most righteous actions as a result of his faith, and we expect that the one who would be able to be best in righteous action or best in deeds would be the one who is strongest in his faith and love for God, the Creator and Sustainer of all. The respected reader is referred to meditation of Day 3 for a more comprehensive discussion of worship. At death, one's examination is completed and the results will be known to him when he is resurrected with everyone else who ever lived, on the Day of Judgment. For anyone who ever wondered why he exists – and we all ask that question as part of our ongoing spiritual development – the beautiful selected passage of today is the most excellent response.

The seeker of success who wishes to reach his goal has uncompromising faith in God, the Most Great, the Most exalted in Might, and the Most Forgiving One, and in His beloved messenger, Muhammad. He knows that God created life and death to see who is best in deed, and that he will be rewarded or punished accordingly on the Day of Judgment, based on his performance during his life on earth. He knows that the best deed an individual can perform is praise and worship of his Lord.

## Day 332

**(Blessed be) He who created the seven heavens, one above another; no want of proportion will you see in the creation of (God) Most Gracious. So turn your vision – do you see any flaw?**

**Turn your vision again a second time; your vision will come back to you in a state of humiliation and worn out.**

(67: 3-4)

# Day 332

The beautiful selected passage of today is a continuation of yesterday's passage. Its main focus is on the beauty and perfection of God's work, i.e. what we see on earth and beyond. The logical conclusion of one who reflects on the works of God, the Most Praiseworthy and Most Glorious, is praise and glorification of Him, which is how the beautiful selected passage of today begins. The end result for the reader should be acquisition of faith, if one does not already possess it, or strengthening of it, if one is already blessed with it – and which is the most valuable component of success.

God, the Originator of all, the Creator of order, and the Shaper of beauty, informs us that He has created the seven heavens one above another. We are still in the process of learning about the details of the earth and its immediate vicinity in space. As we learn further about the marvelous nature of space, we will find the information of heavens or space being found in seven layers to be of great use for us. In the region of space we are able to study including the entire creation that we know of, we see everything made in perfection, with no want of proportion: the predictability of the stars' and planets' motion, the beauty of the entire creation of earth and heaven, and the sustenance for all of creation with no flaw at all. The creator of such beauty and perfection deserves our highest praises and glorification – indeed, this is the essence of faith. The acquisition of faith is completed when we accept the message of the noble prophet Mohammed as the messenger of God, the Most Holy and the Best Guide.

For those who resist the existence of God, the Ever-living and Self-existing one, they are challenged to look again and again for flaws in creation. They can look inside their bodies at microscopic levels, the work of perfection and amazement; they can look at the sky at macroscopic level and see the beauty and power of the sun and the moon, and how they have been placed in control of God, the Greatest One and He Who is able to enforce His will, for the benefit of man. Their vision will come back to them worn out, in a state of humiliation, from looking for signs of imperfection in existence. The most obstinate individuals should now submit themselves to God, the Creator and Sustainer of all exists, for their own benefit, and if they desire any degree of success.

The seeker of success who wishes to reach his goal has complete faith in God, the Creator of all, the Most Pure and the King of all sovereignty, and in His noble messenger, Muhammad. He sees the perfection everywhere on earth and heavens as a sign of the greatness of God and praises, worship and glorifies Him with sincerity, as a result.

# Day 333

And whether you hide your word or publish it, He certainly has (full) knowledge of the secrets of (all) hearts;

Should He not know – He Who created (the hearts)? And He is the One Most Refined, All-Aware (of everything).

(67:13-14)

# Day 333

The beautiful selected passage of today again reinforces the two fundamental components of success: faith and good actions, for the benefit of the seekers of success. The method of reinforcement differs, although the concept is the same as discussed in the previous meditations, so that it can be grasped by as many people as possible for their benefit.

The divine characteristics of God, glorified be His Name, are enumerated for our benefit, including the description of God as the One Who is All-aware (having knowledge of everything and everyone), the One Most Refined (being kind and courteous to His servants, and understanding the finest mysteries). The divine characteristics are mentioned in God's ability to judge the actions of man and even in reference to one's intentions. As a result of the proper understanding of the beautiful selected passage of today, one should increase his faith leading to engagement in higher intensity of praise and worship of God, the Most Glorious and Most Wise, and other righteous actions henceforth, including purifying the content of one's inner thoughts and intentions, which should reflect the nature of righteousness instead of evil.

Even before a particular action is carried out, it exists first as an intention in the heart of man. And all actions need to be judged in the context of one's intention. In the beautiful selected passage of today, God, the Most Great, the Manifest and the Hidden One, informs us that whether we hide what is in our hearts or make it known to others, He has full knowledge of the secrets of all hearts. Indeed, why should He not know – because it is He Who created the hearts and minds in the first place? The implication this has for our daily life is that one needs to be aware that not only will one's actions be judged by God, the Most Great and the All-encompassing, individually - but also the context in which the actions were carried out. And one needs to be aware that God, the All-Aware and All-Encompassing, knows what is in one's heart, and one should attempt to not only perform righteous actions as a result of faith, but to have righteous and honorable intentions and thoughts from which actions proceed.

The seeker of success who wishes to reach his goal has absolute faith in God, the All-comprehending and the Hearer and Seer of all, and in His beloved messenger, Muhammad. He knows that God is aware of, and judges, not only his actions, but also the context in which the actions are carried out, and that He is aware of his most secret thoughts and intentions, which form the basis for his actions.

# Day 334

Do they not see the birds above them, spreading out their wings and folding them in? None upholds them except the Most Gracious (God); indeed, He is All-seer of everything.

Who is he that can provide for you if He (God) should withhold His provision? But they continue to be in pride, and (they) flee (from the truth).

Is he who walks prone on his face (without seeing ahead) more rightly guided, or he who sees and walks upright on the straight way (i.e. Islamic monotheism)?

Say: "It is He Who created you, and endowed you with hearing (ears) and seeing (eyes), and hearts. Little thanks do you give".

(67:19-23)

# Day 334

The beautiful selected passage of today provides three powerful messages to the seeker of success that can help him to reach his goal. It conveys its messages in a most effective format using unforgettable imagery that stays in one's mind, to help the seeker of success to retain the valuable information for practical daily use.

The first powerful message in the beautiful selected passage of today deals with faith in God, the Most Great and the Creator and Sustainer of all – the most important component of success. We are provided with three awe-inspiring signs of God's presence: 1) the Ability of birds to be sustained in mid-air with use of their wings, requiring complex interaction of forces including gravity, physiological and anatomic components and physical forces; this is not a result of random events, but result of Brilliance and Beneficence of God, the Most Gracious and the All-Seer of everything, 2) consideration of who can be of help to anyone except God, the Most Gracious and Source of all strength; if He were to withhold His assistance, the entire world could not help one individual, and if He were to provide His assistance, the entire world together could not harm the individual, and 3) consideration of who it is that could provide one or the entire mankind with their provision, if God were to withhold it: There is none that can do that. As a matter of fact, the entire world together cannot produce a fly (from nothing) without the assistance of God, the Creator and Sustainer of all. Despite the above, and numerous other signs of the presence of God, there are still some arrogant beings who continue to flee in pride from the truth, but not those who are interested in pursuing success and helping themselves, and others.

The second powerful message in the beautiful selected passage of today that can help the seeker of success to reach his goal is the comparison between one who is walking prone (without seeing ahead) and one who walks upright and is able to see ahead; Which of these two is expected to follow the straight and correct path? We can compare the individual who is walking prone to one who relies on his own intelligence for guidance, and the individual walking upright to one who relies on God, the Most Great and the Creator and Sustainer of all that exists, for guidance.

The third powerful message in the beautiful selected passage of today to help the seeker of success to reach his goal is the appreciation of the valuable assets he has been provided with by God, i.e. hearing, seeing and reasoning. Often, man tends to realize the importance of these valuable assets only after losing one of them. However, if man realizes the value of these assets while not having lost any one of them, then success would be more easily attainable to the largest number of people. One should give thanks to God who provided these valuable assets, and use them in the service of the One who provided these, by praising, worshipping, glorifying and serving Him, consistent with His Greatness and Glory.

The seeker of success who wishes to reach his goal has uncompromising faith in God, the Most Great and the Creator and Sustainer of all, and in His noble messenger, Muhammad. He thanks God for the invaluable gifts He provided him with, including hearing, seeing and reasoning, and uses them to praise, worship, and serve Him. He relies consistently on God, the Best Guide and the Most Righteous Teacher, for Guidance - and has more trust in Him than anyone or anything else.

# Day 335

Say (O Muhammad): "Do you see? If God destroys me, and those with me, or He bestows His Mercy on us – who can save the disbelievers from a painful torment?".

Say: "He (God) is Most Gracious; we have believed in Him, and in Him have we put our trust. So you will come to know who it is that is in manifest error".

Say: "Tell me! If (all) your water were to sink away, then who can supply you with flowing (spring) water?".

(67:28-30)

# Day 335

The beautiful selected passage of today contains three powerful messages that can help the seeker of success to reach his goal - the first of which is the knowledge that whether people suffer or prosper – is dependent on the will of God, the Most Great, the Rewarder of good and the Avenger of wrong. The intelligent reader is referred to the earlier meditations where it is discussed that the first step in change must come from the individual level, which is not inconsistent with today's powerful message that even though the first step comes from the individual regarding any change in his condition, the fact that it is seen to its fruition or not, is dependent on the will of God, the Most Powerful and the Most Wise. Those refusing to accept the superiority of God and their submission to Him are asked to consider who it is that can save them from a painful torment that is the prescribed penalty for their refusal to carry out the duties for which they were created, disobeying God, and behaving arrogantly, like the accursed Satan?

The second powerful message in the beautiful selected passage of today to help the seeker of success to reach his goal is the instruction from God, the Most Gracious and the Creator and Sustainer of all, for man and the seeker of success to believe in God and to put his trust in Him (only). Those who refuse to do so and refuse to submit to His authority will eventually come to know their manifest error, when it will be too late.

The third powerful message in the beautiful selected passage of today to help the seeker of success to reach his goal is to engage in an exercise that helps one to understand the Glory of God. Imagine if all of our water supply were to vanish, who is it, then, that could provide us with the flowing water necessary for survival and for life afterwards? There is no other that can do so except God, the Most Beneficent, the Nourisher and the Provider, and the Lord of the worlds; it is to Him that the seeker of success submits, turns to for guidance, and praises, worships and glorifies – as He is deserving of.

The seeker of success who wishes to reach his goal has complete faith in God, the Most Glorious, the First, the Last and the Sustainer of all, and in His beloved messenger, Muhammad. He knows that whatever good or evil befalls him, it cannot be without the permission of God, the Creator of all and the Most Trustworthy, and puts his complete trust in Him. He knows everything in existence came from God.

# Day 336

Truly man was created very impatient –

Fretful (discontented) when evil touches him,

And miserly when good reaches him;

Not so those devoted to prayer;

Those who remain steadfast to their prayer;

And those in whose wealth is a recognized right,

For (the needy) who asks, and him who is prevented (for some reason from asking);

And those who guard their chastity,

Except with their wives and those whom their right hands possess – for (then) they are not to be blamed –

But those who trespass beyond this are transgressors;

And those who respect their trusts and covenants;

And those who stand firm in their testimonies;

And those who guard (the sacredness) of their worship;

Such will be the honored ones in the gardens (of bliss).

(70:19-35)

# Day 336

The beautiful selected passage of today compares the undesirable actions in the sight of God, the Most Great and the Best Judge, with the desirable actions, for the benefit of the seeker of success.

The undesirable actions for man tend to be predictable – for that is the nature of man, until he attains faith in God, the primary ingredient of success. The undesirable actions of man, which are typical prior to acquiring faith, include a sense of impatience, being fretful, irritable, or discontent when afflicted with evil or suffering, and being callous or miserly when good reaches him.

In contrast, after a person attains faith, he exhibits particular desirable qualities or actions as a manifestation of his faith, as instructed by God, the Most Great, the Owner and Inheritor of all. These desirable actions and traits include being devoted and constant in prayer and praise for God, the Creator and Sustainer of all, being charitable, fearing the displeasure of God, the Most Strong, the Most Forceful and the Most Loving, guarding one's chastity, respecting one's trusts and covenants, standing firm in one's testimonies, and guarding the sacredness of one's worship. Those individuals who have faith and exhibit the above qualities as a manifestation of their faith will be rewarded with **lasting success**, attaining an honorable position in the gardens of bliss in the hereafter, for eternity.

The seeker of success who wishes to reach his goal has absolute faith in God, the Most Praiseworthy, the Best Guide and the Most Righteous Teacher, and in His noble messenger, Muhammad. He exhibits patience and constancy in praise for his Lord, in good times and bad, and exhibits the desirable actions noted in the above paragraph, making them a part of his personality.

# Day 337

**Truly the rising by night is most potent for governing (the soul), and most suitable for (framing) the word (of prayer and praise).**

(73:6)

# Day 337

    The beautiful selected passage of today would be categorized in the advanced level of components for those interested in the pursuit of success. As we have learned in the earlier meditations and which has been repeated a number of times, both in them and the Holy Quran, signifying their importance, the most fundamental components of success – and the foundation to build on – are faith and the performance of good actions as a result of faith.

    As for the individual who is fortunate to have a firm grasp of faith in God, the Most Great and the Creator and Sustainer of all that exists, and in His message, as relayed to mankind through His beloved messenger, Muhammad, he realizes that the most righteous of actions which can be performed by him is praise, worship and glorification of his Lord in prayer. Prayer at regular intervals throughout the day is a requirement for an individual whose faith leads him to a formal declaration of submission of himself to God, the Almighty and the Lord of the worlds. However, there are men whose degree of faith leads them to perform acts greater than the minimum requirements.

    The level of participation in any righteous activity will be noted by God, the Most Glorious, Who is All-hearing and All-seeing, and will be rewarded accordingly. All men and women are expected to fulfill the requirements for which they were created, i.e. to praise, worship and serve their Lord, and will be judged accordingly on their performance. There is no special class of worshippers or priests in the religion of Islam, as relayed to us through His noble messenger, Muhammad. Indeed, as we learned earlier, and which has been reinforced a number of times in this collection, worship of the Creator, is the reason for the existence of man. The honorable reader is referred to the meditation on Day 3 of this collection for a more detailed discussion on worship.

    Those individuals whose faith and love of God, the Most Magnificent and the All-knowing One, lead them to be engaged in extra devotion to Him – beyond the requirements of worship in daytime – are encouraged to continue their business and attention to their daytime duties and rise at nighttimes to engage in extra worship. In the nighttime, one is typically not preoccupied with the responsibilities of work and livelihood, and can devote all his attention to God, the Most Great and the Creator and Sustainer of all, with the highest degree of praises, without being preoccupied with other matters. It is also an excellent training in being able to control one's self in order to be able to perform other righteous actions in a consistent manner.

    The seeker of success who wishes to reach his goal has uncompromising faith in God, the Most Loving One, the Best Guide and the Most Righteous Teacher, and in His beloved messenger, Muhammad. In addition to the regular worship of his Lord in the daytime, along with his worldly obligations, he rises in the night for extra worship and praise of his Lord, due to the intensity of his faith in, and Love of God, the Most Compassionate and the Source of all that is good.

# Day 338

Every soul will be (held in hell) in pledge for its deeds,

Except the companions of the Right Hand;

(They will be) in (gardens of delight); they will question each other,

And (ask) of the sinners:

"What led you into the hell?"

They will answer: "We were not of those who prayed;

Nor were we of those who fed the poor;

"But we used to talk vanities with vain talkers;"

"And we used to deny the Day of Judgment,"

"Until there came to us (the Hour) that is certain".

Then will no intercession of (any) intercessors profit them.

(74:38-48)

# Day 338

    An important part of the strategy towards attainment of success is avoidance of those factors which contribute to failure. In the beautiful selected passage of today, we learn about those factors or actions that lead one towards **the ultimate failure**, i.e. being sent to hell for eternity as a result of failure in the test of life- and which is the complete opposite of the ultimate success (or being sent to paradise for eternity for passing the test of life).

    Those fortunate individuals who have succeeded in the test of life will be separated and placed on the right hand side of God, the Most Great and the Most Just, being sent to paradise in the gardens of delight for eternity, while the failures are placed on the left hand side, and are sent to be held in hell, in pledge for their deeds. An example is provided for our benefit, of a conversation between those who succeeded and those who failed on the Day of Judgment. Those who failed in the test of life will recognize the actions that led them to failure and these include: 1) not participating praise and worship of God, the Creator and Sustainer of all, which, along with serving God, is the reason for man's existence, 2) not feeding the poor, 3) participating in useless and false talk and conversations with those who are in such habits, and 4) denying the Day of Judgment, so that they had no understanding of what was expected from them in order to succeed in life. And when the test of life is over – either with death or the arrival of the Day of Judgment, it will be too late to avert the consequences of failure.

    The seeker of success who wishes to reach his goal has complete faith in God, the Most Great, the Best Appraiser and the Most Equitable One, and in His noble messenger, Muhammad. He participates in praise to his Lord with sincerity in prayer and worship, feeds the poor, and avoids useless and false talk with those who are in the habit of engaging in such activity. He is certain of the Day of Judgment, and prepares for it accordingly.

# Day 339

Does man think that he will be left uncontrolled (without purpose and accountability)?

Was he not a drop of sperm emitted (in lowly form)?

Then did he become a clinging clot; then did (God) make and fashion (him) in due proportion;

And made of (that) two sexes, male and female; Has not He (God), the power to give life to the dead?

(75:36-40)

# Day 339

The beautiful selected passage of today again reinforces the two fundamental components of success: faith and good actions; and it does so in a truly impressive, concise, and memorable format. The concern of God, the Most Beneficent and Most Merciful One, for the success of man is evident in how often He emphasizes the most important components of success in remarkably different variations and in truly beautiful imagery and examples, to help us to understand and retain the necessary information for maximal benefit.

The first and most fundamental component of success, i.e. faith in God, the Most Great and the Creator and Sustainer of all, as relayed to us through His noble messenger, Muhammad, is reinforced by the explanation of the development of man from a mere drop of sperm, when combined with a similar component of material in woman, which then becomes a clot, proceeding to be fashioned in due proportion, and continuing to gain in strength and form into adulthood. Man is encouraged to reflect on who causes all these remarkable and miraculous events daily and countless times throughout the world: It is to Him, the Creator and Sustainer of all, that one should turn in awe, praise, and worship and for Guidance. This is the essence of faith, the most important component of success.

The second of the two fundamental components of success, i.e. performance of good actions and righteous deeds as a result of faith, is reinforced by two points in the beautiful selected passage of today: 1) that the Most Great and Most Wise Creator, Who created a miracle with every living individual, would do so for no significant purpose, would indeed seem ludicrous, and 2) that God, the Most Glorious and All-powerful, Who is able to give life to drops of fluid, is able to give life to the dead again. If man is to attain any measure of success, he must be able to appreciate that he was created for a purpose, and that he is accountable for all his actions in the life of this world to his Creator. The intelligent seeker of success will have realized from the earlier meditations in this collection that worship of God, the Most Beneficent and Most Merciful, constitutes the highest example of good action that he can perform, and is the reason for his creation. The esteemed reader is referred to the meditation of Day 3 in this collection for a more detailed discussion of worship.

The seeker of success who wishes to reach his goal has absolute faith in God, the Most Great, the Originator and the Restorer, and in His beloved messenger, Muhammad. He knows that he was created with a purpose – to praise, worship and serve his Lord, that he is accountable to Him for all his actions, and that this life is a test and preparation for the hereafter, which is more important than the life of this world.

# Day 340

But, when there comes the greatest catastrophe (the Day of Judgment) –

The day when man shall remember (all) that he strove for,

And hell-fire shall be placed in full view for (all) to see;

Then, for such as had transgressed all bounds (in disbelief, oppression, and evil deeds of disobedience of God),

And had preferred the life of this world;

Indeed, his abode will be hell-fire.

And for such as had entertained the fear of standing before his Lord's (tribunal) and had restrained (his) soul from the lower desires;

Indeed his abode will be paradise.

They ask you (O Muhammad) about the (Ending) Hour: "When will be its appointed time?"

You have no knowledge to say anything about it;

With your Lord is the (knowledge) of its term –

You are but a warner of such as (those who) fear it;

The day they see it, (it will be) as if they had spent but a single evening – or (at most till) the following morning!

(79:34-46)

# Day 340

The beautiful selected passage of today is of great importance due to its powerful and clear description of certain events and concepts which are crucial to both faith and the performance of good actions or righteous deeds, the two primary components of success. Its distinctiveness lies in its brilliant description of when the truly important event of the Day of Judgment is expected to occur, and in its relevance to our present life.

The concept of the resurrection of all individuals who ever lived, to be raised again, in addition to those living at that moment, on the Day of Judgment, to be judged in the presence of God, the Most Great, the Giver and Taker of life and the Resurrector, is a crucial component of faith. With a proper understanding of faith and the expectation of Resurrection by God, glorified be His Name, one is able to appreciate the importance of good actions or righteous deeds, performed as manifestation of faith, for the pleasure of God, the Most Magnificent and the Best Rewarder. Those fortunate individuals who had entertained the fear of standing before God's tribunal and restrained their soul from lower desires, will be rewarded by God, the Most Rich and the Most Generous One, with paradise for eternity, ***the ultimate mark of success***. On the other hand, those unfortunate individuals who lacked faith, and therefore transgressed in disbelief, oppression, and evil deeds of disobedience to God, the Source of all Power and the Judge, and preferred the life of the world and its immediate gratification, would not have saved anything of value to be judged favorably, i.e. righteous deeds done for the sake of God, the Creator and Sustainer of all. Therefore, they will have deserved their punishment for the waste of the precious resources granted to them - including their sight, hearing and reasoning, and will find themselves in the hell-fire.

In the time of the beloved prophet Muhammad, as well as today, those who are simply curious, or otherwise in contempt of faith, would mockingly ask: "When is this Day of Judgment going to occur?". God, the Most Patient and the Most Righteous Teacher, informs us in the beautiful selected passage of today that it will be the event of the greatest catastrophe, when man will remember all that he strove for, and the hell-fire will be placed in full view for all to see, and those deserving of it, as described above, will be sent there for eternity. Even the noble prophet Muhammad had no knowledge of when the Day of Judgment would occur, except to give warning of its occurrence. God, the Most Pure and Most Wise, informs us that the day one sees the Day of Judgment, compared with when one was living in the world, he would feel as if he had spent a single evening, or less than a day. This should help the seeker of success realize the importance of delayed gratification and preparation for the afterlife, and to avoid wishing for the pleasures of this life at the expense of the hereafter.

The seeker of success who wishes to reach his goal has uncompromising faith in God, the Most Great, the Gatherer and the Most Just, and in His noble messenger, Muhammad. He knows that the Day of Judgment will occur with certainty, fears standing before God's tribunal, and restrains his soul from the lower desires. He knows that this entire life consists of less than a day in duration of the afterlife.

# Day 341

Be cursed (the disbelieving) man!

How ungrateful he is!

From what stuff has He (God) created him?

From a sperm-drop He has created him, and then molded him in due proportions.

Then does He make his path smooth for him.

Then He causes him to die, and puts him in his grave.

Then, when it is His will, He will raise him up (again).

By no means has he fulfilled what God has commanded him.

(80:17-23)

# Day 341

The importance of the beautiful selected passage of today lies in its addressing the two major components of success: faith and performance of righteous deeds, at the elementary level. The unfortunate individual who is lacking in faith will find it extremely useful, for it addresses the major issues related to faith in a comprehensive, yet concise and effective, manner. The fortunate individual who already possesses faith will find that he will have his faith further strengthened.

All men and women with intelligence will ask themselves the questions "Where did I come from?", "What is my purpose in life?", and "Where am I going from here?". All men and women who have eyes to see would marvel at the beauty and perfection they observe within themselves, on earth, and in the sky and heavens. For many individuals who are fortunate, their queries lead them to the door-step of faith. However, there are some individuals who refuse to believe in God, the Most Great and the Creator and Sustainer of all; it is these individuals to whom the beautiful selected passage of today is especially addressed.

Does man really consider from where he came? Does he consider how he came into existence from a drop of sperm and the microscopic egg? Who is it that caused such a perfect organization of tissues and organs and repeats it over and over, and provides for all their sustenance? Who is it that causes him to die? And is not He who gave him life in the first place able to give him life again? Indeed, the individual who denies God, the Most Great, the Giver and Taker of life, is most ungrateful in that he cannot thank the One Who provided him with the treasures of sight, hearing and reasoning; and he is ungrateful in that he refuses to realize the reason for his existence and to fulfill the duties for which he was created, i.e. to praise, worship and serve his Lord.

The seeker of success who wishes to reach his goal has complete faith in God, the Most Great, the Originator and the Restorer, and in His beloved messenger, Muhammad. He is grateful to God (glorified be His Name) for the gift of life and lives it in giving Him praise, worshipping and serving Him. He knows that God, the Almighty and the Most Praiseworthy, Who has given him life, will cause him to die and will raise him up again on the Day of Judgment, to be held accountable for his actions in life. And he prepares himself accordingly for success.

# Day 342

Indeed, this is the word of a most honorable messenger,

Endowed with power, and (high) rank before the Lord of the throne;

With authority there, (and) faithful to his trust.

And (O people)! Your companion is not one possessed;

And without doubt, he (the prophet Muhammad) saw him (Gabriel) in the clear horizon.

Neither does he withhold grudgingly, knowledge of the unseen;

Nor is it the word of the outcast Satan.

Then where are you going?

Indeed this is no less than a message to (all) the worlds.

(With profit) to whoever among you wills to go straight;

But you cannot will except as God wills – the Cherisher of the worlds.

(81:19-29)

# Day 342

The beautiful selected passage of today is at the high-primary to intermediate level of understanding in matters related to success. As we have learned previously, and repeated a number of times in this collection of meditations, the primary ingredient of success is faith in God, the Most Great and the Creator and Sustainer of all that exists. However, faith cannot be said to be complete and genuine unless the belief in God, the Most Great, the One and the Only One, is also coupled with the belief in His beloved prophet Muhammad, as His messenger who brought to all the message and Guidance from God, the Almighty, the First and the Last.

If one is about to take an examination, it is one's responsibility to make himself aware of the requirements, material covered, and the recommendations of the teacher or the examiner on adequate preparation. One cannot expect to do well in the examination relying only on his intuition as to what is important. One cannot expect to pass even if he relies on the older versions of the examination by the same teacher, especially if the examiner warns the students that the older versions of exam requirements have not been understood appropriately and have been corrupted.

Therefore, an individual who denies the prophethood of the beloved prophet of God, Muhammad, with or without the belief in God, the Most Pure and the Source of peace, is ill-prepared in passing the test of life. God, the Most Wise and the Most Loving One, relays to us in the beautiful selected passage of today that His noble messenger, Muhammad, has brought to all, His word (the Holy Quran) through the angel Gabriel, for the benefit of all the worlds. Those who would discount the message of the beloved prophet Muhammad as emanating from one who was possessed, or as from the accursed Satan, and who refuse to recognize the word of God, would therefore fail to prepare themselves accordingly for a successful outcome in the test of life. Because all things are under the control of God, the Source of all power and the Cherisher of the world at all times, even the ability of an individual to recognize His word, thus a great Mercy and of immense profit to himself, requires one to be deserving of it, and requires God's permission (glorified be His Name).

The seeker of success who wishes to reach his goal has absolute faith in God, the Owner of all sovereignty and the Cherisher of the worlds, and in His noble messenger, Muhammad. He wishes to follow the straight and honorable path that leads to his Lord and serve Him, and therefore refers to the Holy Quran often, containing His word and Guidance with message to all the worlds and mankind, as conveyed through His beloved prophet, Muhammad.

# Day 343

O Man! What has made you careless about your Lord, the Most Generous -

Who created you, fashioned you perfectly, and gave you due proportion?

(82:6-7)

# Day 343

The beautiful selected passage of today reinforces again the two fundamental components of success, i.e. faith and righteous deeds, for our benefit in a memorable, beautiful, concise and very effective manner. A proper understanding of it should lead to a vital assessment and renewed vigor for proper action on the path to success. God, the Most Wise, Most Loving and the Best Guide, reminds man to consider who it is that created him, fashioned him perfectly so that every organ and component of his body works to benefit and serve him, and gave him symmetry and beauty – each individual being truly a testimony of thousands and thousands of miracles. Each individual being, therefore, has countless reasons for being thankful to the One Who has provided him with a multitude of gifts, which are better termed miracles. How should one express his thanks to Him who is entitled to it?

Man has been instructed by God, the Most Great and the Most Righteous Teacher, in the Holy Quran, and as reviewed in the appropriate meditations in this collection, that he has been created to worship his Lord, and that He has created life and death to see which of them would best carry out his duties, and that he will be resurrected on the Day of Judgment, to have his performance judged, and be either rewarded or punished accordingly. **The highest form of success** for an individual is, therefore, if one has been deemed successful by his Creator, and is saved from the punishment of hell-fire, and rewarded accordingly, to live in paradise for eternity. The esteemed reader is referred to the meditation of Day 3 in this collection, for a more detailed discussion on worship.

In the beautiful selected passage of today, we are asked to stop and consider what it is that makes us careless about our Lord, the Creator and Sustainer. Is it our preoccupation with the short-term pleasures of the life of this world? Is it our arrogance that holds us back in thanking and praising the One Who is deserving of it and whose right it is? There could be other reasons as well, but the wise individual should stop and take notice and stop being careless about his duties towards his Lord.

The seeker of success who wishes to reach his goal has uncompromising faith in God, the Creator, the Fashioner, and the Most Generous One, and in His beloved messenger, Muhammad. He praises and worships his Lord and strives to serve Him diligently, with the attention and intensity He is deserving of, and which is His right – and he is not careless about it.

# Day 344

**Woe to those that deal in fraud;**

**Those who, when they are to receive by measure from men, exact full measure –**

**But when they have to give by measure or weight to men, give less than due;**

**Do they not think that they will be called to account?**

(83:1-4)

# Day 344

    The beautiful selected passage of today again reinforces to us the two fundamental components of success, i.e. faith and performance of righteous deeds as a manifestation of faith, for our benefit. It concentrates more heavily on the component dealing with performance of righteous deeds and instructs us in avoidance of a particular practice that is incongruent with honorable and righteous action. The understanding and appreciation of the plan of God, the Most Great and the Most High, to resurrect man on the Day of Judgment, to be held accountable for his performance during his life on earth, and to be rewarded or punished accordingly, is an important component of faith and is reviewed in the beautiful selected passage of today for reinforcement.

    With the understanding that man is held accountable for his actions by God, the All-seeing and All-knowing One, a particular undesirable action that can hold us back from attaining success is mentioned that is to be avoided: Dealing in fraud. Man seeks from others that they should give him the full amount that is due to him in measure and weight. However, unless he has faith and a sense of accountability to his Lord, and if he thinks he can get away with it, he can engage in fraud, i.e. giving to others less in weight and measure than is their due. God is Just and enjoins man to do justice. God, the Most Wise and the Most Righteous Teacher, reminds man to deal justly with others and informs us that we will be called to account on the Day of Judgment for dealing unjustly with others by engaging in fraud.

    The seeker of success who wishes to reach his goal has complete faith in God, the Most Kind and the Most Equitable, and in His noble messenger, Muhammad. He knows he will be held accountable for all his actions to God, glorified be His Name, on the Day of Judgment. He gives to others what is their just due and does not deal in fraud.

# Day 345

For those who believe and do righteous deeds, will be gardens beneath which rivers flow (paradise); <u>that is the Great Success (the fulfillment of all desires).</u>

Indeed, truly strong is the grip (and punishment) of your Lord;

Indeed it is He Who creates from the very beginning, and He can restore (life).

And He is the Most Forgiving, full of loving Kindness;

Lord of the throne of glory;

Doer (without let) of all that He intends.

(85:11-16)

# Day 345

    The beautiful selected passage of today again reinforces the two most vital components of success for our benefit: Faith and righteous deeds, and with an emphasis on faith, the precursor to performance of righteous deeds, that can benefit an individual. The use of the term "great success" is of particular significance to those in pursuit of success, especially as defined by God, the Most Praiseworthy and the Most Wise One.

    The characteristics of God enumerated in the beautiful selected passage of today include "Most Forgiving" and "Full of loving kindness", and His abilities that are specified include "Lord of the throne of glory", "Doer of all that He intends", and "the Originator and Restorer (of life)". Even from the limited descriptions used regarding God's abilities and characteristics, one senses an obligation and service that is due to Him Who created all, is Full of love, and is able to do all that He intends.

    Progressing onwards from being a believer in God, the Most Great and Most Beneficent and Merciful, if one goes the next step to doing righteous deeds, as a result of that faith, we are informed in the beautiful selected passage of today, one will be appropriately rewarded with gardens beneath which rivers flow – to live in eternity, known as paradise. **This is termed "great success" by God, the Almighty and the First and the Last, and this should be the fulfillment of all desires**. However, failure to recognize God's signs in one's life and failure to attain faith, leading to not believing in God, and not serving, or doing righteous deeds for the sake of God, the Creator and Sustainer of all, will result in equally severe punishment, as described in the beautiful selected passage of today. The esteemed reader is referred to earlier meditations on understanding the reasons for the severity of expected punishment from God, Who is Most Kind and Most Just, for those who fail in fulfilling their duties on earth.

    The seeker of success who wishes to reach his goal has absolute faith in God, the Most Great, Most Loving and Most Kind, and in His beloved messenger, Muhammad. He performs righteous deeds as a result of his faith and knows that praise and worship of God constitutes the highest form of righteous deeds. He knows performance of righteous deeds inspired by faith will lead to great success as promised by God, the Truth and the Most Trustworthy

# Day 346

**Now let man think from what he is created!**

**He is created from a drop emitted –**

**Proceeding from between the backbone and the ribs;**

**Surely (God) is able to bring him back (to life)!**

**The Day that (all) things secret will be examined.**

(86:5-9)

# Day 346

Today's beautiful selected passage again reinforces for our benefit, the two vital components of success: Faith and performance of righteous deeds as a result of faith. Reinforcements are not mere repetitions, but attempts at relaying the same concept for one's benefit, usually involving a different method of explanation, for greater likelihood of understanding and retention of the important concepts. The method of relaying the important concepts in today's beautiful selected passage is concise, effective and memorable.

First, the focus is on faith in God, the Most Great, the Creator, the Maker of order and the Shaper of beauty, as relayed to us through His beloved prophet Muhammad. Man is asked to imagine from where he arose – from a mere drop of fluid in the male, which, after being combined with similar material from the female, forms a being with thousands of miracles. This is a remarkable feat, worthy of our greatest thanks and appreciation. It is also one of the most obvious signs of the presence of God, the Most Glorious and the Most Praiseworthy. The foundation is now laid for one to be receptive to the second of the two vital components of success, i.e. performance of righteous deeds and accountability. If one is able to imagine the origination of life as described above, then the resurrection of man again by the same Magnificent and All-powerful Being, or God, becomes a totally reasonable plausibility; and that is important, for a vital component of faith is belief that God, glorified be His Name, will bring man back to life on the Day of Judgment, when he will be held accountable for all his actions during his life. Thus we can realize the importance of performance of righteous deeds during one's life on earth. On the Day of Judgment, all things will be examined – including all secrets, and rewarded or punished accordingly.

The seeker of success who wishes to reach his goal has complete faith in God, the Almighty, the Originator, the Restorer and the Best of those who keep account, and in His noble messenger, Muhammad. He knows for certainty that he will be brought back to life after his death on the Day of Judgment, when all his actions, including things secret, will be examined, and rewarded or punished accordingly.

# Day 347

Glorify the name of your Guardian-Lord Most High,

Who has created – and further, given order and proportion;

And Who has ordained laws, and granted Guidance;

And Who brings out the (green and luscious) pasture;

And then makes it (but) dark stubble.

(87:1-4)

# Day 347

If two people are on an assigned mission, chances are much higher that the one who will succeed is the one who not only is aware of his mission, but believes in it with his heart – and is therefore able to add enthusiasm, love, and concern, in addition to following the rules for completion of the mission. Therefore, in matters of faith, the most vital ingredient of success, God, the Most Great and the Inspirer and Guardian of faith, has not only recommended that man have faith, but that he should have full conviction regarding it. It is for this purpose that the topic of faith is not just mentioned once or a few times in the Holy Quran and also in this collection of meditations, but it is reinforced repeatedly, with the use of the best of examples, terms and concepts that man can understand with the precious gifts that God, the Most Beneficent and Merciful One, has provided him, including sight, hearing and reasoning.

All classes of people can benefit from the beautiful selected passage of today – both in attaining faith and strengthening it, from the farmer who is able to finally see the Hand of God, the Creator, the Shaper of beauty and the Giver and Taker of life, as he observes the green and luscious pasture which becomes dark stubble, to the astrophysicist, who is able to appreciate the Power of God, the Creator of all, and the Maker of order, in the ordained laws, order, and proportion on earth and in the universes. As a result, the farmer and the astrophysicist, and indeed all classes of individuals, should glorify the Name of God, Most High and Deserving of all praise and glory, if they are to attain any degree of success. Everything in existence already does so; nothing should hold man back from doing the same.

The seeker of success who wishes to reach his goal has absolute faith in God, the Most Great and the Manifest and the Hidden One, and in His beloved messenger, Muhammad. His faith arises from personal observation of signs of God's existence within his universe, world, and his own body, and as a result of which he glorifies the Name of His Guardian-Lord Most High – not just as a duty, but with full conviction, enthusiasm and love.

# Day 348

**Indeed, those will succeed who purify themselves (by accepting Islam),**

**And glorify the name of their Guardian-Lord, and (lift their hearts) in prayer.**

**But you prefer the life of this world;**

**Although the hereafter is better and more enduring.**

(87:14-17)

# Day 348

The beautiful selected passage of today again reinforces for our benefit the two vital components of success: faith and righteous deeds or good actions as a result of faith. It is of particular interest for clearly identifying success in relation to the above factors. It is one of the most beautiful, concise yet comprehensive, memorable and very effective passages of the Holy Quran. The first step towards success is identified as purification of oneself. In the context of similar passages in the Holy Quran, this would be indicative of acquisition of faith in God, the Most Beneficent and Most Merciful. In the context of the other verses associated with the beautiful selected passage of today, purification of oneself reflects acceptance of the message of the noble prophet Muhammad and invitation to submit oneself to God, the Creator and sustainer of all, in the religion of Islam. Both of the explanations for purification of oneself, as mentioned above for the acquisition of faith, are congruent with each other.

The next step in the acquisition of success is identified as glorification of the Name of the Lord of all that exists, and lifting of one's heart in prayer. In the context of the numerous other passages in the Holy Quran associating faith with righteous deeds for attainment of success, we can conclude that glorification of the Name of God, the Most Pure, the Eternal, and the Self-existing One, and lifting one's heart in prayer, worship, and adoration to Him, is the most important of the righteous deeds as we have reviewed earlier in this collection of meditations, and is the logical result of the acquisition of faith as described above.

The barriers to the attainment of success are brilliantly identified as preference of the life of this world, and failure to recognize that the hereafter is better and more enduring than the life of this world. This is of great help to all of us, because barriers can only be overcome once they have been identified.

The seeker of success who wishes to reach his goal has uncompromising faith in God, the Lord of all Majesty and Reward and the Satisfier of all needs, and in His noble messenger, Muhammad. He submits himself and his life to God, the Most Glorious and the Most Praiseworthy, as a result of his faith and glorifies His Name, lifting his heart in prayer enthusiastically. He knows that the hereafter is better and more enduring than the life of this world, and prepares himself accordingly.

# Day 349

Has the story reached you, of the overwhelming (i.e. Day of Resurrection)?

Some faces that day will be humiliated –

Laboring hard, weary.

They will enter in the hot blazing fire.

They will be given to drink from a boiling spring.

No food will there be for them but a poisonous thorny plant,

Which will neither nourish nor avail against hunger.

Other faces that day will be joyful,

Pleased with their striving –

In a Garden on high,

Where they shall hear no harmful speech;

Therein will be a running spring;

Therein will be thrones (of dignity) raised on high;

Goblets placed (ready);
And cushions set in rows;

And rich carpets (all) spread out.

(Cont'd)

# Day 349

    The beautiful selected passage of today reinforces the importance of faith, the most vital component of success, very beautifully and effectively, using examples that are most fitting and that everyone can relate to. In regard to the other vital component of success, i.e. performance of righteous deeds or good actions as a result of faith, we are provided with the examples of what to expect as a result of performing them as a manifestation of faith. The examples given of a camel (or indeed any living being ), the sky (and its beauty, vastness and the order in it), the mountains (and their strength and how they are fixed firmly), and the earth (with its beauty, vastness and all the wonders that it holds) should encourage all individuals to ask themselves where such wonders come from. They should ask themselves "Who created these wonders, provided order from disorder, and sustains them?" Certainly it cannot be by chance. Certainly it cannot be from several, or a multitude of sources, due to the obvious likelihood of conflict among them. The only logical conclusion remains, from the senses endowed to us of seeing, hearing, and reasoning, for the Source for those and everything else in existence: God, the Most Great, the Creator of all that exists, and the Creator of order. Once an individual attains faith, the performance of righteous deeds, and praise, glorification and worship of God, is the next logical step – which is the reason for man's - and indeed all - creation and existence. All of mankind will be judged on the Day of Judgment by God – the day that will be overwhelming in nature, and every soul will be rewarded or punished accordingly. Those who desire success must keep this day in mind.

    On the Day of Judgment, those who denied faith and refused to submit themselves to God, the Creator and Sustainer of all, will be weary and laboring hard. They will be informed of their failure and their severe punishment in hell, where they will abide for eternity – including the worst food, drink, hunger and suffering. One can ask "Why does God, Who is Most Loving and Most Kind, dispense such suffering?" The answer lies in the severity of the offenses by the man or woman who denied faith and God, denied His authority and did not serve Him, while enjoying His Beneficence and Mercy every moment of his life, and at the same time working against Him. Additionally, having been assigned with the most precious assets throughout his person, including sight, hearing and reasoning, he wasted them, instead of thanking and using them to serve the One Who provided them. Certainly the punishment is fitting of the degree of offense. As for those fortunate individuals who attained faith, they will recognize the Day of Judgment as per their preparation, being joyful and pleased with their striving, in a garden with running springs, on thrones with cushions, rich carpets and goblets of pleasant drink which will not make them drowsy, and therein they will hear no ill speech: **this is success,** a fitting reward for those who strived in their life to serve and please God, the Most Great, the Creator and Sustainer of all.

    The seeker of success who wishes to reach his goal has absolute faith in God, the Most Glorious, the Giver of life and the Creator of death, and in His beloved messenger, Muhammad. He appreciates the marvels in living beings, as well as other creations, such as the earth, mountains, and the sky, pointing towards the Glory and Magnificence of their Creator; he praises and worships God, the Creator and Sustainer of all that exists often, and strives to serve Him with righteous deeds, with awe and gratefulness. He is certain of the Day of Judgment and prepares for it accordingly.

**Do they not look at the camels, how they are made?**

**And at the sky, how it is raised high?**

**And at the mountains, how they are fixed firm?**

**And the earth, how it is spread out?**

(88:1-20)

# Day 350

(To the righteous soul will be said:) "O you, the one in (complete) rest and satisfaction!

"Come back to your Lord, well pleased (yourself) and well pleasing (into him)!

"Enter, then, among My (honored) devotees!

"And, enter My paradise!".

(89:28-30)

# Day 350

    The beautiful selected passage of today gives an excellent description of the end result that one would hope for in his pursuit of success; it gives a general description of the factors required for reaching that end point. It relies on imagery and visualization of already having attained the point of highest of success, so the pursuant could then be sufficiently motivated to find his path to the desired point. Further details on how to reach the blessed state of success are amply available in numerous other passages in the Holy Quran as well as this collection of meditations.

    The date of reference for the beautiful selected passage of today is the Day of Judgment, a day of great calamity and destruction throughout the earth. Arising from the great calamity will be the resurrection of every individual who ever lived, to be held accountable for all his actions during his life on earth, in front of God, the Most Great, the Gatherer and Restorer. Those who denied faith or God and the Day of Judgment, will recognize their folly – but it will be too late, for that is the Day for results to be known and the exam of life would have been over just prior to its start. Those who believed in God, the Almighty, the Bestower of Honors and the Humiliator, and performed righteous deeds as a manifestation of their faith, will also recognize the events of the Day of Judgment– serene and joyful, for having prepared themselves throughout their life for that event. It will be said to such fortunate individuals: "Come back to your Lord well-pleased (yourself) and well-pleasing (into Him)!". The righteous believers will then be honored by God, the Most Magnificent and the Best Rewarder, with the most coveted reward and invitation: "Enter then among my (honored) devotees! And enter my paradise!". **This is the highest success, and should be the object of all desire.**

    The seeker of success who wishes to reach his goal has absolute faith in God, the Most Great, the Creator of all that exists, the Giver of life, Creator of death, and the Resurrector, and in His noble messenger, Muhammad. He knows for certainty of the Day of Judgment, when he will appear before his God's tribunal (blessed be His Name), to account for his acts in the life of this world, and prepares himself in this life accordingly.

# Day 351

I do call to witness this city (Makkah);

And you (O Muhammad) are a freeman of this city.

And by (the mystic ties of) parent and child.
Indeed we have created man into toil and struggle.

Does he think that none has power over him?
He may say (boastfully): "I have wasted wealth in abundance!".

Does he think that none sees him?

Have We not made for him a pair of eyes?

And a tongue, and a pair of lips?

And shown him the two highways (the steep or difficult path of virtue, and the easy path of vice or rejection of God)?

But he has made no haste on the path that is steep.

And what will explain to you the path that is steep?

(It is) freeing a neck (of a slave);

Or the giving of food in a day of hunger (famine)

(Cont'd)

# Day 351

The beautiful selected passage of today again reinforces the two primary components of success for our benefit: Faith and performance of righteous deeds or good actions. Like some other chapters of the Holy Quran, it opens with reference to particular things of wonder. In today's beautiful selected passage, it is the city of Mecca and the mystic ties of parent and child, signifying evidence of God's involvement in such things. After a brief but notable introduction to faith and accountability for one's actions, it goes into more details, specifying what constitutes righteous actions.

Man is reminded in the beautiful selected passage of today that his life is expected to consist of toil and struggle. We are reminded that every individual will be held accountable for his actions, and how man will regret wasting an opportunity to do good with the wealth that he had in the world, upon reflection on the Day of Judgment, when he will be called to account for his actions and how he used the resources (wealth) provided to him. He is reminded of the treasures bestowed on him – of eyes to see, and tongue and lips to speak. This is an invitation to faith in God, the All-seeing and the All-hearing, and man's accountability to Him. Along with the precious gifts of seeing and speaking, it also refers to man having been shown two paths – a steep and difficult path of virtue, and an easy path of vice – and indicates man's preference for the easy path, although the steep path is more beneficial for him.

Examples of righteous actions on the path that is steep but virtuous and desirable that are listed in the beautiful selected passage of today include easing others' hardships, such as freeing of a slave, and giving of food to the hungry orphan and the poor. Performance of these kind acts indicates one who has attained faith, and who recommends to another the virtue of patience and the performance of deeds of kindness and compassion, including charity. Such individuals will, then, be among those who attain **success of the highest kind**, and will become the dwellers of paradise forever. On the other hand, those who reject the signs of God, the Most Great and the Creator and Sustainer of all, and who choose the easy path of vice, will become in the life after death, the dwellers of hell, with the misery from fire all around over them.

The seeker of success who wishes to reach his goal has uncompromising faith in God, the All-powerful, the Best Guide and the Light, and in His beloved messenger, Muhammad. He knows that success is hard work, requiring struggle throughout life, and chooses the steep path of virtue over the easy path of vice - utilizing the wealth and other treasures that have been provided to him by God, the Most Rich and the Best Judge.

To the orphan with claims of relationship,

Or to the poor (down) in the dust.
Then will he be of those who believed, and recommended one another to patience (constancy and self-restraint) and recommended one another to deeds of kindness and compassion.

Such are the companions of the right hand (the dwellers of paradise).

But those who reject Our signs, they are the (unhappy) companions of the left hand (the dwellers of hell) –

On them will be fire vaulted over (all around).

(90:1-20)

# Day 352

By the sun and its brightness.

By the moon as it follows it (the sun).

By the day as it shows up (the sun's) brightness.

By the night as it conceals it (the sun).

By the heaven and Him Who built it.

By the earth and Him Who spread it.

By the soul, and the proportion and order given to it;

And its enlightenment as to wrong and right.

<u>Truly, he succeeds who purifies it (the soul).</u>

<u>And he fails who corrupts it (soul).</u>

(91:1-10)

# Day 352

    The beautiful selected passage of today again reinforces the two most vital components of success for our benefit: faith and righteous deeds or good actions. Its emphasis is on acquisition of faith for the unfortunate individual who lacks it, and on strengthening of faith for the fortunate individual who is already in possession of it. It is one of the most beautiful and moving passages in the Holy Quran, and also one of the most memorable and effective ones - especially as it pertains to attainment of success.

    The most awe-inspiring things in routine observation are first listed, including the sun and the moon, the day as it shows the sun's brightness and the night as it conceals it, along with heaven (the sky) and earth. By these verses, we can follow the enlightenment of the beloved prophet Abraham, when he progressed from dissociating himself from worship of particular things, no matter how magnificent they are, to the worship and devotion only to the One Who created all that is in existence: This is the essence of faith; and acquisition of it, in addition to the above, includes recognition that the noble messenger Muhammad completed the line of prophethood by transmitting the final and perfected message to mankind from God, the Creator and Sustainer of all that exists, as Mercy for the benefit to the worlds, as described in the Holy Quran.

    The climax of the beautiful selected passage of today is related to the identification of the soul as one of the signs and wonders of the existence of God, and the proportion and order given to it in what we observe as human form. It is also given enlightenment as to wrong and right, indicating, perhaps, the ability of the soul to distinguish between right and wrong, or to recognize guidance sent to man subsequently by God, the Most Wise and the Best Guide, through His messengers to mankind. However, there is no question about the conclusion of the beautiful selected passage of today, which is of utmost importance to the seeker of success, specifically that truly he succeeds who "purifies it (his soul)" and he fails who "corrupts it". This reference is clearly made to the acceptance of the message of the noble prophet Muhammad to have faith in God, the Most Pure, the Exalter and the Abaser, submitting to God Almighty (rather than his base desires or the accursed Satan) and performing righteous deeds as a result. The reference to corrupting one's soul is to the denying of the message of the noble prophet Muhammad of having faith in and refusal in submitting oneself to God, the Most Glorious and the Compeller.

    The seeker of success who wishes to reach his goal has complete faith in God, the Most Great, the Creator and the Best Guide, and in His beloved messenger, Muhammad. He submits himself to God, Who is the Lord of all that exists, glorifies His name, and performs righteous deeds as a manifestation of his faith - as a result of which he purifies his soul.

# Day 353

By the night as it conceals (the light);

By the day as it appears in glory;

By (the mystery of) the Creator of male and female;

Indeed (the ends) you strive for are diverse.

So he who gives (in charity) and fears (God),

And (in all sincerity) testifies to the best -

We will indeed make smooth for him the path for ease (goodness).

But he who is a greedy miser and thinks himself self-sufficient,

And gives lie to the best -

We will indeed make smooth for him the path to misery.

Nor will his wealth profit him when he falls headlong (in destruction in hell).

Indeed we take upon Ourself to guide, and certainly unto Us (belongs) the end and the beginning.

Therefore, I do warn you of a fire blazing fiercely;

None shall reach it but those most unfortunate ones -

(Cont'd)

# Day 353

    The two fundamental components of success - faith in God the Most Beneficent and Merciful as relayed to us through His noble messenger Muhammad, and performance of righteous deeds or good actions as a result of faith, are again reinforced in the beautiful selected passage of today for our benefit. It focuses an actions performed by men (both good and bad) and makes relatively useful and detailed comparisons and contrasts between those actions which will lead to failure and those which will lead to the attainment of success. In regards to faith, we are asked to think about the multitude of signs of God's presence: the night, the day, and the mystery of the creation of male and female and the role of God the Almighty, Knower of all and the Manifest and Hidden, in these examples, through the message relayed to us by the noble prophet Muhammad. Next, peoples' actions as groups are examined and it is recognized that the ends for which they strive are diverse. This provides an excellent opportunity for us to benefit from knowing which actions are desirable and which are undesirable in the sight of God the Most Righteous Teacher and the Best Guide to repentance.

    The undesirable actions in the sight of God, the Most Great, the Judge, and the Just, are listed as being miserly, being arrogant and thinking oneself to be self sufficient, and giving lie to the best - most likely reference to denying the message of the noble prophet Muhammad in submitting oneself to God, the Source of all power and the Compeller. A reference is made the second time to those "who give lie to the truth and turn their backs", again referring to those denying the message from God, glorified be His Name, by His beloved prophet Muhammad in accepting God, the Creator and Sustainer of all, and refusal to living one's life to praise, worship and serve Him - their path to misery and further evil deeds in this life will be made easier for them. The wealth that those engaging in undesirable actions accumulate - and cite as proof of their success, will be of no use to them on the Day of Judgment, when they will be thrown into the pit of destruction - for eternity.

    The desirable actions in the sight of God the Most Loving and Most Patient, are listed as being one who fears God, giving charity, testifying sincerely in the message brought by the noble prophet Muhammad to worship none but God, submitting oneself to Him and performing righteous deeds as a manifestation of his faith, devoting himself to his Lord, and spending one's wealth only to seek the pleasure of his Lord Most High, and not expecting a reward or favor from anyone else in return; such will find the path to ease and goodness further made easier, and be saved from a terrible destruction in hell reserved for those engaging in undesirable actions, and they are reassured of having attainment of complete satisfaction in the near future. One should note that it is up to God the All-knowing and Most Wise, to guide man by His Mercy - but man's intentions, actions and sincerity will determine to which direction he will be guided, as we reviewed in the earlier meditations.

    The seeker of success who wishes to reach his goal has absolute faith in God the Most Magnificent, the Highest, the Most Glorious and the Best Guide, and in His noble messenger Muhammad, and in the message brought by him for worshipping none except God, the Most Holy and the Source of all that exists, performing righteous deeds as a manifestation of his faith, devoting himself to his Lord, and spending from his wealth only for the pleasure of his Lord and not expecting a reward or favor from anyone else. He refrains from arrogance and miserliness.

Who give the lie to the truth and turn their backs.
But those most devoted to God shall be removed far from it –

Those who spend their wealth for increase in self-purification;

And have in their minds no favor from anyone for which a reward is expected in return –

But only the desire to seek the pleasure of their Lord Most High;

**<u>And soon will they attain (complete) Satisfaction.</u>**

(92:1-21)

# Day 354

Have We not opened your breast for you (O Muhammad)?

And removed from you your burden,

Which weighed down your back?

And have We not raised high your fame?

Indeed with every hardship there is relief;

Indeed with every hardship there is relief.

Therefore, when you are finished (from your task), devote yourself in God's worship;

And to your Lord (Alone), turn (all) your intentions and hopes.

(94:1–8)

# Day 354

The beautiful selected passage of today takes an example from the beloved prophet Muhammad's life, which was used by God, the Most Great, the Best Guide and the Most Righteous teacher, in providing him with further guidance. This example was additionally used to provide guidance to all, as well, in their pursuit of success. It is one of the most beautiful, effective, practical and useful passages for all – and especially for those in pursuit of success. It can be considered a great motivational passage, in addition to containing invaluable Guidance.

The early part of the beloved prophet Muhammad's life, when he first started receiving revelations from God, the Most Beneficent and Most Merciful, to deliver His message to the worlds for Guidance from their Lord, was quite difficult – with great resistance from various quarters; one of the most ardent foes being his own uncle. With persistence, over many years, and with the help of God, the Almighty and the Best Friend and Protector, the noble prophet Muhammad was successful in his endeavor in delivering God's message, blessed be His Name, and in his own lifetime attained significant fame. At the point that the noble prophet had been successful in his task of delivering God' message, the Most Merciful and the Best Guide, had attained relief of hardship, and had elevation of his fame, he was instructed through today's beautiful selected passage, that in his time of ease, he should turn to God for continued devotion and worship and continue to strive to please Him. This also applies to the rest of the faithful.

In the beautiful selected passage of today, using the example of the beloved prophet Muhammad's life, a generalization and observation for reflection for all mankind was made: That with every hardship there is relief. The level of hardship has a great range, but its importance lies in guidance on what to do after the relief from hardship: Devote yourself to the worship of God, the Most Forbearing and Most Compassionate, turning all intentions and hopes towards Him, and hoping to please Him. It is also useful to reinforce, especially during the suffering of hardship, that with every hardship there is relief; this is a promise from God, the Most Kind, Most Loving, the Truth and the Most Trustworthy.

The seeker of success who wishes to reach his goal has uncompromising faith in God, the Most Great, the Constrictor and the Reliever, and in His noble messenger, Muhammad. When experiencing hardship, he remembers that with every hardship, God, the Most Merciful and the Most Kind, has promised him relief. After attaining relief from the hardship, he devotes himself to the worship of God, blessed be His Name, turning all his intentions and hopes towards Him, and strives to attain His pleasure.

# Day 355

By the fig and the olive;

And the Mount Sinai;

And this city of security (Makkah).

We have indeed created man in the best of moulds,

Then do we abase him (to be) the lowest of the low,

Except such as believe and do righteous deeds, for they shall have a reward unfailing.

Then what can, after this, contradict you as to the Judgment (to come)?

Is not God the Wisest of judges?

(95:1-8)

# Day 355

The beautiful selected passage of today again reinforces the two primary components of success for our benefit: Faith and righteous deeds as a result of faith. It is concise, yet effective in covering the most important components of success. It is memorable in its use of language, imagery and example for persuasion. First, faith and belief in God, the All-powerful and Most Great, is invoked, with the reminder of some things known to the initial audience in Makkah of the signs of God's existence, glorified be His Name: the fig and the olive (and their beauty and usefulness), the Mount Sinai (with the great event associated with it, of the meeting there between the honorable prophet Moses and God, the Creator and Sustainer of all), and the great city of Makkah itself, with its security and the blessings of God, the Almighty and the Source of peace.

Next, the importance of righteous deeds is stated. God, the Most Glorious and the Truth, informs us that man is created in the best of moulds, and that he has the capacity to become the lowest of the low, unless he believes in God, the Most Great and Most Glorious, as relayed through the message of the noble prophet Muhammad, and does righteous deeds. If left to his own accord, man's actions are selfish, base, and harmful to himself and others, congruent with the lowest ethical standards, described as a "dog-eat-dog" philosophy.

The beautiful selected passage of today closes by informing us about the consequence of striving against one's own self and whatever stands in the way of faith, and consequently performing righteous deeds: for such will be a reward unfailing - both in this life, and on the Day of Judgment, when man will be held accountable for all his actions by God, Who is the Wisest Judge, and is Most Just. The consequences of rejecting faith and God (blessed be His Name) are alluded to, by the terminology used for such individuals, who become the "lowest of the low". What is it, then, that prevents an individual from having faith and preparing himself for the Day of Judgment?

The seeker of success who wishes to reach his goal has complete faith in God, the Light, the Guide, and the Wisest of judges, and in His beloved prophet, Muhammad. He strives against his own self and whatever else stands in his way, with faith in God, the Creator and Sustainer of all, and performance of righteous deeds. He is certain of the Day of Judgment, and prepares himself accordingly.

# Day 356

Read! In the name of your Lord and Cherisher Who created (all that exists);

Created man, out of a (mere) clot of congealed blood.

Read! And your Lord is Most Generous, (It is He) Who taught (man the use of writing by the pen);

Taught man that which he knew not.

(96:1-5)

# Day 356

The beautiful selected passage of today again reinforces the two primary components of success: faith and righteous deeds or good actions. It has great significance also because these were the first verses revealed to the noble prophet Muhammad from God, the Creator, Owner and Sustainer of all that exists, through the angel Gabriel.

Faith in God, the Lord and Cherisher of all that exists, is relayed in the beautiful selected passage of today, with the use of the example of the creation of man and all his intricate organs and body parts out of a mere clot of congealed blood. The use of the example of the development of man in the fascinating and informative verses is brilliance par excellence, for even though the signs of God's existence are everywhere, and He is the Creator of all that exists, man need not look any further than his own body for the existence of God, Who fashioned the clot into different body parts with wonderful symmetry, and breath-taking intricacies in every portion of the body. He also fashioned the mere clot with the most valuable assets, including eyes to see, ears to hear, tongue and lips to speak, mind and heart to reason.

In order to further strengthen man's faith, he is instructed to read – which will open up for him countless arenas leading to the signs of existence of God, the All- Encompassing and the Most Glorious. The fact that man is able to read in and of itself is a sign of God's existence, blessed be His Name, and it is referred to in the beautiful selected passage of today as an example of His generosity. Reading can also fall among the performance of righteous deeds when it is used to seek Guidance in the Holy Quran, from God, the All-knowing and the Most Righteous Teacher, to read the works of others in praise of God, the Most Praiseworthy and most Great, and to increase one's knowledge in anything else that will help him to better appreciate and understand the world and existence. All increase in knowledge leads to better appreciation for God's existence and abilities, and to engage in increased praise, worship and ability to serve God, the Most Glorious and the One deserving of all praise

The seeker of success who wishes to reach his goal has absolute faith in God, the Most Generous, the Lord and Cherisher, Who created and sustains all that exists, and in His noble messenger, Muhammad. He engages in reading generally to learn, and specifically to reading the Holy Quran to obtain Guidance from God, the Most Wise and the Most Righteous Teacher- which can better help him to praise, worship and serve his Lord and Cherisher.

# Day 357

We have indeed revealed this (Quran) in the night of power.

And what will explain to you what the night of power is?

The night of power is better than a thousand months.

In it descend the angels and the spirit (Gabriel) by their Lord's permission, with all commands (for the coming year).

Peace (all that night)! Until the appearance of dawn.

(97:1-5)

# Day 357

Although all days are important and provide an opportunity to praise, worship, perform righteous deeds, and seek the rewards from God, the Owner of all and the Lord of all majesty and reward, certain days carry more significance than others. For the student, the day of the exam carries more significance than other days; and for the politician, the day of election carries more significance. In the beautiful selected passage of today, we are informed of a night of great significance in the entire year – this is the night in which the Holy Quran, with its message to mankind and the worlds, was first revealed. It is generally one of the last ten nights of the holy month of Ramadan in the Arabic calendar, expected in the odd nights, and is known as the Night of Power.

In the Night of Power, we are informed that the angels and the spirit (Gabriel) descend with all commands and decrees from God, the Source of all power, the King, and the Creator and Sustainer of all that exists, for the coming year. The commands and decrees for the coming year are specified as "all commands" and this would signify major and minor issues. It is reported to be better than a thousand months. Therefore, if we count the time spent in one night spent in praise, glorification and worship of God, glorified be His Name – which falls in the highest forms of righteous deeds that will be rewarded by God, the Owner of all and the Most Generous One – then the night spent in praise, glorification, and worship of God, the Truth and the Most Trustworthy, would be equal to one thousand months, or eighty three years. Throughout the night is reported to be peace, until the appearance of dawn. An individual interested in the pursuit of success, based on its significance and the return compared to investment, would indeed pay special attention to the Night of Power in the end of Ramadan.

The seeker of success who wishes to reach his goal has uncompromising faith in God, the Most Pure, the Owner of all, and the Lord of all majesty and reward, and in His beloved messenger, Muhammad. He realizes the special significance of the Night of Power generally expected to occur in one of the last ten nights of the holy month of Ramadan (in the odd nights), and he spends that night in extra praise, worship and devotion to his Lord.

# Day 358

**<u>Those who have faith and do righteous deeds – they are the best of creatures.</u>**

**Their reward is with their Lord: gardens of eternity, beneath which rivers flow; they will dwell therein forever – God well-pleased with them, and they with Him; all this for such as fear their Lord and Cherisher.**

(98:7-8)

# Day 358

    The primary ingredients of success – faith and performance of righteous deeds or good actions as a manifestation of faith – are again reinforced for our benefit in the beautiful selected passage of today, with some distinguishing features that give it its uniqueness, and also add further information to help us in the pursuit of success. In regard to knowledge that is reinforced for our benefit and mentioned a number of times earlier, faith (in God and in his noble messenger, Muhammad) and performance of righteous deeds (as a manifestation of the faith) are the primary requirements for success, for which one will be rewarded by God, the Best Guide and the Most Generous, on the Day of Judgment– with gardens of eternity, beneath which rivers flow, to abide therein forever. It is worth mentioning again that reinforcement of important points previously elucidated is an indication of their importance and of a concern for successful outcome by the teacher for his students, and God is indeed the Most Kind and the Most Righteous Teacher.

    In regard to the distinguishing features of the beautiful selected passage of today, beyond the reinforced points that are of vital importance, it is worth noting that those who have faith and perform righteous deeds as a result of it, are classified as the best of creatures. This is indeed an honor, considering that it is coming from God, the Greatest and the Owner of all that exists. Additionally, besides the reward of paradise with gardens of eternity, beneath which rivers flow, to dwell therein forever, one who has faith and performs righteous deeds, keeping in mind the Day of Judgment and thus the fear of his Lord, will be pleased with God, the Most Generous and the Most Appreciative One, and God (Glorified be His Name) will be pleased with him. As any typical child knows, far better than any reward he receives from his parent, is typically the approval and pleasure he senses from the parent who is pleased with his actions. Then how much greater would be man's reaction, when his Creator and the Creator and Sustainer of all that exists, expresses His pleasure with an individual and congratulates him or her on a job well done? That may indeed be worth greater than the reward of paradise itself for someone who has a great degree of love for God the Most Compassionate and the Most Loving .

    The seeker of success who wishes to reach his goal has complete faith in God, the Most Beneficent, Most Merciful and the Lord and Cherisher of the worlds, and in His noble messenger, Muhammad. He performs righteous deeds as a manifestation of his faith and fears meeting with his Lord on the Day of Judgment, when he will be brought in His presence, to be held accountable for all his actions in the life of this world. He is reassured that having faith and performing righteous deeds as a manifestation of faith, places him in the category of the best among creation, as designated by God, the Creator and Sustainer of all.

# Day 359

When the earth is shaken to its (final) convulsion,

And the earth throws up its contents (from within);

And man cries (distressed): "What is the matter with it?"

On that day will it declare its tidings (about all that happened over it of good or evil);

Because your Lord will inspire it.

On that day will men proceed in companies sorted out, to be shown the deeds that they had done.

Then shall anyone who has done an atom's weight of good, see it!

And anyone who has done an atom's weight of evil, shall see it!

(99:1-8)

# Day 359

The beautiful selected passage of today again reinforces the two primary components of success for our benefit: Faith and performance of righteous deeds as a result of faith - which it does in a memorable and effective manner, and relays the grave nature of the events associated with the Day of Judgment, and which is its distinguishing feature. It provides additional information, along with the reinforced material, that is useful for one in pursuit of success. The belief in the end of life as we know it, on a day of catastrophe and resurrection of all individuals who ever lived, to account for their action in life – also known as the Day of Judgment– is a crucial component of faith, because God is the Creator, Giver and Taker of life, as well as the Resurrector; it is to Him and no one else that man should turn for help, give praise, serve, and worship. This is the essence of faith (while believing in God's message (blessed be His Name) to mankind through His beloved prophet, Muhammad). Performance of righteous deeds for the sake of God, the Wisest Judge and the All-Aware, is of importance – for He will judge every individual on the Day of Judgment, and reward or punish him or her accordingly. Briefly, this is how the vital components – faith and righteous deeds – are related to success, and why, therefore, they are reinforced throughout the Holy Quran and this collection of meditations for the benefit of the seeker of success.

We find particular details in the beautiful selected passage of today that are of interest, particularly that the final event signaling the end of life will be a convulsion, meaning earthquake or earth quakes. Additionally, we are informed that men will be placed in groups and shown the results of their performance i.e., poor, good, or excellent. The most distinguishing characteristic of the beautiful selected passage of today, differentiating it from others containing similar information, and which is of significant benefit to one in pursuit of success, is the information that anyone who has done an atom's weight of good shall see it (and be recompensed for it) on that day, and that anyone who has done an atom's weight of evil shall also see it (and be recompensed for it). This signifies that we should be careful of all our actions - no matter how small, because they either help us or harm us when it counts most, i.e. on the Day of Judgment.

The seeker of success who wishes to reach his goal has absolute faith in God, the Most Great, the Giver and Taker of life, the Resurrector and the Judge, and in His beloved messenger, Muhammad. He performs righteous deeds as a manifestation of his faith. He is certain of the occurrence of the Day of Judgment and prepares himself accordingly; he knows that anyone who has done an atom's weight of good or evil will see it that day and be recompensed for it.

# Day 360

Truly man is to his Lord, ungrateful;

And to that (fact) he bears witness (by his deeds);

And passionate is he in his love of wealth.

Does he not know that when the contents of the graves are poured forth (all mankind is resurrected);

And that which is (locked up) in (human) breasts is made manifest;

That their Lord had been well-acquainted with them (even to) that day?

(100: 6-11)

# Day 360

The beautiful selected passage of today again reinforces the two primary components of success for our benefit: Faith and performance of righteous deeds. It has much in common with the meditation of yesterday. Its distinctiveness relates to the additional information related to the main topic of reinforcement and which makes it quite memorable and effective in highlighting the importance of the main topic, i.e. faith and action.

As we reviewed in yesterday's beautiful selected passage, the belief in God's abilities as All-powerful, Creator of all, the Giver and Taker of life, Who will resurrect all individuals to account for their actions on the Day of Judgment, while believing in the prophethood of the noble Muhammad, is a central component of faith; this is related to the relationship of the performance of righteous deeds, as one of the two primary components of success – although a case can be made that one whose faith and love for God, Who created him and everything else that exists, will praise, worship, and serve Him only for the sake of his love and pleasure, regardless of whether he will be recompensed for it or not.

The knowledge that is reinforced in the beautiful selected passage of today, and has been cited in the passage reviewed yesterday, is that all of mankind will be resurrected (on the Day of Judgment), that everyone's secrets (intentions) will become manifest, and that it will become known that God, the Almighty, the All-seeing, and All-hearing, had been acquainted with all that they did - in open and secret, and all they intended (and which will be rewarded or punished accordingly).

The knowledge that is distinctive in the beautiful selected passage of today and makes the above points memorable is the reference to man's passion for wealth in the life of this world, which makes him forget his duties to his Lord and his purpose in life, which is truly a sign of ungratefulness to God, Who created him, and provided him with countless treasures, including eyes to see, ears to hear, tongue to speak, and a mind and heart to reason, and Who provides sustenance and nourishment to him, and that man bears witness to his ungratefulness by his deeds, i.e. including the tendency to give priority to accumulating wealth in the world and to forget his duties to his Lord.

The seeker of success who wishes to reach his goal has uncompromising faith in God, the Almighty, the Creator of all, the Originator and the Restorer, and in His noble messenger, Muhammad. He performs righteous deeds as a manifestation of his faith. The love of this world does not supersede for him the love he has for his Lord.

# Day 361

The striking hour (i.e. the Day of Judgment).

What is the striking hour?

And what will explain to you what the striking hour is?

(It is) a day in which men will be like moths scattered about.

And the mountains will be like carded wool.

Then he whose balance (of good deeds) will be (found) heavy,

Will be in a life of good pleasure and satisfaction.

But he whose balance (of good deeds) will be (found) light,

Will have his home in a (bottomless) pit (hell).

And what will explain to you what this is?

(It is) a fire blazing fiercely!

(101:1-11)

# Day 361

The beautiful selected passage of today again reinforces the two primary components of success for our benefit: Faith in God, the Originator and the Resurrector, as relayed to us through His noble messenger, Muhammad, and the performance of righteous deeds as a manifestation of faith. The most fundamental component of success, faith, is conveyed in the beautiful selected passage of today with reference to God's ability and plan to cause an end to current life as we know it, on the Day of Judgment, and to resurrect all individuals who ever lived, to judge their actions in the life of this world, and either reward or punish them accordingly. This is the fundamental component of faith (when it exists with the belief in the prophethood of the beloved Muhammad), and is therefore repeated and reinforced to the extent we find in the Holy Quran. Therefore, the second vital component of success, performance of righteous deeds is closely linked to the first vital component, i.e. faith, as its manifestation. The end of our current life and beginning of a new, more important one, will begin in a catastrophic manner, as described in the Holy Quran. We can expect a series of cataclysmic events, heralded by the blowing of a trumpet, with severe earthquakes, the splitting of the sky, which will become red like red-oil, as described in various passages in the Holy Quran, and referred to as the striking hour in the very important passage of today. It is a terrible day in which men will be like moths scattered about, and the mountains will become like carded wool.

Although we have a general picture of what will follow on the Day of Judgment, when every individual will be presented before God, the Creator of all, the Judge and the Most Just, to be held accountable for all his actions in the life of this world, the distinctive feature of the very important passage of today, is the explanation comparing the weight of one's good deeds to that of one's bad deeds. The individuals whose balance of good deeds outweigh the bad deeds will be deemed successful, to live in the hereafter for eternity a life of good pleasure and satisfaction; and those whose balance of good deeds will be lighter than bad deeds, sent to reside in hell – as in a bottomless pit of fire blazing fiercely. The presence of some bad deeds even in those who are successful, is indicative of the human nature of imperfection. However, the outweighing of the bad deeds by good ones is indicative of one's striving, and of being successful in overcoming the base aspects of oneself, as well as the evil in the world. But why such a severe punishment in the blazing fire? The answer is that the nature of the offenses calls for such a severe punishment. The offenses include taking responsibility of priceless treasures, such as sight, hearing, speaking and reasoning, and then wasting them for one's pleasure; dereliction of duty that one has been charged with and created for; and treason, for working against the One Who created and sustained him and provided nourishment to him throughout his life.

The seeker of success who wishes to reach his goal has complete faith in God, the Greatest, the Maker of order, the Shaper of beauty, the Giver and Taker of life, the Restorer and the Most equitable One, and in His beloved messenger, Muhammad. He performs righteous deeds as a manifestation of his faith. He knows of the certainty of the Day of Judgment, and that he will be held accountable for all his actions on the Day of Judgment, and prepares himself accordingly. Although he knows that he is not perfect, he strives against his base self and the evil of the world, and seeks forgiveness from his Lord for his imperfections, and seeks His Guidance. The balance of his good deeds, on the Day of Judgment, outweighs that of the balance of his bad deeds.

# Day 362

The mutual rivalry for piling up (the good things of this world), diverts you (from the more serious things) —

Until you enter the graves.

But you soon shall know!

Again, you soon shall know!

And, were you to know with certainty of mind, (you would beware!)

You shall certainly see hell-fire!

And again you shall see it with certainty of sight!

Then you shall be questioned that day (Day of Judgment) about the joy (you indulged in)!

(102: 1-8)

# Day 362

The beautiful selected passage of today again reinforces, for our benefit, the two primary components of success: faith and performance of righteous deeds as a manifestation of faith. In addition, it provides insight into a common and often overlooked practice that can be a significant impediment to the attainment of success, which is the distinguishing feature of the beautiful selected passage of today, and helps to highlight and retain the main point for practical daily use. The points reinforced from the previous passages involve faith in God, the All-Seeing and All-Hearing, as relayed to us through His beloved prophet, Muhammad, and performance of righteous deeds as a result of this faith. It also includes reminder about the important concept of resurrection and in being held accountable to God, the Most Great and the Most Just, on the Day of Judgment for all of one's actions in life, and to be punished or rewarded accordingly.

The distinguishing feature of today's beautiful selected passage, which is a short chapter in the Holy Quran, with the title "The Piling Up", refers to the accumulation of material things of this world – and the mutual rivalry for this purpose, which is often mistaken as pursuit of success; this tends to divert man from engaging in more serious things – actually, the things required from him and the reason for his existence, i.e. to worship his Creator and Sustainer, and the performance of righteous deeds to serve Him. If man persists on this dangerous track, he will have failed to fulfill the purpose for which he was created, because of his distraction from the pursuit of piling up of the material things in life, in rivalry with others, for which he will be questioned on the Day of Judgment. If man is not careful in regard to pursuing the duties for which he was created and neglects them for the sake of the life of this world, he will incur an appropriate punishment, which is listed as hell-fire (for eternity), and God is the Knower of all, Most Wise.

The seeker of success who wishes to reach his goal has absolute faith in God, the Light, the Guide, and the Most Righteous Teacher, and in His noble messenger, Muhammad. He participates in praise, worship, and performance of other righteous deeds in the service of his Lord, and does not let the desire for the piling up of material things in this life, in mutual rivalry with others, divert him from more serious things and from the reason for his existence.

# Day 363

By (the token of) time.

Indeed, man is in a state of loss,

Except such as those who have faith, and do righteous deeds, and (join together) in the mutual teaching of the Truth and of patience and constancy.

(103:1-3)

# Day 363

    The beautiful selected passage of today is relatively short. However, it summarizes some of the most important concepts of success in an extraordinarily brilliant form. The beautiful selected passage of today opens with the mention of time, and how, with the passing of it, man is in a state of loss. Certainly, man is no angel – for angels have no choice in their behavior; they behave only in a way and purpose for which God, the Most Great and the Creator of all, has created them. Man, however, has a choice to make at every second of his existence: Will he choose what is easy for him in the short term, but can be harmful in the long run? And what will be the cumulative end result?

    The perceptive reader will have noted that God, the Most Wise and the All-Aware swears by certain important things in the Holy Quran such as the sun, moon, and the stars. Here is a good opportunity to understand the importance - which is so valuable that once it is gone, it can never be returned. Therefore, the fact that we can either use it for our benefit or for our harm by performing good actions, or neglecting our duties, is something that the seeker of success must appreciate as a fundamental component of success. Indeed, on the Day of Judgment, those who are deemed failures, will beg to be placed back in time, so they can perform good actions based on faith in God, the Most Holy and the Source of all that exists.

    In one of the earlier passages that we also reflected on ( Day # 355), God, the All-knowing and Most Wise, informs us that He created man in the best of moulds, then abased him to be the lowest of the low, except for those who believe and do righteous deeds. Therefore, if left to his own accord, man will prefer what is beneficial for him in the short term and in the life of this world. In the sight of God, the Lord of the worlds and the Best Judge, this is a state of loss for man. We find the same answer in the beautiful selected passage of today as cited earlier regarding how to prevent this state of degradation in man: By having faith in God, the Creator and Sustainer of all, and performing righteous deeds. These are also the two primary components of success that we have noted to be reinforced throughout the Holy Quran, for our benefit. In addition to these two vital components frequently cited in the attainment of success, people are also instructed to exhort one another to truth and patience – so as to protect themselves from degradation, which leads to success, and to help others to also attain success.

    The seeker of success who wishes to reach his goal has uncompromising faith in God, the Most Great, the Best Guide, and the Most Patient One, and in His beloved messenger, Muhammad. He performs righteous deeds as a manifestation of his faith. He recommends others to attain and strengthen their faith, which leads them to perform righteous deeds, to search for the truth, and to practice patience.

# Day 364

Say: "He is God, the One and Only;

"God the Eternal, Absolute (Satisfier of all needs, Self-sufficient).

"He begets not, nor is He begotten;

"And there is none other like Him".

(112:1-4)

# Day 364

The beautiful selected passage of today consists of an entire chapter, which is one of the smallest ones in the Holy Quran. However, its significance to someone in pursuit of success is truly great from all aspects – literal, historical and spiritual. It is very appropriately titled "The Purity", for it purifies the faith and worship of God, the Most Great and the One and Only One, which had been misunderstood up to that time (of its revelation), when it was clarified or purified. How is this of importance to one in pursuit of success? As we have learned and seen reinforced a great number of times in this collection of passages and meditations, faith is the primary ingredient of success. Hence, the importance of purity in pursuit of success is based on its relationship to faith.

Considered from a purely literal aspect, the beautiful selected passage of today provides an excellent and thorough description of God as the Absolute Authority, signifying Self-sufficiency and not requiring anyone's assistance. God is Eternal, the One and Only – neither begetting nor having been begotten – and the Only One Who is deserving of our praise, worship, and devotion, for He is the Creator and Sustainer of all that exists. This is the essence of faith (along with the belief in the prophethood of the beloved Muhammad), the most vital component of success. Considered from historical aspects, although all communities, as we have been informed in the Holy Quran, by God, the All-Hearing and All-Seeing One, were sent guidance from Him, this guidance became corrupted with time, so that faith and worship were no longer for God Alone, blessed be His Name - but ranged from associating others in worship of God, as in polytheism, to worshipping an entity or entities based on the interpretation and reinterpretation of scholars, to confusing a messenger with, and worshipping him as God – a "milder" form of polytheism. Regardless, with the simple and pure declaration of the beautiful selected passage of today, worship has been restored to He Whose right it is Alone, and the path to success cleared of impediments – for the benefit of all future generations.

Considered from the spiritual aspect, two statements from the noble prophet Muhammad, who received the revelations from, God, the Creator and Sustainer of the worlds, to relay to mankind, and who has been recommended as the best example for man to follow by God Himself, in the Holy Quran, are worth reviewing: 1) the right of God on His slaves is that they should join none in worship with Him, and their right upon Him is that He will not punish them if they did so, and 2) his declaration that "By Him in Whose Hand is my soul, "It (the chapter of the Purity) is equal to one-third of the Quran". This relays to us the importance of the contents of beautiful selected passage of today and its relevance to the seekers of success. An important sign of an effective teacher is the relaying of the most profound concepts in the simplest possible format, losing none of their significance – but rather enhancing them, and of which, today's beautiful selected passage is an excellent example. And God is indeed the Most Wise and the Most Righteous Teacher.

The seeker of success who wishes to reach his goal has complete faith in God, the One and Only, the Eternal and the Only Self-sufficient One in existence, and in His noble messenger, Muhammad. He recognizes the folly of using impure ingredients in the pursuit of success, and utilizes the most pure form of faith (meaning worshipping and serving none besides God, the Most Holy and the Only One) – free of any adulterations, knowing that it is the most vital component of success.

# Day 365

Say: "I seek protection with (God), the Lord of mankind,

"The King of mankind,

"The God of mankind -

"From the evil of the whisperer (Satan, who withdraws after his whispering, after one remembers God),

"Who whispers into the hearts of mankind -

"Among jinn and among men".

(114:1-6)

# Day 365

    It is fitting that the last chapter in the Holy Quran, and the last passage selected for review in this collection of meditations on success, reinforces the two primary components of success: Faith and the performance of righteous deeds, striving against evil - both within oneself and externally, and invariably inspired by the accursed Satan. It used to be recited by the noble prophet Muhammad before going to sleep, and also when he became ill, signifying its importance and practical use. It is in itself a prayer, instructed by God, the Most Beneficent and Merciful, to the beloved prophet Muhammad and mankind, to assist in the pursuit of success.

    Faith in God, the Most Great and Most Powerful, is brilliantly explained in the beautiful selected passage of today, by reference to seeking His help and protection - referring to Him as King and Lord of mankind, which are titles sometimes given to men, but which the individuals possessing faith understand only belongs to God, the Owner of all that exists, and the Absolute King. Notice that reliance on only God is instructed, glorified be His Name, and that reliance on anyone else would be contrary to God's qualities as All-powerful and Supreme. Although reference is made to overcoming evil in today's beautiful selected passage (seeking only God's help and not of any other one or anything), it is an important component of faith that God, the Source of all power and the Best Protector, is sufficient for help in all circumstances.

    The main focus in today's beautiful selected passage is the solution to the main impediment that stands in our path to success, i.e. the accursed Satan, who has a lofty strategy to undermine our two greatest assets – faith and the performance of righteous deeds – by whispering his evil distractions in the hearts of mankind. However, we are instructed by God, the Most Beneficent and Most Merciful, that when the accursed Satan does engage in his strategy to prevent the attainment of one's success, by whispering evil into man's heart, to undermine his faith or the performance of righteous deeds, that we should seek the protection of God, the Most Great and the Best Protector, and the Satan's distractions will then exit from our heart, just as water extinguishes fire. Reference is made in today's beautiful selected passage to the existence of jinns along with mankind, and the Satan attempting his evil strategies against both man and jinn. As reported earlier in this collection of meditations, with the limited senses that we have, we are not able to sense the presence of jinns, just as we cannot sense the angels, even though they exist, as reported in the Holy Quran

    The seeker of success who wishes to reach his goal has absolute faith in God, the Most Compassionate, the Best Friend and Protector, the King and the Lord of mankind and all else that exists, and in His beloved messenger, Muhammad. When the accursed Satan whispers his evil distractions into his heart to undermine his faith and his plan for righteous actions, and places a barrier on his path to success – he remembers God, the Most Strong, Who is able to enforce His will and One Who is aware of all those who call on Him, and seeks protection with Him. He knows life is a great struggle - but is a test in which he can, and must, succeed.